TEN YEARS' CAPTIVITY

IN THE

MAHDI'S CAMP

1882–1892

FROM THE ORIGINAL MANUSCRIPTS OF
FATHER JOSEPH OHRWALDER
LATE PRIEST OF THE AUSTRIAN MISSION STATION AT
DELEN, IN KORDOFAN

BY

MAJOR F. R. WINGATE, R.A.

DIRECTOR OF MILITARY INTELLIGENCE, EGYPTIAN ARMY; AUTHOR OF 'MAHDIISM AND THE EGYPTIAN SUDAN'

*WITH MAPS AND ILLUSTRATIONS
BY WALTER C. HORSLEY*

DARF PUBLISHERS LIMITED
LONDON
1986

FIRST PUBLISHED 1892
NEW IMPRESSION 1986

ISBN 978 1 85077 120 3

PREFACE.

FATHER OHRWALDER.

AFTER the fall of Khartum in January 1885, various attempts were from time to time made to effect the release of some of the European prisoners who had fallen into the Mahdi's hands during the early stages of the Sudan revolt.

These attempts were for the most part attended with little result. The causes of their failure, and eventual success in one instance, are fully described in the following personal narrative of Father Ohrwalder.

As Father Ohrwalder is the first European who has escaped from the Sudan since 1885, I was fully occupied with him during the few days immediately following his arrival in ascertaining, for official purposes, the actual situation in the Sudan, and that completed, we had many interesting conversations on the historical events which had occurred in these revolted districts during the last ten years.

Having but recently completed a *resumé* of these events,* which had been largely compiled from the statements of natives who had escaped, I was not unnaturally desirous to verify, by the independent witness of Father Ohrwalder, the accounts which they had given, and I further begged Father Ohrwalder to carefully read over the book and point out the errors. It was with considerable satisfaction that I learnt from him that the facts had been faithfully recorded; but the flood of light which he was enabled to throw on many obscure passages, and the great interest attaching to the narrative of an active participator in so many of these now historic occurrences, induced me to suggest that he should set to work, while the memory of these events was fresh in his mind, to write a personal narrative of his varied and terrible experiences, of which the general public have hitherto learnt but the bare outline.

It should be borne in mind that the circumstances under which Father Ohrwalder lived in the Sudan precluded him from keeping any written record of his life; it was therefore agreed that I should supervise his work which, I need scarcely add, it has given me great pleasure to do. Father Ohrwalder's manuscript, which was in the first instance written in German, was roughly translated into English by Yusef Effendi Cudzi, a Syrian; this I entirely rewrote in narrative form. The work does not therefore profess to be a literal translation of the original manuscript, but rather an English version, in which I have sought to reproduce accurately Father Ohrwalder's meaning in the language of simple narration.

England and the British public in general have shown so much interest in the stirring events which have occurred in the Sudan, and in which many gallant British officers and men have lost their lives, that it is Father Ohrwalder's desire that the narrative of his experiences should be published in the first instance in

* Published under the title of 'Mahdiism and the Egyptian Sudan.' London: Macmillan & Co. 1891.

England, as his modest tribute to the nation which struggled so gallantly, and so nearly successfully, to effect the relief of Khartum and the rescue of those unfortunate Europeans who, like himself, had fallen into the hands of a cruel and merciless enemy.

It seems almost incredible that such sufferings as the European captives endured did not long ago bring to them the happy release of death they so ardently longed for; but it was not to be. The door of escape, which they had thought closed to them for ever, suddenly opened, and they did not fear to risk the dangers and perils of that terrible desert journey, with scanty food and water, and the sure knowledge that they must ride for bare life; re-capture would have ended in certain death, or, at best, perpetual incarceration in a prison, the horrors of which beggar description. In spite, however, of all he has endured, Father Ohrwalder longs for the time when it may be possible for him to return to the Sudan and continue the Mission work so suddenly and hopelessly interrupted since 1882.

I am greatly indebted to Mr. Walter C. Horsley for the admirable manner in which he has executed his portion of the illustrations. The remainder are chiefly from photographs, taken by Mr. Lekegian in his photographic studio in Cairo, of Dervish prisoners captured at the action of Toski, and of refugees who have recently reached Cairo from Equatoria, through the territory administered by the Imperial British East Africa Company.

F. R. WINGATE.

CAIRO, 30*th July*, 1892.

CONTENTS.

INTRODUCTION.

FATHER OHRWALDER'S JOURNEY TO THE SUDAN.

Description of Kordofan and Dar Nuba—The Mission Station at Delen 1

CHAPTER I.

THE MAHDI AND HIS RISE TO POWER.

The rise of the Mahdi—Early successes—Personal appearance—His Khalifas described—Military organization—Makes new laws—He summons El Obeid to surrender . . 6

CHAPTER II.

FATHER OHRWALDER AND HIS COMPANIONS TAKEN CAPTIVE.

The storm rises in Dar Nuba—The Baggara begin to raid—Khojur Kakum of Delen—Mek Omar besieges Delen—The slave guard deserts the Mission—The priests and nuns surrender—They are sent to the Mahdi . . 22

CHAPTER III.

THE MISSIONARIES AND THE MAHDI.

Description of El Obeid—Said Pasha's system of defence—The Mahdi's followers encircle the town—Townspeople desert to the Mahdi—Unsuccessful attack on Government buildings—Dervishes driven off with loss of 10,000 men—The missionaries brought before the Mahdi—Threatened with death—Preparations for the execution—Reprieved at the last moment—The Mahdi's camp described—Death of some of the missionaries—Illness of remainder 34

CHAPTER IV.

THE SIEGE OF EL OBEID.

Terrible sufferings of the besieged—The Kababish—Fall of Bara—Fall of El Obeid—The Mahdi enters the town—Fate of the El Obeid Mission—Cold-blooded murder of the brave defenders—The Dervishes live a life of ease in El Obeid—The Mahdi makes laws—He sends out proclamations—Prestige increased by capture of town—News from Khartum—Bonomi and Ohrwalder summoned before the Mahdi—The interview 52

CHAPTER V.

THE MAHDI'S VICTORY OVER HICKS PASHA.

The European captives learn that General Hicks is advancing—Slatin Bey's defence of Darfur—His heroism—The Mahdi prepares to resist Hicks—The march of the Hicks Expedition—Extracts from the diary of Major Herlth—Colonel Farquhar's gallantry at Rahad—Gustav Klootz deserts to the Mahdi—Klootz's interview with the Mahdi in which Ohrwalder and Bonomi act as interpreters—The expedition advances towards Shekan—Is surrounded and annihilated—Description of the battle—The Mahdi victor of Kordofan 72

CHAPTER VI.

THE MAHDI'S TRIUMPHAL ENTRY INTO EL OBEID.

Fall of Darfur—Slatin surrenders—The Mahdi's divinity credited after the annihilation of Hicks—King Adam of Tagalla—Stambuli's kindness to the European captives—Gordon writes to the Mahdi—Power's letter—The sisters seized and distributed amongst the emirs—They are tortured—The missionaries turned into slaves—The terrible journey to Rahad—The Greeks come to the help of the sisters—The proclamation concerning the treatment of priests and hermits by Mohammedans—The Mahdi at Rahad—Ohrwalder's interviews with the Mahdi concerning religion—The Dervishes attack the Nubas . 91

CHAPTER VII.

FATHER OHRWALDER'S VIEWS OF GORDON'S MISSION.

Ohrwalder describes his treatment at the hands of various masters—The Nubas surrender and afterwards desert—News from Khartum—The capture of the English mail—

Its arrival at the Mahdi's camp—The Mahdi decides to advance on Khartum—Brief review of events in Khartum and Berber—Ohrwalder's views on Gordon's mission—The Mahdi sets out for Khartum—Mohammed Ali Pasha's defeat and death—Colonel Stewart, Mr. Power, and others leave Khartum in ss. "Abbas"—Description of their wreck and treacherous murder 114

CHAPTER VIII.

THE SIEGE AND FALL OF KHARTUM.

The surrender of Omdurman fort—Gordon's dispositions for defence—His great personal influence—The night before the assault—The attack and entry of the Dervishes—Gordon's death—The adventures of Domenico Polinari—The massacre in Khartum—How most of the Europeans died—Ruthless cruelty and bloodshed—The fate of the wives and daughters of Khartum—Ohrwalder's views on the situation in Khartum and the chances of relief by the British Expeditionary Force—His description of the town three months after the fall 131

CHAPTER IX.

THE MAHDI'S LAST DAYS.

Ohrwalder's criticisms on certain events connected with the defence of Khartum—The Sudan devastated by small-pox—The Mahdi gives way to a life of pleasure—Description of his harem life—The Mahdi sickens and dies—The effect on his followers—The Khalifa Abdullah succeeds—Party strife and discord—Abdullah prevails—Events in Sennar and Kassala 152

CHAPTER X.

THE ESCAPE OF FATHER BONOMI.

Ohrwalder continues to describe his personal experiences—Mahmud the emir of El Obeid—His unsuccessful attempts to entrap the Nubas—The arrival of Olivier Pain in El Obeid—His motives in joining the Mahdi—His journey towards Omdurman—His sad fate—Lupton Bey arrives at El Obeid from the Bahr el Ghazal—He is sent to Omdurman and thrown into chains—Life in El Obeid—The escape of Father Bonomi—Ohrwalder's solitude—The death of the Khojur Kakum 169

CHAPTER XI.

REVOLT AGAINST THE DERVISHES.

The black soldiers of the old Sudan army—They revolt against the Dervishes in El Obeid—And march off to Dar Nuba—The emir Mahmud pursues and is slain—Ohrwalder quits El Obeid for Omdurman—Zogal and Abu Anga at Bara 189

CHAPTER XII.

OHRWALDER'S IMPRESSIONS OF OMDURMAN.

Ohrwalder's arrival in Omdurman—His first impressions of the Dervish capital—Khalifa Abdullah's intentions to conquer Egypt—Wad Suleiman of the beit el mal—Wad Adlan succeeds — Gordon's clothes, medals, &c.—Adlan reorganizes the beit el mal—The slave market, museum, mint, and system of coinage—Counterfeit coining—The lithograph press—The Khalifa's system of justice . . 204

CHAPTER XIII.

THE KHALIFA DECIDES TO CONQUER ABYSSINIA.

Events subsequent to the fall of Khartum—Capture of Gedaref and Galabat—Dervishes defeated by Abyssinians at Galabat—Abu Anga's victorious expedition to Tagalla—His triumphal return to Omdurman—The Khalifa's grand review—Destruction of the Gehena tribe—The Khalifa decides to send Abu Anga's army to conquer Abyssinia—The battle of Dabra Sin—Abu Anga sacks Gondar—The victorious Dervishes return to Galabat—Rejoicings at Omdurman 216

CHAPTER XIV.

KING JOHN OF ABYSSINIA KILLED IN BATTLE.

Destruction of the Kababish tribe and death of Saleh Bey—Events in Darfur—Revolt of Abu Gemaizeh—His death and destruction of his army—Rabeh Zubeir—King Theodore's son visits Omdurman—The conspiracy of "Sayidna Isa"—Death of Abu Anga—King John of Abyssinia attacks Galabat—Success of Abyssinians, but the king killed—Victory turned to defeat—The king's head sent to Omdurman 232

CHAPTER XV.

DEFEAT OF NEJUMI AT TOSKI, AND OF OSMAN DIGNA AT TOKAR.

The Khalifa's intentions regarding Egypt—Wad en Nejumi despatched north—Various operations on the Egyptian frontier—Battle of Toski—Defeat and death of Nejumi—Subsequent events in Dongola—Osman Digna's operations against Sawakin—Is defeated at Tokar—Emin Pasha and events in Equatoria—Recent events in Uganda and Unyoro 254

CHAPTER XVI.

THE FAMINE AT OMDURMAN—1888–1889.

Ohrwalder describes Omdurman—The Mahdi's tomb, and how it was built—Pilgrimage to Mecca forbidden—A description of the great mosque—The Khalifa's palace—The markets—The population—The Khalifa's tyrannical rule—The terrible famine of 1888–1889—Awful scenes and sufferings—The plague of locusts 273

CHAPTER XVII.

THE KHALIFA AND HIS GOVERNMENT

The Khalifa's system of government—His household—An outline of his character—His system of prayers in the mosque—His visions and dreams—His espionage system—His household troops—His great activity and circumspection—The great Friday review described—The emigration of the Baggara and western tribes to Omdurman—The flight of Sheikh Ghazali—Management of the beit el mal—System of taxation 293

CHAPTER XVIII.

A CHAPTER OF HORRORS.

The revolt of the Batahin tribe—Revolt suppressed with appalling cruelty — Wholesale executions — Method of hanging—Punishment by mutilation—The execution of Abdel Nur—Trade with Egypt—Wad Adlan the emin beit el mal—His imprisonment and death . . . 315

CHAPTER XIX.

SOCIAL LIFE AT OMDURMAN.

System of public security and justice in Omdurman—The court of small causes—Bribery and corruption — The story of the slave and her mistress—How the Khalifa deals with quarrelsome persons — Thieves and pickpockets—The story of Zogheir—Usurers and their trade—The chief of police — Brigandage—Disproportion of males to females in Omdurman—How the Khalifa overcame the difficulty—Immorality—The marriage ceremony 328

CHAPTER XX.

THE KHALIFA'S TREATMENT OF THE WHITE CAPTIVES.

Description of the prison, or "Saier"—The "Abu Haggar"—The imprisonment of Charles Neufeld—Terrible sufferings of the prisoners—Domenico Polinari—The danger of corresponding with the European prisoners—Neufeld threatened with death—He is given charge of the saltpetre pits—The fate of Sheikh Khalil, the Egyptian envoy—The Khalifa's treatment of the "Whites"—Exile to the White Nile 344

CHAPTER XXI.

LUPTON BEY AND THE AMMUNITION.

The Khalifa's powder and ammunition begin to fail—Lupton Bey makes fulminate—Unsuccessful attempts to make powder—Yusef Pertekachi at last succeeds—The explosion in the powder factory 366

CHAPTER XXII.

AGRICULTURE AND COMMERCE IN THE MAHDI'S KINGDOM.

Remarks on the agriculture and commerce of the Mahdiist kingdom—A sandstorm in Omdurman—The paucity of cattle—System of taxation on imports—Provincial beit el mals—Local manufactures—Slavery and the slave-markets—Torture of slaves 376

CHAPTER XXIII.

THE BAGGARA MASTERS OF THE SUDAN.

Relations between Abdullah and the rival Khalifas—Mahdiism practically dead—The Khalifa's son Osman—His marriage to Yakub's daughter — His intentions regarding the succession—The Baggara and the Aulad-Belad—The Baggara masters of the Sudan—Examples of their tyranny—Emigration of the Rizighat tribe—Hostility between the Khalifa's and the late Mahdi's households—The Ashraf conspiracy—Witchcraft—The dispute between the Khalifas—Riots in Omdurman—The Mahdi's widows 387

CHAPTER XXIV.

PREPARATIONS FOR THE FLIGHT.

Ohrwalder forms plans for escape—The fate of other Europeans attempting to fly—Stricter surveillance—Ohrwalder's means of livelihood—Letters from Cairo—The faithful Ahmed Hassan discloses his plan—Archbishop Sogaro—Miseries of captivity in Omdurman—Death of Sister Concetta Corsi—Preparations for flight . . . 408

CHAPTER XXV.

ON CAMELS ACROSS THE GREAT NUBIAN DESERT.

Father Ohrwalder and Sisters Venturini and Chincarini escape—The ride for life—The rencontre with the Dervish guard near Abu Hamed—Alarm of the party—The journey across the great Nubian desert—Five hundred miles on camel-back in seven days—Arrival at the Egyptian outpost at Murat—Safe at last—Arrival in Cairo 424

CHAPTER XXVI.

THE PRESENT KHALIFA'S DESPOTISM IN THE SUDAN.

Reflections on the situation in the Sudan—The horrors of the present Khalifa's rule—How long shall it continue? . 447

LIST OF ILLUSTRATIONS, MAP AND PLAN.

	PAGE
Father Ohrwalder, Sisters Venturini and Chincarini, and their servant Adila (*Frontispiece*).	
Zubeir Pasha	8
A native woman of Dongola	65
Hicks Pasha	74
Colonel Arthur Farquhar (Chief of Staff)	80
A Baggara emir, present at the annihilation of the Hicks Expedition, and afterwards captured at Toski	89
Father Ohrwalder's interview with the Mahdi at Rahad, concerning religion	107
The gold medal struck by Gordon to commemorate the siege of Khartum	122
A Dervish emir present in the attack on Khartum, and afterwards captured at Toski	136
An Egyptian Harem woman	156
"Many a time did I turn round to look back, until Bonomi disappeared from view in the wood"	181
A slave woman from Equatoria	209
Abyssinian dancing girls	243
An Arab sheikh of Upper Egypt	255
Bishir Bey, sheikh of the Ababdeh Arabs	259
Wad en Nejumi (from a photograph of a drawing made by an Egyptian officer of the great Emir, as he lay dead on the field of Toski)	264
A native woman of Makaraka, the wife of one of Emin Pasha's officers, who reached Egypt from Uganda in June 1892.	270
A trophy of arms, banners, and drums, captured from the Dervishes	305
Charles Neufeld	354
A slave girl from Equatoria	382
A Baggara woman	398
The Arab guides who effected the escape of Father Ohrwalder and the Sisters	409
"We had scarcely gone twenty paces from the river, when suddenly we heard the sound of a camel"	435

Plan of Omdurman.
Map of the Nile Basin, showing route taken by Father Ohrwalder.

TEN YEARS'
CAPTIVITY IN THE MAHDI'S CAMP.
1882–1892.

INTRODUCTION.

FATHER OHRWALDER'S JOURNEY TO THE SUDAN.

Description of Kordofan and Dar Nuba—The Mission Station at Delen.

I LEFT Cairo on the 28th of December, 1880, as full of bright hopes for a happy future as any young man could wish to be. I had no thought of the miserable fate which was so soon to overtake me.

Our party consisted of Bishop Comboni, two missionaries, Johann Dichtl and Franz Pimezzoni (these three have long since passed into eternity), and several sisters. We embarked at Suez, and spent the first day of 1881 on the Red Sea. On the 4th of January we landed at Sawakin. At that time the governor of the town was Ala ed Din Pasha, who subsequently accompanied General Hicks as Governor-General of the Sudan, and was eventually killed with him. After a journey of twenty-eight days and travelling *viâ* Berber, we reached Khartum; here the pleasant gardens and shady groves of date-palms impressed us most favourably. Standing on the high river bank, just in front of the Mission gardens, were the various members of the Mission, headed by Father Alois Bonomi, also the Austrian Consul Hansal and the Italian Consul Legnani, who gave us a hearty welcome. The whole city was *en fête*, to celebrate the return of the Governor-General Rauf Pasha from

Gedaref. After landing, we walked through the lovely garden towards the Mission buildings, and here, in the principal parlour, were collected Rauf Pasha, Giegler Pasha, Gessi Pasha, who had just returned quite worn out from his campaigns in the Bahr el Ghazal; the courageous Slatin, fresh from Darfur; Marcopoli Bey, Doctor Zurbuchen, Marquet, the African traveller Jean Maria Schuver, and many others who had come to welcome Bishop Comboni on his arrival.

On the 15th of March we celebrated the fiftieth birthday of Bishop Comboni with general rejoicings: in the evening the European colony dined at the Mission, and then followed a *soirée*. Little did we think of the terrible fate that was in store for the majority of those gathered together on that happy evening!

In the meantime Slatin Bey had been appointed Governor-General of Darfur, and he considered it his duty to proceed as soon as possible to take up his new post. Our bishop accepted Slatin's proffered invitation to travel together as far as El Obeid, and on the 29th of March we embarked on a steamer placed at our disposal by Rauf Pasha and proceeded to Tur el Hadra. We were accompanied thus far by Marcopoli Bey, Dr. Zurbuchen and Marquet, and here, mounting on camels, we made a rapid march across the Kordofan deserts, arriving at El Obeid on the 5th of April. No sooner had we dismounted, than two telegrams were handed to us: one announced the sudden death, on his return to Khartum, of Dr. Zurbuchen, and the other described the death of the Czar Alexander of Russia at the hands of the Nihilists.

We remained at El Obeid while Slatin was making arrangements for his journey to Darfur. Bishop Comboni then made a tour through Jebel Nuba, returned to El Obeid and subsequently to Khartum, where he died on the 10th of October. God, in His mercy, took him away so that he should not behold the terrible events in the Sudan which followed soon after his death.

I left El Obeid on the 28th of November, 1881, and

reached Delen in Dar Nuba on the 5th of December. I was most favourably impressed with the Nuba country. Whilst Kordofan is merely an extensive plain with little change of scenery, Dar Nuba presents an entirely different aspect. Here chains of picturesque hills, running in various directions, rise out of the plain, interspersed with numerous watercourses. Jebel Delen, on which our Mission station was situated, is one of the smallest of the hills. The other principal groups are Naïma, Kurun, Dobab, Dair, Kedaro, Tagalla, Gedir, and Tira, in which gold is found, besides a number of smaller hills. It is estimated that in all there are upwards of one hundred inhabited mountains.

The intervening plains and valleys are rich in vegetation of every description; trees of colossal dimensions are found, more especially in the khors (the beds of perennial streams), and the thick luxuriant growth is so dense that the rays of the sun cannot penetrate. The soil is exceptionally fertile and rain abundant, consequently for six months in the year the density of the undergrowth makes it almost impossible to traverse these rich valleys; but when the rains are over and the grass becomes dry, it is generally fired, and thus the plains and valleys become passable again. A quantity of the rain from these hills flows into Lake Birket, some passes also into the Khor Abu Habl, which becomes lost in the sand before it reaches the White Nile. The rain from the southern Nuba hills finds its way into the Bahr el Arab. The plains abound with quantities of deer, giraffe, antelope, and wild boar, whilst the woods contain myriads of birds of lovely plumage, and apes and monkeys of every description. During the winter season, elephants were frequently to be seen in the neighbourhood of Delen, which also abounds with snakes, amongst which the boa-constrictor is not uncommon.

The population of Dar Nuba, which at one time was considerable, does not now exceed 50,000; the scattered sub-tribes of Baggara, who roam the plains with the Bederieh and Ghodiat Arabs, have decimated the Nubas, and forced those that are left to fly to their mountain recesses, where they eke out a wretched existence, their protection being the inaccessible nature of their retreats.

I found the Nubas a pleasant and well-disposed people; indeed, they have the reputation in the Sudan of being the best of all the negroid races; they cultivate only sufficient quantities of corn, sesame, and beans to serve for their livelihood; whilst the wild fruits and vegetables of their country are so plentiful as to furnish almost sufficient food for their maintenance should they be unable to cultivate. They possess numbers of goats and cattle which supply them with milk and butter; they are much addicted to drinking marissa (a kind of beer made from dhurra), and great quantities of this beverage are consumed at their feasts, principally at the feast known as Zubeir. On this occasion men and women drink and dance together; but notwithstanding this unusual familiarity, I never saw anything which might be considered an outrage to society. With the exception of the Khojur, of whom I shall presently speak, and the head sheikh, monogamy is practised.

The Nubas are governed entirely by their own traditional laws and customs, the Khojur only intervening in case of necessity. The Khojur is in reality a sort of religious chief, whose power over the people depends entirely on his skilfulness and sagacity. During the time I was in this neighbourhood the Khojur was a certain Kakum, known as "Kakum of Delen."

Only a short time had elapsed since the Egyptian Government had made a settlement at Delen. A company of Sudanese soldiers, under the command of a captain who was appointed for the suppression of the slave-trade, had been recently quartered there, and they were also charged with the protection of our Mission station.

I was very happy in Delen, where I found a variety of pursuits to occupy my time. I amused myself in collecting insects, of which I soon had a large selection. I also skinned birds and snakes. The various modes of Nuba life and cultivation were, moreover, an immense interest to me, and the presentation of a few glass beads enabled me to secure many strange objects in return. The natives used to roar with laughter when they saw me examining with interest the curious insects they brought me.

We had quite a colony of blacks in the Mission, and as the number increased, it became necessary to enlarge the accommodation, so we began to make and burn bricks; we obtained lime from the Saburi mountain (I may here say the Nubas gave us this information) and the doleb-palm supplied us with plenty of wood. Assisted by Father Bonomi, our carpenter Gabriel Mariani built a four-wheeled cart, which we drove with two strong mules. We worked along cheerfully and full of hope. We turned out some 2,000 good bricks. Our blacks were quite contented; far removed from the corruption and temptation of the towns, they kept steadily to their work, and tilled their own little patches of ground; everything was going well, and we anticipated great results. But suddenly our tranquillity was disturbed. Early in April 1882, there were perceptible at Delen the first murmurings of the terrible storm which was to deluge the entire Sudan with blood, and to bring misfortune and calamity on the land and on our happy Mission; but these events I will describe in the following pages.

CHAPTER I.

THE MAHDI AND HIS RISE TO POWER.

The rise of the Mahdi—Early successes—Personal appearance—His Khalifas described—Military organization—Makes new laws—He summons El Obeid to surrender.

A FEW years previous to the time of which I speak, an individual who called himself a Dervish had attracted people's attention. He wandered through the Sudan in the garb of a Dervish, and strove to rouse the Moslems to religious fanaticism. He urged that reality no longer existed in the religion; faith was becoming of no account, and this religious decadence was due to a luxurious mode of life and contact with Christians. A number of influential sheikhs and merchants took up his cause, and these he made to swear to remain faithful and true to him. At this time at El Obeid there was a certain Said el Mek, who had the reputation of being a holy man, and the Dervish did all in his power to induce him to espouse his cause. Said el Mek urged that religion had not fallen into such disrepute, and that all would be well if more mosques were built; but the Dervish, with threats that if he refused to join him he would compass his destruction, extracted from him a promise to keep his plans secret. He then prepared the way by continuing his wanderings, preaching everywhere against the oppression of the Turk and the decadence of the true Moslem faith. Under the very nose of the Government he collected a small body of faithful adherents, set off with them for the island of Abba on the White Nile, and there openly declared himself. Rumours that he intended to raise the people to revolt reached Khartum. At this time Rauf Pasha was

Governor-General; he sent a noted Khartum townsman named Abu Saud to Abba, with instructions to invite the Dervish to come and see the Governor-General. Abu Saud nearly succeeded in his mission, and had it not been for the advice of one of his adherents, Ahmed Sharfi, it is probable that the Dervish would have accepted the invitation. Rauf Pasha, on learning of his refusal to obey the summons, despatched two companies of troops to Abba Island at the end of July 1881, with instructions to bring the Dervish forcibly to Khartum. The two captains of the companies had a difference of opinion, and, landing the troops in a most careless manner, they were drawn on by the adherents of the Dervish into a marshy swamp, where they were fallen upon and a number of them killed with simple sticks. Ahmed Sharfi himself told me this. Only a very few succeeded in escaping and returning to the steamer, in which they made their way back to Khartum.

This episode caused great excitement. I was at El Obeid when it happened, and Giegler Pasha, who was also there at the time, told me about it. Giegler despatched Mohammed Said Pasha to the White Nile with orders to prevent the Dervish from escaping south; but Said Pasha soon afterwards returned, having done nothing; probably he did not dare to attack the rebels. In the meantime the Dervish quitted Abba, and succeeded in reaching Tagalla in safety; thence he proceeded to Jebel Gedir, and located himself at the foot of that mountain. The natives of this district are called Kawakla, and dwell on the top of the mountain; they are possessors of a very celebrated and holy stone, on which there is a tradition the prophet Mohammed sat and prayed. Here the Dervish Mohammed Ahmed now took up his abode, and waited to see what action the Government intended to take.

At Delen the news of this Dervish was very meagre, though there was much talk of his wonderful miracles, the most important of which was said to be his power to change the bullets of the Government troops into water. His repute as a worker of miracles grew rapidly, and was the cause of largely increasing the number of his adherents. The malcontents, runaway slaves, criminals evading justice, and religious fanatics, hurried to Gedir; but perhaps the bulk of his adherents were men who lived by theft and robbery, and who were the main supporters of the movement. To all, the Dervish gave promises of enormous shares of loot and everlasting

ZUBEIR PASHA.

happiness in the world to come. But it was to the slave-dealers that Mohammed appeared in the light of a saviour, and it was to them that he owed his subsequent success.

From the time that Gessi Pasha put an end to the slave-trade in the Bahr el Ghazal by conquering

Suleiman, the son of Zubeir Pasha, and dispersing his forces—as Gessi had often related to me—numbers of these runaway slave-dealers (as they afterwards assured me) owed their ruin to him. These men were all warriors, accustomed to every description of hardship, well trained in the use of firearms, and from their constant slave-fights well accustomed to war; they flocked in numbers to the Dervish, and he gave them elaborate promises of quantities of booty and a complete resumption of the slave-trade. Mohammed Ahmed had the power of inspiring these men with an extraordinary amount of fanatical ardour, so much so, indeed, as we shall presently see, that they would not hesitate to rush into certain death at one word from him. He would compare these men with the Government troops, and prove how far inferior were these latter; and, on the other hand, the Government troops made the fatal mistake of underrating their enemies, and conducting their operations with a complete disregard for the wary foes with whom they had to deal. What more obvious example of this blind self-confidence can there be than in the miserable defeat of Rashid Bey, Mudir of Fashoda, who, without any instructions, advanced against the Dervishes, and was cut to pieces on the 9th of December, 1881?

Rashid Bey—so an eye-witness told me—was drawn into the middle of a forest, and there he and his men were massacred, before they could even alight from their camels, so completely taken by surprise were they. Thus the Dervishes gained an important and decisive victory, with, comparatively speaking, no loss at all. The German Berghof, inspector for the suppression of slavery at Fashoda, also fell in this fight. What wonder is it that such successes as these strengthened the belief of the people that the Mahdi could turn Egyptian bullets into water! This victory gave enormous impetus to the cause; not only was a quantity of arms, ammunition, and stores captured, but Mohammed Ahmed's moral influence was greatly increased. He was now believed in as the true Mahdi; men flocked to his standard from all parts, and were ready and willing to lay down their lives in his cause.

Mohammed Ahmed Wad el Bedri, one of the Mahdi's favourite and early adherents, told me that it was the latter's intention to proceed to Dar Fertit, and there organise an extensive revolt against the Government; but Elias Pasha, a Jaali, and former Mudir of El Obeid, urged him against this. Elias Pasha was a bitter enemy of Mohammed Said Pasha, and of Ahmed Bey Dafallah, one of the principal merchants of El Obeid, and he took this opportunity to wreak his vengeance on them. He fully convinced the Mahdi of the inability of the garrison of El Obeid to offer any prolonged resistance, as the troops were few in number, and he could count on all the inhabitants joining him. It was this advice that caused the Mahdi to turn his attention to Kordofan.

During all this time the number of the Mahdi's followers was continually increasing, and the Government at length decided to send an expedition against him. On the 15th of March, 1882, Yussef Pasha Esh Shellali, formerly Gessi's second in command in his campaign against Suleiman Zubeir, left Khartum for the south, in command of some 4,000 men, a large number of whom deserted on the march. About the middle of May, however, he left Fashoda, and advanced towards Gedir. At the same time another expedition under Abdullah, brother of Ahmed Bey Dafallah and Osman, started from El Obeid. This force was composed entirely of volunteers, whom it had taken almost a month to collect, the noggara beating night and day as a summons to arms. They were badly armed, and in spite of Abdullah's well-known bravery, the expedition left with little hope of success. Besides, an event happened which filled the men with gloomy forebodings. Just as the troops were starting, Abdullah fell from his horse, and, according to Sudan superstition, such an untoward event is always a sign that the expedition will meet with misfortunes. Abdullah effected a junction with Yussef Pasha, and the combined force reached Gedir,

THE MAHDI DECIDES TO BESIEGE EL OBEID. 11

where they entrenched themselves in a zariba near the base of the mountain. A body of rebels, noiselessly approaching by night, succeeded unobserved in dragging away some of the thorns forming the zariba, and in the early morning the Dervishes, with fearful yells, broke in and threw themselves on the troops, who, scared by the suddenness of the attack, offered little resistance; they were soon overcome, and fell a prey to the deadly dervish spears. Abdullah alone made a gallant stand, and fought with desperate bravery, but he too fell at last. A few only succeeded in escaping to Fashoda, and Emin Bey, who was there at the time, on his way to the Equatorial Province, was the first to receive the sad news. The account of this massacre, which took place on the 7th of June, 1882, was described to us by an eye-witness.

And now the Mahdi determined to lay siege to El Obeid, a step which was hailed with satisfaction by all his followers. Large numbers of Dar Hamd, Ghodiat, and Bederieh Arabs collected at Birket, which in winter-time becomes a large lake, round which are clustered numerous villages.

In July 1882, Mohammed Said Pasha sent Major Nesim and Osman, the brother of Abdullah who was killed at Gedir, with a force of 1,500 men, with orders to disperse the Arabs. After a stubborn resistance the Arabs were defeated by Nesim, but the latter suffered heavily, and Osman was amongst the killed. Nesim afterwards returned to El Obeid.

Meanwhile the various military stations in Kordofan were falling one by one into the Mahdi's hands. In July Fiki Rahma, at the head of the Gowameh Arabs, assaulted and took Ashaf and razed it to the ground. Here terrible atrocities were committed; not a woman was spared; even those with child were ripped open and the unborn infant impaled on a lance. On the 8th of August Shat was captured and destroyed by Wad Makashif. Fiki Minneh stormed and took Tayara, putting all the inhabitants to the sword. Bara and El Obeid were now the only towns left in the whole province of Kordofan over which the Egyptian flag was still flying; and these two places were gradually being invested, while within lurked the spirit of treachery, and the Mahdi propaganda was being secretly instilled into not unwilling minds. At El Obeid, Elias Pasha was the most active agent, and it was to him that the Mahdi had consigned the medals, watches, and other valuables captured at Gedir, with orders to sell them in El Obeid.

The Mahdi now became a man whose very name was a terror to the Egyptians. The way to El Obeid lay open before him, and when he saw how rapidly he had risen to power, there is no doubt he really believed himself to be the true Mahdi, divinely sent by God to carry out this great revolution, and the fulsome flattery of his numerous adherents must have confirmed him in this idea. Here a few remarks on the Mahdi's antecedents may not be out of place.

Mohammed Ahmed belonged to the race of people known as the Danagla—*i.e.* inhabitants of Dongola—who are notorious in the Sudan as being the cleverest and most determined of the slave-dealers. On the White Nile and in the Bahr el Ghazal they had built numerous zaribas, and it was through their means that this country became first known. In Darfur they always occupied the position of chief ministers or vazirs to the Sultans; even to the present day the prime minister of the Sultan of Borgo is a Dongolawi. In spite, however, of their capacity, the Danagla were rather despised throughout the Sudan, and it was only subsequently that they were created Ashraf (or noble) by the Mahdi. Mohammed Ahmed's age was estimated at his death to have been about forty-five, he must therefore have been born about the year 1840. It appears that his father came into the Sudan when quite a young man, and sent his son to the Mesit or Kuran school at Kererri, and, from what I have heard, there is no doubt that the young Mohammed Ahmed showed signs of a violently fanatical nature at quite an early age. After the fall of El Obeid, his former teacher came to see him, and was received with great solemnity by his early pupil, who at once arranged that he should receive a monthly salary.

Mohammed Ahmed's early youth was spent in learning the Kuran; later on he led the life of a Dervish, moving about from place to place, distributing amulets, and writing on little slips of paper mysterious words, which were supposed to protect the wearer against all the ills and diseases to which human beings are liable. Through constant study, and by leading the life of an ascetic, he acquired a facility of speech which obtained for him a great reputation amongst the uneducated and superstitious classes in which he moved. Before he openly declared himself, he retired for some time to a cave, where he gave himself up entirely to prayer. His repute for sanctity was so great that sailing vessels and even Government steamers stopped to ask his blessing on their journey; in return for which he received many valuable gifts. As I have already said, it was not till after he had prepared the ground by his itinerant preaching that he openly declared himself.

His outward appearance was strangely fascinating; he was a man of strong constitution, very dark complexion, and his face always wore a pleasant smile, to which he had by long practice accustomed himself. Under this smile gleamed a set of singularly white teeth, and between the two upper middle ones was a V-shaped space, which in the Sudan is considered a sign that the owner will be lucky. His mode of conversation too had by training become exceptionally pleasant and sweet. As a messenger of God, he pretended to be in direct communication with the Deity. All orders which he gave were supposed to have come to him by inspiration, and it became therefore a sin to refuse to obey them; disobedience to the Mahdi's orders was tantamount to resistance to the will of God, and was therefore punishable by death.

He called himself Mahdi Khalifat er Rasul (*i.e.* the successor of the Prophet), while his adherents called him "Sayid" (*i.e.* Master); Sayidna el Mahdi (*i.e.* our

Master the Mahdi), or Sayidna el Imam (*i.e.* our Master the head, or one who goes in front). The Mahdi in his every action endeavoured to imitate and follow in the exact footsteps of the Prophet.

Thus he made his hejira or flight to Gedir, and there appointed his four Khalifas. The first of these was the Khalifa Abdullah, who assumed the title of Khalifa Abu Bakr, or Khalifa Es Sadik; he belonged to the Taisha section of the Baggara tribe, and it was through his influence that the Taisha, Rizighat and Homr Baggaras were won over to the Mahdi's cause. It was agreed that Khalifa Abdullah should, in the event of the Mahdi's death, succeed.

The second Khalifa was Ali Wad Helu, the chief of the powerful Degheim and Kenana tribes, who also largely contributed to the Mahdi's success. The third was Ali Esh Sherif, a Dongolawi, and son-in-law of the Mahdi; the title of Sherif, or noble, was given to him as being a member of the Mahdi's family; he was the representative of the Gellabas (or traders), and of the inhabitants of Gezireh,* Berber, and Dongola. Ali Sherif was in reality the last Khalifa, for a fourth was never appointed. The Mahdi asked the son of Sheikh Senussi, as by his influence he thought to win over Egypt, but he refused the honour, and in consequence no one else was nominated to fill the place, though strenuous efforts were made by the more ambitious adherents to secure this much-coveted position; and it is needless to add that several who sought the honour were relegated to prison as possible rivals. The Khalifa Abdullah is now about forty-three years of age, has a dark copper-coloured complexion, much marked by small-pox, an intelligent face, and is a man of great energy. He is gifted by nature with common sense, but he has had no education, and can neither read nor write. The Khalifa Ali is rather short, and if he were only a little taller would pass for a good-looking man; he has a ruddy complexion, and wears a large

---

* The Gezireh or Geziret Meröe is generally applied to the country lying between the Blue and White Niles.

THE MAHDI'S MILITARY ORGANIZATION.

beard; he was educated at the El Azhar university in Cairo, and has a considerable knowledge of Islam theology. He is at present under forty years of age, and should succeed Abdullah. The Khalifa Sherif is not at present more than twenty-one years of age.

These three Khalifas were the commanders-in-chief of the army, of which each section had its own special distinctions, whilst the Mahdi himself had no distinctive military insignia—neither flag nor drum. Each Khalifa had his own Jehadieh, or regular troops, his cavalry and lance-bearers, all from the tribe to which he himself belongs; each had also his own distinctive flag; Abdullah's the Raya Zerga, or black flag; Ali's the Raya el Hamra, or red flag; and Sherif's the Raya el Hadra, or green flag; each Khalifa had in addition his own war-drums made of brass, and which were therefore called "nahas," in contradistinction to the ordinary drums known as "noggara," which are made of wood, over which a piece of skin is tightly stretched; the Khalifa Abdullah had also the onbaïa, a very powerful wind instrument made of an elephant's tusk, hollowed out, and which when blown has a very loud and impressive sound.

The whole of the Mahdi's troops were thus divided into three sections under their respective flags, and each Khalifa was in actual command of his section. The Mahdi and Sherif represented the Gellabas, who are known, in contradistinction to the Baggara, as Aulad-Belad (country people), and Aulad-Bahr (river people), because they dwell on the banks of the Nile; whilst Khalifa Abdullah and Ali Wad Helu represented the Baggara, *i.e.* the Arabs. The former of these two parties was the most capable as well as the most numerous, but, as we shall presently see, Khalifa Abdullah's party, through their leader's immense energy, gained the ascendency. Each Khalifa has numbers of emirs under him, all of whom have their different flags. These banners are quite simple and require no great labour; they are made of varied colours, and on each the Moslem creed is written, with the addition of the words: "Mohammed Ahmed el Mahdi Khalifat er Rasul" (*i.e.* "the successor of the Prophet"). This is specially directed against the Sultan of Turkey, who claims this title. Latterly flags were made to represent certain stated numbers of men; for instance, in the early days of the revolt, Abderrahman en Nejumi was designated Emir el Umara (or Emir-of Emirs), because in the first instance he commanded from 2,000 to 4,000 men, and secondly, these men received a regular rate of pay, which in reality found its way into the emirs' pockets; but latterly many of the emirs command only fifty men. Each emir is assisted by several mukuddums, or under officers, and each mukuddum also has his assistant.

Thus did the Mahdi organise the force which was to conquer the Sudan. He had absolutely no knowledge or system of drill, but he had men in abundance; and taking the proverb, "Nekhrib ed Dunia wa nammir el Akher" (*i.e.* "We shall destroy this and create the next world") as his motto, he thought not of sparing the lives of his men, but rather urged that by dying they should go direct to paradise. His plan, therefore, was to attack in overwhelming numbers with wild shouts, and to be regardless of all loss. Later on, at Abu Kru in the Bayuda desert, they yelled so furiously in the hope that they would alarm the English, that their commander, Nur Angara, tried to make them desist, by telling them that if they continued shouting much longer, the English would laugh at them. In spite, however, of his bold tactics, the Mahdi did not hesitate to practise every possible deception and falsehood—indeed, most of his early successes were secured by these means. At the commencement of the revolt the use of firearms was forbidden; sticks and lances formed the only arms, as it was the Mahdi's intention in this instance also to follow directly in the footsteps of the Prophet who had gained all his victories without firearms.

The Mahdi, however, whilst thus preparing for war, did not relax in any degree his religious fervour. His

THE MAHDI MAKES NEW LAWS. 17

primary object was to be a religious reformer, and to preach that to him was confided the task of bringing back the religion now polluted by the Turks, to its original purity. He therefore formulated many severe orders. The use of alcoholic drinks, to which the Sudanese are much addicted, was entirely forbidden, and any infringement of this order was punished by sixty blows with the kurbash. Smoking and chewing tobacco, a custom much in vogue amongst the Sudanese, was also strictly forbidden; and the use of hashish, to which the Turks and Egyptians were addicted, was entirely prohibited; disobedience to this order was punishable by eighty lashes. Death often ensued before the punishment could be completed, but the full number of lashes was always given. If any one lived through his punishment he was considered purified both externally and internally. Any harmless word of abuse, such as "kelb" (dog), was punishable with twenty-seven lashes. This punishment went by the name of "Hakk-Allah" * (the right of God), and was also inflicted in the time of the Prophet, who, to make it a really mild punishment, ordained that the upper part of the arms and shoulders should be covered with camel's hide, and the punishment inflicted on the lower arm only, the indication that it had been correctly administered being shown by the fact that the camel's hide had not moved from its place. The Mahdiists, however, took quite another view of the matter, and thought that the only correct way of administering "God's right" was to draw blood copiously.

The Mahdi also issued many new orders regarding marriages. Hitherto in the Sudan and in the East generally, the marriage ceremony is accompanied by large feasts. It was the custom of the father on the betrothal of his daughter to obtain in exchange as large a sum of money as possible; that is the reason why fathers greatly preferred their children to be girls, for they made quite a small fortune on their marriages.

* In law, the retributive chastisement which it is the duty of a magistrate to inflict for crime and offences against morality and religion.

But the Mahdi changed all this, and ordered that the bridegroom should expend a sum of ten dollars only, besides providing a korbab (girth) coverlet, perfumes and ointment for the bride's hair, also another sort of ointment which the Sudanese greatly appreciate, and which is generally used for anointing the bridegroom's body; also he must supply a pair of shoes. The ceremonies of betrothal and marriage are very simple. When the contract is completed and the above articles delivered by the bridegroom, his friends and relations assemble, generally on a Friday or Monday (these days being considered lucky); after a good meal the fiki asks the bride or some one appointed to represent her, whether she consents to the marriage, after which the bridegroom repeats the usual saying, in which he mentions the Mahdi's name, the ceremony is thus concluded, and is announced to the neighbours by the women of the party uttering at intervals the shrill cries of joy called "Zagharit." Young women are forbidden by the Mahdi to walk about with uncovered faces; an unveiled woman is considered to be naked; but if she wear a veil and the rest of her body be unclothed, it is not an offence. The wearing of gold and silver ornaments, and of goat's hair curled and plastered with gum (a custom which some of the Sudanese women affect), was strictly forbidden, and woe to the woman who thus adorned herself; not only was her false hair forcibly torn from her, but her real hair as well.

All these innovations the Mahdi justified by the divinity of his mission. He announced that he was the last of the prophets, and that the end of the world was near; further, he said that during his lifetime the prophet Jesus would appear, and that the whole world would become Moslem; he therefore urged the people to repentance and prayer, and do all in their power to further the Jehad (or holy war). Why should they seek after riches when in a very short time the world would cease to exist? It is easy to see how such teaching as this must eventually result in famine and destruction. The Mahdi forbad all weeping and wailing for the dead, on the grounds that to die in such times as the present for the Mahdi's cause was an honour and reward which would without fail secure paradise to them. As for those who did not have the good fortune to die, the Mahdi urged them to show their contempt for the pleasures of this life by continual fasting, prayer, and repentance. If a man were suffering from hunger, he recommended him to tighten his belt, whilst his more fanatical adherents advised placing a heavy stone on the stomach. He further ordained that the poorest of clothes should be worn, the feet bared or in sandals, and, in imitation of the Prophet's example, the hard floor should be chosen as the place on which to sleep. He made curious regulations regarding the manufacture of jibbehs (*i.e.* the Mahdi uniform coat); they should be made of damur, a rough cotton fabric of the Sudan, and if torn, they should be mended with new patches or old rags, but that on no account should a new jibbeh ever be worn.

All these innovations, which were based on religious motives, were intended by him to enforce unity and cohesion amongst his followers, and at the same time they had the effect of hardening them to undergo the perils of war without complaint; for the Mahdi thoroughly understood as long as men were rich they would fear death, and that a luxurious and comfortable mode of life was the worst possible training for war. The Mahdi always conducted prayers in public, and his followers considered it a very great privilege to be permitted to take part in worship with him; consequently, when he prayed, his followers came in their thousands, and ranged themselves in long regular lines behind him. When prayers were concluded, it was his custom to make religious discourses, in which he explained various passages in the sacred books, arguing that they referred to the divine message concerning his mission, and the destruction of the Turks and unbelievers. The people whom he addressed were so ignorant and uneducated that they believed implicitly every word he uttered; these were the guileless, simple folk, and they were entirely deceived by the Mahdi; but there were others who well knew that every word he uttered was a falsehood; nevertheless they listened, and, to flatter him, showed an apparent interest in his new doctrine.

Thus the Mahdi, having prepared himself, as we have seen, and having already been three times victorious over the Egyptian troops, now quitted his place of refuge, Gedir, and set off for Kordofan, which he intended to reduce to entire submission. In order to cover his retreat in case of failure, he left his uncle, Sherif Mahmud, with some troops at Gedir, where he also left the guns, as transport at that time of the year was very difficult, owing to the rain having flooded the khors and valleys; he also left behind the arms captured from the Turks. Hitherto he had not collected any large amount of treasure, and had suffered considerable privations at Gedir.

When the Mahdi announced his departure from Gedir, he wrote letters to the tribes, and soon they flocked to his standards in great numbers and from all directions; Baggara from the plains of Dar Nuba, Miserieh, Dar Abu Dali, and Hawazma Arabs. These hordes assembled, according to the Mahdi's orders, at Birket, and to this place also came the Bederieh, Ghodiat, and Dar Homr Arabs, whilst on the further side of El Obeid, cruel fiki Minneh was gathering the Gowameh, Asaker Abu Kalam and Dar Giumeh Arabs, with whom he intended to assault El Obeid from the north, simultaneously with the Mahdi's attack from the south. The rumours of the enormous quantities of treasure stored in El Obeid misled the Arab hordes, and there is no doubt that the town would not have fallen had the inhabitants remained loyal to the Government. Mohammed Said Pasha had dug a ditch and raised a high parapet round the whole city; but this line of defence was so extensive, that it would have required at least 20,000 men to hold it; besides, the ditch was neither sufficiently deep nor broad, and did not present a very serious obstacle to cross.

From Birket the Mahdi despatched three messengers to Said Pasha, calling on him to surrender, and to acknowledge him as Mahdi; in case he refused he was threatened with instant destruction. The three messengers, clothed in their soiled and tattered jibbehs, were brought before a meeting of all the principal people in El Obeid; but in spite of their dirty appearance, they behaved in such an overbearing and insolent way, that Said Pasha, regardless of the advice and counsel of a number of those present who were in reality in league with the Mahdi, at once ordered Skander Bey to hang them. The order was carried out, and in a few moments their lifeless bodies were dangling on the gallows.

If Said Pasha had taken strong measures in dealing with some of the principal townsmen, he might have saved El Obeid. A certain Ahmed Dafallah, a loyal supporter of the Government, urged him to put all the suspected people including himself in chains in the Mudirieh; this would have disposed of Elias Pasha, Mohammed Wad el Areik, Hajji Khaled, Ben en Naga, and Siwar ed Dahab; and their chiefs once away, it is probable their followers would have returned to their former loyalty; but Said Pasha refused to accept the proposal, and instead of trying to win over his sworn enemy, Elias Pasha, he alienated him still further by taking possession of his newly-built house near the Mudirieh and handing it over to Elias's bitterest enemy, Ahmed Dafallah, to live in, thus entirely disregarding Elias Pasha. Now was Elias Pasha's opportunity to revenge himself on his two adversaries, the garrison of El Obeid was unusually weak, insignificant reinforcements had been sent from Khartum under Mohammed Pasha Khabir, but he also, being an enemy of the Mudir, joined the Mahdi, as I shall narrate in the following chapter.

CHAPTER II.

FATHER OHRWALDER AND HIS COMPANIONS TAKEN CAPTIVE.

The storm rises in Dar Nuba—The Baggara begin to raid—Khojur Kakum of Delen—Mek Omar besieges Delen—The slave guard deserts the Mission—The priests and nuns surrender—They are sent to the Mahdi.

LEAVING the Mahdi at Birket, I shall now return to the narration of the events which befel us in Jebel Nuba.

As I have already said, the first indication of a revolt occurred in our part of the country in April 1882. When the Mahdi had established himself at Gedir, the slave-hunters, whose occupation had been destroyed by the action of the Goverment, and who were therefore greatly incensed, were among the first to join his banners. At that time the most notorious slave-dealer was a certain Ismail Wad el Andok of Haboba, who took the opportunity, when the Government was collecting troops to attack the Mahdi, to assemble about 1,600 men and make a slave raid on Golfan-Naïma. He had already burnt over a hundred houses and captured the inhabitants, when some of the poor Nubas who had escaped, arrived by night at Delen and urgently begged the inspector of slaves, Roversi, for help. This, Roversi gladly promised he would give them, but it required all his powers of persuasion to induce Captain Mohammed Suleiman to consent; and, indeed, there was no small risk in advancing with only eighty men—which was all Roversi could raise—to attack this powerful band of robbers. However, we put our trust in God, and asked His blessing on our humane undertaking. Roversi left that evening, guided by the terror-stricken Nubas.

Golfan-Naïma is about ten hours' journey from Delen, and Roversi, by making a forced march during the night, arrived there at daybreak, and was taken by the Nubas to a high hill, from which he could see the enemy's entire camp without being seen, and, indeed, so close was he that he could hear the horses neighing and the sheep bleating. After the men had taken a short rest, they prepared for the assault. Soon after daybreak, Roversi gave the signal for attack by a trumpet call; the enemy, taken completely by surprise, thought only of flight, but the bullets coming from every direction, gave them no time to think or look from whence they came or how many were opposed to them; they fled as rapidly as they could, leaving behind them all the people and cattle they had captured, as well as a number of their own women. Roversi's men were soon masters of the situation, and were welcomed by the relieved Nubas with every expression of joy and delight; the other Nubas, who had fled to the hills, now came down and cut off the retreat of the Arabs. Roversi captured a large quantity of loot, received the warmest thanks from the captives he had rescued, and soon after he released a number of the women whom he had taken prisoners. The large number of cattle and sheep captured from the Arabs in this expedition proved invaluable during the investment of Delen, which followed shortly afterwards. The little force now returned laden with booty of every description, and was received by the inhabitants with every manifestation of joy. This, however, was our last victory.

I must now give a short description of Delen before I proceed to narrate the events which occurred there later on. Delen, situated five days' journey to the south of El Obeid, is on one of the smallest of the mountain ranges. Jebel Delen itself consists of five hill summits, decreasing in height from south to north, the highest point being scarcely 1,500 feet above the plain. These five hills form a most picturesque group; enormous granite blocks lie piled one over the other, and the spacious cavities thus formed serve as haunts for panthers and other beasts of prey. The rain, which comes down in torrents, has washed all the soil away, leaving only the barren rocks standing in these huge piles; far in the clefts, a sort of wild fig has taken slender root, and, gradually shooting up, gives a pleasant shade, and takes off from the barren aspect which these hills would otherwise present. Of the five hills only two are inhabited, and in all there cannot be more than 2,000 inhabitants, who are remarkable for their tall and graceful figures and unusual bravery. At the foot of the northernmost hill lay our little Mission station, while at the foot of the south-east hill was situated the palisaded zariba of the soldiers; to the west and north, and close to the Mission buildings, stretched the Nuba villages, extending from the base to the summit of the hills.

The second hill from the north, which is about 600 yards from the first hill, was inhabited by the Nubas and their Khojur Kakum. Kakum was at that time a man of about fifty years of age of commanding appearance, and greatly respected by the blacks. He used to wear wide white trousers and a gallabieh, and on his head a nicely embroidered cap with a large tassel which our sisters had made for him. He had passed his youth in Alexandria as a soldier, and acquitted himself admirably as the Khojur, not of Delen only, but also of the neighbouring hills. Numbers of people used to come and seek his blessing and advice, and when our Bishop Comboni arrived at El Obeid, he was there to beg him to send missionaries to teach his people and make men of them. He always remained faithful and loyal to the Government, and when our time of difficulty and hardship came, his continual motto was, "Eed Effendina tawileh" (*i.e.* "Our Khedive's hand is long") —that is to say, his power is great.

The third mountain was occupied by a certain Dogman, with a small following who were for the most part inclined to Mahdiism. For the moment this man was not dangerous, and the people on the two other hills remained loyal to us. When the whole country was up in arms against the Government, this honesty and devotion on the part of these poor Nubas was a bright exception; they would even have fought for us had it been of any use and we had deemed it necessary.

The enemies we most feared were the Baggara of the Nuba plains, who had their headquarters at Singiokai, about six hours north of Delen. These tribesmen had joined in the revolt from the beginning, and had cut off our communication with El Obeid; they had organised themselves into a corps of from 150 to 200 strong, mounted on horses, and they frequently made incursions on the people in the neighbourhood of Delen; they would suddenly appear galloping at full speed, and as suddenly disappear, destroying or seizing everything on their path. Their raids were principally directed against the Nubas who were working in the fields, and on their women who were carrying water from the wells. These robber-dervishes appeared for the first time on the 8th of April, 1882, and a cry of alarm was raised from the mountains, which echoed and re-echoed it back a hundred times.

Every one fled to the mountains, even the cattle instinctively made for their shelters. Some Nubas were attacked and killed in the woods, and twelve of the soldiers, who were out looking after the camels grazing, were all killed, with the exception of one who fell severely wounded in the back; all the camels were captured. When the Baggara had disappeared, the Nubas descended from the hills and came to the scene of the raid. On finding the dead bodies, with weeping and wailing they carried them back to the villages; the women tore their hair, rolled on the ground, and put dust on their heads. The large broad lances had made deep gaping wounds in the unfortunate soldiers who had fallen.

That night, when all was still, the widows of these poor men went to the top of a high rock and there sang a solemn dirge for the dead, which made a melancholy echo in the deep recesses of the hills. I never heard a more touching lamentation for the dead. It was as if all nature joined in sympathy with these poor people, whose happy homes had been destroyed. I was deeply affected, and the more so as I thought over the cruel fate which now seemed to be hanging over our heads.

Soon afterwards the Baggara appeared again, but this time they were seen from a distance, and by a preconcerted signal all fled to places of security, and the robbers returned empty-handed. The Nubas now wanted to lie in wait for the Baggara, and asked the captain commanding the company to assist them with twenty men. This, however, he refused to do, so we gave them twenty rifles from the Mission, and they then prepared an ambush for the unsuspecting Arabs, who a few days afterwards came riding along on their tired horses. The Nubas waited till they came quite close, and then suddenly opened fire; fifteen of the enemy fell, and the remainder galloped off at full speed; eight horses and some booty fell into the hands of the Nubas, who returned in triumph to the village, and were welcomed with great rejoicings. It was interesting to see them as they marched slowly along, leading their captured horses, while the maidens of the village danced in front of them and sang songs in honour of the braves.

We had now a short period of tranquillity, but soon afterwards the Baggara renewed their attacks, and we were in a state of constant alarm. Our information about the Mahdi was distorted and unreliable; we had practically no news from El Obeid, and we could only arrive at the conclusion that the Government was powerless, otherwise why should the Baggara attack us?

One evening the captain told us that he had certain information that we were to be massacred that night; he had heard that the Baggaras had made a compact with the Khojur Kakum and the Nubas, and that our destruction had been agreed upon. The alarm which fell upon our little colony at this news can be readily understood.

It was a very dark night, and in the distance we saw a line of fires which we took to be the Baggara campfires. As we all quite believed in the captain's information, we prepared ourselves for defence; but as we thought over the situation we began to wonder how it was that Kakum, who had hitherto been our sworn friend, and united to us by the tie of blood-brotherhood, should suddenly join with his bitterest enemies, the Baggara, to compass our destruction; then, if the news were false, why should we spend a night of anguish?

After some deliberation, Father Bonomi decided to ascertain the true state of affairs, and taking with him two boys and a lantern, he set off to see the Khojur himself. Full of anxious thoughts, we watched the light as it moved on towards the gap in the hills; at length it reached the base, and then began slowly ascending. An ominous silence pervaded the whole place, which was unusual, for the Nubas love gossiping till a late hour at night. Still we kept our eyes fixed on the light, which eventually disappeared. How anxiously we awaited its reappearance! Should the Khojur intend treachery, we knew we should not see Bonomi again. How slowly the time passed! But at length the light reappeared, and began to descend the hill. We breathed again; after all we should not lose our Father Bonomi.

In a few minutes he was with us again, and with a cheery laugh told us how the captain's information was all wrong, and how angry the Khojur was that we should ever have doubted him. I thereupon hastened to the soldiers' quarters, to reassure the poor captain. Mohammed Suleiman was really a good man, but he was too old and unfitted for his position. Although it was midnight, he and Roversi returned with me to the Mission, and there he related how one of his female slaves, who had a slight knowledge of the Nuba language, had gone to the Khojur to grind some dhurra, and had overheard him talking secretly with some of the Nubas; then some of them had got angry, and, standing up, beat the ground with their spears. This, the woman concluded, must mean an oath that we should be destroyed. As for the rest of the story, it was entirely the woman's invention. Everything was now explained, and our fear gave way to cheerful conversation, which we continued till dawn, when the ringing of the "ave" bell awakened the echoes of the black mountains of Delen.

At sunrise the Khojur arrived, accompanied by a number of followers and many influential Nubas. Not content with his declaration of fidelity made the previous night, the good man had come down to give us his solemn oath that, far from fighting against us, he and his men were ready to fight and die for us. In a grave speech, full of earnest fervour, he assured us of his and of the Nubas' friendship. We, on the other hand, felt certain of his loyalty, and we pledged the success of our compact in a bottle of wine, which our good friend the Khojur greatly enjoyed.

We lived in this state of uncertainty and fear for upwards of five months, not knowing what the next day would bring forth; we were entirely cut off from the rest of the world, and our peaceful work and occupations were all disturbed. We now no longer dared to expose ourselves on the plains, but confined ourselves to the hills, where we sometimes hunted the koodoo. On one occasion, when we went to the Dogman mountain, our suspicions were aroused by the way in which the people gathered round us, and showed a curious desire to examine our arms. As we were returning, the former sheikh of this district—a man named Isa—warned us not to come to the mountain again, as some of the men intended to kill us, and would have done so had they not been afraid of our arms. Roversi's rifle had a magazine for sixteen cartridges.

Early in September our position became very critical. The Mahdi, having quitted Gedir, had advanced into Kordofan; his adherents gathered round him at Birket from all directions, and from here he despatched a certain Mek Omar with letters and a small band of followers to take possession of Delen. Mek Omar arrived, and encamped on the hill with his friend Dogman, and planting his standard, he beat his war-drum incessantly, day and night. He then sent us a letter saying that the Mahdi had captured El Obeid, and that all the inhabitants had joined him, with the exception of Mohammed Said Pasha and a few soldiers who still held out in the Mudirieh buildings; at the same time Omar urged us to submit, as resistance was useless. The fact that Omar, with only fifty men, possibly less, had the audacity to pitch his camp under our very eyes, rather induced us to believe in the truth of his assertions. Roversi, however, determined to attack him, but was dissuaded from doing so by the captain.

We then held a council to consider what would be the best course to follow. After much deliberation (which is always the case in dealing with Arabs) it was unanimously decided to attempt a flight to Fashoda. The Nubas also, who offered us their services as guides, advised us to take this course. It is very probable we should have succeded in this attempt, as almost all the Arabs who wanted to fight had followed the Mahdi to El Obeid, in anticipation of the booty which they thought would so soon be theirs.

The route to Fashoda lay far to the south of the scene of present operations, and with the eighty Remingtons of the soldiers, and our thirty good rifles, we felt confident that we should be able to make our way thither. It was therefore decided that we should start off very quietly in the dead of night. Every one made up a small bundle of the few things he wished to take, which would be required on the journey, either as presents or to buy or offer in exchange for food. We also had a sufficient number of camels, mules, and donkeys for the sisters and sick, and we had made up into bundles all that we required; we gave the rest of our things to the Nubas, so that nothing should fall into Mek Omar's hands. The Nubas gave us every possible assistance, and through the darkness we could see them moving about like ghosts amongst the black rocks, laden with every imaginable thing.

At midnight we quitted the Mission and made our way to the soldiers' zariba, hoping that we should find them all ready to start; but instead we found them all in bed, the captain had given no orders to prepare, and Roversi's influence was gone. We tried in various ways to induce the captain to give orders, but he merely answered that he was waiting till he received a reply from Mek Omar, to whom he had written. Getting impatient, he sent a trustworthy man to Omar, who never returned. It was now nearly sunrise, and all our efforts to move the captain were unavailing. Then the Khedivial National Anthem, which was always blown at reveille, was sounded, but was smothered by the deafening rattle of the noggaras; it was, as it were, a mockery, showing that the light of civilisation was about to be extinguished by the barbaric hordes of Jebel Nuba. In the meantime the soldiers had got ready of their own accord, and declared themselves willing to undergo any fatigue, and, if needs be, die for us; but the fear and irresolution shown by their captain unnerved them, and as the sun rose they one by one left the camp and submitted to Mek Omar. A very few only stayed with Roversi; and when the captain quitted the zariba, these too went over to the enemy.

Thus were we left quite alone—a party of some 200 persons, of whom the greater number were women and children. Flight was now out of the question; there was nothing left for us but to return to our homes. We did so; but what a sight met our eyes! The Nubas had carried off everything. With heavy hearts we returned to the rooms of the Mission; here everything was wrecked and ruined; what the Nubas had thought of no use to themselves they had smashed to pieces. Roversi, who had always been most loyal and true to us, now went to Mek Omar to arrange for his own safety. When the first bitterness of feeling had passed off, we discussed the next step to be taken; there was

THE MISSIONARIES SURRENDER.   31

absolutely nothing left in the station, and we had not a mouthful of food left.

I then went, in company with Bonomi, to Mek Omar. This former slave-dealer—a short, crippled, and dirty old Takruri, who had been well known to us a long time ago—received us in a friendly manner. He had coffee brought to us, and related the great bravery of the Mahdi, and then concluded with the following words : " I know that you will not turn Mohammedans, you must therefore understand that your property and slaves are no longer your own ; at the same time I will give you a letter to the Mahdi regarding your situation." Hard as these conditions were, we had no alternative but to accept ; and when our conference was over, our arms were taken from us, and all our blacks, for whose welfare so many lives had been sacrificed and such trouble expended, were suddenly lost to us at one fell stroke. We then returned to the Mission, where we spent the night alone and on our knees.

These events took place on the 14th of September, 1882. On the morning of the 15th of September we rang for the last time the ave-bell for Heaven knows how many years. At noon Mek Omar arrived with his followers, and, chanting the Mohammedan creed, he first entered the church, and there we had the agony of beholding with our own eyes its destruction. Our blacks were taken over by Omar's troops, and attached to the Government soldiers. Omar thought that he would find some treasure, but here he was mistaken, for we had hidden the little money we had to meet our future wants ; and as we had been cut off from El Obeid for seven months, we had consumed all our reserve stores ; for the fourteen days previous to this we had not even any salt to mix with our food.

We had to stay on at Delen for three long days, awaiting Omar's pleasure to allow us to proceed. It was pitiable to see the cruel and brutal way in which our poor blacks were treated by Omar's followers. Before leaving we paid Khojur Kakum a visit ; the poor man was filled with pity for us, and more especially for the sisters; he longed to stay with us, and, bitterly weeping, bade us farewell. He also fully expected to meet a tragic fate. We finally left our beloved Nuba hills on the 18th of September, and after endless trouble succeeded in procuring from Mek Omar four animals on which the sisters could ride. Father Bonomi, myself, and two lay brothers took it in turns to walk and ride. Our mounts consisted of a camel, a mule, and two donkeys. Mek Omar placed us in charge of his son Naser and a party of Arabs; several of the Nubas accompanied us for some distance, and as we passed Kakum's hill, we could see the poor man standing up and stretching out his hands towards us as a last farewell. Many of our young blacks also followed us, but were forced by their new masters to turn back. Our departure caused us pangs of grief which pierced us to the very core.

In the evening we reached a small hill called Kudru, at the base of which there was a well, and here we encamped for the night. Here also the Nubas came down from the rocks to greet us. We left the next morning, and our road now lay through the great grass plains. At this season of the year, besides the rain, there is always a very heavy dew which wetted us to the skin, besides we often had to ford streams up to our necks, and emerging with dripping clothes, to continue our march. We knew that this was sure to bring on fever and diarrhœa, and so, indeed, it proved, shortly after our arrival at El Obeid.

At length we reached Singiokai, the head-quarters of the Baggara, and we found numbers of nomad Arabs living in tents. On our arrival, every one, old and young, hastened to look at us, and gaze on the hated captured Christians. This inquisitive and motley crowd derided us and heaped insults upon us; the ugly old women, whom one could only compare with hyenas, were perhaps the most bitter in their disgraceful taunts. We stayed here one day, and then continued our journey. Whenever we came to a village we were subjected to the rudest treatment, and had we not been guarded by our escort, we must have inevitably been killed. We were constantly searched, in the hope that money would be found on us. When we got near El Obeid, Naser put us into a hut, where we were told to remain until he should see the Mahdi, and ascertain from him his instructions regarding us. We gathered from what he said that he was going to find out whether we should be killed where we were, or brought first before the Mahdi. Thus Naser left us under strict guard.

CHAPTER III.

THE MISSIONARIES AND THE MAHDI.

Description of El Obeid—Said Pasha's system of defence—The Mahdi's followers encircle the town—Townspeople desert to the Mahdi—Unsuccessful attack on Government buildings—Dervishes driven off with loss of 10,000 men—The missionaries brought before the Mahdi—Threatened with death—Preparations for the execution—Reprieved at the last moment—The Mahdi's camp described—Death of some of the missionaries—Illness of remainder.

DURING our stay in the hut we were told how the inhabitants of El Obeid had joined the Mahdi, and that only the garrison held out; but I will here narrate what had actually occurred.

We left the Mahdi last at Birket, while his three messengers had been hanged in El Obeid. He left Birket on the 4th of September, and encamped at Kaba, a place a few hours' journey from El Obeid. El Obeid is situated in the midst of a vast plain, which in the hot weather is just like a desert. Here and there a few Adansonia trees, transported from Khartum, break the monotony of this dreary scene which is bounded on the south-east by the Kordofan mountains; at a distance of about five kilometres to the north rises the cone-shaped hill known as Korbatsh, while to the north-west appears the small Om Herezeh mountain. El Obeid lies in a sort of hollow in the plain; consequently during the winter-time the wells become full of water, and serve as a sufficient supply for the whole year.

Since the Egyptian occupation of the Sudan, El Obeid had become a town of some importance, but the houses were for the most part built of mud, with the exception of the Government buildings, which were constructed of sun-dried bricks. The entrance to these buildings was through a lofty archway, over which a second story had been raised, thus making it a most conspicuous object, and one which could be seen from a considerable distance. El Obeid, at the time of which I speak, was an important and flourishing city, with a population of about 100,000 souls. It was noted principally for its gum, the best quality of which was known by the name of Kordofan gum. The largest quantities came from Tayara and Dar Homr, where the gum trees were planted in large gardens regularly laid out. Thousands of camels were engaged in the transport of this valuable commodity to Shatt on the White Nile, to Omdurman, and to Dongola. Ostrich feathers also formed another important article of commerce. At Dar Homr there are numbers of ostrich farms, the animals being kept in large zaribas; but as an article of trade, the feathers of the wild ostriches are more valuable than those of the domestic animal. Ostrich feathers are always sold by weight. Other exports from Kordofan are tamarinds, senna, and the skins of animals. Iron is also found in Kordofan; and one day, when we were digging out a well at Delen, we came across quicksilver.

El Obeid was also the supply depôt for Darfur, Shakka, and Dar Nuba, and thus became an important trade centre. Numbers of rich merchants lived here, such as Elias Pasha, Omberer, Hajji Mohammed Ben en Naga, Ahmed Bey Dafallah (who owned thousands of slaves), Mohammed Wad el Areik, Hajji Khaled, Ibrahim wad Adlan, besides numbers of Copts and Egyptians. Several of the principal mercantile houses in Cairo also had their agents—Syrians, Greeks, and Jews—in El Obeid. Kordofan was also rich in cattle. The Kababish, Dar Homr, Beni Jerrar, and Dar Hamed Arabs possessed large numbers of she-camels. These animals are always kept in the deserts, and are retained exclusively for breeding purposes. Quantities of the young camels are killed, and their flesh, which is preferred to any other kind of meat in the Sudan, is considered a great luxury, and is generally eaten uncooked. Corn is largely grown in Kordofan, also sesame, which is preferred to that grown on the White Nile; large white water-melons are also grown in abundance. It may therefore be understood why Kordofan was the richest province in the Sudan and brought in the largest revenue to Government.

The whole of this rich country was now in the hands of the Mahdi, with the exception of El Obeid, which was destined soon to be the scene of bloodshed and fanatical warfare between people of the same race and religion. The Arabs of various tribes, who in peace time had brought their goods to El Obeid to barter and exchange, were now clamouring for the destruction of the town and the slaughter of its inmates. As I have already related, Said Pasha had completely surrounded the town by a ditch and parapet; but as this would require such an enormous number of men to defend it, and knowing that he could place little reliance on the inhabitants, he had strongly entrenched the Mudirieh and Government buildings, and at the same time put into a state of defence the barracks, officers and officials' houses, and those of the Greek and Syrian merchants, The members of our Mission station left their house and pretty church, and hired rooms within the fortifications; the loyal citizens and merchants followed their example, while the remainder of the inhabitants continued to live in the town, and conspired with the Mahdi. On the 7th of December, that is to say, the day on which the Mahdi arrived at Kaba, the whole of these inhabitants quitted the town and joined him in his camp. The wealthy merchants had for long been in communication with the Mahdi, others joined him because they were worked up to a pitch of wild fanaticism; some feared to disobey the summons, for they could see how weak were the Government troops and how successful the Mahdi had been. Amongst the deserters to the Mahdi's side were Mohammed Khabir Pasha of Darfur, and a number of irregular troops who had been despatched from Khartum as reinforcements for El Obeid.

THE MAHDI ATTACKS EL OBEID.

Thus by various means the Mahdi's force now numbered upwards of 30,000 fighting men, and with such an army as that it seemed to him a very easy matter to subdue Said Pasha and his meagre garrison. The Mahdi further incited his people to fight by assuring them that the gates of paradise were open to all those martyrs who should fall, and that each of them should be attended by forty lovely houris when they entered its portals. He also roused their feelings of cupidity by representing, in the most exaggerated terms, the value of the treasure locked up within the Mudirieh, and told them that victory was assured, for God and his Prophet had decreed that they should annihilate their enemies with simple sticks; this he said because he knew that only a few of his followers had firearms. Having thus raised them to a pitch of the wildest excitement, he advanced from Kaba.

In the meantime the Mudir, seeing that he could not rely on the inhabitants, did all in his power to improve the fortifications, and awaited the assault of the enemy. At daybreak the hordes appeared on the rising ground near El Obeid; the defenders heard only the dull roar caused by the mass of voices in the distance, but the clouds of dust prevented them seeing anything; it was only when the fitful gusts of wind blew away the dust that the thousands of horsemen could be seen galloping wildly about and then disappearing again behind the dust. But the noise like approaching thunder became every instant more audible, and soon above the clouds of sand the myriads of flags and banners became visible. Fiki Minneh, with about 10,000 men, approached from the east, whilst the Mahdi's attack was directed on the south-west end of the town. The first ditch was soon crossed, and then the Mahdiists spread out and completely encircled the town; masses of wild fanatics rolled like waves through the deserted streets; they did not advance through these alone, but hurrying on from house to house, wall to wall, and yard to yard, they reached the ditch of the Mudirieh, and like a torrent suddenly let loose, regardless of every obstacle, with wild shouts they dashed across it and up the ramparts, from which the din of a thousand rifles and the booming of the guns suddenly burst forth; but these wild hordes, utterly fearless of death, cared neither for the deadly Remington nor the thunder of the guns, and still swept forward in ever-increasing numbers.

The poor garrison, utterly powerless to resist such an assault, ran to the tops of the houses and kept up an incessant fire on the masses, which now formed such a crowd that they could scarcely move—indeed the barrels of the rifles from the rapidity of the fire became almost red hot; and soon the streets and open spaces became literally choked with the bodies of those who had fallen. There was a momentary pause, and Ali Bey Sherif, seizing this opportunity, collected a party of men and dashed towards the magazine, where a fierce conflict was going on between the guard and the Dervishes. The latter had already become masters of the situation when Ali Bey suddenly appeared on the scene, and firing on the mass, whether friend or foe, he drove the Mahdiists back over the ditch, and then formed up in the breach ready to repel any further attempt to break in.

Meanwhile Said Pasha was heavily engaged in front of the Mudirieh. Here an emir named Wad Gubara broke in, and shouting, "Death to the Turks, those dogs and swine!" he dashed forward at the head of his men, but the determined resistance of the Mudir forced them to retire back across the ditch. Ahmed Dufallah defended that part of the line which was assaulted by Ibrahim Wad Abdullah, an emir who had gained great celebrity amongst the Dervishes. This brave Arab attacked again and again, hoping that the bodies of those who fell would soon fill up the ditch and make a passage which he could cross, but his attempt failed, and he too was forced to retire.

The Mahdi all this time was watching at a safe distance, and kept on ordering the assault to continue; but it was impossible to stand up against the well-directed fire from the defences, and consequently towards the afternoon he was forced to retire. The gallant little garrison seeing this, could not be restrained, and dashing out over the heaps of slain they made a fierce onslaught on the houses in the town, which were filled with Dervishes in search of loot. In their fury they killed all who came in their way, and perhaps they may be excused, for they were in a state of the wildest excitement, occasioned by this fearful scene of bloodshed.

It was impossible not to admire the reckless bravery of these fanatics who, dancing and shouting, rushed up to the very muzzles of the rifles with nothing but a knotty stick in their hands, only to fall dead one over the other. Numbers of them carried large bundles of dhurra stalk, which they threw into the ditch, hoping to fill it up and then cross over. When the town was cleared, the victorious troops had a great feast and general rejoicing. Amongst the dead bodies of the Dervishes were found a near relative of the Mahdi's named Said Mohammed, also Wad Gubara; the latter was a Turk who, with his two brothers, had joined the Mahdi at Gedir; he was one of the fiercest of the emirs. He had fought with the greatest pertinacity in front of the Mudirieh, and, mounted on a horse, he was urging on his followers; but the soldiers, noticing his fair face, persistently aimed at him, and at length he and his horse fell on the top of a heap of dead bodies. When the soldiers subsequently found his body, they were so annoyed that a Turk should have joined the Mahdi that they cut off his head and hacked his body to pieces.

Whilst the soldiers were clearing out the enemy from the houses, the Mahdi was retiring on Kaba with a loss of 10,000 men. Said Pasha then held a council to consider whether they should pursue; but he himself was against pursuit, for he thought that possibly Fiki Minneh might then fall on the defenceless town; besides, in all he had not more than 3,000 men. As for the Mahdi, he and his principal emirs were greatly alarmed, and it is very probable that if they had been pursued, the result would have been a complete victory for Said Pasha. As it was, the Mahdi was on the point of retreating to the mountains, and would have done so had not the inhabitants of El Obeid, who still thought of their houses and property, dissuaded him. The latter still urged him to continue the siege, consequently on the following day he took up a position on a hill called Gianzara, about two kilometres distant to the north-west of the town, and only one kilometre distant from the Oshra Well (so called from the oshra or euphorbia which grows in quantities in the vicinity). Fiki Minneh established himself to the north-west of the town, and soon it was more closely invested than ever; from that date nothing came in and nothing went out of the doomed city.

We had spent one day in the hut, and had learnt all the details about the Mahdi's attack on the town, when a messenger sent by Naser arrived, and ordered us to move on to the Mahdi's camp, as it was his gracious intention to permit us to look upon his face. Shortly after we had set out, we met Naser returning, accompanied by a party of Dervishes.

As we approached El Obeid, the rattle of the rifles, broken every now and then by the boom of a gun, became more and more audible. We were halted under a large Adansonia tree and ordered to rest, but we had scarcely laid down when we were suddenly attacked by Naser and his party, who seized our watches and other valuables, and then stripped off our clothes; they even attempted to remove the veils and outer garments of the sisters, but to this we forcibly objected, and seizing sticks tried to drive them off. At length these wretched thieves, ashamed of the unequal contest, drew off, and Naser ordered our clothes to be returned; but my suit, in which I had stitched thirty dollars, was not given back to me, and I was reduced to appearing before the Mahdi in a shirt and drawers! Our escort having satisfied their cupidity, now mounted our donkeys, and we were obliged to walk; the burning sun beat down on our heads, and the heated ground and heavy sand made our progress intensely laborious.

As we approached the camp, at every step the crowd

grew denser. El Obeid was now visible a short way off, and the sight of the houses and trees was a pleasant break in the monotony of this desolate wilderness. The continuous rattle of the bullets, interrupted by the thunder of the cannon, was an indication that a brisk engagement was going on. As we entered the camp, the crowd was so enormous that we were almost choked with the dust that was raised, and soon became thoroughly exhausted. Our brother Mariani, who was sick at the time we left Delen, could keep up no longer, and we were obliged to almost carry him along

The fanatics now completely surrounded us, and kept on threatening us with their lances, clubs, and sticks. Naser himself, seeing some of the very excited Dervishes pointing their lances at our breasts, greatly feared for our safety, and it seemed to us that there was now not the slightest doubt that they intended to kill us. He therefore ordered our escort to draw their swords and form a square, in the centre of which we walked. The exertions of the last few days, the heat, the yelling of the crowd, the monotonous chants of the Dervishes, and finally the din of this enormous camp of over 100,000 men, exclusive of women and children, reacted on us to such an extent that we were well-nigh speechless. Slowly we made our way towards the centre of the camp where the great Dervish, Mohammed Ahmed, had pitched his tent.

We were taken, in the first instance, to the hut of the Khalifa Sherif. Here we found a lad of twelve or thirteen years of age, lying half-naked on a bedstead, who invited us to come into the shade and rest ourselves, at the same time he drove off with his whip the inquisitive crowd that kept pressing in to look at us. He gave us some water to drink, but we were so utterly weary and exhausted that we could not swallow it for some time, and the heat and dust had literally glued our tongues, so that we were unable to articulate. We were allowed to rest for a short time, as the Mahdi had not risen from his noonday sleep, and this brief respite enabled us to collect our thoughts, which the events of the last few days and the uproar of the camp had caused to wander sadly.

At length an order came that the Madhi was up and wished to see us. We were then taken to a small hut, which had two sides open, through which a cool breeze blew in; close to the hut one of the tents captured from Yusef Pasha Shellali had been pitched, and as we arrived the Mahdi came out of the tent and seated himself, in Arabic fashion, on a straw mat spread on the floor of the hut. He greeted us kindly, and asked us about our nationality and our object in coming to the Sudan, also whether we had ever heard anything about the Mahdi, he then briefly explained to us the nature of his divine message, and recounted his great victories over "the enemies of God and His Prophet," by which name he designated the Turks.

Seeing that we were utterly exhausted, he offered us some kamar-ed-din (dried apricots) mixed with water, but almost before we could put it to our mouths it was full of flies. In the meantime a certain George Stambuli, who had joined the rebels with the other inhabitants of El Obeid, came in, and through him the Mahdi endeavoured to place before us the great advantage of the Islam religion. The Mahdi himself never asked us to adopt the Moslem faith, because he feared that we should answer in the negative. He then stretched himself out on the mat as if he were preparing to behold a vision.

Mohammed Ahmed was a powerfully built man, of dark-brown complexion and carefully kept skin; he had a pleasant smile, which showed to advantage the curious slit between his front teeth. By constant training he had acquired a gentle manner in speaking, and with these exceptions there was nothing unusual in his appearance. He wore a dirty jibbeh, on which particoloured strips of cotton had been sewn; on his head the white skull cap or "takia," round which a broad white turban was bound; he also wore a pair of loose drawers and sandals.

After he had lain for some time with closed eyes, he

rose and offered us some more kamar-ed-din, from which he himself began to take out the flies; but finding it absolutely useless to do so, he gave it up, and then went back to his tent, probably to hold a council. After a short time he again returned, wearing a clean jibbeh patched with pieces of the vestments belonging to our Mission church at El Obeid. He then began to recount to us the history of the numerous conversions which had taken place in the early days of the Prophet. Seeing that we took little interest in what he said, he got up and ordered us to be taken before the Khalifa Abdullah (the present ruler of the Sudan), while he himself retired to his own tent.

On our arrival at Abdullah's hut, we found ourselves in company with twenty robbers who were chained hand and foot. An enormous crowd stood round, and amongst the faces I noticed some of our Delen friends, who had evidently followed us to see what the end would be. Our guard, armed with Remington rifles, stood around us, and close to us was the Khalifa Abdullah's horse, which always remained saddled—a witness to his unbounded energy. A short distance off, about eighty flags were planted in the ground, and beside them were the war-drums. Hardly had we seated ourselves when the Khalifa Abdullah entered. He was at that time a man of about thirty-three years of age, of middle height, very thin—in fact, little else but skin and bone; he greeted us kindly, and invited us to become Moslems. From his bombastic conversation, we soon saw that he was a man of no education whatever, and he ended up by saying that if we refused to obey we had only death to expect. We were then marched off.

On the evening of the 27th of September, when George Stambuli came to tell us that if we did not embrace Islam, we should most certainly die, we gave him no hope that we should change our minds. The Mahdi frequently sent people to teach us the truths of religion, but we soon tired of their nonsensical chattering, and Father Bonomi used to send them away with strong words. Shortly afterwards Abdullah came again, bringing a water-melon with him, and in default of a knife he broke it on the ground; but we refused to take any. Greatly annoyed at this, he went off in a rage, saying that we should be beheaded the following morning.

At midnight Stambuli came to us again, to say that he had offered a considerable sum for our ransom, but that the Mahdi had refused to accept it. We therefore gave him the few dollars we had left, and asked him to come and see us the following morning, which he promised to do. We employed our few remaining hours in preparation for death. The terrors and alarms which we had undergone for the last five months were over at last; in the midst of our sufferings the thought of death, which should soon take us out of the hands of these barbarians, was a comfort to us. A deep quiet had now settled down over the camp, which was only occasionally broken by the clank of the prisoners' chains.

Just before dawn a wonderful comet appeared in the east; its golden tail seemed to project about ten feet into the blue firmament, and was a most striking sight. It brought back to our minds the star in the east which stood over the manger at Bethlehem. The Arabs called it "Nigmet el Mahdi" (the Mahdi's star).

According to Sudan superstition, the appearance of a comet is supposed to forebode evil, and, indeed, what catastrophe could have been greater than that which was now impending over the Sudan? The sudden clang of the war-drum startled me from the meditations which the appearance of that strange comet had produced. The beating of the drums and the blast of the great ivory horn (onbeïa) was the signal for the "Ardeh-Kebir," or grand review, and I now had to bethink me of my own affairs and let the star pursue its way in the heavens.

The emirs' war-drums now took up the signal, and soon people were rushing from all directions towards their particular flags, which were planted to the east of El Obeid. Stambuli again appeared and announced to us

THE MISSIONARIES BROUGHT OUT FOR EXECUTION. 45

that our sufferings were nearly over. We gave him a small piece of paper on which we had written our last farewells to our own loved ones at home, and had signed our names. This we begged him to send on when an opportunity occurred. Weeping bitterly, he took the paper and went to his hut, saying he could not bear to look on at our execution.

We were now all ready, and at about nine o'clock a party of thirty men armed with lances arrived and ordered us to follow them. We were still suffering from fatigue, but we got up and followed. After about half an hour's walk we arrived before the Dervish hosts, and thanked God that victory was now so near. About 40,000 men were standing on parade, and thousands of others were moving about the camp like ants. We were taken to a central position and ordered to bend our necks to receive the death-blow, and without the smallest hesitation we did so. But our hour had not yet come. We were summoned before the Mahdi, who was riding on a magnificent white camel; behind him rode a slave carrying an umbrella to shade him from the sun's rays. As we approached, he turned round to us and said, "May God lead you into the way of truth," and then rode on.

The troops were now dismissed, and we were immediately surrounded by a turbulent crowd, who threatened to crush us to death; but the Mahdi, seeing us in danger, turned back, and ordered us to walk in front of his camel for protection. We did so, but were too weary to keep up, and then the Mahdi gave orders, which we could not understand, to a number of different emirs; the latter ordered us to halt until the great rush of people had passed, then they formed a square and asked each one of us separately whether we agreed to become Moslems or would prefer to suffer death. Each one of us answered resolutely—death! Then, full of anger, we were forced on—exhausted and covered from head to foot with dust—till we reached the Mahdi's hut. Having arrived there he said, "Have you not seen my army?" and then he began to boast of the number of his followers and their great bravery. We said nothing. He then went off, and we were taken back to Khalifa Abdullah's hut.

A council was now held to consider our fate; the majority were for killing us, but a certain Hajji Khaled —now an emir in Omdurman—pointed out that, according to the Moslem law, it was not lawful to kill priests who had not offered any armed resistance, and who were, moreover, captives. His view of the case was accepted, and we were handed over to George Stambuli, who was made responsible for us. We then left Abdullah's hut, and proceeded to Stambuli's, which was barely large enough for himself and his family, so we were obliged to take up our quarters outside in the open, where we remained for fifteen days, exposed to the continual insults of the Arabs, until we were able to build a hut for ourselves. We were now able to take a survey of this gigantic camp. From the sandhill Gianzara almost up to the base of the Om Herezeh mountain, was one mass of small huts, these were merely enclosures made of branches of euphorbia and (sorghum) dhurra stalks, just sufficient to keep off the burning rays of the sun. Here and there a white tent indicated the headquarters of some important emir. Fiki Minneh's camp adjoined that of Gianzara, and extended from Fulla (a small pond which runs dry in the summer months), up to the base of Om Herezeh. The huts were built so close to each other that constant fires took place, which spread rapidly, and caused great destruction.

This enormous camp presented a wonderful spectacle, more especially at night, when almost every one had his own cooking fire, and the whole plain resembled a sea of fires which were lost in the distant horizon. The din and noise created by hundreds of thousands of men, women, and children, can be better imagined than described. Every emir's[*] dwelling was known by two

---

[*] The title "Emir" really means "Prince," and is far too high a title to give to these wretched chiefs ; but as it is the Sudan custom, I must retain it.—J. O.

flags which were always planted near the entrance, and beside them lay the war-drums, which were beaten day and night, almost without intermission. Besides all this, the neighing of thousands of horses rendered the din still more unbearable. The whole air was infected with the most sickening stench; but to these wretched people, pure or impure air makes no difference; they do not mind. All the filth was piled behind the huts, dead donkeys lay about unburied; no attempt was made to keep the place clean, and all this huge mass of people lived in the midst of an ever-increasing heap of rotting impurities. A daily market was held, and the people laid their goods on the ground, sheltering themselves under a strip of cloth, known as "Farda," stretched on the points of lances, the bases of which were stuck in the ground. El Obeid was close by, the great arched gate of the Mudirieh towered above the other houses of the town, and over it floated the red Egyptian flag, which was hoisted every Friday. Some of the Dervishes used to conceal themselves in the deserted houses of the town and fire at the fort, while others pulled down the roofs and walls and dragged away the beams to the camp, and there cut them up for firewood. Our church, which was covered with galvanised iron plates, was completely destroyed; even the mosque was not spared. There was a busy scene day and night at the Oshra well; here thousands of male and female slaves drew water, and frequent quarrels and fights took place.

All this change of scene made a deep impression on me; the strain of the last few days, the tiring journey from Delen to El Obeid, the continual uncertainty as to our fate, anguish, fear, din, tumult, bad food, had already considerably affected our health, and now that we were at rest, and that the Arabs had ceased to molest us, the re-action came, and we fell a prey to disease. The infected atmosphere of El Buka—as the Mahdi's camp is always called—brought on a burning fever and constant diarrhœa. Besides all this, when confined with the robbers in Abdullah's house, we had become covered with horrible vermin; it was impossible to get rid of them—they seemed to increase daily. We had no clothes to change, and as we had scarcely enough water to drink, washing was out of the question. With a feeling of utter despair we lay helpless and comfortless on the floor of that miserable black hut. Our maladies became worse, and ere a month had passed, three of our number were dead. Sister Eulalia Pesavento, of Verona, died of fever on the 28th of October; carpenter Gabriel Mariani died of dysentery on the 31st of the same month, and sister Amelia Andreis died on the 7th of November, while we four who still remained, hovering between life and death, lay helplessly side by side with our dead brothers and sisters. It was a terrible exertion to us to sew the corpses in mats and drag them to the door of the hut. At length some slaves—much against their will, and on the promise of good pay—removed the already decaying bodies, and buried them in shallow pits, which they covered up with sand. No one lent a hand to bury these "Christian dogs," as we were called. It was a terrible grief to us not to accompany our poor companions in adversity to the grave, but we were all too ill to move, and so they were carried away to their last resting-place without prayer or chant; and even to this day I cannot tell if the slaves really buried them, or merely dragged the bodies beyond the huts, and left them lying there on the ground.

The condition of us miserable wretches who were still alive is beyond description; we envied our companions, who were now beyond the reach of human suffering; but our hour had not yet come. Towards the end of November we were somewhat recovered, but our lives seemed to have been spared only to behold more terrible sights and sufferings than we had previously undergone.

Meanwhile, more of our companions in adversity had arrived from Dar Nuba. Shortly after we had been made over to Stambuli, Roversi came, and was interviewed by the Mahdi, who received him well, and

THE SAD FATE OF ROVERSI.   49

presented him with a horse. Roversi recounted to us the story of his misfortunes; during his journey from Delen to El Obeid he was frequently in danger of losing his life; the Baggaras, mindful of their defeat at his hands, thirsted for vengeance. Roversi owed his life to his magazine rifle. He used to visit us daily and tell us of the various plots of which we were the intended victims. He told us how the Arabs had determined to take the sisters, and that they intended to distribute us amongst the various emirs. This news terrified the sisters, and there is little doubt that the bare thought of it hastened the deaths of the two who were so ill. Roversi further informed us that a quarrel had occurred between Mek Omar and the Nubas regarding the distribution of the loot taken from our Delen Mission; a conflict had taken place, in which Mek Omar had lost a number of his men, and had been obliged to retreat from Delen to Singiokai.

After Roversi's arrival the Mahdi wrote to Said Pasha again, summoning him to surrender; Roversi also, by the Mahdi's order, was forced to write to the Mudir, telling him that resistance was useless, as it was out of the question to hope for reinforcements from Khartum. Towards the end of October Roversi fell ill with dysentery, caused by the infected and foul atmosphere of the camp; the last time he came to see us he was very weak; then we heard that the Mahdi had suddenly ordered him to Kashgil for change of air, and a few days later we heard that he was dead. Some said he had been killed, others said that he had been poisoned by Ismail Wad el Andok, in revenge for his defeat at Golfan-Naïma. Roversi's maid-servant, Aisha —a black girl brought up in Constantinople—and his man-servant, Hajji Selim, reported that they had found his shoes in the forest, and his dead body in a hut. The unfortunate young Roversi was barely thirty years of age, a Protestant by religion, and a man for whom we all cherished a great affection. The date of his death was probably the 3rd of November, 1882. A few days after this date Mek Omar and his men arrived in the camp, bringing our Delen blacks with them. The latter at once came to see us, and soon afterwards all of them—both boys and girls—were sold as slaves, whilst the more grown-up youths were drafted into the Mahdi's army. Two of the girls, one an Abyssinian and the other a black, became concubines of the Mahdi. A cruel fate soon overtook Mek Omar : it was reported that he had concealed some of the captured booty, and he was at once put in chains by the Mahdi's order. Shortly afterwards he sent for us, and Bonomi and I paid him a visit. We found him shackled with two chains on his feet, and a chain about fifteen feet long round his neck; the poor man was completely bowed down with the weight of these chains, and begged us most humbly to intercede for him, as he told us it was the Mahdi's intention to have him beheaded. The condition of this unfortunate individual so touched us, that Bonomi went to the Mahdi and represented that it was really the Nubas who had stolen the booty, and so Mek Omar was released.

As we slowly began to recover from our illness, the thought of release was constantly in our minds. We applied to the powerful Elias Pasha, whom we had known very well in El Obeid. This blind old pasha received us kindly, but said that Abdel Kader Pasha in Khartum, was furious with him for having joined the rebels ; he therefore said that our best course was to apply daily to the Mahdi, who in time might perhaps be moved to grant our release. We followed his advice, but it was no easy matter to make our way through the crowd of fanatics who surrounded his hut day and night, all struggling to get a sight of his face which, it was said, shed rays of light. Pushed about, shoved in every direction, and insulted, we might perhaps succeed in reaching the doorway ; but here we were stopped by the guards, and it was almost impossible to pass them. However, after superhuman efforts, we succeeded twice in interviewing the Mahdi. He listened kindly to our entreaty, and then said, " At present the roads are dangerous, and I wish no harm to come upon you; when El Obeid has surrendered, we will permit you to go to your own country." He advised us to wear kuftans (the Arab outer garment), for hitherto we wore merely a shirt and drawers, as he said that, dressed in this way, we should escape the inquisitive glances of the multitude and we took his good advice.

CHAPTER IV.

THE SIEGE OF EL OBEID.

Terrible sufferings of the besieged—The Kababish—Fall of Bara—Fall of El Obeid—The Mahdi enters the town—Fate of the El Obeid Mission—Cold-blooded murder of the brave defenders—The Dervishes live a life of ease in El Obeid—The Mahdi makes laws—He sends out proclamations—Prestige increased by capture of town—News from Khartum—Bonomi and Ohrwalder summoned before the Mahdi—The interview.

THE garrison in El Obeid now began to suffer from the effects of this close siege and blockade. The necessaries of life were failing rapidly; the price of provisions had gone up enormously. The commonest food, known as "dokhn" (a kind of millet) rose to 150 dollars, and eventually to 500 dollars the ardeb. Meat had almost entirely given out. Our Mission brethren in the fort possessed one camel, which was nothing but skin and bone, and which was sold for 1,000 dollars, and two days afterwards the purchaser offered it for sale for 1,500 dollars. Eventually the butcher bought it for 2,000 dollars. A chicken went for thirty dollars; eggs a dollar apiece; a loaf of sugar fifty dollars, and twenty dollars for a pound of coffee. A thimbleful of salt cost a dollar. The above were the prices a month after the close investment had begun. Butter and oil could not be had for any money. The poor began to starve quite at the beginning of the siege, and soon were dying in considerable numbers. A little later, matters came to a terrible pass. All the camels and cattle being finished, donkeys, dogs, mice, and even crickets were consumed, as well as cockroaches, which were considered quite tit-bits; white ants, too, were eaten.

And now the deaths by starvation had reached an appalling figure. The dead and dying filled the streets; the space within the fortifications being so limited, there was not room for all the people, and in consequence many lay about in the streets and open spaces. The air was poisoned by the numbers of dead bodies lying unburied, while the ditch was half full of mortifying corpses. Scurvy and dysentery were rife; the air was black with the scores of carrion-kites, which feasted on the dead bodies; these ugly birds became so distended by constant gorging that they could not even fly away, and were killed in numbers by the soldiers, who devoured them with avidity.

Later on gum became the only food; there was a quantity of this, but it brought on diarrhœa, and caused the bodies to distend—indeed, numbers died from eating it. The ground was dug up in all directions in search of the white ants' nests; and the food which they had collected for the winter was greedily consumed. Some poor sufferers eked out a miserable existence by living on the undigested food found in the excrement of animals; all sorts of leather, shoes and sandals, were boiled and eaten. It was a terrible sight to see these human skeletons—their eyes sunk into the backs of their heads, wandering about in search of food. The Mudir extorted all the corn and money he could from the rich merchants, but of what good was a mere handful of corn to the soldiers? They became desperate, all discipline was at an end and they often broke into the houses by night in search of food.

During all this time the Dervishes outside kept on shouting out curses and insults, deriding those within for eating dog's-meat, for, during all this terrible famine in the city, there was abundance of food in the Dervish camp, and this made the besiegers bolder and more insulting than ever, for they knew that the town was practically in their hands. We often tried to establish some sort of communication with our Mission brethren in the city, but we never succeeded in getting any reliable information about them. At length, towards the end of December, we managed, through the kind offices of George Stambuli, to send in a letter and received a reply from the Father Superior, Johann Losi, which was brought to us by one of our female slaves. The news it contained was heart-rending; all our brethren were down with scurvy—that is to say, Father Rossignoli, brother Locatelli, and four sisters, whilst Father Losi himself was on the point of death. For a month they had lived on nothing but dokhn and rice; everything else was gone. Father Losi sent us some clothes, which were a godsend to us, and also 200 dollars, while we in return could do nothing for our poor besieged brethren. A few days later we heard that Father Losi died on the 27th of December of scurvy.

The garrrison frequently attempted small sorties, in the hope that they might be able to secure a sheep or bullock, or some wood, and these always caused some excitement in the camp. When anything of this sort took place, the usual cry was "Et Turki Marak" ("The Turks are coming out"), then the camp suddenly woke up, and, like a swarm of ants, moved towards the town to drive the garrison in again. On these occasions quantities of ammunition were expended without much result. In the meantime the Mahdi continued his daily preaching against the vanities of this life, of his divine message, and of the approaching end of the world. During these sermons the people stood wrapped in wonder and astonishment at the Mahdi's great wisdom.

The Egyptian guns frequently fired into the camp, and on two occasions shells burst close to our hut, but did no harm. The Dervishes also returned the fire, but their shots always fell far beyond; had they only been skilled in the working of the guns they had, the fortifications would have become untenable in a day, but the Mahdi seemed purposely to wish to prolong the siege, and to thus compass the death of its defenders through famine. The wells were only about one kilometre distant from the forts, and in consequence within easy range of the fire of the besieged; but the Mahdi was quite regardless of this, and often formed up his troops there—a proceeding which generally resulted in his losing some men.

It was about this time that the principal sheikhs of the powerful Kababish tribe, viz. Saleh and Tome, the sons of Sheikh Salem, came to pay their allegiance to the Mahdi. As a gift they brought him two hundred camels, and he in return ordered a great military display and a special bombardment of El Obeid in their honour. The two sheikhs did not, however, take a great interest in these proceedings; and one day Saleh suddenly took himself off, and from that date became the Mahdi's sworn enemy, until the day of his death, when, as we shall presently see, he was one of the last of the great sheikhs who was overthrown by the Mahdi. His brother Tome was suddenly thrown into chains without any warning, the Mahdi giving as his reason that the Prophet had appeared to him in a vision and told him to do so.

Towards the end of November, news arrived that a further reinforcement of troops had left Khartum for El Obeid. This information occasioned a great stir in the camp, because there was some idea that English troops had been sent. These must have been the arrival of the first batch of troops destined eventually to form part of the Hicks Expedition; but even then it was too late to send any help to El Obeid.

One day it came to the Mahdi's ears that provisions were being smuggled into El Obeid, where they were sold at enormous prices, and to stop this he made the investment still closer. Some of the smugglers were caught, and as a punishment their right hands were cut off, and their handless arms tied to their necks; they were then led round the camp as a warning to others.

Meanwhile, as the siege of El Obeid was drawing to a close, other places in Kordofan were falling into the Mahdi's hands. The town of Bara had been reduced to great straits. A force marching to its relief under Abu Kuka, was attacked by Fiki Minneh: the majority were killed, and it was only through the bravery of Surur Effendi that a few hundred of them succeeded in reaching the town. The notorious Nur Angar, who was on the walls of the town, rendered no assistance during the siege, and went over to the enemy. At length, on the 5th of January, Bara was forced to capitulate through famine, and the garrison was sent to the Mahdi's camp.

The victory was celebrated by a salute of guns, and the unfortunate garrison in El Obeid took this to be the approach of relieving troops; but the Mahdi made it known to Said Pasha that, on the contrary, it was in celebration of the fall of Bara—an incident which caused the gloom to deepen over the doomed city; and all hope of delivery was abandoned. Yet the Mudir still continued to hope against hope that he should be relieved from Khartum, and his sanguine spirit kept up the courage of the garrison. But it could not last much longer; the soldiers were too weak even to hold their rifles in their hands, and Said Pasha realized that further resistance was useless. In desperation, therefore, he proposed to blow himself up in the powder magazine, and this he certainly would have done had not the senior officers urged that in doing so numbers of other lives would have been sacrificed as well. There was now nothing left to be done but to surrender, and this event took place on the 19th of January, 1883.

The Mahdi and his hordes now entered El Obeid, and he made the Mudirieh his residence. Guards under the command of mukuddums were posted outside every large house, to prevent the notables escaping, to further extort money and to search for treasure. Children, servants, and slaves were kept aside, and by continual flogging were obliged to divulge the secret hiding-places. The Mission buildings were of course entered by thousands of Mahdiists. Father Bonomi and brother Locatelli lay sick, and the sisters were completely exhausted. Hundreds of Dervishes struggled to break into the narrow enclosure where the unfortunate brethren lay ill. The crosses which the sisters wore round their necks were wrenched off and broken to pieces with axes. Sister Concetta Corsi, who was then one of the strongest, flew at these cruel intruders and made them wonder at the boldness of a poor weak woman. Some of them then entered with drawn swords, and, pointing their lances within an inch of her bosom, they threatened her with instant death if she made the slightest resistance ; but she answered, "You are dogs, and not men!" whereupon one of those standing near her gave her a blow on the face, which broke several of her teeth and made her mouth pour with blood.

Three days after the Mahdi's entry into El Obeid, our missionaries were taken before him, and in a solemn assembly he tried in vain to force them to become Moslems. They were then sent forth with nothing but the clothes they wore, in company with the other survivors of the siege, to the Dervish camp.

Our little party was now increased by the arrival of Father Rossignoli, brother Locatelli, who was then more dead than alive being carried on an angarib (native bedstead), and four sisters, who were all suffering from scurvy. They were brought to our hut, and our meeting could not be otherwise than a sad one. The sisters were accompanied by a girl named Bianca Limona, who, though a Sudanese, had quite a fair face, and resembled an Albino. Gordon, when travelling from Darfur to El Obeid, came across a youth of a similar type, whom he brought to the Mission, and suggested that he should marry the girl ; but he being a fanatical Mussulman, the girl absolutely refused.

Bianca, being of no trade value, was permitted by the Dervishes to remain with the sisters. All the other Mission blacks remained with the soldiers, but the young ones were sold. From amongst the Christian girls the Mahdi selected two as concubines—an Abyssinian and a black ; the latter had been well brought up, had learnt handiwork of different sorts, and she soon became the head of all the concubines.

The Dervishes captured quantities of arms and ammunition in the fort, also a considerable amount of rough gold, goods of all sorts, and furniture. This was all carried off to the beit el mal; the floors were all dug up in search of hidden treasure, and even dead bodies were disentombed and examined. The body of Father Losi, who had died a month before, was pulled up and searched, as it was believed he had a quantity of money. I must here recount an episode which will give an idea of the wonderful fidelity of our poor blacks, and their affection for us. Father Losi had purchased a little black boy in El Obeid, and for the ten long years during which this brave missionary had worked continuously for the welfare and happiness of the blacks, his boy Said served him most faithfully, and during all the horrors of that dreadful siege this boy never left the side of his "Father," as he used to call Father Losi. When Losi died, the boy used to spend most of the day weeping over his grave, and one day he was found lying stretched on the grave quite dead—he had died of grief.

The Mudir, Said Pasha, and the senior officers were, for a time, placed under guard, and refused, even on pain of death, to say where the treasure was; but when Said Pasha heard that his concubine and servants had been cruelly flogged and beaten to make them divulge, he at length handed over all his property to the Mahdi, and £6,000.

A few days after the fall of El Obeid a fire broke out on the north side of the camp; the strong wind drove the flames to the adjoining huts, and soon half the camp was ablaze. We had to run from our hut, which was soon afterwards enveloped in flames, and we were again obliged to encamp in the open. However, our good friend Stambuli succeeded in procuring a small tent for us. The Mahdi now ordered the whole town of El Obeid to be occupied by the Arabs, but it was not nearly large enough to hold all the people, consequently

THE MURDER OF THE DEFENDERS OF EL OBEID. 59

an enormous circle of huts soon surrounded the town, and we ourselves erected a small one, just beyond the precincts of the Mahdi's camp, having some Greeks and Syrians, who had been turned out of El Obeid, as our neighbours.

For about fifteen days most of the inhabitants of the town—clerks, Government officials, and Copts, were closely guarded and continually flogged to make them disclose the hiding-places of their treasure. Most of the principal people were handed over to the emirs. Said Pasha was placed in charge of Ismail Wad el Andok, and sent to Aluba; Ali Bey Sherif was sent to Birket, and several of the Coptic clerks were sent to Singiokai. Ahmed Bey Dafallah and Major Yesin were dragged to Shakka. Evil reports were spread about them, and it was rumoured that both the Mudir and Ali Bey Sherif had written to Khartum, consequently the Mahdi issued orders that the gallant defenders should be killed, justifying his action by saying that the Prophet had, in a vision, ordered him to do so. Ali Bey Sherif was beheaded close to the tent occupied by his wife and two children, who were afterwards taken over by Sayid Abdel Kader, the Mahdi's uncle. Said Pasha was most cruelly slaughtered with axes at Aluba; he was greatly disliked by the people, who called him "Jurab el Ful" ("Sack of beans") because he was so stout. Ahmed Bey Dafallah and Major Yesin were executed at Shakka. Such was the end of the brave defenders of El Obeid, who, in truth, deserved a better fate.

The Mahdi, having thus made away with his enemies, was able to breathe more freely, and, as if to excuse himself for his horrible cruelty, he published a vision, in which he said that he had been told that Said Pasha did not go to hell, but as he (the Mahdi) had earnestly begged it, he was permitted to go to paradise.

During the siege there was much friction between the Mahdi and Fiki Minneh, whose capacity for drinking marissa and stealing booty came to the Mahdi's ears. As long as Minneh was useful to the Mahdi he forbore with him; but when El Obeid fell, he sent for him and forcibly made him divide his booty. Fiki Minneh therefore returned in a sulky mood to Tayara, and from that time became the Mahdi's enemy. He openly collected a quantity of dokhn, and brought together his fighting force. The Mahdi therefore despatched Abu Anga, the Commander-in-chief of his forces, Abderrahman en Nejumi and Abdullah Wad en Nur, with a large number of men. Making a forced march, they appeared suddenly at Tayara, and the Gowameh followers of Minneh fled on the first volley. Minneh's brother, uncle, and two sons were captured and beheaded on the same spot where Minneh himself had slain the soldiers and their wives and children the previous year; their heads were hung up in the market-place at El Obeid as a warning to others.

The Mahdi and his emirs now began to live a life of ease; the latter occupied the various buildings around the Mudirieh and made themselves comfortable: they placed no restrictions on themselves in the way of food and drink; there was money in abundance and supplies were plentiful, consequently sensuality and luxurious living were substituted for the abstemious life which the Mahdi doctrine had at first inculcated. The principal emirs delighted in extensive harems and a show of splendour. Jibbehs were still worn, but their ragged condition, which was essential in the early days, gave way to as much embellishment as such a garment would admit of. The emirs vied with one another in their wealth of slaves, cattle, horses and donkeys; their sword-hilts were now embellished with silver. In place of lying on the dirty ground, their clothes full of vermin, they assumed the luxurious and comfortable mode of life of the Turks and Egyptians. So shocked, indeed, was the Mahdi's uncle, Sherif Mahmud, when he arrived from Gedir to see the drunken and debauched lives led by the emirs, more especially by Wad en Nejumi, that he induced the Mahdi to order the latter to reduce his harem by twenty wives, who were subsequently sold in the beit el mal as slaves. At the same time the Mahdi issued the strictest orders against luxurious living, and insisted that no gold and silver ornaments should be worn. He further ordained that in future the dress should consist of a takia (or skull cap) made of the leaves of the dwarf-palm, round which a turban should be worn with end hanging down; the jibbeh (or coat); a pair of drawers; and a girdle made of straw. This made rather a becoming uniform to these swarthy warriors.

The rules regarding smoking and drinking were reiterated with greater severity. It was next to impossible to induce the Sudanese to give up smoking and chewing tobacco: a man would willingly give all the money he had to secure even a small quantity. Then the blacks, and especially the emirs, are much addicted to marissa drinking, which it was found still more difficult to stop; if men or women were caught in the act of smoking or drinking, they were obliged to walk through the market with the drinking bowl or tobacco on their heads, followed by an insulting and hooting crowd. It was sometimes the custom to break the bowl on the marissa drinker's head and drench him with its contents; this was the signal for all the children to throw mud and dust at the culprit until he became almost unrecognisable; he was then dragged before the kadi (or judge) in the market-place, where he received eighty unusually heavy blows, the first of which generally drew blood. The place was full of spies, who were always on the lookout to report smokers and drinkers to the Mahdi. Sometimes they forced their way into the houses, and finding nothing, would surreptitiously throw some tobacco on the floor, which they would then suddenly discover, and declare it to be the property of the owner of the house, who would be forthwith dragged off and thrashed unmercifully although perfectly innocent.

Justice was administered according to the Moslem law. Blasphemers of God or the religion were punished with instant death, as well as all those who disbelieved in the Mahdi. A murderer was at once beheaded, no extenuating circumstances were ever admitted. A thief was deprived of a hand and a foot; adultery between married persons was punished by beheading the man and stoning the woman, but in the latter case a necessary proof was that the woman should be with child. Illicit intercourse between unmarried persons was punished with eighty lashes; these laws regarding immorality were, however, in the case of slaves, relaxed to some extent, and they were, as a rule, punished by flogging only. Persons found concerned in the making of eunuchs were beheaded, though curiously enough the khalifas and emirs all retained eunuchs for their harems. Slaves freed by the Egyptian Government were not recognised as such, and were again forced to become slaves. A slave's witness was not accepted in a trial. All important cases were judged before the Mahdi, who sentenced persons as he thought fit. The Mosaic law—an eye for an eye and a tooth for a tooth—was generally practised. The relations of murdered persons generally carried out the sentences on the criminal, provided that the judge approved. Punishment could be modified or cancelled altogether by the payment of money. In addition to the Mahdi, his relatives and the khalifas were permitted to judge cases—a proceeding which resulted in great confusion and miscarriage of justice. The marketplace was the chief centre of activity; here the judge held his court, and a profitable business he made of it by substituting money for punishments.

Shortly after the fall of El Obeid the Mahdi set himself to regulate his finances. The Kordofan Arabs, who had gained many successes over the Government, and who had really taken up the Mahdi's cause in anticipation of the loot they would acquire, were ordered to bring all their booty—down to the smallest article—to the Mahdi at El Obeid, and to enforce this order, parties of Dervishes were sent out in various directions to forcibly drive in the Arabs, who now regretted that they had so precipitately joined the Mahdi in the first instance. Everything was brought to the beit el mal, and there publicly sold; of the proceeds, one-fifth was given to the Mahdi personally, and the remaining four-fifths were set aside as administrative revenue, but in point of fact a considerable portion of this sum also found its way into the Mahdi's private treasury. A native of Dar Mahas, named Ahmed wad Suleiman and a great favourite of the Mahdi, was given unlimited control over the beit el mal treasury. His master had had a divine revelation, pointing out that he was the one man to hold this responsible position, and in consequence he was unassailable. Whenever the Mahdi rode out on horseback, Ahmed held the reins and walked barefooted at the horse's side.

All learned men were despised and disliked by the Mahdi, for he not unnaturally recognised a danger in their combating his claims by reference to divine books. Consequently all such documents were ordered to be burnt, and any one who concealed a book did so at the risk of his life. The Mahdi's object was to keep the people in ignorance by proclaiming that he was the centre of all light and knowledge; there were even flatterers to be found who asserted that they had seen flashes of light darting out of his head! He frequently indulged in visions, sometimes representing that he had been taken up in the spirit to the heavens, where he conversed with God and His Prophet. To doubt the truth of these visions was an unpardonable offence. He entirely abolished all the rules and customs practised by the Government. The wearing of the tarbush (fez) was strictly forbidden; if any one was seen wearing one, it was instantly pulled off and torn to shreds. All Government registers were burnt, and debts contracted with the Government considered cancelled. He ordered his adherents to call themselves Foggara * or Asyad.†

His usual custom was to pray on a small straw mat placed in the divan of the Mudirieh and in the presence of all his followers; a slave generally stood beside him with a pillow on which he either sat or knelt, as the

* Pl. of Fakir, *i.e.* a poor religious mendicant—one who has renounced the world.

† Pl. of Sayid, *i.e.* a master.

case might be. When the prayers were over he received the visitors, conversed on matters of general interest, read his letters, and discoursed on the manners and customs of the Turks with the object of making his hearers despise and laugh at them. He plunged wildly into the sensual delights of his immense harem. In place of wine he substituted a drink much appreciated in the Sudan, consisting of date syrup mixed with ginger, of which he drank quantities out of the silver cups taken from the Mission Church in El Obeid.

In spite, however, of all this luxurious living, the Mahdi did not omit to publish his new propaganda far and wide. He wrote several letters to the inhabitants of the Gezireh (the country between the Blue and White Niles), calling on them to rise, and threatening all those who refused to obey the summons. Numbers flocked to his standards, partly through fear and partly because they recognised the inability of the Government to cope with the revolt. It was at this time that he despatched Osman Digna, who afterwards became so notorious, to the Eastern Sudan. This fanatical adherent of the Mahdi copied the example of his master in every respect, wearing neither shoes nor sandals, and only riding during exceptionally long marches, his argument being that as the Mahdi deigned to walk the earth, he thereby made it holy. A force was now despatched to capture Sheikh Tome of the Kababish, who was reported to be in friendly communication with Khartum. The unfortunate man was attacked by night, captured and dragged off in chains with his wife, child, slaves, and camels to El Obeid. The Mahdi was prepared to pardon him, but Khalifa Abdullah insisted on beheading him, which was done; this cruel act terrified the remainder of the tribe. During the last fifteen days of Ramadan the Mahdi attended to no public business, but gave himself up to fasting and prayer. The holidays following Ramadan were set aside for military parades and manœuvres, which served to rouse the fanatical ardour of his now numerous followers.

About this time a letter came from Mustafa Yawer,

the Mudir of Dongola, to Osman Tobji; the latter was a most generous man, who gave much of his money to the poor and to widows and orphans, especially during the siege of El Obeid; Tobji had thus won the honour and respect of all, and on the fall of the town the Mahdi

A NATIVE WOMAN OF DONGOLA.

returned to him the property he had captured; thereupon he at once set to work to relieve the distressed Egyptian families who had been turned out of house and home, and whose property had been taken. In his letter Mustafa Yawer asked his friend Tobji if Mohammed Ahmed were the real Mahdi or not ; this letter came into the Mahdi's hands, and Tobji was at once sent for and asked what reply he intended to give. Osman answered, "When the sun has risen over the horizon it is visible to all, and no further proof of its existence is required—thus if the Mahdi be the true Mahdi, his works will bear witness of the truth." This evasive answer did not however satisfy the Mahdi, who obliged Tobji to sign a letter declaring that Mohammed Ahmed was the true Mahdi, and this letter was then despatched to the Mudir of Dongola.

The Mahdi was well versed in the art of winning over people. His unruffled smile, pleasant manners, generosity and equable temperament, though at times somewhat severe, all tended to enhance the popular idea of him. He attributed the execution of Said Pasha and Ali Bey Sherif to the Khalifa Abdullah, and when the two little sons of the latter were brought to him, the smiling hypocrite wept for their father's fate. The popular belief in him and his cause almost amounted to worship : women especially raved about him and thought him the most handsome of men. They swore by him in the words "Hakk rabb el Mahdi (By the Mahdi's God) or "Hakk Sayidna el Imam" (By our Lord, the Imam); all solemn oaths and statements began with the words "Aleik el Mahdi el Muntaser" (By the Victorious Mahdi) ; his virtues were extolled in poems, and constant reference was made to his good looks, wisdom, stature and to his repeated victories over the Turks. The beggars used to learn off by heart special laudatory verses, and by reciting them from house to house they were sure to be given alms ; to such an extent was this laudation carried that if a beggar sang songs in which the Prophet's name occurred, he was at once interrupted and told to substitute the Mahdi's for the Prophet's name ; at every street corner his praises were sung ; soldiers on the march sang of his glorious victories ; female slaves gathering wood, or laden with corn, or grinding it between the stones—all sang the same refrain, which indeed might be called the

Mahdi's national anthem, and began with the words "Mahdi Nur Ainana" (the Mahdi is the light of our eyes), or "El Mahdi kammal et Turk fi Kana" (the Mahdi conquered—lit. gave their full to—the Turks at Kana).

The Arabs delight in poetry, and during the night generally collected in parties, and seated on the sand sang the Mahdi's praises, the two principal singers keeping time by beating the ground with their sticks, while the rest joined in the chorus at the end of each verse. Inspired sometimes by their theme, they would stand up and flourish their swords in the air as if combating the Turks, shouting "Fi Shan Allah" (for God's cause). Thus the adulation of the Mahdi extended from the highest emir to the lowest slave, and woe to him who was ever heard to utter one word in deprecation or blame of the new Prophet, he would at once be pounced upon and beaten to death with sticks.

Sometimes the Mahdi was called "Khalifat er Rasul" (the successor of the Prophet), and sometimes even they dignified him with the sacred title of Nebbi (Prophet). In truth the Prophet Mohammed occupied in the people's minds quite a secondary position, and the celebration of his birthday was forbidden by the Mahdi.

On one occasion a dispute occurred between two men; one argued that the Mahdi would have a higher seat in heaven than the Prophet, while the other maintained that "God was higher than the Mahdi." The dispute waxed hot, and the case was referred to the judge, who settled the matter by saying that "the living was better than the dead," but at the same time the man who advocated the Prophet's claims was relegated to prison, not so much for asserting what was perfectly true, that "God was higher than the Mahdi," but that the tone in which he had said it was tantamount to an insult to the Mahdi. Naturally those Moslems who still had some sense of the orthodox creed were much annoyed at this decision.

Early in April a messenger arrived from Khartum with a letter from the Austrian Consul Hansal. Now as we were perfect strangers in El Obeid, people did not dare to associate with us; the messenger therefore handed over the letter to George Stambuli, who was then a man well known to every one. Stambuli, who supplied us with all the necessaries of life, now came to us in a state of great excitement, bringing the letter in which he hoped to find some news of the outside world. We opened the letter, which was long and well-written, and found that it was directed to the Mahdi. We read it and considered it a well-written letter; in it Hansal called the Mahdi "Sheikh," and begged him to release us, receiving as a ransom such a sum as he should demand, and which he (Hansal) was prepared to give. The bearer of the letter was then ordered to take it direct to the Mahdi, but fearing that its contents might compromise him, he gave it to Stambuli, who gave it as his opinion that the letter was useless, as he himself had been doing all in his power to effect our release, but was unable to do so. Father Bonomi, however, urged that as the letter was useless it was therefore harmless, and that there could be no objection to giving it to the Mahdi; consequently it was taken to him, and he expressed himself much pleased with it; although he admitted that the system of ransoming was in vogue during the days of the Prophet, he stated that it had been changed by him, as also was the tax per head formerly paid by Christians.

He, however, promised to give us protection until the coming of Sayidna Isa (Jesus Christ), when we should either have to turn Moslems or die; thus the letter was of no good to us, and on the following day a rumour was spread abroad that the Austrian Consul had joined the Mahdi. The messenger asked us to give him a few lines to take back, and thus prove that he had delivered the letter to us; so we and Stambuli complied, and the messenger left for Khartum; but he was followed by spies, and when at Korsi—one and a half day's journey distant—he was searched by them, and the letters found in the saddle-bag on the donkey, consequently he was arrested, brought back, and thrown into chains.

The false news was now rapidly circulated that an English post had arrived. Father Bonomi and I were at once summoned to read the letters. It occurred to us that our letters had probably been seized and that we were in some danger. I was not alarmed about my letter to Hansal, for I had written in German, and there was no one besides myself in El Obeid who understood German; but Bonomi's letters had been written in Italian, and there were several people who understood that language. As we entered the Mudirieh we saw Stambuli also coming. We were first taken to the Khalifa Sherif, who was lying on a straw mat in his hut; after greeting us, he lifted up the mat and drew out several letters, which we at once recognised as those we had written. The Khalifa asked us if we had written them, and we replied in the affirmative. He thereupon produced a piece of paper on which Bonomi had written that the messenger should receive six pounds. Father Bonomi translated this to the Khalifa; Stambuli was then called in, as he pretended to know a number of European languages, while in point of fact he knew little or nothing; when the paper was given to him to read he said that it contained a medical prescription, and this translation did not of course agree with Bonomi's version. Amidst the murmuring of the bystanders the Khalifa now rose and bid us follow him into the divan of the Mudirieh, and thence into the room adjoining that in which the Mahdi was sitting with the Khalifa Abdullah. The latter had to keep his bed, for his leg had been broken by a fall from a horse; he had collided with another horseman, and in falling had been badly kicked. Father Bonomi and Stambuli only were taken before the Mahdi, whilst I was left in the room outside; there were a Dervish and a Greek also in the room, and as I was sitting on the ground near the door, the Greek came up to me and told me that a sheikh wished to speak to me. I replied, "Let the sheikh come to me if he wants to speak to me; I have nothing to ask of him."

A few moments afterwards the sheikh came up to me

in a furious rage, and without further ado attacked me with his fists, kicked me, and called me a Christian dog; then seizing me by the leg he dragged me out towards the gate, where he said he intended to cut off my head.

The sound of this struggle reached the Mahdi's ears, and he sent a eunuch to take me out of the sheikh's hands. Shortly afterwards the Mahdi himself, Bonomi, and Stambuli came out, and were rather pleased than otherwise that my incident with the sheikh had interrupted their somewhat painful conversation. The Mahdi did not appear angry, and as usual, smiled pleasantly all round; then, surrounded by his principal emirs, he performed the noonday prayers in the divan, while the multitude conformed to the prayers in the Mudirieh courtyard. This over, he sat down on his mat and opened his audience, whilst a slave standing behind him fanned him and drove off the flies. Numbers of people submitted their cases to him in a very low and humble tone of voice, and from the various gestures which took place, I concluded that he had given satisfaction to all. He then read aloud a letter from an influential sheikh in Khartum, whose name I have forgotten; after which a number of sheikhs came in to take the oath of allegiance.

During this ceremony the man taking the oath had to place his hand in the Mahdi's right hand; then the latter repeated the oath in the following words: "Thou consecratest thyself, thy children and thy property to the Mahdi. Thou shalt be guilty of no impurity; thou shalt not steal, nor drink alcohol; and thou shalt bind thyself to do thy duty in the Jehad." The person to whom the oath was administered sealed it with a solemn "Amen." If several persons took the oath together, they were obliged to repeat it in chorus, and at the conclusion they shouted "Fi Shan Allah." When the audience was over, we asked the Mahdi's permission to retire, which he allowed us to do.

Bonomi now gave us an account of his interview with the Mahdi and Khalifa Abdullah. They had thought that we had written letters to the Government at Khartum, but they could not read the letters which, in point of fact, contained nothing political. Bonomi had given the Mahdi a short resumé of their contents with which he seemed pleased, but Abdullah appeared dissatisfied.

For the next eight days we were in considerable danger, and the one topic of conversation was what should be done to us. It was the general idea that we were to be beheaded; but Stambuli was working his friends, and by dint of bribes the matter was hushed up, although I believe that we owed it principally to the good will and kindly disposition of the Mahdi. After about ten days we were summoned before a certain emir named Hajji Khaled, who made enquiries about the letters, and we told him that we were prepared to translate literally every word. Our fearless persistence impressed him, and he did not trouble us further.

Some of the European merchants could have translated the letters, but Stambuli bribed them with twenty pounds, and on the 26th of April, thirteen days after the letters had been intercepted, the Mahdi pardoned Stambuli at a public meeting, and handed them back to him; then in the presence of two trustworthy friends of the Mahdi, we translated them word for word into Arabic, and gave them back to the Mahdi, who, judging from their general tenour, appeared convinced of their harmlessness.

CHAPTER V.

THE MAHDI'S VICTORY OVER HICKS PASHA.

The European captives learn that General Hicks is advancing—Slatin Bey's defence of Darfur—His heroism—The Mahdi prepares to resist Hicks—The march of the Hicks Expedition—Extracts from the diary of Major Herlth—Colonel Farquhar's gallantry at Rahad—Gustav Klootz deserts to the Mahdi—Klootz's interview with the Mahdi in which Ohrwalder and Bonomi act as interpreters—The expedition advances towards Shekan—Is surrounded and annihilated—Description of the battle—The Mahdi victor of Kordofan.

IN our present miserable plight all our hopes were directed on Khartum, from whence we expected succour. Hitherto we heard only vague rumours, but the news of the defeat and death of Wad Makashef on the White Nile encouraged us to hope on. We had no idea who commanded the Egyptian troops in this action. We were quite uncertain as to what policy the Government would adopt regarding Kordofan; and of course, at this time, false reports were flying about everywhere, and it was quite impossible to arrive at the truth. At first we were inclined to believe everything we heard, but gradually we found that we lived in such an atmosphere of lying and deceit that we arrived at believing almost nothing we heard. The Sudanese proverb, "Consider all news to be good and true, even if it be false," is universally acted on in the Moslem world; and those who looked for help from the Government always hoped for good news, and seized on the smallest pretext to give colour to their expectations; their belief in dreams which never came true accentuated their misery. It was useless to try and enlighten these poor ignorant people, contradiction only made them annoyed. Fortune-tellers were often consulted about the future, and naturally they foretold what they thought their interrogators wanted to hear, and thus gave them hope for a short time; but when it turned out incorrect—as was invariably the case—it only increased their depression.

God, in His mercy, sent a ray of light into the darkness of our captivity, which again kindled the hope of succour which had been well-nigh quite extinguished. On the 21st of June, 1883, a man came into our little hut and asked in a scared sort of way if we were the missionaries. After repeated assurances that we were, the man took courage and withdrew from his trousers a little note, which he had concealed very carefully, and handed it to Father Bonomi, who at once tore it open in nervous haste and eagerly scanned the few lines which were to give us a new life. The note was signed by Marcopoli Bey, by order of General Hicks, and was to the effect that we should not abandon hope, for as soon as the winter season began, a large army would advance into the Sudan to attack the Mahdi. We kissed that dirty little bit of paper, and thanked God most heartily for sending us news so full of comfort. We became reassured, and now our dark future gave place to cheerful hopes which brightened the few months of anxious delay which followed the receipt of this note. The letter was dated from the White Nile, where the General had already gained a victory over Wad Makashef, and soon the news of the intended expedition against the Mahdi spread like wildfire through the camp.

It appears that Consul Hansal also wrote a letter to the Mahdi, but the latter said nothing to us about it. Amina, one of our black girls whom the Mahdi had taken as a concubine, said she saw in the Mahdi's hand a letter with a large seal, on which the "double-headed eagle" was represented; but the Mahdi does not appear to have taken much notice of it. In Darfur the news of the intended Hicks expedition had considerable effect. Slatin, the Governor-General, had been fighting continuously against the natives of Darfur and against the Rizighat, Habbanieh, and other Arab tribes; he was now in the north, then in the south, combating with bravery and unusual rapidity the various revolts which sprang up throughout his province. He was a scourge to the Arabs and killed thousands of them; he even pursued them into the almost inaccessible hills and valleys of Jebel Marra. His powers of endurance were

HICKS PASHA.

wonderful, and he would often be twenty-four hours in the saddle, constantly fighting, and with nothing to eat or drink. He slept on the bare floor or ground beside his native soldiers, and lived on dhurra soaked in water; he was just, never took bribes, generous, ever ready to assist the poor and needy, and never refused admittance to old and young who sought his help. In

spite, however, of his having—as he himself told me—
fought in twenty-seven battles against the Arabs, he
could not crush them, for they were like fungus growing
out of the earth.

In action Slatin was most heroic. On one occasion
he was struck by a bullet which shattered one of his
fingers; but, undismayed, he seized the hanging remnant
with his other hand and ordered the man standing next
him to cut it off with his knife; then he joined again
in the fight, and cheered his men on to victory. Not
only in Kordofan, but throughout the entire Sudan, he
was celebrated for his bravery in the face of the enemy.
Still he was powerless to cope with the extensive revolt
in his province, and obtained little support from his
Egyptian officers, who were jealous and constantly
intrigued against him; yet it was the wonder of all
that he succeeded in holding out so long. At length,
when his ammunition was almost finished, came the
news of Hicks's projected expedition, and to gain time he
resorted to the following expedient. His vakil was a
man named Mohammed Zogal, uncle to the Mahdi, and
a man of sense; with him Slatin came to a private
understanding, and it was agreed that Zogal should pay
a visit to the Mahdi, inform him that Slatin was prepared to submit, provided he was permitted to hold his
present position, and then he was to return and bring
back full information regarding the Mahdi, his power,
&c., and at the same time endeavour to arrange for a
suspension of hostilities pending the arrival of Hicks.
Should Hicks be victorious then Slatin and Darfur
would be saved, otherwise all would be lost; but this
plan, if successful, would enable Slatin to hold out until
Hicks came, which he could not otherwise have done.
Zogal set out on his journey and arrived at El Obeid
early in September 1883, where he was warmly welcomed by the Mahdi. The latter was much pleased
with Slatin's proposition, and ordered a salute of one
hundred guns to be fired to announce his surrender.

The Mahdi could now turn his entire attention to his
preparations to resist the advance of General Hicks,

concerning the number of whose troops the wildest reports were circulated. On learning of his departure from Omdurman on the 9th of September, he issued a proclamation instructing his emirs to read it to their followers. In it he, as usual, styled himself the Mahdi sent by God to defeat the Turks, who were the enemies of God and His Prophet, and that his mission was to conquer the world; he extolled the virtues of holy war and promised paradise and its joys to all those who fell fighting in the holy cause. He now quitted El Obeid and pitched his tent under a large Adansonia tree outside the walls; his three Khalifas and their followers copied his example, and this was the signal for the whole town to be evacuated. The life of ease and comfort was abandoned and people collected round their emirs' flags, so that in a short time an enormous camp was formed in anticipation of the great battle. Couriers were sent in all directions to proclaim that anyone who refused to follow the Mahdi would have his hand and foot cut off; all men joined willingly, the Mahdi's camp daily grew larger, and straw huts (or tokuls) soon covered the plain, though the people were allowed in turns to go back to the town at night. Detachments of troops were sent to various parts of Kordofan to collect the Dervishes, and whole tribes streamed from all directions towards El Obeid. Daily manœuvres and reviews were held, and guns fired repeatedly so that the horses should get accustomed to the noise. Thus the Mahdi instilled great enthusiasm into the masses, and we began to have some fear for Hicks.

The Mahdi now despatched the three emirs, Abdel Halim Wad el Hashmi, Hajji Mohammed Abu Girgeh, and Omar Elias Pasha, with their followers, to Duem. They were instructed to watch the movements of Hicks's force, and when it left the White Nile, to cut his communication; they were then to harass his march as much as possible, but not to bring on a general engagement. All these orders were admirably carried out.

General Hicks left Duem on the 24th of September, 1883, and marched in a south-westerly direction through

Shatt, Zeregga, Aigella, Shirkeleh, and Rahad, which he reached on the 20th of October, leaving Tagalla and Jebel Dair on the left. The inhabitants of the districts through which the troops passed, quitted their villages and carried off all their goods, so that when the troops arrived they found nothing but straw huts, which the soldiers at first set fire to; but General Hicks soon forbade this practice. The ill-fated army scarcely met a living soul, but flocks of vultures followed them as if waiting for their prey. Shortly after the annihilation of the army, a small and incomplete diary belonging to an Austrian officer, Major Herlth, came into my hands, but it was sufficient to give me an insight into the wretched condition of this force. The facts were briefly as follows: It was expected that on the arrival of the army at Shirkeleh, it would be joined by several thousand Tagalla people, and it was hoped that this reinforcement would inspire the troops with some life and energy, which they entirely lacked; but these reinforcements never appeared.

Major Herlth described the troops as anything but good, and frequently refers to the want of agreement between the two commanders—General Hicks with his small body of European officers on the one hand, and Ala ed Din Pasha, Governor-General of the Sudan, a man imbued with the old Turkish system, on the other. The European officers were convinced that the expedition would not be successful; the camels were badly looked after, hundreds died every day, and their loads were piled on to the others which were still alive; saddles were for the most part without straw, so that the bare wood rubbing on their backs made terrible wounds. Almost all the horses had died before the force reached Rahad. General Hicks had also great trouble in keeping the men together; numbers of them had recently been fighting against the English with Arabi Pasha, and had been forcibly sent to the Sudan. It is also strange that the shorter route from Duem to Bara, on which there was plenty of water, was not chosen in preference to the long roundabout road they took. While the latter route led through forests and long grass, the former was entirely free from these obstructions, and, moreover, the friendly Kababish tribe would have supported them on their northern flank. There was still another circumstance which contributed to the final disaster—the guides were treacherous, and led the army into the hands of the Dervishes; indeed, it was an open secret in the camp at El Obeid that the guides had been sent by the Mahdi.

At Rahad, Hicks expected to have been joined by five hundred Baggara horsemen, and it is true a number of horsemen were seen in the distance, and a white flag was shown; but the riders did not approach, and it was soon evident that they were enemies. The force was in such a miserable and wretched condition that the emir, Abdel Halim, begged permission of the Mahdi to be allowed to attack it with his own followers; but this the Mahdi would not permit him to do, as he wanted to have all the honour and glory of victory for himself. Every day information about the movements of the Egyptian troops was sent to the Mahdi; sometimes reports reached him twice a day, and were always of the same tenour, viz. that the men had no heart to fight. Had an expedition been coming which had the elements of success in it, public opinion would have shown itself by numbers deserting the Mahdi's standards; but they had heard nothing of Hicks's early successes, and now the only reports that reached them were that the army was in a hopeless condition. All this only made the Mahdi's prestige the greater, and it must be remembered that the latter was an adept at inspiring fanaticism. One of General Hicks's spies was captured, and he was at once impaled on lances. The following extracts, which I give from memory, from Major Herlth's diary will show how demoralised the expedition had become. The camp was pitched at Rahad on a small eminence near the Khor Abu Habl, whilst the enemy, who were concealed on the opposite side in the high grass and under the trees, fired incessantly at the Egyptians and killed a number of them. One bullet entered Hicks's tent and struck the seat on which he was sitting; he then gave orders that the grass and woods should be at once cleared of the enemy. There was still a little water in the Khor, and as it seemed to be deep, a consultation was held as to how it should best be crossed. The discussion lasted an hour. At length a few, more courageous than the rest, decided to try and wade across, and to their intense surprise found that it was quite shallow and easily fordable; they then crossed over and drove back the enemy, killing seven of them.

While at Rahad, it was discovered that the camp out of which they had marched the previous day had been entered, and everything that they had left behind had been taken. It was now evident that the enemy were in greater force than they had thought, and in consequence General Hicks made an entrenchment and put guns into position, which were fired with some effect, as one shell killed no less than thirteen men. This news was sent to the Mahdi.

At El Obeid the slow advance of the troops could not be understood, and this had a still more convincing effect on the Dervishes that the expedition must be in a bad way. It was a matter of no surprise that the troops had not been victorious, as it was known that every element of success was wanting; as for the poor Egyptians, the capture of a cow was an event of great importance, and General Hicks ordered every officer to be given a piece of it.

Colonel Farquhar, chief of the staff, did all he could to raise the courage of the soldiers. On one occasion some horsemen were seen a short distance away sitting fearlessly on their horses as if challenging anyone to come out and fight them. When Farquhar saw them he mounted his horse and advanced straight on them. When he approached they began to retire, but he went in pursuit, and coming up with them killed two, the third he pulled off his horse, and capturing the horses brought them back to camp. In spite, however, of such a gallant example, the men were listless and out of heart; the long marches had thoroughly exhausted them.

At Rahad, Gustav Klootz, a native of Berlin, deserted the army. He was Baron Seckendorf's servant; but at Shirkeleh he quitted his master's service, and became the servant of Mr. O'Donovan, correspondent of the *Daily News*. Klootz had certain socialistic tendencies, which caused him to change masters, and there is no

COLONEL ARTHUR FARQUHAR.
(*Chief of the Staff.*)

doubt that these ideas had much to do with his desertion. He and a native of Saxony determined to escape secretly, and on the plea of gathering wood outside the camp, these two men succeeded one evening in passing the outposts. No sooner had they gone beyond the line than they heard firing, and the Saxony man, fearing a sudden attack, at once turned back to camp, whilst

Klootz continued his flight. When he had gone a short distance he fired two shots, one to make the Egyptians believe that the enemy was close to them, and the other to make the enemy think that they were close to the Egyptian outposts. When night came on he lay down under a tree to sleep, regardless of the fact that he was between two enemies; and the next morning he began to debate with himself whether, after all, it would not be better to return. He would not have hesitated for an instant had he not thought that perhaps the Saxony man had betrayed his desertion. At length he decided there was nothing for it but to go on towards the Dervishes.

After going some distance he saw three dirty-looking men who pointed their rifles at him; but he signed to them that he was not coming as an enemy, and to further reassure them, he threw down his rifle and revolver on the ground, and advanced towards them. The Arabs also approached; but Klootz, who did not understand a word of Arabic, called out, "Dervish—where is the Dervish?" (by "Dervish" he meant the Mahdi.) The Arabs understood perfectly what he wanted to say, but at that moment they were thinking much more of the loot they saw before them than of the Mahdi; so they seized the little money Klootz had, and took possession of his watch, rifle, revolver, and even his boots. Klootz soon realised into whose hands he had fallen, for these Arabs, having taken everything from him, then directed him towards the Dervish camp. On he plodded barefooted, through the long grass, and often over thorns, until at last he met an old woman, who made him understand by gestures that he was close on the camp. A few moments later several horsemen appeared, and, surrounding him, took him in triumph to Abu Girgeh; for they thought at length they had captured a hated Englishman. Klootz, to his astonishment, now found himself in a large entrenched camp, where the Dervishes were living in perfect safety. The horsemen had told Abu Girgeh that they had found him sitting in a tree writing, so he was at once put in chains, tied tightly to a bedstead, and then interrogated about Hicks's troops. At the same time a messenger was sent to the Mahdi to inquire what should be done with the Englishman. The Mahdi ordered that he should be at once brought to El Obeid; the chains were therefore removed, and a rope put round his neck, by which he was drawn by horsemen to the Mahdi's camp. The journey lasted a day and a half, and he was obliged to walk the whole way barefooted in the burning sun, so that when he reached El Obeid his feet were swollen up and in a dreadful condition.

As swift as lightning the news now spread through the camp that an English officer had been captured. Who could the unfortunate man be? we wondered. When Klootz was brought before the Mahdi all he could say was that he was Nimsawi (a German). The Mahdi therefore summoned Stambuli, Bonomi, and myself, to act as interpreters. When we entered the crowded enclosure everyone understood the object of our coming; most of them were busy cleaning their lances, and shouted out after us, "Mind you make careful inquiries of him." There was such a crowd in front of the Mahdi's tent that it was almost impossible to make our way through; but at last there was a cry of "Ahl Delen" ("Here are the Delen people"), and they made way for us. We took off our shoes, and were shown into the Mahdi's presence. I was intensely anxious to see who this Englishman might be; we had seen nothing but black faces for so long, that had he been a creature from the other world, we could not have been more interested; then we were on tenter-hooks to know how the expedition was progressing, whether it was under English command, &c., &c. Of course General Hicks's name was well known, but we knew nothing about the composition of his force.

When we entered we saw the Mahdi, the supposed English officer, and Ahmed Wad Suleiman sitting on a straw mat. We saluted the Mahdi, who returned our salute in a most gracious manner. He was smiling, and seemed much pleased. He introduced the Englishman to me, and asked me to question him about his coming. My imagination, in which I had pictured an Englishman, received a rude shock, for I beheld before me a young man with blonde hair, blue eyes, a sunburnt face, and a nose from which the skin was peeled off. He wore a dirty tarbush; his clothes were made of rough canvas, and he looked very much like the fireman of an engine. Before anything else I expressed to him my sincere pity at his having fallen into the hands of savages, for I did not then know that he had come of his own accord. I asked him his name; he replied, "Gustav Klootz, of Berlin," and said that he was the correspondent of an important newspaper. He afterwards gave me a true account of himself. I translated everything to the Mahdi. I then asked him about the state of the army. He said that it consisted of barely 10,000 men, and he added that it was generally believed by the European officers that they would be defeated. It was with the greatest difficulty that I concealed the blow to my feelings which this news occasioned. I asked him why he deserted, and he excused himself by saying that he did so to save his life. I now knew that he could be no soldier; but, of course, I did not translate to the Mahdi the wretched account he gave of the army. At this moment I received a kick in the ribs from Ahmed Wad Suleiman, who cried out, "Ask him how many guns are in possession of the unbelievers?" I was then given a small book, which turned out to be Klootz's diary, and was told to translate it. There were only a few leaves, in which the date of departure from Shatt and other places was noted; the number of camels that died daily; a few observations on his master, and sundry other things.

The Mahdi then asked whether, if he wrote to Hicks, he would be likely to surrender, to which Klootz naturally replied that he was sure nothing would induce him to do so.

The Mahdi further asked whether Klootz thought he or General Hicks was the more powerful, to which Klootz answered that he thought the Mahdi would be successful; but that he would probably lose a number of his followers, as Hicks's force was well supplied with good firearms, to which Wad Suleiman added, "Death will be our reward."

The Mahdi seemed delighted with the news he had received, and ordered a plate of fried meat to be brought, which he shared with us, eating with his fingers. It was considered a very high favour when he touched the plate with his hand, and handed a small piece of meat to those who sat with him, and this favour he conferred on us. It was rather striking that he should have done this, for many Moslems consider it wrong even to eat in the presence of Christians. When the meal was over he dismissed us, and Klootz was handed over to Stambuli till further orders.

Just as we got outside the hut, Klootz and I were called in again. The Mahdi was now quite alone. He ordered us to sit down on the floor, and then whispered in my ear, "Tell this man he may count on the best of treatment if he will turn Moslem; if not, he must die." I explained this to Klootz in German, and he replied that he was quite prepared to do anything the Mahdi required; whereupon the latter presented him with his shoes and a jibbeh, and named him "Mustafa," as it struck him that there was a similarity of sound between Mustafa and Gustav.

When we left the hut we found an enormous crowd of people all clamouring to know what the Englishman had said. Of course everyone wanted to see him, and it was impossible for us to move a step. Stambuli, therefore, procured a horse, mounted Klootz upon it, and in this manner we proceeded to Stambuli's house.

We did not at first believe in Klootz's statement, and thought that he must have purposely given the Mahdi false information, so as to gain favour and save his own skin; but when we were alone together, I bound him by a solemn oath to tell me the absolute truth, and, to my astonishment, he told me he had nothing to add to what he had already said. It is impossible to describe our misery when we heard Klootz's report. We had counted for months on the success of the expedition to deliver us from the hands of our enemies, and now all our bright hopes were rapidly fading away, and again a gloomy future yawned in front of us.

General Hicks left Rahad on the 26th of October, and arrived at Aluba on the 29th; here he received the Mahdi's letter summoning him to submit. Of course this was taken no notice of, and on the 3rd of November the army advanced towards Kashgeil, which is about twelve miles south of El Obeid.

In the meantime the Mahdi had been collecting his followers, and doing all in his power to inspire them with wild fanaticism; anyone who saw the enormous hordes of savages which were brought together, must have trembled for the fate of Hicks. It was said that the Mahdi had been promised the assistance of 40,000 angels from paradise, and everyone quite believed in the truth of this assertion. Anyone beholding this immense multitude of fanatics of every race and age, even though he had formerly been a disbeliever in the Mahdi, must now have been convinced of his divinity. The uneducated masses of the Sudan are entirely governed by the influence of external appearances, they had never heard or seen anything of this description before; now heralds were going from end to end of the camp foretelling the death of everyone who refused to follow the Mahdi.

On the 1st of November, Mohammed Ahmed quitted El Obeid, and everyone—man, woman, and child— followed him. Every house was evacuated, and woe to him who attempted to hide himself! Wad Gubara and his flag alone remained behind as garrison of El Obeid. The throng, noisy bustle and din of the camp suddenly gave way to almost absolute silence—the silence of the grave. The days which followed were for us a period of terrible anxiety. Although we felt almost certain that a terrible catastrophe was about to take place, yet we still had a slight hope that, with the help of European leaders, good rifles, and machine-guns, the result might be different. Abu Anga, who had separated from his Jehadieh (black troops) just the day before, now joined the powerful division of Abdel Halim, and on the 3rd of November the Mahdi's followers also joined this division, whilst the Mahdi himself, accompanied by his Khalifas, set out for Birket.

It was on the 3rd of November that the action actually began, for, in accordance with the Mahdi's orders, his followers had gradually completely encircled the troops, who were now opposed by black soldiers with Remington rifles, Wad en Nejumi's Gellabas, and the flags of Abdel Halim, Sherif Mahmud, and many others. In the attack which occurred on this date, the Dervishes were forced back with the loss of Fauzi, one of the Mahdi's katibs, Elias Pasha's son, and the son of Hajji Khaled; but General Hicks's losses were considerably greater; he had also run short of water, and was doing his utmost to dig wells, though he did not know that within fifteen minutes' walk of him there was a large reservoir of rain-water. What days of terrible anxiety these must have been for the principal officers, and especially for General Hicks, on whom the entire responsibility rested!

Major Herlth's diary stops abruptly on the 4th of November; he writes on that day that Dr. Georges Bey was wounded the previous day and died shortly afterwards. As far as I can remember, the Major then continues:—"These are bad times; we are in a forest, and everyone very depressed. The general orders the band to play, hoping that the music may enliven us a little; but the bands soon stop, for the bullets are flying from all directions, and camels, mules, and men keep dropping down; we are all cramped up together, so the bullets cannot fail to strike. We are faint and weary, and have no idea what to do. The general gives the order to halt and make a zariba. It is Sunday, and my dear brother's birthday. Would to God that I could sit down and talk to him for an hour! The bullets are falling thicker . . . ."

Here the writer suddenly breaks off; possibly a bullet had penetrated his weary heart.

The ring of encircling Dervishes was gradually drawing in and enclosing the ill-fated troops. The greatest destruction was done by Abu Anga's men who may be said to have destroyed the army; hidden behind shrubs and bushes, they fired incessantly at very close range into the midst of the Egyptians. One of Abu Anga's men told me that he alone had fired one hundred and fifty rounds. On that terrible Sunday General Hicks had to abandon a number of guns, for he had no mules to carry them. Dire confusion prevailed everywhere, the troops were suffering terribly from thirst, discipline was gone, and the men could not even lay their guns properly.

Klootz, whom the Khalifa Abdullah took with him, told me that he was some way from the place where the actual fighting was going on, and that the shells were striking the branches overhead. It would seem that the army made three attempts to break through the Dervish lines, but failed, and Klootz told me that the bodies were scattered in three large heaps extending over a distance of nearly two miles. The largest heap was in the forest of Shekan near Kashgeil, and it was here that the Dervishes fell on the remainder of the force and the European officers, and killed them with their lances on the 5th of November.

According to the evidence of the Dervishes themselves, the European officers fought most heroically. General Hicks was one of the last to fall; he had emptied his revolver, and, holding his sword in his right hand, waited for the rush of the enemy; he was soon surrounded and his horse wounded in the back; he then dismounted and fought most gallantly with his sword until he fell, pierced by several spears. The heroism of these brave men was the admiration of all. After the massacre the bodies were stripped and mutilated. Even long after the battle those who were present used to talk of the terrible spectacle of all these bodies lying with their mouths gaping open and covered with blood. These savages used to plunge their spears into the bodies of the dead so as to dip them in the bloody entrails of their enemies, and for long after they talked and revelled over the yellow-looking fat of the "Turks," which protruded through their gaping wounds. Baron Seckendorf, who was remarkable for his enormous size, had been beheaded, and his head was taken to the Mahdi ; it was thought that he must have been General Hicks. A few escaped by hiding themselves under the heaps of dead bodies or behind guns or waggons ; at the end of the action these were all collected, and numbered one hundred persons. During the actual fighting no quarter was given. An Egyptian soldier pursued by some Dervishes fled towards the Khalifa Sherif and begged to be spared ; but the latter laughed at his fear, and he was at once despatched with spears.

The Dervishes then collected their dead and laid them out in a line. It seems almost incredible to say so, but there were only three hundred and fifty in all killed. The Mahdi offered up a prayer over them, and then they were buried.

The dead bodies of the Egyptians were left a prey to the vultures and hyenas. Klootz, who said that he understood doctoring, was permitted by the Mahdi to collect all the medicines in the field, and when doing so he was enabled to examine the bodies of the Europeans. He told me that it was with the greatest difficulty he kept himself from breaking down when he saw the mutilated corpses of those with whom he had but a short time ago laughed and spoken. The body of a soldier was seen hanging between earth and sky ; he had evidently climbed up an Adansonia tree in search of water, when a bullet must have killed him, and in falling he was caught by the branches.

Amongst those who escaped was a man named Abderrahman Ben en Naga Bey, whose father, then in El Obeid, had entreated the Mahdi to spare him. A few days before the catastrophe he was found writing letters to Omar Wad Elias Pasha, then with Abdel Halim's force ; in consequence he and his men had been put in irons, and it was Ala ed Din Pasha's intention to execute him ; but Hicks would not allow it, saying that he would be fairly tried after El Obeid was captured. Ben en Naga was in the thickest of the fight, and had already lost an eye, when his father's slaves succeeded in reaching him and saving his life.

The Mahdi and his followers were greatly delighted,

A BAGGARA EMIR, PRESENT AT THE ANNIHILATION OF THE HICKS EXPEDITION, AND AFTERWARDS CAPTURED AT TOSKI.

for they had not calculated on such a complete victory, and a messenger was at once despatched to El Obeid to order a salute of one hundred guns to be fired.

It was early on Tuesday morning, the 6th of November,

that the thunder of the guns was heard in the camp, and our alarm at this terrible news can well be understood. Our bright hopes, which enabled us to support a wretched existence for more than a year, were rudely dashed to the ground. We now gave up all idea of the Government sending a second expedition. It was clear that Khartum must look to its own safety, and as the Mahdi had in the first instance gained possession of Kordofan through his victory over Yusef Pasha Esh Shellali, so now his annihilation of General Hicks's force placed almost the entire Sudan in his hands.

CHAPTER VI.

THE MAHDI'S TRIUMPHAL ENTRY INTO EL OBEID.

Fall of Darfur—Slatin surrenders—The Mahdi's divinity credited after the annihilation of Hicks—King Adam of Tagalla—Stambuli's kindness to the European captives—Gordon writes to the Mahdi—Power's letter—The sisters seized and distributed amongst the emirs—They are tortured—The missionaries turned into slaves—The terrible journey to Rahad—The Greeks come to the help of the sisters—The proclamation concerning the treatment of priests and hermits by Mohammedans—The Mahdi at Rahad—Ohrwalder's interviews with the Mahdi concerning religion—The Dervishes attack the Nubas.

The Mahdi remained seven days with his entire force at Birket, so as to collect families and stragglers and to take possession of the loot which the greedy Arabs had seized and refused to give up. Several of the latter were flogged, and seven slaves belonging to the Mahdi's uncle, Sayid Mohammed Taha, suffered the loss of a hand and a foot because they had kept for themselves some of the Mahdi's booty.

The loot referred to consisted of war material, such as Krupp guns, machine guns, and Remington rifles, besides a number of axes, pickaxes, and shovels, which were required for making zaribas; a quantity of money, watches, and clothing, was also included, and the whole was carried off to the beit el mal.

Some of the dead bodies were secretly set fire to, so as to make the ignorant people think that these unbelievers were being consumed by hell-fire. General Hicks's white horse was handed over to Klootz with orders to cure the wound in its back.

At length the pestilential smell of thousands of dead bodies of men and animals drove the conquerors forward.

The Mahdi's entry into El Obeid was a scene of wild enthusiasm and excitement. The many-coloured flags came first, then followed thousands upon thousands of Dervishes moving to the ever-swelling murmur of "La Ilaha il'lallah" ("There is no god but God"), whilst others danced out of the ranks and shook their blood-bespotted spears, uttering fearful yells. After them followed the cavalry with the three Khalifas. Every now and then a halt was made, when a number of riders would dash forward at full gallop, poising their lances ready for the thrust, and then would return to the ranks amidst the loud applause of the others.

After the cavalry followed a few prisoners, the wretched remnant of Hicks's army. Most of them were naked, and were being dragged forward under the continual insults of the Dervishes; then came the guns drawn by wounded mules, and last of all came the Mahdi himself, riding a magnificent white camel, and surrounded by his most fanatical adherents, whose monotonous "La Ilaha il'lallah" resembled the sound of a rushing stream. Clouds of dust filled the air, and as the Mahdi passed by, the spectators threw themselves down and kissed the ground, whilst the women shouted "Mahdi Allah" ("The Mahdi of God").

Such a scene of wild triumph had never before been witnessed. The Mahdi was now honoured almost as a god. This victory gained for him an enormous increase of power and respect. The fear of his name sped like wildfire throughout every province and district in the Sudan. He was now regarded as the true Mahdi, every Moslem believed in him, and all doubt was put aside.

At the battle near Shekan numbers of people said they saw the angels whom the Mahdi had summoned to fight against the Turks. He now became the object of almost superhuman adoration; even the water with which he washed himself was handed by the eunuchs to the believers, who drank it with avidity as an antidote to all ills and diseases.

After a time the captured Egyptians were released,

and many died in a state of beggary in the marketplace at El Obeid. The captured blacks were distributed amongst the beit el mal soldiers, and were known by the name of "Hiksani," for example, Morgan Hiksani. It was one of the Mahdi institutions that slaves should—besides their own names—bear also the names of their masters. Our Delen blacks were also given my name, "Yusef." Of course it would have been more correct if they had called them after our chief, Luigi Bonomi, but the Arabs found this name rather difficult to pronounce.

The Mahdi now became more imperious, and his success made him bolder and more confident. He despatched letters to various parts of the world, proving the divinity of his mission by his success in arms, and summoning all to rise against the Turks. He wrote very strongly to the inhabitants of the Gezireh, threatening them with fire and sword if they refused to rise against the Government and join him.

Having rid himself of his enemies, the Mahdi now turned his attention to Darfur. He appointed his uncle, Zogal Bey, who was known as Sayid Mohammed Khaled, emir of Darfur, and sent him to that province, accompanied by Abdel Samad, the son of Ahmed Sharfi, and Omar Wad Elias.

Khalifa Sherif, immediately after the victory over Hicks, urged the Mahdi to advance to the White Nile and attack Khartum, which he might easily have done, but the Mahdi was anxious first of all to secure Darfur, and he also wished to rest on his laurels a little longer. He wrote to Slatin Bey informing him of the destruction of Hicks's army, and he also forced Klootz to write to the same effect. Zogal started on the 16th of December, 1883, and proceeded in the first instance to Dara, where Slatin was at that time. He then sent in a messenger with the Mahdi's letter, in which he was called upon to surrender. Zogal well knew that this was a mere formality, for Slatin was quite unable to hold out any longer, and he had only five cartridges per man left; his men too refused to make any further stand. Slatin, therefore, on receipt of the letter, rode out to Zogal and submitted. The Dervishes then entered Dara, and as usual began to plunder. Zogal subsequently proceeded to El Fasher, which was at that time commanded by the Mudir, Said Bey Guma, who had put the town in a state of defence.

In spite of the wells being beyond the lines, Said Bey offered a resistance which from the outset was hopeless; seven days later, that is to say on the 15th of January, 1884, he surrendered. Kebkebieh also yielded to Zogal, and Omshanga had already submitted. Thus the populous and valuable province of Darfur, which had cost Egypt much blood and money, was entirely lost in the short space of eight days. In the meantime the Mahdi had despatched his son-in-law, Wad el Beshir, to the Gezireh to head the revolt against the Government in that district.

The Mahdi showed his wisdom in never attempting to invade a district which had not previously declared in his favour. When he heard of the submission of El Fasher and Dara, he despatched Abu Girgeh to undertake the siege of Khartum. The latter left with only a small body of troops, but numbers joined him on the way, especially when he reached the White Nile; so that he was not afraid of advancing towards the capital.

Thus through his victory at Shekan, the Mahdi had virtually made himself master of the whole Sudan from the Red Sea to the boundaries of Waddai, and from the Bahr el Ghazal to Dongola. All eyes were turned to him, and the majority of the people believed him to be the true Mahdi; some thought he must be a great magician. Even now at the present time, when he has already been six years in his grave, and the fallacy and misery wrought by Mahdiism are thoroughly admitted, still his wonderful success is attributed to witchcraft. His own countrymen—the Danagla—although they now admit he was not the Mahdi, say that he was undoubtedly a very holy man, and was supernaturally endowed by God with extraordinary authority and wisdom. Amongst others who feared the Mahdi's power was King Adam of Tagalla, who with his wife, child, and slaves, came down from his mountain retreat and surrendered.

For a long time the King's Kadi had endeavoured to convince his master that Mohammed Ahmed was not the true Mahdi, and did his utmost to dissuade him from joining; but after the defeat of Hicks, Adam delayed no longer, and moreover took his Kadi with him. When they reached Melbeis, about three hours' journey from El Obeid, the Kadi deserted, but he was recaptured, put in chains, and brought with the king to El Obeid.

On their arrival near the town, Khalifa Abdullah went out with a large retinue to meet Adam, who had a great reputation throughout Kordofan, and greeted him most cordially. A salute was fired, and every one rejoiced at the Mahdi's bloodless victory. King Adam was warmly welcomed by the Mahdi, given a special place to live in, and treated with the greatest respect. To gain still more favour in the Mahdi's eyes, Adam sent him six of his prettiest young girls as concubines. After a short time, however, the mountain king seemed to tire of residence in El Obeid and began to suffer from melancholia. In his mountains he was absolute master, here in El Obeid he was nothing but a slave. At first he thought he would be permitted to return to his mountains, but soon he had to give up all hope of this; and before long he realised that one of the first principles of Mahdiism was that those who were fortunate enough to behold its light would never be permitted to wander back into darkness. Now he bitterly repented that he had not accepted his Kadi's advice, while the spies by whom he was surrounded soon let the Madhi know what the Kadi's opinions were; and when Khalifa Abdullah learnt that he meditated flight, he at once had him seized and beheaded. Thus was the unfortunate Adam intimidated; then his horses were taken from him, and last of all, to save his life, he had to sell his wives.

Almost all the inhabitants of Jebel Nuba sent messengers to say that they were the Mahdi's subjects.

Even in Khartum already numbers were inclined to him. In proof of this statement, the case of the Sub-Mudir of the town, Wad Gesuli, may be quoted. When this individual heard of Gordon's arrival at Berber, he at once fled from Khartum and came to El Obeid, where he threw himself at the Mahdi's feet and assured him that the inhabitants of Khartum to a man were on his side.

All hope of release now seemed at an end. Our pitiful condition was somewhat lightened through the kind offices of our Syrian friend, George Stambuli, who was both the Mahdi's favourite and our benefactor at the same time, and he supplied us with the necessaries of life. The sisters made jibbehs (Dervish coats), which Stambuli sold and gave us the proceeds. We obtained the material chiefly from the clothes of the soldiers who had been killed, and from the officers' tunics. O'Donovan's mackintosh and some other articles of clothing which Klootz recognised came into our hands and were soon cut up. Most of the clothing was stained with blood, which we were obliged to wash out; but what bitter thoughts occupied our minds in this sad task!

Towards the end of January 1884 an unfortunate incident occurred which brought us into difficulties. One of Stambuli's female slaves, having come to an understanding with his Dongolawi servant, went to the Khalifa Abdullah and reported that her master was a Christian, and prayed daily. Stambuli's suspicions were aroused, and that evening he hid away everything which could be brought up against him, except a small silver cross which his little daughter wore round her neck. Almost before dawn his house was surrounded by a number of Dervishes, and Nejumi with Wad Suleiman, who had been ordered to take possession of his house, broke into it and began a thorough search.

Stambuli who, since the fall of El Obeid, had never been questioned, had his house full of all sorts of things, and was also in possession of a quantity of gum and ostrich feathers. The house was turned upside down, but nothing of an implicating nature could be found:

the slave had, however, mentioned the little girl's cross, and the inquisitors demanded to see the children; when they saw the cross they at once asked what it was. Stambuli replied that it was an ornament which had no special signification, and Wad Suleiman then pulled it off the child's neck and kept it.

I must here remark that numbers of people were very envious and jealous of Stambuli, and did not at all care to see a white man in possession of all this property; they therefore took every occasion to rob and steal from him. Stambuli was now put into chains, whilst his property was carried off to the beit el mal. It was decided that he was to be beheaded, but his Syrian countrymen and the Greeks consulted together, then went to the Mahdi and begged for his life. They were kindly received by the latter, who gave them some hope, and fifteen days later Stambuli was pardoned. He was obliged to appear before the Mahdi with a shebba (*i.e.* a long piece of forked wood in which the neck was placed, and which had the effect of forcing the head back), and in this condition he was obliged to implore the Mahdi's forgiveness. His property was never returned to him, and he could support us no more.

Father Bonomi seized this opportunity to write to the Mahdi and beg for our release, which he had so frequently promised. The Mahdi wrote several kind words on the reverse of the petition, but they meant nothing; he said Father Bonomi was aware with what affection he regarded him, and that, therefore, he could not bear the thought of losing him. At the same time he instructed Wad Suleiman to give us whatever was necessary for our sustenance from the beit el mal; this occurred on the 5th of February, 1884.

Just at this time, when all hopes of release seemed at an end, God sent us light in the midst of our darkness. Some people arrived from Khartum and reported that Gordon Pasha had reached there and had been received with great enthusiasm.

The alarm with which this news was received by the Mahdi and his adherents, and the delight which it occasioned to those who still hoped for deliverance, can readily be understood. The Mahdi, who thought the Sudan was actually in his grasp, was thoroughly upset, for it was generally believed that Gordon had brought Englishmen with him. A few days later he received a letter from Gordon, and the anxiety to know what it contained was enormous. Nothing else was talked about, and when the Mahdi ordered the letter to be read in public the disappointment was very great.

In this letter Gordon offered the Mahdi the whole of the Western Sudan, of which he said he should be considered the Sultan. He authorised the continuance of the slave trade, and free transit to all pilgrims going to Mecca; and, in conclusion, he asked for the release of the prisoners. The Mahdi laughed at Gordon's proposals, and thought him a very cunning unbeliever, who was attempting to delude him with vain promises merely to gain time. He could not understand how it was Gordon came to offer him what he already possessed some time ago; and he remarked that the very ground on which Gordon was standing was practically in his hands. The fact that Gordon had brought no troops with him served to further increase his pride, and his reply was couched in the following terms:—He said that when he was at Abba Island he had warned the Government officials that if they refused to recognise him as the Mahdi, they would undoubtedly perish. He had repeated the same warning to Yusef Pasha Esh Shellali, and to Hicks Pasha. He informed him of the surrender of Darfur, and concluded by saying that he had no desire for worldly benefits. His object was to reform the people, and he invited Gordon to come and join him. With the letter the Mahdi sent him a complete set of Dervish garments, viz., a jibbeh, takia, turban, girth, and pair of sandals.

Meanwhile the Mahdi had despatched the emir Abu Anga with some troops, also the emirs Wad Nejumi and Abdullah Wad en Nur to Jebel Dair, where the king (Mek) Kumbo was still offering resistance. It was thought that the number of troops would alarm these mountaineers; but they successfully resisted the first attack, and then withdrew to their mountain fastnesses where the troops could not follow them.

On the 23rd of March, 1884, a man arrived from Khartum with a small note from Consul Power. It was written in English on one side, and in French on the other: " Courage pour un peu. Gordon est ici. Courage tout ira bien," was what this good man wrote. He also asked for the names of the survivors of Hicks's expedition, and the names of the European prisoners in Kordofan. We answered all his questions. These few words of the consul gave us no little comfort and encouragement.

The time of the Mahdi's departure from El Obeid was now drawing near. The crowd of people who had been collected was so enormous that the water in the wells was insufficient, and rose greatly in price, and anyone with slaves had to pay dearly for the luxury.

Disturbances frequently took place round the wells, and often people fell in. The wells were from 150 to 160 feet deep.

The Mahdi's further stay at El Obeid was now useless, and he decided to advance on Khartum. He issued a proclamation summoning all people to join him, and heralds were despatched in all directions with the Mahdi's orders. At the same time it was announced that all people should follow in the Mahdi's track via Rahad, and Arabs living to the north and east of El Obeid were instructed to fall upon any travellers, put them in chains, and drag them to that town.

Provisions now became very cheap, such as coffee, wheat, dates, &c.; but, on the other hand, the rates of hire of camels and donkeys increased enormously. Money was distributed to everyone for the journey.

With regard to ourselves, however, as we were not permitted to leave, we resolved to try and escape; but this was most difficult, for we were avoided by everyone and no one dared associate with us. We managed, however, to procure a trustworthy man, who succeeded n getting us camels and guides; but God had disposed otherwise. Khalifa Abdullah, accompanied by a number of followers, suddenly appeared at our huts on the 28th of March, and Father Bonomi, brother Joseph Rognotto and myself were summoned before him. We found him seated on his sheepskin in the midst of a circle of emirs, and when he had beckoned to us to sit down, he then began to address to us a heap of questions, all leading up to the one important point—that we should accept his faith. His arguments were valueless, and had no effect upon us, so we were sent back to our huts.

That evening, at about sunset, some thirty men, mounted on horses, broke into our humble abode, and said that they had orders to remove the sisters, assuring us with mock modesty that no harm should happen to them. We, however, well knew what would happen, and absolutely refused to be separated, saying that if they wished they could kill us, and cut off our heads; but that it would be a cruel shame for the Mahdi to ill-treat these poor women after all his solemn promises and assurances. But of what avail could our protests be against brutal violence! They forced their way in, seized the sisters, and took them before the Khalifa Abdullah. He and Khalifa Sherif used every means of cruel barbarity to shake the faith of these poor sisters, and the latter, seizing a pair of scissors, which one of the sisters was carrying, cut the partition between her nostrils. The Khalifa's wives also howled and insulted them in every base way, and then they were distributed amongst the emirs, and sent to Rahad.

We spent that night in our own huts, but early the following morning the Dervishes came and took us to the Khalifa, who made us over to various emirs. My master was to be Abdullah Wad en Nur; but as at that time he happened to be at Jebel Dair, I was made over to his brother Makin, who was then occupying Mohammed Said Pasha's house. Father Bonomi, together with the little property we had left, was put into the beit el mal; but my diary, which I had now written for the third time, also Herlth's diary, General Hicks's Bible and prayer book, and a sandwich case and small bundle, belonging to O'Donovan, were all lost. We were now exposed to ill-treatment and insult from all sides. The Mahdi's three sons, ranging from seven to ten years of age, used to come and insult me daily; but I cannot mention the details, which will for ever remain engraven on my memory.

At length, on the 7th of April, 1884, the Mahdi set out, and we with him. The huge camp, swarming with thousands and thousands of people, became empty in a few days, and each one, as he left his hut, set fire to it, so that nothing was to be seen but clouds of smoke and flames darting upwards to the sky.

Just as we were leaving I was made over to another master, Idris Wad el Hashmi. When I arrived at his house, I found everything ready for the journey; numbers of well-bound books were lying about on the floor. I picked one up, and found it was 'The Soldier's Pocket Book,' by Lord Wolseley. I would like to have searched amongst these books for a diary, but they turned me out: Idris had taken them out of some good leather trunks, which he had filled with his own effects. Three days after the Mahdi's departure my master and I quitted El Obeid. The road to Rahad was one uninterrupted stream of human beings—men, women, and children; camels carrying the household goods, on the top of which were fastened angaribs, on which women were seated; oxen and donkeys, all heavily laden; numbers of Arabs were driving along their flocks with them; here one would see a camel fallen prone under its heavy load, there a child or a slave vainly seeking in the crowd for his lost master. Of course I had to walk, and to act as a camel-driver as well, subject to continual insult and threatening. I moved along as best I could; the Arabs applauded my master's good sense in making me his camel-driver, and urged that I should carry a load as well. We had to halt frequently, as the camels were so heavily laden.

The burning sun and fatigue were terribly oppressive, and it is always a wonder to me how I escaped sunstroke. As to food, I had a share of my master's

horses' meal. In the evening I was obliged to clean
the dokhn, which was given to the horse, and the
pangs of hunger made me covet even this, while I was
obliged to ask my master's slave to occasionally give me
a gulp of water; indeed, this slave pitied my wretched
state.

It took us three days to reach Rahad, though, under
ordinary circumstances, the journey could easily be
performed in one and a half days. The burning sand
had blistered my feet, and caused my legs to swell.
One day I saw the unfortunate King Adam, of Tagalla,
riding by; he was mounted on a mule, and his feet
heavily chained. They thought that the sight of his
native mountains might make him wish to desert.
Soon after his arrival at Rahad the poor king died,
heart-broken, and to him death must have come as a
happy deliverance; while to us, who also longed for it,
death would never come.

Rahad is situated in a depression, which in winter
becomes a swamp; the water remains standing for some
time, and there are numerous wells, which are sufficient
for a large number of men and animals. During the
dry season, Rahad is a centre in which large numbers of
Arab tribes collect, and about four hours to the south
rises the great Dobab mountain (called by the Arabs
Dair, because of its semicircular shape). Dobab is
perhaps the best naturally-fortified hill of the entire
Nuba group. It is accessible from one side only, and is
easily defensible; there are quantities of water, which
would enable the inhabitants to stand a prolonged siege.
The circumference of the base of the mountain is about
eighteen miles, and the inhabitants live on the top.

Already the Dervishes had constructed their rude
barracks under the shady trees of Rahad, and soon an
enormous camp sprang up. Shortly after my arrival,
I was again obliged to change masters; the one with
whom I had recently been was not really bad, but my
new master, Abdel Halim Wad Id, was a very great
and fanatical emir.

Before, however, I proceed to describe the events

which occurred at Rahad, I must give a brief outline of what had happened to the sisters since they were so cruelly wrenched away from us. They had set out from Rahad with the various emirs amongst whom they had been distributed; on the journey they suffered greatly; they were obliged to walk the whole distance barefooted, over thorns and burning sand; they underwent the agonies of hunger and thirst, and some of them had to carry loads; one of them, for a whole day, had not a drop of water to drink. These brutal savages were continually beating, insulting, and abusing them, and when, tired and weary, they sat down for a moment, they were driven forward under the lash of the cruel whip. On their arrival at Rahad they scarcely looked like human beings, with their faces all scorched and peeled by the burning sun; and here new tortures awaited them. One of them was suspended from a tree, and beaten on the soles of the feet until they became swollen and black, and soon afterwards the nails dropped off. In spite of all this suffering, and notwithstanding the continual threats of these barbarians that they would be violated, these sisters clung firmly to their faith and belief.

One night, one of the sisters succeeded in escaping to the Mahdi's hut, and, forcing her way into his presence, appealed vehemently to him against the cruel treatment which she and her companions were suffering at the hands of his tyrannical emirs, and that their only fault was that they resolved to adhere to their own faith. Under other circumstances the Mahdi would never have forgiven this bitter reproach, but when he saw this poor sister wounded and bleeding, he pretended that he knew nothing of the matter, and at once ordered all the sisters to be brought to his enclosure, where they were, to some extent, safe from ill-treatment; yet they were in constant terror of being dishonoured, and therefore decided to seek the protection of some of the Greeks who were in favour with the Mahdi, and who, at the sisters' request, sought his permission to take charge of them and care for them. The Mahdi, who really pitied them from his heart, sanctioned the proposal of the Greeks, to whom the sisters were duly handed over; but it was not, of course, admitted that pity for them had induced this decision.

It is a well-known fact that in the Kuran the Prophet Mohammed enjoins respect and toleration of the ministers of Christianity, whom he calls "Rahban," or pious persons consecrated to God's service; and, moreover, he tells his followers that it is their duty to do so. In support of this I may here quote a translation of the celebrated passage which occurs in the manuscripts kept in the Greek convent on Mount Sinai. It is as follows :—

"In the name of the merciful God, Mohammed Ibn Abdullah issues this proclamation to all. He announces that he is the trusted one of God, by whom he has been placed over his creatures. No one, therefore, can shelter himself under the plea of ignorance.

"I have written this proclamation in the form of an order to my nation, and to all Christians in the East and West, far and near, young and old, known and unknown. He who fails to follow the instructions laid down in this order is conducting himself contrary to God's will, and renders himself liable to a curse, whoever he may be, whether Sultan or any other Moslem.

"If a priest or a monk retire to a mountain, grotto, cave, plain, desert, city, village, or church, I myself am prepared to follow them with my army and my subjects, to protect them against any enemies they may meet, for these priests are my rayas (subjects), and I myself will prevent any harm coming to them. Taxes shall not be taken from them, except those which they may give of their own free will and accord, not being compelled to do so by any one. It is not permissible to remove a bishop from his bishopric, a priest from his church, or a monk from his retreat. No objects shall be removed from their churches and used in the construction of mosques, nor, indeed, for the construction of the houses of Mussulmans. Whoso doth not act in accordance with this, acteth contrary to the law of God and His

Prophet. It is forbidden to burden bishops or other holy men with taxes. I shall uphold these their privileges everywhere, on land or sea, in the East or West, North or South. They shall enjoy my favour and protection against anything harmful, disagreeable, or unpleasant to them.

"Those who cultivate on mountains or distant places shall not be burdened with the tithe or tenth-tax, even if they give it of their own free will and accord, provided that what they cultivate is for their own maintenance. If there is a scarcity of corn, they shall be supported each with one quart of corn for each house. It shall never be necessary for them to go to war or to pay tribute. Those in possession of unmovable goods shall not pay more than twelve drams of silver annually. No one shall be burdened. No discussions will take place with those who follow the teaching of the Gospels, they should rather be in some degree sympathized with so as to put aside all enmity and to cause the wings of mercy to spread out.

"Should a Christian woman go amongst Moslems, they shall treat her well and permit her to go through her prayers in church, and allow nothing to come between her and her religion. Whoso acteth contrary to these orders acteth in rebellion to God and His Prophet.

"Christians should be supported in the maintenance of their churches and houses; their religion should help them to do so. It is not their duty to carry arms, the Moslems shall do that for them, and Moslems should ever hold firmly this order until the world's end.

"The witnesses who confirm the truth of this proclamation, which is hereby issued by Mohammed Ibn Abdallah, the messenger of God to all Christians, which proclamation is to seal their privileges, are, Ali Ibn Abu Taleb, Bakr Ibn Ali Kohaifi, Omar Ibn El Khattab, Othman Ibn Affan, Abu El Darda, Abu Horeireh, Abdullah Abu Masaud, Abbas Ibn Abdel Muttaleb, Fodeil Ibn Abbas, Zoheir Ibn Awan, Talaat Ibn Obeidallah, Saad Ibn Maaz, Saad Ibn Obadi, Tabet Ibn Kais,

Abu Khayetma, Hashim Ibn Omaya, Hareth Ibn Tabet, Abdallah Ibn Amr Bin el Aas, Amr Ibn Yasin, Moazzam Ibn Koreishi, Abdel Azim Ibn Hassan.

"This proclamation is written by the hand of Ali Taleb on the 3rd Moharrem of the second year of the Hejira corresponding with the 1st of August, 622 of the Christian Era. It is signed by the Prophet himself.

"Blessed be he who followeth the contents thereof, and cursed be he who acteth contrary to them."

No doubt the precepts enjoined in the above proclamation weighed with the Mahdi in his decision to hand over the sisters to the Greeks, and thus it was that the danger was for the time tided over. Later on, when Khartum fell and hundreds of the young women who had been in the harems of the principal people of the town fell into the hands of the emirs, the persecution of the sisters was entirely stopped, and in retirement they at length secured some rest and quietude, gaining their daily bread by sewing and other handiwork.

After this digression, let us return to Rahad, where numbers of straw huts were now erected. A market was opened and provisions were cheap. Various Arab tribes—the Dar Homr, Bederieh, Ghodiat, Baggara Howazma, Miserieh, and Dar Nauli—streamed hither with their flocks and herds, and soon the camp extended greatly. Sherif Mahmud, whom the Mahdi had left behind in El Obeid, was instructed to send all the people on from there.

The Mahdi set up his abode between two large trees, and the Khalifas lived around him. The combined movements of this enormous crowd were most impressive. At prayer-time thousands upon thousands of Dervishes ranged themselves in well-ordered lines behind the Mahdi, and the shout of "Allahu Akbar" resounded through the air. Often the singers of the Mahdi's praises would go on till long after midnight, and thus did he continue to inspire his gigantic audience.

I was also twice summoned by the Mahdi; on one

FATHER OHRWALDER'S INTERVIEW WITH THE MAHDI AT RAHAD, CONCERNING RELIGION.

occasion two of his body-guard rushed up to me quite out of breath, just to show how expeditiously they carried out the Mahdi's orders, and brandishing their swords over my head shouted, "Get up, the Mahdi wishes to speak to you." As a matter of fact I had no desire to see him, but I had to get up, and this I did as slowly as I possibly could, and then I was pushed forward in the direction I had to go. At length I reached the two large trees, and sitting down beside them I leaned against the roots. The Mahdi had not arrived. Close to me was a hut roughly built of dokhn reeds, which I was told was the fort, around which a small thorn zariba had been constructed to keep off the crowding Dervishes who were collected in their thousands, most of them seated in long lines on the sand and repeating their "subhan allah." The Mahdi's huts and tents were close by.

It was then the time for noonday prayers, and as the Mahdi approached there was a short buzz and hum followed by a deep silence.

When the Mahdi came to the place where the sheepskin was stretched out on the ground, a slave came up and took off his sandals, after which he conducted prayers. These over, he turned round and greeted me. Then some of his favourites came forward and presented petitions to him, some of which he approved at once by writing a few words on the back of the paper, while the remainder were put aside for consideration.

Since the occasion on which the Mahdi had interviewed Klootz, I had not seen him. I now saw a considerable change in him; he had grown much stouter, but he still wore the same clothes of rough damur, consisting of drawers, jibbeh, girth, and turban. His conversation soon turned on religion, and he asked me if we Christians used the "Hamdu" (a form used by the Moslems as they bow in prayer) in our prayers. I replied that not only had we one but several, and at his request I repeated the Lord's Prayer in Arabic.

This created much surprise amongst the ignorant listeners, who believe that Christians do not know how to pray, and I was thought quite "fasieh" (*i.e.* educated). After a long conversation on the Psalms of David, the Mahdi said, "I know that you Christians are very good people, and that you feed the hungry." He then told me about "deeds of mercy," and added that all such acts were useless, as anyone who did not believe in the Mahdi was but "wood for the fire." Our conversation was interrupted by the Aser or afternoon prayers, after which the Mahdi again held a reception. Amongst others a small dwarf appeared, and the Mahdi spoke to him about his tribe and asked if he were married. The dwarf replied that he had come to ask for a wife, and explained that the possession of one was the desire of his heart, whereupon the Mahdi gave orders that he should at once be provided with one. He then rose up to leave, and I was permitted to go home.

On the following day I was again summoned before him, and he explained that through the noonday prayers he knew he should win over the whole world. He said that God had given him a period of forty years (as a matter of fact he only lived four years, but a cypher more or less is of no consequence) during which he should make all people believe on him and acknowledge that he was the Mahdi. He added that after the subjugation of the Sudan he would take Egypt, which would only offer a weak resistance, and that afterwards he would attack Mecca, where the most bloody battle which the world had ever seen would take place; from Mecca he should proceed to Jerusalem, where Jesus Christ should descend from heaven. "Of course," I said, "Christ will possess all the characteristics which the Gospel attributes to Him;" but the Mahdi continued, "Would Christ not fight with anti-Christ? If I do not believe in Him He will kill me."

The Mahdi then asked me if I ever had dreams, and I replied that even if I did have dreams I did not believe in them. Then the Mahdi turned round to those who were near and said, "Assuredly the Turks do not believe in dreams, or they would have admitted that I am the Mahdi." It is said that Mahmud Bey Ahmedani,

Mudir of Khartum, who had accompanied Hicks and had fallen near Shekan, had seen the Mahdi's shadow on the wall surrounded with a halo of light, but in his obstinacy he still refused to acknowledge him.

Just then a Sherif of Syria came in, and, making obeisance to the Mahdi, said, " Sire, you are my relation !" (By this he meant that as he belonged to the Prophet's tribe, and as the Mahdi had sprung from the Prophet, that therefore they were connected.) The Mahdi was much gratified by this flattery, and ordered Wad Suleiman to give him fifty dollars and a concubine. The conversation was then turned on Gordon. The Mahdi remarked he was full of pity for him, for he said that he was convinced it was the Ulema's arguments which had made Gordon believe that he was not the true Mahdi. He then asked me what was the object of the wires with which Gordon had surrounded Khartum. I replied that I knew nothing of the art of war, but others said that this was telegraph wire, which Gordon had put down so that in case of attack the horses would stumble over it. The Mahdi smiled, and remarked that God was more mighty than all the tricks and artifices of Gordon.

It was now evening, and the Mahdi got up to go, so I went home, and when I returned to Sheikh Idris, several came up and congratulated me for having had the good fortune to talk with the Mahdi. For my own part I would gladly have dispensed with this good fortune. When I was summoned the next day I sent word that I was very ill, and by this means secured some rest.

Whilst at Rahad, the Mahdi's eyes were continually directed on Jebel Dair, and when Abu Anga and the emirs who were sent to subjugate these districts, returned, defeated in their attempts to scale the mountain, the Mahdi then despatched every man fit for war to reinforce him. He excused himself for this unusual measure by saying that all persons should be exercised in war, and that, moreover, this was penance to those who had only recently joined him, to purify them from the sin of not having joined him earlier. As a matter of fact, these Arabs were a source of great trouble and annoyance to the Mahdi, for they did nothing but wander about the market-place begging, and it was no small difficulty to keep such vast crowds in order.

The war against the Nubas was waged in the most cruel manner; the proud Dervishes were incensed at the stubborn resistance of these poor black slaves, as they used to call the Nubas. On one occasion, when the Dervishes, led by Abu Anga and followed by the Gellabas, attempted to ascend the mountain, the Nubas allowed them to advance some way and then pounced down upon the Gellabas in the narrowest pass; these men were badly armed, and four hundred of them were killed. Abu Anga seeing this beat a rapid retreat, and on coming into the pass was implored by the wretched wounded Gellabas to carry them away, but Abu Anga's men jeeringly replied that they must die "in God's cause," and left them to the tender mercies of the Nuba lances.

I may here remark that there was great ill-feeling between the blacks and the Dervishes, for the black soldiers complained that they were always placed in the forefront of the battle. In another attack the Dervishes succeeded in reaching the Nuba village, burning the huts, killing a large number of them and carrying off their wives and children as captives to Rahad, where they were sold as slaves. On this occasion Nur Angar cut off the heads of three Nubas who had already submitted, while Abu Anga's men seized the little children by the feet and dashed their brains to pieces on the rocks. At Rahad a special zariba was built for the Nuba captives, who were driven like cattle into a pen to be sold. These poor creatures, without covering from the sun or rain, suffered terribly from hunger and thirst; each evening they were given a handful of dhurra and some water, but that was quite insufficient, and in a few days mothers had to see their children slowly starving to death, while the little suckling babes gathered round their mothers in the vain search for food. Each morning the guards looked in to inquire if there were any dead or dying, and then ordered the wretched survivors, who had scarcely the strength to get up, to drag out their dead and dying friends and relations.

It would take a long time to tell of all the horrible atrocities and cruelties which these poor Nubas suffered at the hands of the Dervishes—and why? because they tried to retain their freedom and defend their fatherland, refusing to follow that base liar who called himself the Mahdi, to the siege of Khartum. Amongst the captives in the zariba was a man and his wife and two small children. The sight of his starving children was breaking the father's heart; the view of his native mountain so affected him that he became desperate, and knowing that he would probably be separated from his wife and children and sold the next day, he took a terrible resolution: in the middle of the night he embraced his wife, kissed his little children, and then plunged his knife into each of them, preferring rather that they should die than become slaves; he then broke out of the zariba and fled, the guards fired and missed him; thus the wretched man succeeded in reaching his beloved hills.

CHAPTER VII.

FATHER OHRWALDER'S VIEWS OF GORDON'S MISSION.

Ohrwalder describes his treatment at the hands of various masters—
The Nubas surrender and afterwards desert—News from Khartum—The capture of the English mail—Its arrival at the Mahdi's camp—The Mahdi decides to advance on Khartum—Brief review of events in Khartum and Berber—Ohrwalder's views on Gordon's mission—The Mahdi sets out for Khartum—Mohammed Ali Pasha's defeat and death—Colonel Stewart, Mr. Power, and others leave Khartum in ss. " Abbas "—Description of their wreck and treacherous murder.

THE war with Jebel Dair dragged on a long time; the Nubas fought with desperate courage. I used to hear of their bravery from the Dervishes who frequented my master's house. After about a month my master was sent to Birket, where he was ordered to collect the Arabs and send them on to Rahad. At this place he practised unprecedented cruelty. A man found drinking marissa he ordered to be flogged with eighty lashes, until the poor victim's bowels fell out. During his absence I was sent back to my old master, Sheikh Idris, where I continued to lead a wretched existence, eating out of the horses' nose-bag and quenching my thirst from the share of water which was allotted to the animals. The ground was my bed, the sky my roof.

Every morning when I got up I had to shake off the scorpions from my clothes, into which they had crept during the night. It is curious that the sting of these animals, which at other times was always most painful, caused me little trouble or irritation. The filth in the camp, owing to the entire absence of all sanitary rules, caused the flies to increase prodigiously; eating during the daytime was impossible, for one would have eaten as many flies as food.

I still suffered threats and insults here as in other places, and many a time did I intentionally put my head in danger in the hope that death would release me from these savages. Sheikh Idris was annoyed at my ill-treatment, but what could one man do with these hordes of fanatics? One day after a review I was asked by Idris to have breakfast with him in his hut; after breakfast he began to talk confidentially with me, and said that the Prophet Mohammed had expressly forbidden the ill-treatment of priests and hermits. He then said that Egypt had lost the Sudan, and that Gordon would not be able to withstand the Mahdi; most of the fikis and sheikhs had already submitted to the Mahdi, and the Sudan was in their hands. When I pointed out the great difficulties he would have in traversing the deserts to Wadi Halfa, he remarked that the Mahdi's undertaking was not likely to be hindered by the death of a few thousand men? I then argued that it was most unlikely that the white Moslems would ever accept a black Mahdi; and that, moreover, according to the traditions, the Mahdi would appear in Mecca. He replied, "God is the Lord of all," by which he meant to say that God can make a black Mahdi.

We had a long conversation about the Mahdi, and it seemed to me that Sheikh Idris did not believe in him, but had merely joined him in the hope of gain and rewards. Idris also added, "By what right should we be ruled by the Turks? can we not govern ourselves?" If there had been many more sensible and enlightened men like Sheikh Idris, it is probable that Mahdiism would have taken a very different form; but Idris was an exception—most of the principal emirs were uneducated and ignorant savages. It was God's will that this Idris should fall later on in the battle of Argin in 1889, fighting against Wodehouse Pasha.

A few days after this conversation, my original master, Abdullah Wad en Nur, arrived from Jebel Dair to obtain the Mahdi's instructions as to the future conduct of the war. The Mahdi presented him with a very good horse. Khalifa Abdullah asked him what he intended to do with me, and advised him that when he again went to the Nuba country he should take me with him and put me in the front so that the Nubas might kill me. Sheikh Idris told me this, and Khalil Hassanein, Roversi's old clerk, who had obtained a good place in the beit el mal, brought me three dollars for the journey. I was delighted with the idea of a change, for I could not have been worse off than I was at Rahad.

At first I was handed over to a fiki, who bothered me with his useless and nonsensical talk; his name was Mahmud, and he came from Tuti Island, near Khartum; he joined the Mahdi after Hicks's defeat, and brought a donkey and a few dollars with him. The first thing he did was to sell his donkey and purchase a concubine, but in two days the latter purchase ran away, so he lost both his donkey and his money. He then joined the Khalifa Abdullah, who recommended him to Idris as a good man to instruct me in the right way; but instead of convincing me of the Mahdi's divinity, I very soon convinced him of the reverse, and it was by no means difficult to do so; the fiki used frequently to go to the beit el mal to try and get a concubine, but no one took the smallest notice of him. On the other hand he used constantly to see the numerous concubines of Idris, who was rich, while he was but a poor man. From this I made him understand that the chiefs of Mahdieh sought only how they could best gain riches and honour at the expense of their poorer brethren. Soon afterwards he fell sick at Rahad, and there was no one to look after him or care for him; I knew that in his heart he had had quite enough of the Mahdi, but he was ashamed to acknowledge it before me. One night, not hearing his voice in the miserable hut which had been given to him, I looked in and found him lying stretched out dead on the ground. I felt sorry for the poor creature who had died away from his own home.

Another reason which made me glad to go away to

Dair, was that I was ill and suffering much from my old complaint, which forced me to frequently retire outside the camp amidst the jeers of the Arabs; but suddenly the ray of hope which had come to me with the thought of a change to the mountain, was as suddenly extinguished, for it transpired that Idris had arranged with Abdullah, without my knowledge, to leave me at Rahad.

The war against the Nubas was continued, and from Rahad I could see the columns of smoke ascending, showing where the villages had been burnt by these cruel Dervishes. At length these poor but brave mountaineers, overwhelmed by superior numbers, became discouraged, and agreed to submit on condition that they should remain free, and be allowed to live in their mountains. The Mahdi approved, for the Dervishes were quite worn out with their long and bloody war. The brave inhabitants descended from their hills—men, women, and children—in astonishing numbers, and established themselves at the foot of the mountain, and near the Dervish camp, while Mek Kumbo and the principal chiefs went to the Mahdi to take the Bea'a (oath of allegiance).

There was now great rejoicing. The Mahdi received them kindly, gave them presents, and handed back to them those who still remained in the beit el mal; but before they left his presence he ordered them and their wives and children to follow him to the White Nile. This was quite contrary to the agreement made between them, but the Mahdi cared little about honour and keeping his word, his main object was to attain his point by any fraud or deception he could practise. The Nubas promised to do so, and went back to their camp; but on talking to their people, they agreed to escape during the night, preferring rather to starve in the caves and recesses of their own mountains, than to leave their native country. Like one man, they rose and fled to the hills, and the fight was once more renewed. Many of them fought with the most stubborn desperation; several were killed, but the Dervish loss was also very heavy. The Nubas retired into the inmost recesses of the hills, where the enemy could not possibly follow them. On one occasion the Dervishes all but captured Mek Kumbo; his horse and lance fell into their hands, but he himself escaped.

At length, thoroughly exhausted by this tedious and interminable war, they returned to Rahad; but heavy rain had fallen, the Khor was now a rushing torrent, and here hundreds of Mahdiists were drowned—victims to their rash fanaticism—for they believed that the Mahdi's power could save them from the wild impetuous stream. Many of them crossed on angaribs (native beds), to each post of which an inflated skin was attached.

Towards the end of June, 1884, Slatin Bey arrived at Rahad. The Khalifa Abdullah ordered the big wardrums to be beaten, and the whole of the cavalry left the camp to meet him and escort him in. The Mahdi received Slatin very kindly, and he was attached to Khalifa Abdullah's followers.

Abdullah delighted in collecting foreigners around him. One day Father Bonomi and I were summoned by Abdullah to meet Slatin, and this gave me a chance of meeting Father Bonomi, whom I had not seen for months.

It was about this time that Marietta Combotti, one of our black girls, came from Khartum to Rahad. After Hicks's defeat we sent her to Khartum to inform our people there about our condition and about the Mahdi's power, and urged everyone to leave Khartum as soon as possible. We gave her some letters which were sewn into the end of a mat. Consul Hansal had assisted Combotti in every way, and had given her several things for us, such as clothes, money, and medicines. She had suffered greatly on the journey, had been put in chains, and all she had succeeded in saving was her money. She had been away seven months.

Amongst other things Consul Hansal sent us a photograph of our new and highly-honoured bishop, Monsignor Imbrien, of the Tyrol. Marietta also brought a letter from the consul to me describing the condition of Khartum, and the defeat of Baker Pasha, about which we had heard nothing. The consul further added: "We hope that the English will energetically push forward into the Sudan, or we shall be lost. Our condition is desperate." This letter was dated early in January, 1884. Hansal also sent us the *Tyroler Volksblatt* newspaper, published in Posen, and in it I was surprised to read an account of my own death. The paper said I had been captured by the Mahdiists, and had died of fatigue and ill-treatment. So my friends believed I was dead! and, indeed, I felt then that death could not be far distant. My complaint was worse than ever, and I was suffering from scurvy as well. We did indeed feel grateful to the unfortunate Hansal who had done all he could to alleviate our distress; but God has disposed otherwise. How I wish poor Hansal had taken our advice and gone home.

The state of moral darkness in which we lived, the constant insults, being gazed upon by such multitudes, being at the mercy and sport of these savages, just as if one were a monkey or other curious animal, all had a dulling effect on one's spiritual nature, and I felt that I must be losing my mind; but yet in all these trials and afflictions God did not leave us. Again a ray of hope shone through the obscurity.

We had already heard something about English troops, but the information was very vague. One of the Mahdi's messengers, who took the Mahdi's answer back to Gordon in Khartum, told me that Gordon had received him well, had given him some bakshish, not like the God-forsaken Mohammed Said Pasha, who had executed the Mahdi's messengers; but, prior to his departure, Gordon had warned him in the following words:—" Go, tell the Mahdi that I have only to stamp my feet on the ground, and thousands of Englishmen will at once spring up." I believed this story, for I did not think the messenger was clever enough to invent it; besides, I felt sure that Gordon must have known quite well that he alone was utterly unable to extinguish the fire of this gigantic revolt. But at length all these reports were fully confirmed.

It was Friday. The Khalifas were out on parade, when two camels, carrying an English mail, arrived. Khalifa Abdullah at once left the review, and sent for Klootz to read the letters. Klootz came at once to me and said that an entire English mail for Gordon had been captured near Omdurman. It was clear from several letters that English troops were advancing into the Sudan from three directions; that is to say, from Suakin to Berber, from Korosko to Abu Hamed, and from Dongola, where there were 20,000 infantry and 10,000 cavalry. There was a telegram from Cairo to Assuan announcing General Graham's advance; a touching little letter from a young girl to her father in Khartum, whose name I forget. In this letter she told of the alarm she felt for her father's safety, and how she prayed daily that her father might not meet the same fate as General Hicks. In another letter Gordon was informed that £60,000 had been sent to him.

All these letters had been sent from Berber to General Gordon by Joseph Cuzzi, who had written a letter to Gordon to that effect in Italian. One letter said that it was well known that the Khalifa Abdullah was the moving spirit of the revolt, and that the Mahdi merely supplied the religious element; but Klootz did not translate this in the Mahdi's presence. When the latter got up to go, Klootz translated this sentence to the Khalifa Abdullah, who was delighted with this flattering remark. Cuzzi's Italian letter was concealed by Klootz, who afterwards brought it to me. In this letter Cuzzi briefly informed General Gordon that he was forwarding the letters; that he had sent a messenger to Sawakin to come to an understanding with General Graham, and that the rebels at Abu Hamed had seized a number of the Government boats. He added that Gordon should have no anxiety about Berber, as long as Hussein Pasha Khalifa was Mudir. But in this matter he proved to have been completely deceived.

The general import of all these letters convinced the

Mahdi that the English were in earnest. He therefore decided to take no action for a time, and to remove the camp to the foot of the mountain, where it was his intention to await their advance.

But soon after came the news that Berber had fallen, and that General Graham had returned to Sawakin, and this decided the Mahdi to advance on Khartum.

The Nubas now began to give some difficulty. No sooner had the Dervishes abandoned their camp at the foot of the mountain, than the Nubas rendered all roads in the vicinity of Rahad, and for a considerable distance, unsafe. Slaves going out to gather wood or straw were suddenly swooped down upon by these bold mountaineers, who killed or captured them. In this way they revenged the cruelties which they had suffered. The Mahdi was quite unable to subdue these blacks, and his failure to do so was a great blow to his pride.

I may here remark that at this period of the Mahdieh religion, violation of moral laws was very severely punished. One of the Mahdi's bodyguard caught *in flagrante* in the practice of a species of immorality by no means uncommon in Eastern countries, both culprits were led out in chains and beheaded in the presence of the assembled multitudes.

Before following the Mahdi on his march to Khartum, it is advisable here to take a brief review of the events which had occurred in Khartum, Berber, and the Gezireh.

The catastrophe which had overtaken General Hicks's force filled the inhabitants of Khartum with indescribable dismay. Several of them returned to Egypt, and the members of the Austrian Mission, with their blacks, quitted Khartum on the 11th of December, 1883. Fortunate were those who seized this chance of escape before the roads became blocked!

General Gordon's arrival in Khartum gave fresh life and hope to the inhabitants. Great were the rejoicings, and a magnificent reception was prepared for the long-expected deliverer. This reception took place on the

18th of February, 1884, and must have greatly encouraged General Gordon in his undertaking; but it was not Gordon's individual presence which so greatly inspired the people. What could Gordon do alone, against the now universally worshipped Mahdi? The nature of the revolt was not political; the Sudanese had no intention of establishing an empire under the Mahdi's rule, and, even had this been the case, it is very improbable that Gordon's mediation would have been of any avail.

The movement was a religious movement, and was not limited to the Sudan alone; the Mahdi's intention was to subdue the world. He was a prophet, and in his

THE GOLD MEDAL STRUCK BY GORDON TO COMMEMORATE THE SIEGE OF KHARTUM.

own and the estimation of his followers he was a greater man than the Prophet Mohammed. The world was to come to an end in his time. Had Gordon only known beforehand how boundless was the wild fanaticism, and how completely the Mahdi's followers were intoxicated by it, he would never have accepted the mission. As it appeared to us in Kordofan, and to the Mahdi himself, Gordon's undertaking was very strange; it was just as if a man were attempting to put out an enormous fire with a drop of water. Gordon's name alone could not suppress the revolt, and it was not on account of his name that the Khartum people rejoiced at his arrival;

it was because they looked on Gordon as an English representative, and that he was only the precursor of an English expedition sent to take possession of the Sudan for England. That is what made the people glad, and caused them to put aside all idea of departure. Had they not been certain that an English expedition was coming, not a soul would have remained in Khartum, and I have no hesitation in saying that had the Egyptian Government not sent Gordon, then undoubtedly the evacuation originally ordered could have been carried out without difficulty.

Those who escaped massacre in Khartum have often told me that they were perfectly ready to leave, and it was only Gordon's arrival that kept them back; but Gordon's arrival without troops had rather disappointed them. Had he been accompanied by five hundred British bayonets, his reputation in the Sudan might have been maintained, and probably the Mahdi would never have left Kordofan.

Gordon himself committed a mistake, by which he gave a death-blow to himself and his mission. On his way to Khartum he stopped at Berber and interviewed the Mudir Hussein Pasha Khalifa; he imprudently told him that he had come up to remove the Egyptian garrisons, as Egypt had abandoned the Sudan. At Metemmeh also—a strong place between Berber and Khartum, and the headquarters of the powerful Jaalin tribe—he committed a similar imprudence, by giving the same information to Haj Ali Wad Saad, the emir of Metemmeh.

This Haj Ali was a man held in great respect, on account of his just dealings, and afterwards, when he died in Omdurman, there was public mourning for him. The fact, indeed, that the Khalifa had pardoned him after "marissa" had been found in his house, sufficiently indicates how greatly he was respected. Both Haj Ali and Hussein Pasha Khalifa informed all their principal people about the decision of the Government, and it was this announcement that made these faithful sheikhs, who were then trembling in the balance, throw in their lot with the Mahdi. Why should they remain loyal to a Government which had decided to give up their land? Had they remained faithful, what had they to expect when the Mahdi prevailed? It was this announcement of Gordon's which was the main cause of the fall of Berber, which place was essential for Gordon's plan of operations.

Haj Ali, shortly before his death, and when in great suffering, reviewed the misery which the Mahdi had brought upon the Sudan, and the part he himself had taken in it, and he then said that it was nothing but the knowledge of the intention of the Government to abandon the Sudan which made him join the Mahdi. "How," he said, "could I have remained loyal to a Government which I knew intended to leave me in the lurch afterwards? I would only have been paving the way for the Mahdi's vengeance."

At the time Haj Ali said this he was in doubt about the Divine nature of the Mahdi, and spoke openly to people on these matters. "But," he added, "at that time every one thought only of himself. Gordon thought only how he could save himself and the Egyptians, and we thought how we could save ourselves and avert the Mahdi's vengeance by taking his part; so we went to Berber, joined with the Ababdeh, besieged and took the town, and then cut Gordon's communications with Egypt."

Gordon was soon destined to see with his own eyes what a fatal mistake he had made, but only when it was too late.

No notice was taken of Gordon's peaceful proclamations; the revolt was now widespread, and masses of fanatical Dervishes were gradually encircling Khartum. Mohammed Wad el Besir, the sheikh El Obeid—a man held in great respect in the Gezireh—his sons, and the Fiki Medawi advanced on the town from the south. On the 16th of March, 1884, Gordon's troops were heavily defeated, and their leaders were executed by Gordon for treachery.

Another blow fell on Gordon by the surrender, at

THE FALL OF BERBER.

Fedasi, of Saleh Wad el Mek, with 1,400 men, to the emir Abu Girgeh. Still Gordon did not despair of success, and it was his individuality which inspired the inhabitants of Khartum with hope.

Saleh Wad el Mek's surrender greatly encouraged the Dervishes. Rebels were also gathering to the north of Khartum. The Jaalin of Metemmeh and the Ababdeh, as I previously stated, prepared to attack Berber. Hussein Pasha Khalifa, Sheikh of the Ababdeh, who had been Mudir there since the 18th of December, 1883, remained faithful to the Government, but his subordinates paid no attention to him; and it was largely due to the influence of these officials that numbers of local sheikhs joined the Mahdi.

The Ababdeh, Barabra, and Jaalin, under the supreme command of Mohammed el Kheir, now besieged Berber. Eight days later the town was taken by storm, and most of the garrison and a number of inhabitants were massacred. Joseph Cuzzi had attempted to escape, but he was caught and sent to Khartum to endeavour to induce Gordon to surrender. He was subsequently sent on to the Mahdi at Rahad.

Gordon's communications with the north were now cut. After Saleh Pasha's surrender, the number of besieging Dervishes increased greatly, and Abu Girgeh growing bolder, seized the village of Buri, where he built a fort and began to shell the town. Gordon therefore, on the 2nd of May, sent out a considerable force, which attacked Abu Girgeh, drove him out of his position, and all but succeeded in capturing him. Thus did Gordon, although hemmed in on all sides, maintain a bold front, and employed every art of war to keep the Dervishes from investing the town more closely.

To return now to the Mahdi at Rahad. He was at this time in full preparation for departure to the siege of Khartum, and, as usual, he despatched Abu Anga, Wad Nejumi, Wad En Nur, and Wad Gubara, with all his best troops in advance. As I have previously related, Cuzzi, who arrived at Rahad at the end of June, had been previously sent by the Dervishes to Khartum to try and induce Gordon to surrender, and Gordon had given strict orders that he should not be permitted within the walls. When, therefore, he arrived at Rahad, the Mahdi received him very well, loaded him with presents and then sent him back with George Clementino to Khartum as bearer of letters to Gordon. He arrived at the Dervish camp at the same time as Nejumi. Clementino was permitted to converse with the Greek consul, Leontides, but Cuzzi returned to Berber.

The Mahdi passed the month of Ramadan in Rahad, and it was not until the 8th of August that he set out for Khartum. The whole population, like a swarm of bees, accompanied him on the same road which Hicks had taken. The people joyfully undertook this long journey through pathless districts, and at a time when the rainfall was heaviest. Camels, too, were expensive and difficult to procure; but, in spite of all these obstacles, fanaticism was more pronounced than ever. There were in all upwards of 200,000 people, and at Shirkeleh the cavalry numbered 4,000. To defeat such an enormous force as this, a European expedition was necessary, not the weak force at Gordon's disposal.

Throughout the entire route fresh cavalry joined, whilst the herds of cattle which the Arabs drove along served as food, and meat was then cheap enough. Numbers of animals died during the march, and the road was plainly marked by an unbroken line of dead camels, donkeys, horses, and oxen. The route lay from Shirkeleh to Shatt, and thence to Duem. Here a halt was called for a few days to collect stragglers. All notion of working in the fields was abandoned, and agricultural pursuits were entirely dispensed with. Thus it happened that on the Mahdi's arrival at Omdurman the Dervishes were in great want of grain.

The Mahdi arrived at Omdurman on the 23rd of October, 1884, but the whole of the stragglers did not reach it till early in November. Everything had been prepared. Gordon was surrounded by numerous enemies, still he did not despair.

THE SIEGE OF KHARTUM.

In August both Niles had risen considerably; the Blue Nile had arrived almost at its full height, while the White Nile had overflowed its low bank, and now swept past Fort Mukran and the houses in Khartum. So high was it, that a dam had to be constructed to keep the water within bounds. At high Nile the White river is very broad; and at a later date, when I crossed over from Omdurman to the roughly built fort which has long since been destroyed, I was sea-sick. But as the river fell it left the ditch full of mud, and this proved a source of great danger. When the river was high, Gordon made several successful counter-attacks. Mohammed Ali Pasha went up the Blue Nile to a place near Gereif, and on the 30th of August fell upon the Arabs, utterly defeating them. This brave leader also attacked the old Sheikh El Obeid at Halfaya, and captured a quantity of dhurra and cattle. Khartum breathed once more, and it seemed as if all would be well; the bands played in the evening, and the town was full of joy, which, alas, was soon to be turned to sadness.

Mohammed Ali Pasha, emboldened by his late successes, advanced again on the Sheikh El Obeid, whom he defeated near El Eilafun; but, advancing into the desert to renew the attack on the 4th of September, he and upwards of 800 of his troops fell into an ambush and were slaughtered. This proved a very severe blow to Gordon, and Khartum being now closely invested, he decided to send a steamer north to communicate with the Government, and give them full information of the state of affairs.

As the Nile was now high, it was thought the small steamer *Abbas* would be able to make her way safely to Dongola. The *Abbas* left Khartum on the 10th of September, and was accompanied by two other steamers towing boats, in one of which were a number of Greek, and in the other Syrian merchants. These steamers ran the gauntlet of shot and shell till past Berber. When a short way beyond that town, the steamers *Mansureh* and *Safia* turned back, and reached Khartum only with the greatest difficulty, being fired upon throughout almost the entire distance. The *Abbas* continued her journey north, and drew up for the night at a small island. The two boats which had been cast off when the other steamers left, now passed the *Abbas*, but were driven on to some rocks by the wind, and here they had to stop for the night to repair. The next morning the *Abbas* passed them, and Colonel Stewart urged them to push forward. The Greek boat started, but it was some time before the Syrians could set sail; and again they were driven on to the rocks, where they remained firmly fixed.

In the meantime the Dervishes at Berber, who had gained possession of the steamer *El Fasher* when the town fell into their hands, at once sent her off in pursuit, together with two large sailing boats. The *Fasher* soon came up with the wrecked Syrian boat, which now made a sign of truce, was boarded and taken possession of. The Dervishes, having obtained all information, left one of their boats in charge of their capture, and then pursued the Greek boat, with which they soon came up, and, having secured her, the *Fasher* continued her pursuit of the *Abbas*. She proceeded almost as far as Abu Hamed, but here the captain refused to take her any further, as he feared running her on to a rock. So she returned to Berber with her captured boats, in which there were in all twelve Greeks and fifteen Syrians. Of the latter, eight were males, five females, and two children.

The steamer *Abbas*, after passing Abu Hamed, entered the Wadi Gamr cataracts, which are very rocky and dangerous, and here she struck on a rock near the village of Hebbeh, the inhabitants of which belong to the Monasir tribe. Colonel Stewart had the baggage disembarked on an island, on which the travellers now took up their abode until the expected Greek and Syrian boats should arrive; but, after waiting two days, Stewart sent his interpreter, Hassan Husni, with Mohammed Hilmi Gorab and the captain, ashore, with instructions to see the sheikhs, and, by the offer of presents and the promise of a good reward from the Government, to induce them to supply camels to enable the shipwrecked party to continue their journey to Dongola.

These messengers were well received by Sheikh Suleiman Wad Naaman, and neither he nor his people were wearing jibbehs; they asserted that they were thoroughly loyal to the Government, and added that it was only the arrival of Sheikh Heddai that had made them pretend to be against the Government. Suleiman said that he would assist the shipwrecked passengers with the greatest pleasure, and so well did he conceal his wicked treachery that the messengers returned to Stewart greatly elated with their success. But in the meantime Suleiman had prepared a treacherous trap, into which the over-confident passengers blindly fell. He sent secret orders to all the people round about to prepare for a fight, and then drove some camels along the river bank, to show that he was preparing for the journey. Colonel Stewart ordered all the spare ammunition to be thrown into the river, and then landed with the other passengers.

Suleiman invited him and the consuls, Power and Herbin, to go into his house, so as to make final arrangements with the camel-owners, and at the same time he begged them to remove their arms, as the Arabs might get alarmed and make difficulties about hiring their camels. An artillery captain who was with Stewart begged him not to let go his arms, as there might be treachery; but Stewart laughed at his fears, and he, with the two consuls and the interpreter, entered the house, while the others remained outside; they still retained their revolvers. Suleiman begged them to be seated, and proceeded to present to them a number of Arabs, who, he asserted, were the camel-owners.

The traitor had dates brought to them, and, so as not to offend him, they took some. Then Suleiman stood up and lifted his leather water-bottle, which was the prearranged signal for the Arabs to rush out of their hiding-places and attack the guests. In a second the house was full of armed men, who called upon them to throw down their revolvers and submit; but before they had even time to do this, the Arabs rushed upon them with their swords. Consul Herbin, who was standing near the door, was the first to fall; his head was chopped off with an axe. Consul Power and Colonel Stewart were soon cut to pieces. The interpreter, Hassan, begged to be spared, crying out, "I am a Moslem! I am a Moslem, and my name is Hassan!" So he was not killed, but received a wound in the shoulder. The murderers then rushed off to the river bank to attack the others, who were soon killed, except two artillerymen, who jumped into the river, and a few servants. It was said that the interpreter, Hassan, had arranged the betrayal, and I was afterwards told that when he got into difficulties later, he sent a petition to Mohammed el Kheir, in which he said that he was entitled to reward for having secured Colonel Stewart's death. He is still living in Omdurman.

Suleiman sent all the correspondence he captured to the Mahdi, who thus became thoroughly aware of Gordon's desperate condition. On the 22nd of October he wrote to Gordon, informing him of the event, and summoned him to submit, as he had no hope of receiving any relief.

This catastrophe was another terrible blow to Gordon. He had counted on Stewart being able to inform the Government of the straits to which Khartum was reduced, and the necessity of sending immediate help. The state of Khartum now became very serious. Nejumi and the other forces were clustering round Kalakala; there was daily fighting, and bullets fell in the streets of Khartum. There were upwards of 10,000 Dervishes, extending from Kalakala to Buri. Wad Gubara and Wad Sheikh el Obeid had their camp at Khojali, on the right bank of the Nile, to the north. Thus was Khartum surrounded by hordes of fanatical Arabs, who attacked the starved and forsaken town from morning till night.

CHAPTER VIII.

THE SIEGE AND FALL OF KHARTUM.

The surrender of Omdurman fort—Gordon's dispositions for defence —His great personal influence—The night before the assault— The attack and entry of the Dervishes—Gordon's death—The adventures of Domenico Polinari—The massacre in Khartum— How most of the Europeans died—Ruthless cruelty and bloodshed—The fate of the wives and daughters of Khartum— —Ohrwalder's views on the situation in Khartum and the chances of relief by the British Expeditionary Force—His description of the town three months after the fall.

THE Mahdi camped on the south side of Omdurman fort, and at once began to direct the siege, the command of his troops was vested in Abu Anga; but he did not dare to send his black troops, who had previously fought in the Egyptian service under Gordon, against Khartum, fearing that, owing to the influence which Gordon had formerly exercised over them, they might desert to him.

Omdurman Fort, which was then under the command of Faragallah Pasha, was soon reduced to great straits, and the Mahdiists threw up trenches, in which they were comparatively safe from the continuous fire. Eventually they succeeded in entrenching themselves between the fort and the river, thus cutting the communications, which Gordon was unable to restore. Consequently, the garrison soon began to starve; but they still fought courageously, and inflicted great loss on the Dervishes. Amongst the latter was a certain emir, named Mohammed Wad el Areik, who, while in the act of laying a gun at Omdurman, was struck in the back of the neck by a bullet. He was visited by the Khalifa Abdullah, who promised that he should recover; but, in spite of this promise, he died the following day.

Faragallah, having now no food left, was obliged to surrender, and thus the Mahdi was enabled to press the siege of Khartum more closely than ever.

The town itself was full of traitors; almost all the important townsmen had written to the Mahdi from time to time, to the effect that they wished to submit to him, and that they believed in him. Gordon was, so to speak, alone in the midst of enemies, but the expected arrival of the English kept the inhabitants from surrendering.

Every day Gordon invented some means of making the people believe that their deliverers were near; he frequently had the walls placarded with announcements that they were very near Khartum, but all his promises came to nothing.

Gordon was almost superhuman in his efforts to keep up hope. Every day, and many and many a time during the day, did he look towards the north from the roof of the palace for the relief which never arrived. He overcame the want of money by issuing paper bonds; but soon the people refused to accept them, and to enforce his order he sent fourteen merchants to the east bank, just in front of the enemy's guns; this he did to frighten them, and when they agreed to accept the bonds he had them brought back to the town. To further strengthen the belief of the people in the speedy arrival of the English, he hired all the best houses along the river bank, and had them prepared for their occupation. He was sure they would come—but when? The time was pressing. How eagerly he searched the distant horizon for the English flag he longed to see, but every day he was doomed to disappointment.

The troops were famine-stricken, and began to lose heart, whilst the enemy without the walls daily grew bolder in anticipation of the plunder they hoped so soon would be theirs. From Buri to Kalakala the Dervishes extended in one unbroken mass, whilst their hundreds of noggaras never ceased beating in Gordon's ears night and day.

The town was closely hemmed in on three sides.

Wad Gubara on the north was near enough to shell his palace; and under the hole where the first shot struck the wall Gordon inscribed the date as a remembrance. None of us can realize how heavily his terrible responsibilities weighed upon him. Despair had seized upon the town. The unreliable nature of the Sudanese was a constant source of anxiety to him, and enhanced the critical situation. Those in charge of the biscuits and dhurra stole quantities of it on every possible occasion, and tried to deceive Gordon by assuring him that there were millions of okes in store, when in reality there was almost nothing. In their endeavours to enrich themselves they forgot that they were only preparing the way for their ultimate destruction.

The officer in charge of the dhurra store was arrested and brought before a Court of Inquiry; but Gordon had to point out to those who were making the investigation that they should not inquire too critically into the matter. He knew all that had taken place, but he was powerless to stop it. He won the people's hearts by his generosity; and even to this day all who knew him never cease speaking of his kindness. His endeavours to recompense the Greeks for their honesty are affecting in the extreme. He elaborated numerous plans for their escape. His first intention was to place a steamer at their disposal to convey them to Emin Pasha in Equatoria; and, to avoid ill-feeling and jealousy, he made known his plans to them at a public meeting, remarking that as most of them were natives of the Greek islands, they had necessarily considerable experience of boats and navigation, and that therefore it became their duty to patrol with the steamers on the Blue and White Niles, and watch the enemy's movements; but secretly he warned them that they should be in readiness, as soon as they saw Khartum was lost, to set off and join Emin Pasha.

This plan did not, however, please the Greeks, so Gordon proposed another, which was that, in case of great danger, they should proceed north; and for this purpose he kept a steamer moored off the palace, well stocked with biscuits and other necessaries. To enable them to get their families on board during the night without the other townspeople knowing about it, he gave orders that after 9 P.M. all traffic along the roads leading to the Blue Nile should be stopped, and that no persons were to be allowed out of their houses after that hour. In this way, should the Dervishes enter the town by night, the Greeks could easily escape to the steamer, start down stream, and meet the English. Some of them resolved that, should the Mahdiists effect an entrance, they would forcibly carry off Gordon and put him on board the steamer, for they felt sure he would not leave Khartum of his own accord. Everything was carefully prearranged and considered; and all would have been well but for a disagreement amongst the Greeks themselves, which mainly arose through the phlegmatic and short-sighted conduct of their consul Nicola Leontides.

On that fatal Sunday evening one of the principal Greeks came to the consul and begged him urgently to spend that night on the steamer. The consul refused, arguing that there was no imminent danger, and that he was sure the troops could hold out a few days longer. The Greek argued in vain, and at length left him; and that was the last time they saw each other.

That night proved to be the last night on earth for Gordon and thousands of others. While they were sleeping soundly, and dreaming perhaps of the arrival of the English, the Dervishes were creeping like snakes towards the parapets. It is hardly likely Gordon could have slept. For two days he had remarked considerable movement in the Mahdi's camp; he had observed numbers of boats passing to and fro on the White and Blue Niles. He could not have doubted that the Mahdi was preparing to strike the final blow. And so it proved, for he was planning the assault on Khartum. He had received news of the destruction of his troops at Abu Klea and Abu Kru, and of the advance of the English.

The Mahdi was convinced that if one Englishman

THE ASSAULT ON KHARTUM. 135

reached Khartum his chance of success was gone, and that he must retire to Kordofan. That was his reason for attempting the assault. Gordon, on the other hand, expected the arrival of the English at any moment; and while he was counting the hours which might elapse ere they could reach him, his enemies were shaking their lances with which they should pierce him.

The moon had gone down, deep obscurity reigned; and now the Dervishes stealthily advanced in perfect silence towards that portion of the defence which had been destroyed during the high Nile, and which, as the river receded, had left an open space in which ditch and parapet had almost disappeared. Here there was little to impede their entry; and the Dervishes, shouting their wild battle-cry, dashed in wild disorder over this open ground.

Farag Pasha commanded the whole of this portion of the defences. Many people in the Sudan, more especially those who used to be in the Government service, say that Farag Pasha betrayed the town; but the fact that he was killed almost immediately after the fall points to his not having done so.

It is a well-known fact that many of the senior officers were wavering, and numbers of Khartum merchants were in correspondence with the Mahdi. It is possible that their action may have assisted the Dervishes. The latter naturally assert that Khartum was captured entirely by force of arms, for any acknowledgment on their part of treachery within the town would tend to detract from the effect of the Mahdi's success. The matter stands thus: the parapet which had been destroyed had never been repaired. This was not Gordon's fault; in his desperate position he could not be everywhere. It is a thousand pities that he had not a few trusty European officers with him. With the exception of this defective portion near the White Nile, the whole line of defence was almost impregnable; the ditch was so deep and the parapet so high that it would have been next to impossible to cross it.

On coming through the open space the Dervishes

A DERVISH EMIR, PRESENT IN THE ATTACK ON KHARTUM, AND AFTERWARDS CAPTURED AT TOSKI.

broke up into two parties. One party dashed along the parapet, breaking all resistance, and slaughtering the soldiers in all directions; the other party made for the town. The inhabitants, roused from their sleep by the shouts of the Arabs and the din of rifle-shots, hurried out, anticipating what had occurred. Like a pent-up stream suddenly released, over 50,000 wild Dervishes, with hideous yells, rushed upon the 40,000 inhabitants of Khartum, besides the 5,000 soldiers—all that was left of the 9,000 at the commencement of the siege. The only cry of these fanatical hordes was "Kenisa! Saraya!" ("To the church! the palace!")—*i.e.* the Austrian Mission Church and Gordon's palace, where they expected to find treasure stored up in the cellars, and priests and sisters.

The surging mass threw itself on the palace, overflowed into the lovely garden, and burst through the doors in wild search for their prey; but Gordon went alone to meet them. As they rushed up the stairs, he came towards them and tried to speak to them; but they could not or would not listen, and the first Arab plunged his huge spear into his body. He fell forward on his face, was dragged down the stairs, many stabbed him with their spears, and his head was cut off and sent to the Mahdi.

Such was the end of the brave defender of Khartum. When I came from El Obeid to Omdurman I visited Khartum, and went to the palace, where I was shown some black spots on the stairs which they told me were the traces of Gordon's blood.

On Gordon's head being brought to the Mahdi, he appeared to have been much displeased at his death— not because he felt pity for him, but he believed that Gordon might join his army. Had he not done so, he would have imprisoned him and reduced him to slavery. It was much better that Gordon should have died when he did than have remained a captive in the hands of these cruel and fanatical Arabs. Gordon's head was hung on a tree in Omdurman, and the wild multitude rejoiced in heaping curses on it and insulting it.

After the palace, the Mission building was the next principal object on which the wild, plunder-seeking Arabs vented their fury. General Gordon had some time previously hired this building, which was of stone and bomb-proof, and turned it into a powder magazine and ammunition store. The Dervishes killed the guards mounted outside the garden, and then broke in, while others clambered over the high wall. A black who was employed in the Mission garden was lying on the point of death on his mattrass in the garden; the Dervishes ended his life by ripping open his body.

The Mission gardener, brother Domenico Polinari, who had been left to take charge of the Mission property, on the first alarm, had rushed to the main gate of the garden to see what was the matter. He opened the gate slightly, and, seeing an array of lances, he slammed to the gate with all his might, and fled to a small hut in the garden which was full of hay, and he hid himself in the corner underneath the hay. Several slaves who were working in the garden followed his example; but they did not stay long, for, thinking it was not a sufficiently good hiding-place, they were running off to another hut when they were fallen upon and massacred. Domenico heard their shrieks and the click of the sword which beheaded them from his place of concealment; but he dared not move from the spot, though half choked with the dry grass in which he lay. Several Dervishes entered the hut and thrust their spears into the hay to search for any one in concealment.

One can realize the terror of poor Domenico as the naked spear-heads were forced through and almost touched him. He lay, however, undiscovered for some hours, and at last the noise and din of rifle-shots grew less. Though suffering agonies from thirst, he still did not dare to move till close on midnight, when he emerged from his bed of hay. All was still, the stillness of death. He could see the Dervish guard fires; and, as he crept along, he stumbled over the dead body of the black who had been working in the garden. Horror-stricken, he slowly moved forward again. At every step he saw a dead man, all of them labourers and watchmen who had attempted to escape when the Dervishes entered. Creeping under the shadow of the large lemon-trees, he reached the main gate, above which was a small hut which had been occupied by one of the black families belonging to the Mission. The windows of the hut looked into the garden, and Domenico scrambled through one of these into the room. Here he found one of the women, Halima, and begged her to give him some bread and water. He questioned her about the entrance of the Dervishes and the fate of the inhabitants. She replied in a few words that the town had been stormed, and numbers of the inhabitants, as well as General Gordon, Consul Hansal, and most of the Europeans, had been killed.

This was a new shock to the already terror-stricken Domenico. He threw himself on the bed and begged that Halima would not betray him; but she, fearing to be found out, crept out of the hut, went up to the Dervishes who were collected round the camp fire, and told them that there was a Turk in her cottage. Some of them jumped up, and, following Halima into the hut, they drove out the unfortunate Domenico with the butt ends of their lances. He was brought in front of the camp fire and carefully searched for money; but he at once drew forty pounds out of his pocket, which he distributed amongst them, and they were satisfied and did not ill-treat him.

On the following day he was taken before Ahmed Wad Suleiman, the Emin beit el mal, who made full inquiries of him regarding the Mission money. Domenico said that when the Mission left Khartum they took all the money with them, and had left nothing. Domenico was then sent to the garden to work there for his new master, but soon afterwards was betrayed a second time, and fell into grievous trouble and danger.

A few days before the fall of Khartum he had buried £150 in the garden, intending to make use of it when the needful time came; but one of the blacks who was working at the steam-pump in the garden, to whom Domenico had confided his secret, and who was one of the garden labourers who had escaped the massacre, went and told Ahmed Sharfi (one of the Mahdi's nearest relations) that Domenico had concealed money. This he did to ensure his own safety, for the Dervishes had been greatly disappointed in the quantity of loot they expected to find. In the palace they had discovered only paper money, and in the Mission some furniture, instead of the treasure they had been led to expect. Ahmed Sharfi was therefore much pleased with the black's information, himself came to Domenico and asked to be shown the place where the money was buried. In vain Domenico protested that he had given all the money to Gordon. He was at once knocked down and flogged with a kurbash; but the first stroke, which drew blood, made him cry for mercy; he disclosed the hiding-place, and, when Ahmed Sharfi had secured the money, he was released.

The ruthless bloodshed and cruelty exercised by the Dervishes in Khartum is beyond description. I will briefly describe the deaths of the best-known people. Nicola Leontides, the Greek consul, who, on account of his amiable character, was much respected in Khartum, had his hands cut off first, and was then beheaded. Martin Hansal, the Austrian consul, who was the oldest member of the European colony, was alive up till 2 P.M., when some Arabs from Buri, led by his chief kavass, who was on bad terms with him, entered the courtyard of the house, and, on Hansal being summoned to come down, he was at once beheaded. At the same time Mulatte Skander, a carpenter who lived with him, was killed in the same way. His body, together with that of his dog and parrot, were then taken out, alcohol poured over them, and set fire to. After a time, when the body had become like a red-hot coal, it was thrown into the river.

Human blood and ruthless cruelty alone seemed to satisfy the Dervishes. The Austrian tailor, Klein, on making the sign of the cross, had his throat cut from ear to 'ear with a knife which was used to slaughter animals, and his life-blood was poured out before the eyes of his horror-stricken wife and children. Not satisfied with the death of the father, they seized his son, a youth of eighteen, and, burying their lances in his body, they stretched him out at his mother's feet, a corpse! They then took counsel as to how they should kill the next son, a lad of fifteen. But by this time the mother, a daughter of Cattarina Nobili, of Venice, was worked up into a state of mad despair. Seizing her son of five years old with her right hand, while she held her suckling babe to her breast with her left, she fought against these murderers like a tigress being robbed of her young, and they could not wrest her children from her; but they seized her daughter, a girl of eighteen, who became the wife of an Arab.

The son-in-law of Doctor Georges Bey (who had been killed in the Hicks's expedition) was roused from sleep by the noise of the Arabs breaking in. He rose from his bed, and, making the sign of the cross, rushed to the window, where he shouted "Aman" ("Security of life"); but a bullet struck him in the forehead, and he fell dead at the feet of his young wife. The Dervishes forced their way into the house, broke in the door of the room where the dead man lay stretched out on the bed, killed another Greek, and clove open the head of the little son, a boy of twelve years of age, with an axe, scattering his brains over his unfortunate mother, who was sitting beside him. She saved her little son of six months old by saying he was a girl. The mother herself was not killed, as she was with child, but she was reserved to become the wife of Abderrahman Wad en Nejumi.

Aser, the American consul, fell down dead on seeing his brother beheaded before his eyes. The males of most of the Coptic families were massacred, but the women were spared. I know several of these poor women who, from continuously weeping over the cruelties of that terrible 26th of January, have become quite blind.

Those men whose lives were spared have to thank Providence that either they fell into the hands of those less cruel than their comrades, or that they did not quit their houses for two days, at the end of which time the first wild passions of these murderers had cooled down.

The fate of seven Greeks was a sad one; these were all together in one house, for, through a merciful Providence, they had fallen into less cruel hands. It was past noon, and they were rejoicing at having escaped from the general massacre. Then a certain George Clementino entered. This Clementino had originally come from El Obeid, and had frequently been sent by the Mahdi with messages to Gordon, and when he returned from Khartum to the Mahdi, the latter treated him with much favour.

When the capture of Khartum was known in Omdurman, Clementino hastened to the town, with the intention of rescuing any compatriots he could find, and he soon heard of the seven surviving Greeks. Full of delight at their safety, he congratulated them, and advised them to make their way to the house of Manoli, the Greek who, with his wife and nephew, had escaped by concealing themselves in the dove-cot.

It was Clementino's intention to collect all the Greeks here, and then take them to Omdurman. The seven Greeks trusted to their compatriot's name and influence to protect them, but Dervishes were on the watch to stop them. As they were following Clementino to Manoli's house, which was only a short distance off—indeed, they had only gone a few steps—they were met by a party of Ahmed Sharfi's Danagla, who were searching the streets filled with the dead and wounded, with the object of giving the *coup de grâce* to any who might still be alive.

When these murderers espied the party of white men from a short distance, they shouted, "Look! Some of these dogs, these unbelievers, are still alive," and, full of anger, they rushed upon the unfortunate Greeks. Clementino begged and prayed that they might be spared, but they were beheaded before his eyes, and he himself barely escaped with his life. Pale, terror-stricken, and trembling, he fled to Omdurman, and for some months he lay on the point of death, so great had been the shock of witnessing the massacre of his fellow-countrymen.

Numbers even of women and little children were not spared, and the torture which the survivors had to undergo, to force them to produce their money, are scarcely credible. Ibrahim Pasha Fauzi (the favourite of Gordon) was tied for several days to a date-palm and flogged till he gave up all his money. The old widow of Mustafa Tiranis was flogged almost to death. She was a rich Circassian lady, and had supplied Gordon with money in donkey loads, and had been decorated by him with the Khartum medal.

Slaves were most cruelly tortured, beaten, and forced to disclose the hiding-places of their masters' money and treasures. The Shaigieh tribe in particular was most harshly dealt with; this was the only tribe which remained loyal to the Government, and even eight days after the fall of Khartum, if a Shaigi was seen, he was instantly killed; hence the Dervish proverb, "Esh Shaigi, Wad er Rif el Kelb ma yelga raha fil Mahadieh" ("The Shaigi, the Egyptian, *i.e.*, the white one, the dog, no rest shall he find in Mahdieh").*

Farag Pasha did not live long after the fall; some still said he had betrayed the town, and the Dervishes were furious with him because, some ten days before the assault, during one of the preliminary attacks, he had shot Abdullah Wad en Nur, an emir of great repute, and much beloved by the Ansar. Farag was summoned before Wad Suleiman, who ordered him to produce all the money he had. Incensed at his treatment and at the charge of treachery, he fell into a hot dispute with Wad Suleiman, who had him forthwith beheaded as an unbeliever and an obstinate man. If he was really a

* According to the Mahdi doctrine, dogs, being considered impure animals, are destroyed; but this subject will be considered in another chapter.

traitor, he richly deserved his fate; but if not, his death was that of a brave man.

When the massacre in Khartum was at an end, the Mahdi himself gave orders that the survivors should be spared, but the wild fury of these fanatical Arabs had been satiated at the cost of 10,000 lives; the streets were filled with headless corpses, which were left unburied until the plunder had been distributed.

The whole of Khartum was now divided up amongst hundreds of emirs and their mukuddums. Every emir planted his flag in the midst of the quarter captured by his men, and then the work of collecting the survivors was begun. Ahmed Wad Suleiman ordered all free women and slaves to be brought to the beit el mal; here the young and good-looking fair women were locked up in a separate enclosure, the good-looking, unmarried Sudanese girls in another zariba, and in a third were placed black slave girls, suitable as concubines.

It is deplorable to think that at such a time were found certain of the well-known townsmen of Khartum who assisted the Dervishes to lay hands on all the prettiest girls in Khartum; through their intermediary, many of the women who had cut off their hair, and in other ways concealed their beauty and sex by disguising themselves as men, fell into the hands of the Ansar.

May God's curse fall on those wicked traitors who delivered up these unfortunates in order to gain favour with the Mahdi! What sufferings these miserable creatures underwent when they lay huddled together like cattle in a pen, awaiting their cruel fate! Many of them were still in their silken robes, all bespattered with the blood of their husbands and children, and there they lay, awaiting their turn to become the wives of those who had murdered their husbands and their offspring!

The first selection was, of course, made for the Mahdi, who took for himself all girls of five years of age and upwards, who, in a few years' time, he would take to his harem; then came the turn of the three Khalifas, whose selections were made especially under the direction of Wad Suleiman; then followed the emirs, each in the order of his rank, and one by one they made their choice of these wretched women. Those that were left were distributed amongst the Ansar. Then were openly enacted sights which would have melted hearts of stone. The weeping and lamentation of the white women, as they prayed and besought the pity of their masters, the rough jeering and foul replies of these monsters, it is all too horrible to relate.

The old unmarried women were given a few rags with which to partially cover themselves, and were sent to Nejumi's camp, where they were kept in captivity for a few days. All suffered the agonies of hunger and thirst, heat and cold. Little babies, not yet weaned, were left to die of hunger, and for weeks after the fall young widowed mothers could be seen wandering naked through the market at Omdurman, begging. Some poor women brought forth children in the streets, and there they would lie, mother and child, naked and foodless, until death came as a happy release from their misery.

The Mahdi had directed that all gold and silver jewellery, precious stones and ornaments, should be collected in the beit el mal; but of course most of this had already found its way into the pockets of the emirs; and, in spite of the Mahdi's most stringent orders, and his threats that those who concealed the booty would be punished in hell-fire, still the Ansar kept the loot and risked the eternal flames.

Considerable quantities of treasure were, however, collected in the beit el mal, for Khartum was wealthy, and the women especially had quantities of gold and silver ornaments; but so much loot soon reduced the currency, and a sovereign was now valued at two and a half dollars. Every penny was extracted from the prisoners by the lash, and all were reduced to complete beggary. They were then sent to Nejumi's camp; and on their way thither they were again beaten and searched. They were kept a few days longer as prisoners in that camp, and then those who had the fortune to meet with relations or friends who had been released would weep together over their wretched state. The confusion was terrible. Women wandered through the camps in search of their children, children sought their parents; but how few ever found them!

After a time all the prisoners were permitted to live in Omdurman, where they eked out a miserable existence by begging; but hunger, disease, and all the sufferings they had undergone carried off hundreds. For days they remained naked, scorched under the burning sun by day, and perished with cold at night. How could people accustomed to ease and comfort bear up against such hardships?

When at length all the houses in Khartum had been evacuated, the furniture, &c., removed, and their owners robbed of all they possessed, the effects were sold from the beit el mal at a low price. The various coloured stuffs were cut up and utilised for making the patches on the jibbehs (Dervish uniform), gold brocades were purchased by those who knew their real value for a mere trifle, and the gold melted down and made into ornaments. Mirrors and looking-glasses were chopped in pieces with axes, and valuable china and pottery articles, which might have been sold for much, were smashed in pieces. The beautiful Khartum gardens were divided up amongst the chiefs; the Khalifa Abdullah became the possessor of Gordon's garden, Khalifa Sherif took that of the Roman Catholic Mission, and Khalifa Ali Wad Helu became owner of Albert Marquet's. Every emir selected the best house he could find, and there he installed himself with his wives and slaves; while the Ansar took the houses of the poorer Copts and Egyptians. But Omdurman, and not Khartum, was now considered the Dervish capital.

Intoxicated by their success, and insatiable in their desire for women and plunder, the Dervishes had forgotten altogether about the English, for whom Gordon had waited so long. How cruel is fate! Two days after the fall, on the 28th of January, 1885, two steamers were seen slowly making their way along the western shore of Tuti Island.

Khartum and Omdurman were electrified; a consultation was quickly held, and it was at once decided to prevent their landing. The English could be seen searching in all directions for some sign to show them that Gordon was still alive; but the only answer they got was the rain of thousands of bullets fired from thousands upon thousands of rifles and guns at Omdurman and Fort Mukrun. All rushed to the river bank. The women, seizing sticks and waving them over their heads, shrieked and yelled like hyenas, " Mót lil Inglez !" ("Death to the English!") and they were prepared to rush at them with their sticks if they attempted to land. When the English saw this, they could have had little doubt as to what had happened; they turned back and disappeared. The rage of the Dervishes at their departure was unbounded. They rained bullets and shell after them; but they were soon out of sight.

Let us now consider for a moment the chances of success of the English relief expedition. The defeat at Abu Klea struck terror into the Mahdiists gathered round Khartum; the arrival of some wounded men at Omdurman added to the general alarm. Had twenty redcoats arrived at Khartum, it would have been saved. Their presence would have given fresh courage to the inhabitants; and, confident of their approaching deliverance, they would have striven might and main to hold out longer. General Gordon, assisted by the advice and energy of a few English officers, would have completely regained his influence. It is true, indeed, that the soldiers were weary of the long siege and continual fighting, and they had lost all faith in Gordon's repeated promises that the English were coming. They became heart-broken and in despair; but Khartum was not for long in the state of distress which prevailed in El Obeid before that town fell. In Khartum they had only been eating gum for a few days previous to the fall, while in El Obeid they had existed on it for months, and had practically nothing else to live upon.

Had the Khartum people but seen one Englishman with their own eyes, they would have taken fresh courage, and would in all probability have held out for another month, until the relief for which they had waited so long was a *fait accompli*. The Mahdi would not have dared to assault Khartum; and even if he had, it is most probable he would have been beaten back. Many survivors of Khartum often said to me, "Had we seen one Englishman, we should have been saved; but our doubt that the English were really coming, and the feeling that Gordon must be deceiving us, made us discouraged, and we felt that death would be preferable to the life of constant war and daily suffering we were leading during the siege."

The unaccountable delay of the English was the cause of the fall of Khartum, the death of Gordon, and the fate of the Sudan. The Mahdi only made up his mind to attack when he heard that they had delayed at Gubat. He did not begin to cross over his troops till the 24th of January, and it was not till Sunday night that the crossing was complete. He could not have attacked earlier than he did. When the first news of his defeat at Abu Klea reached him he wished to raise the siege and retire to Kordofan. If the English had appeared at any time before he delivered the attack he would have raised the siege and retired. Indeed, it was always his intention to revisit El Obeid before he made his attack.

Even to the present day people in the Sudan cannot understand the reason for the delay. Some say that the English general was wounded at Abu Klea, and was lying insensible, and that those who were acting for him did not dare to undertake any operations until he was sufficiently recovered to be able to give his own orders.

The Sudanese wondered why Europeans, who generally take precautions for every eventuality, should not have done so in this case. Others thought that Kashm el Mus Pasha must have urged the English to attack the Arabs about Metemmeh and Shendi, in revenge for the persistency with which they had attacked and harassed the steamers. The above are only some of the many reasons by which the Sudanese seek to explain the delay after the battle of Abu Klea.

When the English were convinced that Khartum had fallen, they retreated north. Once the town had fallen, the little English fighting force was in the gravest peril; the Mahdi had now his entire force at his disposal to combat them. He at once despatched Nejumi and a large number of his best emirs with a large force; and had not the English already retreated before he reached Metemmeh, they could not have escaped.

The Mahdi was furious when he heard that the English, who had killed such numbers of his best troops, had retired; and, though the latter failed in their object, still their bold attempt to snatch the prey from the lion's mouth must remain for ever a grand exploit. The bravery of the English in advancing on Khartum with such a small number of men is always a source of wonder to the Sudanese. But, alas, what a useless sacrifice of blood and money! The relief came too late.

The memory of Gordon, the heroic defender of Khartum, is still held in respectful remembrance in the Sudan. His bravery, generosity, and voluntary self-sacrifice have won the admiration of his bitterest enemies. It is the common saying amongst Moslems, "Had Gordon been one of us, he would have been a perfect man." I will now give a slight sketch of the events subsequent to the fall, and the fate of the town.

After the retreat of the English, the new masters of Khartum settled down and made themselves comfortable. The Ashraf, *i.e.* the Mahdi's relatives, especially made themselves at home in the best houses and gardens, the best dancers entertained them by night, and they lived a life of ease and luxury. After the death of the Mahdi, which occurred on the 22nd of June, 1885, his successor, the Khalifa Abdullah, looked on the prosperity of Khartum with jealous eyes.

When I arrived in Khartum from El Obeid in April

1886, I visited every part of the town, and examined it most carefully; very few houses had been destroyed, and the town was thickly populated. I also visited the lines of defence between the Blue and White Niles, they extended about six kilometres. The impression I gathered from the appearance of the ditch, which at that time had been much damaged by the heavy rains, was that it could not have been crossed, except near the White Nile where it was quite choked up with mud and sand. At various points along the line there were strongly-built forts manned with guns, and a little in rear of the parapets were high structures which commanded the ditch; behind every loophole were small mud shelters, evidently made by the troops to protect themselves from the cold and strong winds.

The Messalamieh gate was built of burnt bricks and cement and was then in a good state, but the iron gate lay unopened against the side of the ditch. I counted about 150 bodies along the parapet; there they lay, shrivelled up like mummies, while rats and mice had made their homes in them. In one place I saw two bodies tied together by the feet, they had evidently been killed in this position. It was impossible to distinguish the Egyptians from the blacks, for the sun had burnt up and shrivelled the skin into one black colour. Here, where there had been such bustling activity, now only the stillness of the tomb prevailed. As one walked along, lizards and other reptiles would creep from beneath the skeletons and dart off to take refuge under others.

I strolled on from the Messalamieh gate to the European cemetery. Here what desolation and desecration met my eyes! The crosses had been smashed to pieces and lay strewn about in little bits. Graves had been dug up and the bodies pulled out. I recognised from their clothes three who had died in January 1881. The grave of Bishop Comboni, who had died on the 11th of October, 1881, and had been buried in the Mission garden, had also been opened, but the obelisk erected to his memory by the townspeople of Khartum had not been destroyed. The church bells had been pulled down, but lay there in the garden undamaged.

Shortly after my visit, Khartum was reduced to ruins. The Khalifa Abdullah, jealous of the Ashraf, who had completely established themselves in the town, and whose actions he could not therefore sufficiently supervise, determined to order its evacuation. In August the command was given to all to quit the town within three days; it was carried out at once, and on the fourth day the destruction of Khartum began. Houses were pulled down, the wood of the windows, balconies, and doors was transported to Omdurman, and within a very short time the whole place was in ruins; the burnt bricks were for the most part brought to Omdurman; the only buildings which were spared were the Arsenal, in which work still continues to be done, Gordon's palace, and the Mission house. In fact, Khartum is now nothing but a heap of mud ruins, here and there a wall is left standing, everywhere large prickly thorn bushes have sprung up and cover as with a veil the sad remnants of the once thriving and populous metropolis of the Sudan.

CHAPTER IX.

THE MAHDI'S LAST DAYS.

Ohrwalder's criticisms on certain events connected with the defence of Khartum—The Sudan devastated by small-pox—The Mahdi gives way to a life of pleasure—Description of his harem life——The Mahdi sickens and dies—The effect on his followers—The Khalifa Abdullah succeeds—Party strife and discord—Abdullah prevails—Events in Sennar and Kassala.

LOOKING back on the events which occurred during the siege of Khartum, I cannot refrain from saying that I consider Gordon carried his humanitarian views too far, and that this excessive forbearance on his part both injured the cause and considerably added to his difficulties. It was Gordon's first and paramount duty to rescue the Europeans, Christians, and Egyptians from the fanatical fury of the Mahdi, which was specially directed against them. This was Gordon's clear duty, but unfortunately he allowed his kindness of heart to be made use of to his enemy's advantage.

Khartum during the siege was full of the wives, relations, and children of men who had joined the Dervishes, and were foremost in their efforts to harass and attack the town. These crafty people thus assured themselves that should the Mahdi be victorious, their loyalty to him would ensure the safety of their families and property in Khartum, while, on the other hand, should Gordon be victorious then their wives and families would be able to mediate for them with the conquerors. Thus in his kindness of heart did Gordon feed and support the families of his enemies. It was quite sufficient for a number of women to appeal to Gordon with tears in their eyes, that they were starving, for him to order that rations of corn should at once be issued to them, and thus it was that the supplies in the hands of the Government were enormously reduced.

Had Gordon, in the early stages of the siege, relieved Khartum of the presence of these people, as he subsequently was forced to do, he would have had supplies sufficient to prolong the resistance of his troops far beyond the limits at which they had arrived when the assault took place, and, after all, should not Gordon's first care have been for his troops? His men clamoured against the lavish way in which Gordon distributed what should have been their rations amongst the families of the besiegers, but it was of no avail.

Gordon should have recognised that the laws of humanity differ in war from peace time, more especially when the war he was waging was especially directed against wild fanatical savages who were enemies to all peace. He was entirely deceived if he believed that by the exercise of kindness and humanity he was likely to win over these people to his side; on the contrary, they ridiculed his generosity and only thought it a sign of weakness. The Sudanese respect and regard only those whom they fear, and surely those cruel and hypocritical Mahdiists should have received very different treatment to civilized Europeans.

I also think that Gordon brought harm on himself and his cause by another action which I am convinced led to a great extent to his final overthrow. Such men as Slatin, Lupton, Saleh Wad el Mek, and others had offered at the risk of their lives to come and serve him. It is almost certain that some means could have been found of rescuing from slavery these brave men who had defended their provinces with the greatest determination against treachery from within and overwhelming numbers from without, and they could have rendered him most valuable and useful services. None knew better than these men the weak and the strong points of the Mahdi's rule and his method of warfare, and it is quite possible that they might have been able to alter the fate of Khartum. In the Mahdi's camp they were looked upon as brave and skilful leaders, indeed they were feared, and that is why they were put in chains, as it was thought they might attempt to escape. Had they been permitted to enter Khartum they would not only have been able to assist in the Mahdi's overthrow, but they would have been able to encourage the garrison.

Gordon would not, however, even vouchsafe an answer to the letters of appeal these men wrote to him. He could not have believed they were traitors, such an idea could not have entered into the mind of an European. The Mahdi never for an instant doubted their inclinations, and treated them with the greatest mistrust; but even to these savages the idea of killing men who had been loyal to the Government, and had fought bravely for their provinces, was objectionable, unless they could have produced a really valid reason for doing so. How was it possible Gordon could be for an instant in doubt as to the inclinations and intentions of these men? I feel strongly on these points, and therefore cannot refrain from mentioning them.

After the fall of Khartum only two strong places remained in the hands of the Government, Kassala and Sennar, both of which were closely besieged. The English had retired north, and the Mahdi could rest at last, assured that he was now possessor of the Sudan.

The enormous multitudes around Khartum had been engaged during the whole of the winter season in war, consequently cultivation was neglected, and had it not been for the quantities of cattle available, a disastrous famine must have occurred. As it was, there was a great deal of distress, and numbers died of starvation. Famine and war had brought disease in their train. In addition to fever and dysentery, small-pox, which in the Sudan is endemic, increased with fearful rapidity. In Omdurman hundreds died, and the principal business of the beit el mal was distributing "kafans" (shrouds).

It was curious that the Sudanese, who much dread this disease, should have attributed it to the English; but that they did so is a fact, and this is how it came about. When the English retired from Gubat, they left behind them a quantity of preserved stores and tinned meat. The Dervishes, in spite of the belief that they contained pork, which is an abomination to them, were so hungry that they consumed almost everything they found, and it is said that almost immediately afterwards they were attacked by small-pox, which gave rise to the idea that the English had mixed their food with the germs of the disease, and this was implicitly believed in.

Owing to the prevalence of small-pox in Omdurman, many people fled to Kordofan, Darfur, and other places, and consequently caused the disease to spread over the whole country. Several false doctors, with the sole object of making money, guaranteed to check the disease by inoculation; but as the inoculated matter was frequently in itself diseased, the epidemic was still further increased.

Notwithstanding this national calamity, the Mahdi now gave himself up to a life of ease and luxury, in which the unfortunate women captured in Khartum played a prominent part. He represented that all those who died of small-pox were suffering God's punishment for being evil-minded or having appropriated the booty. People believed what he said, and would still believe him, if he were alive and told them even more incredible things. The capture of Khartum had, of course, raised his prestige enormously, and now the belief in his Divine message needed no furthur confirmation. Before the assault took place he said that he would divide the river into two parts, just as Moses had divided the Red Sea, so that his followers could cross to Khartum on dry land if they failed to take it by assault. His promise, too, that very few should fall by the sword, not only encouraged them in the attack, but its verification served only to further prove his divinity. His uncle, Sayid Abdel Kader, up to the time of the fall of Khartum, still doubted that he was the true Mahdi; but, once the town was taken, he doubted no longer.

All this success increased the adulation and worship of the Mahdi to an extraordinary extent, and as for himself, although he was continually warning his followers to despise the good things of this world, and to abandon all luxurious modes of life, he surrounded himself with every sort of comfort and luxury, appreciating to the utmost the very pleasures which he

AN EGYPTIAN HAREM WOMAN.

declaimed so violently. He urged moderation in eating and drinking, yet he secured for himself every dainty which Khartum could possibly produce. He now wore shirts and trousers of the finest material, and, before putting them on, his wives were obliged to perfume them with incense and other costly fragrances. His wives attended on him in turns, but no regularity was preserved. They anointed his body with all sorts of precious unguents, but his speciality was the expensive "Sandalia" (a perfume prepared from sandal-wood and oil), and so saturated was he with these perfumes that when he went forth the air was laden with sweet-smelling odours.

The courtyard of his harem was full of women, from little Turkish girls of eight years old to the pitch-black Dinka negress or copper-coloured Abyssinian; almost every tribe in the Sudan supplied its representative, so that one might say the entire Sudanese woman-world was to be seen here.

Amongst this vast concourse four only were lawful wives; the remainder were considered as "ghenima," or booty, and were looked upon as slaves and concubines. His principal wife was called "Aisha," or, as she is better known in Omdurman, "Om el Muminin" (the Mother of the Faithful). She was a woman of considerable influence, for the wives of all the principal emirs visited her, and she was assisted by them in elaborating an extensive system of espionage. Alas, how many unfortunate girls were left weeping day and night for their miserable state, robbed by this Aisha of their happiness and liberty!

The Mahdi's dwelling was built for the most part of the captured loot. From the boards of General Hicks's stable he had two huts built, and near these a hut made of mortar and a small magazine. This man, who hitherto had but a small straw mat, now lay on fine bedsteads originally brought from Jedda and captured in Khartum, while the floors were spread with Persian carpets. Here was this Divine Mahdi leading indoors a life of the most immoderate uxoriousness, whilst outside his fanatical followers hailed him as the direct messenger of God, sent to purge the world from the evil practices of the hated Turk.

Two persons whom I knew well, and who had visited

the Mahdi less than three weeks before his death, gave me an account of the sort of life he was then leading. It was the month of Ramadan, the great fast, and any one who failed to keep it strictly was punishable by death. From noon till midnight people used to crowd to the mosque, which was then only a large enclosure surrounded by a zariba. Thousands of Dervishes could be accommodated in this large rectangular space, in which the clash of a forest of spears indicated their impatience to see the Mahdi as he came to prayers; they had seen him hundreds and hundreds of times before, but they seemed never tired of gazing at him, and often fought to get a place near the mihrab (niche) where he prayed.

Whilst the impatient murmur of thousands of voices indicates that the time of his approach has almost arrived, let us for a moment turn into the Mahdi's harem, and here is a true picture of what my friends there beheld. The Mahdi reclining on a magnificent carpet, his head propped up by a pillow covered with gold brocade; he is clothed in a linen shirt of finest texture, a pair of drawers, and a gallabieh; his shaved head covered by a takia of embroidered silk. Upwards of thirty women stand around him; some fan him with great ostrich feathers, others gently rub his feet (a practice in which the Sudanese delight), without in any way disturbing his slumber; others gently smooth his hands, and Aisha lies beside him, covering his head and neck with loving embraces.

Meanwhile hundreds of Ansar are shouting outside his zariba, impatiently awaiting his blessing, and anxiously expecting to hear his voice. The eunuchs are trying to drive off this importunate crowd with whips, but they will not leave until they have obtained the earnestly sought blessing. At length one of the eunuchs enters, and receives from Aisha the blessing, which she gives without disturbing the Mahdi. He then returns and tells the impatient crowd that the Mahdi is at present in deep contemplation, but that he is graciously pleased to give them his blessing, which is then repeated. This is the signal for a wild shout of joy, and then they return to the mosque to range themselves in their appointed lines for prayers. And now those who were not present to receive the blessing press forward to touch the others, and thus obtain some of its virtue.

The Mahdi is gradually sinking from his half doze into a sound slumber, when Aisha very gently rouses him and tells him that the appointed time for ablutions and prayers is already passed. The women now assist him to rise, his red shoes are brought, and then he proceeds to the place of ablution, followed by four women carrying his water-bottle. On his return the women throw themselves down frantically on the spots which his feet have touched, and struggle with each other in their endeavours to embrace the ground on which he has trodden.

It is believed that the earth touched by the Mahdi's foot has healing properties, and has, moreover, the effect of ensuring a quick and painless delivery; it is therefore distributed amongst holy women, and even to this day is carefully preserved for the purpose which I have cited. Not a drop, too, of the water with which the Mahdi has washed is allowed to be wasted, but is hoarded with the greatest care, and drunk as an unfailing remedy for every sort of illness and malady.

But to return to my friends' description. The Mahdi's ablutions over, his son Bashra runs up to him and shows him a golden ring his mother has given him. Bashra asks permission to wear the ring, but the Mahdi, who has by this time noticed the presence of two strangers, says, " Oh, my son, only the Turks wear such ornaments, because they love the things of this world; but it is not becoming in us to wear such ornaments, which are perishable; we strive to obtain things imperishable. Give the ring back to your mother." The little hypocrite well understands what his father means, and obeys.

Aisha then clothes the Mahdi in his Dervish jibbeh, girdle, and turban, and in this godly raiment he marches off to the mosque. As he quits the palace, his body-guard surround him and keep off the crowd. On reaching the mihrab he is received with a shout by the assembled multitude. After prayers he gives a short sermon, and then returns to his wives.

Thus did the Mahdi enjoy the sweets of victory indoors, whilst outside he practised the most abominable hypocrisy. Most of his principal emirs (with the exception of his uncle, Sayid Abdel Karim, who had been sent to reduce Sennar) followed in their divine master's footsteps, and led a life of pleasure and debauchery. Sometimes the Mahdi used to cross over to Khartum and disport himself in Gordon's palace, whither he ordered a portion of his harem to be transferred.

But all this good living and unbridled sensuality were to be the cause of his speedy dissolution. He grew enormously fat. The two visitors, whom I mentioned above, saw him only eight days before his death, and told me that they believed then he could not live much longer. Early in Ramadan he fell sick, and soon became dangerously ill. The hand of God's justice fell heavily upon him; and it was decreed that he should no longer enjoy the empire which he had raised on the dead bodies of thousands of the victims to his wretched hypocrisy and deceit.

It is, indeed, terrible to think of the awful misery and distress brought upon his own country by this one man. His disease grew rapidly worse; he complained of pain in the heart, and died, on the 22nd of June, 1885, of fatty degeneration of the heart. Some say that he was a victim to the vengeance of a woman who had lost husband and children in the fall of Khartum, and who repaid the Mahdi's outrage on her own person by giving him poison in his food. This may be so; and it is true, poison is generally used in the Sudan to put people out of the way; but I am rather inclined to think that it was outraged nature that took vengeance on its victim; and that it was the Mahdi's debauched and dissolute mode of life which caused his early death. He died in the mortar hut, which I previously described; and his adherents gave out that he was about to travel through the heavens for a space of three years. People were not allowed to say "The Mahdi is dead," but "El Mahdi intakal" (*i.e.* "The Mahdi has been removed").

The shock of his death was terrible. The wild fanatics were, so to speak, struck dumb; their eyes were suddenly opened; and their very confusion showed that they had realized the Mahdi was a liar. Omdurman was full of suppressed murmuring; and the people were collected in groups, talking of this awful catastrophe.

Those who were oppressed believed that the sudden collapse of Mahdieh must result in a revolution. No one believed that the Mahdi's party could continue ruling in his name. Would that some good man could have been found to rapidly seize this opportunity of putting himself at the head of the anti-Mahdiists; he must have been successful!

The confusion in the Mahdi's household was beyond description; his women wept and wailed in the wildest grief. Ahmed Wad Suleiman and the Mahdi's nearest relatives prepared a grave immediately beneath the bed on which he had died; the body was washed, wrapped in a shroud, according to the Moslem custom, and, in the presence of the Khalifas and all the members of the Mahdi's family, it was lowered into the grave, amidst the lamentations and wailing of the enormous crowd collected outside the building. Before the grave was filled in, the body was sprinkled with perfumes; then each person present took a handful of earth and threw it into the grave, amidst murmurs of "Ya Rahman, Ya Rahim!" (*i.e.* O merciful, O gracious God!) A simple monument was erected over the tomb.

Thus ended the Mahdi—a man who left behind him a hundred thousand murdered men, women, and children, hundreds of devastated towns and villages, poverty, and famine. Upon his devoted head lies the curse of his people whom he had forced into a wild and fanatical war, which brought indescribable ruin upon the country, and which exposed his countrymen to the rule of a cruel tyrant, from whom it was impossible to free themselves.

Before his death, the Mahdi had nominated the Khalifa Abdullah as his successor; he saw that this was the only man capable of holding in check the rapacious Sudanese tribes, and of governing the strange empire which he had raised; but the selection of this "foreigner" was a bitter disappointment to the Danagla and Jaalin, who, hitherto rulers, had now to become the ruled; and from whose hands their authority was transferred to the cruel and tyrannical Baggaras, who henceforth became the conquerors of the Sudan, and who governed its inhabitants with a rod of iron.

In nominating the Khalifa Abdullah, the Mahdi threw the firebrand of discord amongst the hitherto united ranks of Mahdieh, and thereby greatly weakened his cause. It was hard for the Mahdi to die, just when he had established an empire stretching from the Bahr el Ghazal to Egypt, and from Darfur to the Red Sea; he had neither had the time nor the inclination to try and govern it; his mission had been the destruction of all existing forms of government; and he had carried it out to the letter.

Immediately after the Mahdi's death, the Khalifa Abdullah summoned a meeting, and then and there insisted on the two Khalifas and the Ashraf acknowledging him as the Khalifat el Mahdi (or Mahdi's successor). After a long discussion it was at length agreed to, and he gave a solemn assurance that he would follow absolutely in the Mahdi's footsteps. Just at this time the agitation was too great for him to think of introducing the selfish and ambitious plans which he had already formulated. Moreover, Sennar and Kassala were still holding out; it was therefore the first necessary step to be most conciliating on all sides, and to all parties.

The Mahdi's name was still paramount in inspiring fanaticism; and therefore the Khalifa's watchword became "Ed din mansur" (Religion is victorious); thus he sought to establish unity and concord by means of the new religion which the Mahdi had founded, and which, now that its originator was dead, he sought to make unassailable.

Nevertheless, discord very soon sprang up. The Khalifa Sherif and the Ashraf were furious at being out of power, and they could not long conceal their discontent. Each Khalifa now did his utmost to show his independence of the other; each of them rode about in Omdurman in the greatest splendour, as if he were a king, and ordered his own great war-drum to be beaten. Jealousy, hatred, and discontent spread rapidly amongst the people; and soon Omdurman was divided into two distinct camps: Khalifas Sherif and Ali Wad Helu in the one, and Khalifa Abdullah in the other.

Both parties now prepared for battle. Abdullah had the Baggaras and blacks, under Fadl Maula (Abu Anga's brother). There were frequent disputes in the market-place; and every day it was thought a fight must take place. At length matters reached such a stage that Abdullah challenged the two other Khalifas to fight on the open plain, on which the great reviews usually take place, just outside the town.

The two parties collected their entire forces; but it was evident the Baggaras were by far the stronger; and as they marched out they shouted "Môt el Gellaba" ("Death to the Gellabas!" *i.e.* the Danagla, in contradistinction to the Baggara). Khalifa Wad Helu now acted the part of mediator, and went across to confer with Abdullah; the troops of the latter were drawn up in battle-array, and quite prepared for the fray. Khalifa Sherif feared to enter the lists alone, and therefore he submitted; he was obliged to hand over his soldiers, arms, ammunition, flags, and war-drums, which Abdullah took possession of, and was allowed to retain only fifty men, with firearms, as a bodyguard.

Thus Abdullah constituted himself the one and only ruler, and showed that he was quite resolved to allow no one else to share his authority with him. Gradually he reduced the power of the two other Khalifas and of the Ashraf, and in a short time they became men of little influence. The Mahdi's two uncles, Abdel Karim and Abdel Kader, who showed the most open and violent animosity, were at once thrown into chains, their houses destroyed, and themselves declared enemies of the Mahdi; and, as we shall presently relate, he ordered Abu Anga to secure Zogal and put him in prison.

Whilst all these disturbances were going on in Omdurman, the two places, Sennar and Kassala, in which Government troops were still holding out, were now in the greatest straits; and I will here give a brief account of the events which occurred.

Sennar had suffered from the Mahdiists for a very long time. Ahmed Wad el Makashef had besieged it in 1883; Abdel Kader Pasha, Governor-General of the Sudan, had advanced to its relief with a large force, had defeated the Makashef, and then raised the siege. Abdel Kader himself was wounded in this fight, and his watch was broken to pieces by a bullet. Sennar and Khartum were once more in communication. It is unfortunate that Abdel Kader, who was greatly feared by the Sudanese, was recalled to Egypt.

In 1884 the rebels again attacked Sennar, but were repulsed. It was then besieged by El Mehrdi Abu Rof, who succeeded in defeating the Egyptian troops under Nur Bey. I shall presently relate how this Mehrdi was afterwards treated by the Sudanese.

Some say that the fall of Khartum had a very discouraging effect on the gallant garrison of Sennar; but this was not so—they determined to make a stand. The Mudir, Hassan Sadik, who had been put in chains by Nur Bey, volunteered, if he should be released, to attack the rebels, and, in fact, he succeeded in driving them off; but on his return to the town he fell into an ambush and was killed. Brave Nur Bey again pursued the enemy, and succeeded in inflicting a further defeat on them.

Abdel Karim now arrived with a large force, and

summoned the garrison to surrender. Nur Bey refused, and on the 16th of June the city was assaulted; but Abdel Karim was driven back, and was himself wounded in the thigh. He then decided to make the garrison capitulate by famine. The siege was pressed very closely, and on the 18th of July Nur Bey made a successful sortie, inflicting considerable loss on the enemy; but he too was wounded in the leg, and was rendered permanently lame.

The determined defence of the town now induced the Khalifa to despatch Wad En Nejumi with large reinforcements. Meanwhile the garrison had been suffering greatly from famine, and Nur Bey had decided to make a last sortie, which should be under the command of Hassan Bey Osman; but this proved unsuccessful, the commander was killed on the 19th of August, 1885, and Nur Bey was forced to capitulate. Of the 3,000 men of whom the garrison had originally consisted, 700 only remained — a tangible proof of the vigorous and determined resistance they had made.

It is thought throughout the Sudan that the defence of Sennar was most praiseworthy. Nur Bey still lives in Omdurman. Only last year his old wound was cut open to remove the splinters of bone. He was better again when I escaped, but is still lame. Wad En Nejumi arrived two days after the fall of the town and found it in ruins. All that is left of Sennar are a few mud and sand heaps, and its very name has ceased to exist, although early in this century it was better known even than Dongola or Kordofan.

Kassala alone was left. This town is situated on the Khor el Gash, not far from the Atbara River, and about midway between Khartum and Massawah. It had a population of 13,000, and was surrounded by a wall. Here the celebrated moslem, Sid el Hassan, is buried, and a dome is erected over his grave. This man was greatly venerated in the Eastern Sudan; and if any one swears by his name, it is believed that he must be speaking the truth. One of his pupils, whom I met in

Omdurman, told me of his miracles, of which I will quote one or two examples. One day he was preaching a sermon; and when it was over, several of the listeners came to him and begged for alms. Sid el Hassan struck his knee, and forthwith a number of dollars fell out—the exact sum for which the beggars had asked. Amongst the bystanders was a poor shame-faced man, who immediately begged that he might have one dollar. Sid el Hassan again struck his knee, and one dollar fell out, which he at once handed to the man, saying, "This is for the poor shame-faced one." The man at once fell at his feet and gratefully kissed his hands. All who were present were greatly astonished at this miracle, and some, bolder than the rest, approached Sid el Hassan and touched him, when they found, to their wonder, that he felt just like a sack full of dollars.

On another occasion two travellers arrived, with the intention of making a map of the country. Having failed in their purpose, they applied to Sid el Hassan for advice, and, after offering them food and drink, he handed to them the map they required. He performed many different miracles, and was, moreover, a very tolerant man, rendering the Government many valuable services, especially when he succeeded in stopping a revolt of the soldiers. During all the recent events, his relations remained perfectly loyal.

But to return to my narrative. When Osman Digna came to the Sawakin neighbourhood, he sent the emir, Mustafa Hadal, to commence the siege of Kassala; but, as the Shukrieh tribe supplied quantities of corn, it was enabled to stand a very prolonged siege. In January 1884, it was assaulted, and the Mudir suffered serious loss. The Arabs, who had hitherto remained loyal, seeing no hope of help from the Government, also deserted.

The siege was now more closely pressed, and the suburb of Khatmieh was nearly captured; but the enemy were at length driven back. A treaty was concluded with Abyssinia to relieve the Egyptian garrisons and bring them through that country to Massawah; and though at that time all the donkeys in the town had been eaten, they still hoped for relief.

In June 1885, the city was hemmed in on all sides, and was in a desperate condition. Nevertheless the attempted assault on the 15th of the month was successfully repulsed, and the Mudir pursued the enemy, of whom he killed 300. He also succeeded in capturing 1,000 head of cattle. This enabled the town to hold out for a short time; and the news of the Mahdi's death served to further encourage the garrison.

But at last the town was reduced to absolute starvation, and, on condition that the lives of the inhabitants should be spared, the Mudir surrendered. No sooner, however, were the arms given up than the conquerors began to pillage the town and inflict all sorts of cruelties on the people. Osman Digna, who was at that time furious on account of his defeat by Ras Alula on the 22nd of September at Kufit, vented his wrath on the unfortunate Mudir, Ahmed Bey Effat, Hassan Agha, and Ibrahim Eff Shawki, and also on two Greeks, Stello Apostolidi and Tadros Manioseh, whom he caused to be beheaded on the 30th of September, 1885.

From that time Kassala remained under Osman Digna; but in 1886, when the latter was fully occupied in his operations against Sawakin, the Khalifa sent Abu Girgeh there as emir. When Abu Girgeh was subsequently sent to Tokar, Sayid Hamed became emir of Kassala, which from that time formed a part of the province of Galabat, of which Sheikh Nasri, of the Bederieh tribe, became emir.

Abu Girgeh was eventually sent to Berber to replace Osman Wad Dekeim, who had fallen into disgrace. This Osman was very anxious to marry a pretty woman he had seen in Berber, and had frequently visited her in the hope that she would consent; but the woman, who did not want to marry him, decided on a stratagem, and agreed to have a rendezvous on a certain day. She, however, told her brothers and relations to lie in wait; and when Osman arrived at the appointed hour, and was almost sure that he had succeeded, the brothers suddenly broke into the hut and thrashed him so soundly that he made off, and resolved not to urge his suit a second time.

Abu Girgeh did not long remain on good terms with this low Arab, and soon they were both recalled to Omdurman ; the former was again sent to Kassala, where he accused Nasri of having oppressed the inhabitants, and appropriated a quantity of money ; the latter fled to Omdurman, where the Khalifa pardoned him.

Sayid Hamid also quarrelled with Abu Girgeh, and just before I left the Sudan I was told that the Khalifa had recalled him on suspicion that he was in league with the Italians. It is generally believed in the Sudan that Italy will shortly take possession of the weakly defended Kassala, but accurate information of occurrences in the Eastern Sudan is more likely to be received in Cairo than in Omdurman.

CHAPTER X.

THE ESCAPE OF FATHER BONOMI.

Ohrwalder continues to describe his personal experiences—Mahmud the emir of El Obeid—His unsuccessful attempts to entrap the Nubas—The arrival of Olivier Pain in El Obeid—His motives in joining the Mahdi—His journey towards Omdurman—His sad fate—Lupton Bey arrives at El Obeid from the Bahr el Ghazal—He is sent to Omdurman and thrown into chains—Life in El Obeid—The escape of Father Bonomi—Ohrwalder's solitude—The death of the Khojur Kakum.

I MUST now return to the narrative of my own personal experiences, which I broke off in order to follow those events of the Mahdi's career in which I did not take part.

Before the Mahdi left Rahad, I was again handed over to yet another master; this was Sherif Mahmud, the Mahdi's uncle, and Governor of Kordofan, and I was put into his charge when he came to Rahad to see the Mahdi off. I stayed a few days with Mahmud at Rahad. I was then in a wretched state of health; to my horror I discovered black spots on my body, my teeth were chattering, and then I knew that I had scurvy. I longed to escape to the Dobab hills, but my guards were always with me, and I could not succeed.

At length Mahmud started back for El Obeid, and he gave me one of the few surviving mules of the Hicks expedition, which had been wounded by a bullet in the neck and which had never healed. The heavy rain had entirely changed the aspect of the country, which was now a mass of green, and under any other circumstances the journey would have been pleasant enough. We were twice overtaken by terrible thunder-storms, which obliged us to halt, as the heavy rain made travelling impossible; at night we had to sleep on the wet ground.

As we approached El Obeid we heard the war-drums beating, to announce the Governor's arrival. The great sandy plain around was transformed into green fields planted with dokhn. We halted for a time under the leafy Adansonia tree, under which the Mahdi's tent had been pitched, and I noticed that the entire bark of the tree had been peeled off. I afterwards learnt that the people believed the Mahdi's presence had hallowed the tree, and that in consequence the bark had been stripped off and boiled, the liquid being used as medicine or for witchcraft purposes.

Only a few huts were left standing in El Obeid, and Mahmud went to live in the Mudirieh. He had a great reception on his arrival, and the most profuse flattery was showered upon him. It was the usual thing to say that "during his absence the town had been as still as the grave and as dark as night, but, thanks be to God, on his return light was once more restored," &c., &c. The Sherif delighted in this adulation.

A few days after our arrival, Father Bonomi was brought from Rahad to El Obeid in chains, and he and I were given a small hut in the midst of his slaves' quarters, where it was thought we would be in safe custody.

Sherif Mahmud was a small thin man about fifty years of age, full of wiry strength and with evil, malignant-looking eyes. He had formerly been a slave-dealer in Dar Fertit and had then joined Zubeir Pasha's army. Even at Abba he was one of the Mahdi's most fanatical adherents. He pretended to hate the things of this world, was always poorly dressed, and before others always eat of the worst and humblest food. But he was inordinately proud, and loved the power of commanding. During his prayers he used to throw about his arms and legs and shout "Hoa! Hoa!" ("It is He! it is He!" *i.e.* God). His followers used to say that when he did this he saw God in his vision; but others who knew him of old laughed at these antics, though at the same time they were afraid of him and indulged him with flattery. He was excessively severe and strict, but was impartial in his administration of justice.

He dealt very severely with the robbers who now infested El Obeid, and cut off a number of hands and feet. He thoroughly believed in the Mahdi's divine message, and had the reputation of being the bravest of the family. He had received a bullet wound at Gedir, and at Shekan he was always in front, carrying a flag, until he disappeared in the smoke; he fell pierced by two bullets and was thought to have been killed; after the battle, however, his people found him lying on the ground with both legs broken; but he recovered. He carried such a number of arms that men laughed at him. In addition to the two broad-bladed spears, he carried two smaller ones, as well as a number of javelins in a quiver; from his shoulder hung his sword and a small Remington rifle, while his girdle was stuck all over with revolvers and knives. Women always fled out of his path, for he whipped them ruthlessly; sometimes he would dash amongst a crowd of women on his horse and lay about him right and left. He had a very choice harem, and amongst his women was a young Egyptian girl; it is the great desire of a Mahdiist to possess a fair woman, and they often have recourse to the most violent and cruel practices in order to acquire what they want.

Mahmud frequently went through his prayers with his wives and concubines, and on one occasion they began to laugh, in consequence of which the Egyptian girl was sent away and the rest flogged. From this date he took an intense dislike to all the fair-skinned people, and the few Egyptian families who still lived in El Obeid were banished from it

He flattered himself that neither Abu Anga nor Nejumi understood how to wage war against the Nubas, and therefore he once more determined to attack these mountaineers; but he set about it in a very different manner from his predecessors. He armed 400 Takruris and instructed them to encamp at the foot of the mountain ; they were to say they were at enmity with the Dervishes and desired the friendship and assistance of the Nubas.

Meanwhile Mahmud pitched his camp at Rahad, and was in constant readiness for the attack. At first the Nubas were inclined to fall into the trap, and made a treaty of friendship with the Takruris ; but they too had recourse to a still more successful stratagem, and when the Takruris seemed quite certain of their prey, the Nubas suddenly fell upon them during a wild, stormy night and killed almost all of them, very few escaped, and Mahmud was obliged to return crestfallen to El Obeid.

On the 15th of August, 1884, a great surprise came upon El Obeid. Quite unexpectedly, at about two o'clock in the afternoon, a European and three Arabs, mounted on good camels, entered the open yard of the Mudirieh, where Ali Bakhit, the chiefs, and a number of Dervishes were assembled. The European dismounted, and boldly advanced towards the crowd. He was tall, and gave one the impression of being a powerful and energetic man ; he had a fair beard, and his face was very sunburnt. His appearance made a great commotion amongst the Dervishes.

Immediately all sorts of wild rumours were flying about; some said he was the King of France ; others that he was one of the principal ministers of that nation. He wore a jibbeh, white cap and turban, and at once was directed to Ali Bakhit. Being unable to speak Arabic, Father Bonomi was immediately summoned to act as interpreter ; but he had much difficulty in making himself understood.

The stranger informed Bonomi that he had marched from Dongola to El Obeid in thirteen days ; that he had escaped from Dongola, as the English had endeavoured to thwart him in his projects ; that his name was Olivier Pain, and that he was the bearer of letters from Zubeir Pasha to the Mahdi ; but that fear of the English had obliged him to destroy them. He said that he came in the name of France, to place his nation's submission in the Mahdi's hands; and that he was prepared to assist the Mahdi, both by advice and, if required, by deeds.

After this statement Olivier Pain was searched, and at once relieved of his money; a small hut was then pointed out, in which he was to live, in charge of a guard; the three guides were also secured in another place. The Dervishes did not credit Pain's statement; they could not believe it possible that a European would voluntarily come into the Sudan to join the Mahdi; they entirely distrusted Europeans, whose mental superiority they thoroughly recognised; they therefore concluded that Pain was a spy sent by the English to take stock of the situation.

On the following day Bonomi was again summoned; the various articles Pain had brought with him were laid before him, such as books of travels in the Sudan, an Arabic dictionary, a Kuran in French, a few maps, letters, and a passport. Bonomi had to explain these various articles to the Dervishes, who were not a little surprised about the maps of the Sudan, and more especially that of Kordofan. It is true there was nothing found in Pain's baggage of a suspicious nature; still, the Dervishes did not trust him; and he was kept under a very strict guard; we were not permitted to visit him.

The next day Pain complained of the bad food he was given; but the Dervishes gave him wholesome instruction: they told him that the true adherents of the Mahdi were dead to the things of this world. Poor Pain's mind must have been sadly disabused by this reception.

The Dervishes were full of curiosity about this strange Frenchman's doings and intentions, and kept worrying us to know why he should have come; but it was also a mystery to us; and when they asked him, he always gave the same answer—"The whole of the European nations, more especially France, and with the one exception of England, entirely sympathised with the Mahdi." He was asked if the Senussi had risen against the unbelievers in Egypt; but he replied that the Senussi feared the English. When asked what the English were doing, he replied that they were building forts at Assuan; whereupon Ali Bakhit observed—"May God destroy their forts." But, question as they would, Pain's arrival and his reasons for coming still remained a mystery to them. He was therefore sent, in charge of a large escort, to Mahmud at Rahad; Mahmud received him well, gave him a horse and a female slave, and sent him on to the Mahdi, who was then on his march to Omdurman.

On the 28th of August Pain arrived at Aigella, where one of our El Obeid Mission brothers was staying; the latter at once inquired of Pain what he was going to do. On this occasion, it appears, he spoke more openly; he asked if the brother understood French; but the latter replied that he could not speak it, though he understood it. Then Pain proceeded to say that he was correspondent of a newspaper, and came to see the Mahdi and his empire, about which he intended to write full accounts to his paper.

This brother endeavoured to explain to him the difficulties he would be sure to meet with, and on what dangerous ground he was treading, adding that it was most unlikely he would ever return; but Pain replied that if he succeeded in his undertaking, he would receive an immense reward; and that hitherto the Dervishes had not treated him badly; moreover, he was full of energy, and would not give up hope of escape in the future. Pain also explained to the brother the difficulties with which the English expedition would be sure to meet, and how he believed Khartum would certainly be lost.

Pain caught up the Mahdi at the village of Busata. Various were the surmises of those in camp regarding his intentions. Slatin, Klootz, and the other Europeans were especially perplexed. Olivier Pain had imagined that the immense services which he would be able to render the Mahdi would cause the latter to receive him with open arms; but the poor man was sadly deluded.

He was presented to the Mahdi, who greeted him coldly, and asked him his reasons for coming. Pain replied— "To acknowledge you as Mahdi, and to lay before you the submission of the French nation." The Mahdi gave an ironic smile, as much as to say he did not believe a word Pain was saying; and then he ordered Abu Anga to take charge of him, guard him most carefully, and permit no one to see him.

During the march to Shatt, Klootz managed to approach Pain, and began talking to him; but for this disobedience he was at once seized and put in chains. On Slatin's representations, however, to the Khalifa Abdullah, he was released.

At Shatt, Pain began to suffer from dysentery and fever, brought on by over-fatigue and bad water. The Mahdi permitted Slatin to visit him; and Pain's wretched condition so disturbed Slatin that he begged the Mahdi to give him a little money, with which he could buy some better food, which it was absolutely necessary Pain should have.

But his disease became worse; and it was with the greatest difficulty he could continue his march to Om Sadik. Here his condition became hopeless; he explained that he could go on no longer, and begged for some medicine. The custom in the Sudan is to drink melted butter; and after Pain had taken a little, he was placed on a camel; but it had scarcely gone a few steps, when he was seized with a fainting fit, and fell off. As he lay unconscious on the ground, and was deathly pale, his guards believed that he must be dead; so they dug a rough grave, in which poor Pain was laid, covered him over with sand, and then hurried on. It is quite possible the unfortunate man was not dead. They marked his grave by planting his stick in the sand, and tying his sandals to it. This event occurred on the 15th of November, 1884.

Early in September, Lupton Bey, Mudir of Bahr el Ghazal arrived at El Obeid; he had been permitted to retain his property, and he was most kind to us; indeed, I have no words to express our gratitude to him for his unvarying generosity to us. He told us a great deal about his own fights, and related how, after the destruction of General Hicks, the Mahdi had despatched the two slave-dealer brothers Karamallah and Kirkesawi from Dongola to the Bahr el Ghazal. Karamallah had summoned Lupton Bey to surrender; but Lupton, as his letters to Emin Pasha show, determined to fight; his subordinate officers, however, almost all deserted him, and joined the Mahdiists, and the few who remained loyal eventually refused to fight. Indeed, I have seen the actual document they drew up and signed to that effect. Lupton, who at that time was thoroughly exhausted by his constant warfare against the Dinkas, had therefore no alternative but to submit, which he did on the the 28th of April, 1884.

A few days later Lupton, with his kavass and clerk, were sent as prisoners to El Obeid, *viâ* Shakka. His arrival was a welcome addition to our little circle, and it was a very great comfort to us to have the society of such a genuine and kind friend as Lupton in these times of trial. He remained with us for about a month; at that time we had daily information about the movements of the English expedition, and we now hoped that the time for our deliverance was approaching. Many of the Mahdiists themselves were getting tired of the new *régime*, which gave neither rest nor security of property to anyone. It was through these malcontents that we obtained news which gave us food for argument and speculation during the long and weary days of our captivity.

This life of a slave was terribly obnoxious to poor Lupton, who frequently gave way to bursts of indignation, and in one of these Sherif Mahmud arrested him, and in the first week of October he despatched him under escort to the Mahdi. On his arrival at Omdurman he was put in chains, where he remained for ten months, as he had attempted to escape to Khartum. During this period of captivity, Lupton underwent terrible sufferings, which I could not possibly describe.

Shortly after Lupton left us, we received a letter

from Slatin, saying that Gordon intended holding out until the English arrived, at the same time he urged us to try and obtain leave to come to Omdurman; but this was impossible. Another friend also told us that he hoped shortly to be able to effect our release; but in his letter he wrote in such a manner that we alone were able to grasp his meaning, for he feared that what he had written might fall into the hands of the Dervishes.

Our anxiety can readily be understood, for we felt certain that if the English were victorious, we should be killed in revenge. Sherif Mahmud had already received orders from the Mahdi to encamp outside the town, and be prepared for any eventuality. So our days passed in a whirl of hopes and fears, and death would have been welcome.

But now a new disaster occurred; the circumstantial account of the death of Colonel Stewart and his party, and the fact that the state of Khartum was rapidly becoming desperate, made us full of doubt as to Gordon's fate. The fall of Omdurman further confirmed our fears, and we trembled to think that Khartum would fall before the English arrived. The prolonged resistance of the town, and the knowledge that the English were almost there, caused no small alarm amongst the people in El Obeid; when, therefore, Sherif Mahmud ordered a salute of one hundred guns to be fired to announce a great victory, the reaction was tremendous.

The news of the fall of Khartum and of the English victory at Abu Klea reached El Obeid the same day. Mahmud held a great review, and the Mahdiists were wild with joy. Thus the last bulwark of Egyptian authority in the Sudan had disappeared; the English turned back and left the Sudan to its fate. The Mahdi rested for a time on his laurels, and occupied himself with bringing into subjection the few who still resisted.

Sherif Mahmud now determined to make himself famous for his bravery, and resolved to conquer the whole of Nuba, and convert the inhabitants. As a first step, he proceeded with a force of two thousand men straight to Delen ; these good people had been left unmolested since Mek Omar had taken his departure, and had gone back to their peaceful ways and former mode of life, which consisted largely of breeding swine, planting tobacco, and drinking marissa to their heart's content.

The Baggaras, who lived in Nuba, and of whom many had been unwillingly forced to follow the Mahdi, were getting somewhat tired of the new faith. Khojur Kakum was just in the same position as before, and had gained considerably in reputation, as he had foretold correctly how the Mahdi would conduct himself. Mahmud duly arrived at Delen, and encamped at the foot of the hills.

On Mahmud's departure, we thought the time had at length arrived when we might attempt to escape, for long ago we had projected a plan to get the Kababish to assist us. Formerly this tribe did much of the carrying trade between Dongola and El Obeid, and they had already proved that they were loyal to the Government. It was said that when the English came to Dongola, this tribe was bringing thousands of camels laden with corn from Dar Hamer ; but when Mahmud heard of it, he sent after them, and captured two thousand five hundred loads, so from that time no Kababish ever came to El Obeid. This, therefore, greatly interfered with our plans ; besides, we had no money either to buy camels or pay the guides, so I reverted to my old idea, which I had formulated at Rahad, to escape to Jebel Dobab and live with the brave Nubas.

I was thinking over this plan, and casting up in my mind the chances of success, when, on the 4th of June, 1885, a Coptic friend of ours called Sideham arrived, and handed Father Bonomi a small note, saying at the same time that a man had come to take him back to Dongola, and that he would meet him in the market next day. Bonomi and I then retired to a place where we knew no one would see us, and there in fear and trembling we tore open the letter; then Bonomi, in the deepest agitation, read as follows :—

" Dear Friend, I am sending this man so that you

may escape with him. Trust him—he is honest. Monsignor Sogaro awaits you in Cairo with outstretched arms. Your fellow-countryman, ALOIS SANTONI."

For some moments we were so excited we could scarcely speak; but my first thought was, "Why is Bonomi only sent for?" and the feeling that flight was debarred from me, filled me with the most utter dejection.

It was to be my sad fate to see my companion in adversity start without me; then a ray of hope flashed across my mind, possibly the man might be the bearer of a verbal message. It was the very moment for flight; there were very few Dervishes in El Obeid. Oh, the terrible length of that day and night! How slowly the hours went by!

The next morning Bonomi went alone to the place of rendezvous. I thought if I went with him it might create suspicion; but at the same time I begged him to urge the man to take me with him as well. Bonomi met the man, and it required only a very few moments to come to an arrangement. How I longed for him to return and know the result. At length he came, looking very pleased; but the man, he said, had definitely declined to take me with him; however, he promised that if he succeeded in conducting Bonomi safely, he would return for me in fifteen days.

I grieved terribly at the news that my flight must be deferred; but, on the other hand, I rejoiced that one of us should be fortunate enough to escape from this terrible bondage. The man told Father Bonomi not to trouble about anything, but merely to meet him on Mount Korbatsh, where he would find him with the camels.

On the afternoon of the 5th of June, Bonomi prepared himself for flight, taking a large knife with him. We left our huts, and proceeded to the rendezvous; our hearts were too full to speak. At last I left him; and pressing him to my heart, bade him farewell, saying— "Do not forget your poor companion in adversity, who is left behind."

Many a time did I turn round to look back, until Bonomi disappeared from view in the wood. It was just sunset, and a lovely evening, which made even that dull plain look beautiful. Wild, anxious thoughts kept careering through my brain, as I walked back to my wretched and solitary home. Would Bonomi succeed, and what would happen to me? for I knew that the Dervishes must conclude that I knew about Bonomi's flight. So immersed was I in these thoughts that I kept on losing my way, and did not get back till late.

My delay had already caused some suspicion; but I found a ready excuse. I said that I had been searching for corn; for at that time there was famine; and nothing was to be had in the market. My excuse was accepted, and fortunately they did not think of asking for Bonomi. I now threw myself down on my hard bed; but my weary eyes found no sleep. I kept revolving in my mind all that had occurred; but at length I determined to pluck up courage and put my trust in God; and then my thoughts turned to more practical considerations. How should I explain Bonomi's absence to the emir without saying anything which would implicate myself?

It was a hot, sultry night, but a refreshing shower fell just then; and in the midst of the patter of the rain-drops, I thought I heard Bonomi's voice in the hut. What could it be? Had he returned? A thousand wild thoughts crowded into my mind; but I did not dare make a noise, though it was all I could do to control my curiosity.

I rose very early the next morning, and searched about the hut; but found no one. It was at any rate quite certain Bonomi had gone; but yet I felt sure he must have come back during the night. It was not until six long years afterwards, when I returned to Cairo, that I solved the mystery; and then he himself told me how, after parting from me, he had lost his way, and could not find the guide or camels; after vainly wandering about, he had returned to the hut, where the Copt who had given him the note found

"MANY A TIME DID I TURN ROUND TO LOOK BACK, UNTIL BONOMI
DISAPPEARED FROM VIEW IN THE WOOD."

him, and conducted him to the Arab with whom he had escaped.

I must here explain why it was the messenger had only been commissioned to rescue Father Bonomi; and this I did not learn till after my own escape. News had reached Cairo that I was in Omdurman, and that Bonomi had been left alone in El Obeid; and therefore arrangements had been made for his rescue only.*

Meanwhile, I kept Bonomi's escape concealed; and it was not until the fourth day after he had left, and when I was assured of his safety, that I informed the emin beit el mal† that he had gone to Khartum to fetch some medicine. I believe this man thoroughly knew that he had escaped; but he did not show the slightest suspicion, and ordered us to go to Khartum as well; and we were placed under close surveillance. He also wrote to Sherif Mahmud at Delen, and to Khartum; a few days later orders came from Mahmud that we were to be imprisoned in the zariba of the beit el mal. That evening, soldiers came and dragged us and our slender property to the zariba; and while waiting till huts should be made for us, we were housed with slaves suffering from small-pox.

This disease was then very prevalent in El Obeid, and horrible sights continually met our eyes. These unfortunate sufferers had no one to help them, and they were left to die, either of the disease, or of hunger; they lay about under the trees in the market-place, shunned by every one; often, when still living, they were dragged off by men, who tied ropes round their bodies, and pulled them along the ground till they were beyond the outskirts of the town; and there they were left to be devoured by the hyenas.

A dreadful famine prevailed, and the population was

---

* Father Bonomi arrived safely in Dongola, and Mr. Santoni, who is now director of posts at Assiut, was rewarded by His Holiness Pope Leo XIII. with the Order of Gregory the Great, in recognition of the humane service he had rendered.

† I.e. the official in charge of the beit el mal or Dervish storehouse and treasury.

decimated by hunger; ten to twelve pounds of corn were sold for a dollar, and the man was fortunate who could buy it at this price. In the market, fights were frequent; meat, however, was not so expensive, and we lived for days on meat only, without any bread. The poor people used to dig about the streets and in the houses for gum, which they knew had been concealed during the siege; and this unwholesome food frequently caused their death.

The air in the zariba was poisoned by the number of people suffering from small-pox; but curiously enough, the disease never seemed to touch the white people. My new abode turned out to be not so bad as I expected. I became friends with some of the soldiers who used to be in the Government service, and sympathised with them in their wretched state; these poor men often tried to do me any little service they could.

It was about this time that Sultan Dud Benga, flying from Zogal, arrived, on his way to give himself up to the Mahdi in Omdurman, and also a certain Sherif, who set himself up to be the fourth Khalifa—Osman. The latter, however, on his arrival in Omdurman, was thrown into chains, and his wives, horses, and slaves confiscated. I planted a few water-melons round my hut, which grew well; and I used to amuse myself by watching the movements of the chameleons which disported themselves underneath the leaves; but one day a fire broke out, which destroyed my hut, water-melons, chameleons, and all; and so this little dissipation was denied me. However, I built a new hut in a few days.

Almost a month had now passed since Bonomi's departure, and I began to look about anxiously for the return of the Arab who was to help me to escape. During the night I had cautiously loosened the zariba hedge, so that I could easily get out, when the time came; but day by day passed, and I began to lose hope. I did hear a rumour once that a man had come to help us to escape, but that on hearing we were locked up in the zariba, he had gone away. This was very probably true; for the Arabs are excessively timid;

and we were as universally shunned by all as if we were infested with a plague ; if anyone dared to speak to us, he was almost sure to be arrested and locked up.

Thus we dragged out a miserable existence, devoid of hope, shunned by all, and suffering much from continual sickness. One event, however, unexpectedly occurred, which we thought would completely alter the state of affairs, and would produce a revolution, in which we again thought we saw some chance of escape.

Early in July 1885, the news of the Mahdi's death arrived. At first it was not credited, and the leading people thought it better to keep it a strict secret, but their dismal countenances belied them. It was a terrible blow to the Dervishes, and they themselves believed that disturbances would undoubtedly take place, for the number of malcontents was by no means small. The truth, however, soon came out, and the immediate effect on the ignorant masses was the realization that they had been deceived, and that the Mahdi was no Mahdi at all. Hitherto Mahdiism had been thoroughly admitted, and it was their belief in the Mahdi's divine mission which had given birth to the fanaticism which had made them so bold and fearless— the belief that to die in battle as martyrs assured them paradise with its myriads of lovely houris, its lovely gardens, laden with milk and honey, fruits and flowers.

All this was implicitly believed. What wonder then that they should throw themselves into the very thickest of the fight in the sure and certain hope that to die in the Mahdi's cause ensured eternal delights and pleasures! Now all these glorious visions had collapsed like a house of cards, and in the future Mahdiism to live would have to be enforced. From this time forth there was no voluntary seeking to obey, and it was clear that the new Religion was on the wane.

The family and adherents of the Mahdi were at variance with the followers of Khalifa Abdullah, the latter by his immense energy had made himself master of the situation. But the glow and fervour of religious enthusiasm was gone.

The blow of the Mahdi's death almost killed Sherif Mahmud; many of his chiefs and emirs muttered: "See how the Mahdi has deceived us. Had he been the real Mahdi he would not have died in Omdurman. Alas! what thousands of human lives have been sacrificed to this false Mahdi's caprice." Mahmud was at a loss to know what to say and contented himself with murmuring: "Even if the Mahdi be dead, his religion did not die with him; let us therefore fight in the cause of religion."

Nevertheless all obedience and discipline did not disappear, for these men had still their own interests to look after: but it was unfortunate there was no one to place himself at the head of the malcontents and openly declare that the Mahdi was no Mahdi.

Mahmud now returned without delay to El Obeid, and immediately on his arrival he ordered the criers to announce that he required some account of Father Bonomi's escape. He was furious at his flight; he sent for me and asked where he had gone; I simply replied, that he had disappeared one night and that the next morning I could find no trace of him in the hut. If Mahmud had not been so upset by the Mahdi's death, I believe I should have had to pay dearly for his flight. As it was he believed that Bonomi would be seized by the Dervishes in Dongola, and at the same time he sent out spies to try and discover who had assisted him to escape. Suspicion fell on Mohammed Suleiman, who had been our old captain at Delen and who was now the kadi's clerk; he was threatened with a flogging, which he would certainly have received had not his master begged him off.

Mahmud brought with him from Delen the unfortunate Khojur Kakum; this poor man was thrown into chains soon after his arrival, and his hut and the chair which he used for his religious ceremonies were burnt. The Nubas were solemnly abjured to desist from their superstitious beliefs, and Mahmud made a small straw mosque for them in which they were obliged to say prayers; but the Nubas set fire to it, and after Mahmud's departure they named their pigs after the Mahdi's important emirs.

When Kakum was on his way to El Obeid, he had had a bad fall from a bullock, which had injured him internally and made it almost impossible for him to move: he was put into our zariba, and soon after he came I went to see him and found him in a state of profound dejection. He was very pleased to see me, and the tears rolled down his black cheeks; he was so affected he could barely speak, and lost all control over himself. His two wives were sitting near him—one of them, Mea, was a thoroughly good woman, and many a happy hour did I spend playing with her little child of six years old. Kakum gave me coffee, and we talked over the old days at the Mission, then I left him to rest. That same night I was suddenly summoned by Mea, who said that Kakum was seriously ill; I hastened to the hut and found him almost unconscious, and in a few hours he was dead. He was a thoroughly good, sensible man, and had been a faithful friend to the Mission and to the Government. He died in July 1885, and I think he must then have been about fifty-five years of age. His second wife married the Khojur of Sobei, who had also been dragged to El Obeid by Mahmud; but Mea did not marry again. She devoted herself to her little child.

The boy delighted in being with me, and said he always wanted to stay with the Christians; but a month later Mea and her child were allowed to return to Delen. I gave the boy a little shirt, and in return Mea promised to send me some tobacco; and, true to her word, a messenger arrived soon afterwards with that luxury, in return for which I sent her some glass beads.

During his stay at Delen, Mahmud had captured Shirra, one of the renegade Baggara chiefs, and his two sons. This man had formerly been our sworn enemy, and had declared that he would kill every one of us Christians; but when this great chief and his sons came into the zariba they greeted me like lambs, and when, in fun, I recalled to them their former oaths, they admitted that they had been completely deceived, and now that they had not words sufficient to praise the Christians or to curse the Mahdi. It was no little satisfaction to me to find such an entire change of mind and purpose in one who had been our bitterest foe. Thus was justice tardily meted out to us.

Meanwhile Khalifa Abdullah had sent an order from Omdurman to Mahmud, telling him to set out forthwith for Omdurman to swear the Bea'a (or oath of allegiance) to the Mahdi's successor. Mahmud therefore, in August 1885, left El Obeid with a large number of followers.

CHAPTER XI.

REVOLT AGAINST THE DERVISHES.

The black soldiers of the old Sudan army—They revolt against the Dervishes in El Obeid—And march off to Dar Nuba—The emir Mahmud pursues and is slain—Ohrwalder quits El Obeid for Omdurman—Zogal and Abu Anga at Bara.

THE old Sudanese soldiers of the Egyptian army were perhaps, of all others, the most dissatisfied with Mahdiism. These brave blacks who, as they say in the Sudan, "had eaten the Khedive's bread," were now in a wretched state compared with the once miserable Gellabas, who now galloped about proudly on horseback, while in former years they had scarcely a donkey to their name. Several of these soldiers had been to Egypt, some had been servants to Europeans, and most of them had been in the various fights which had previously taken place in the Sudan. Sherif Mahmud, it is true, treated them with some deference, and gave them corn when he refused to give it to the Gellabas who were starving; but in spite of this, their previous condition was infinitely preferable to their life under Mahdiist rulers. There were about two hundred of these soldiers in El Obeid; shortly afterwards, a number of slaves arrived, and quite recently their numbers had been further increased by the addition of a company sent by Zogal.

Many of these men had fought under Munzinger Pasha, and under Slatin Bey, and were distinguished for their bravery; their total number was now three hundred, under the command of an Egyptian mowallid,[*]

---

[*] The name given to natives of a mixed parentage; *i.e.*, generally an Egyptian or Turkish father and a Sudanese mother.

named Abdullah. These men used to complain of being always placed in the forefront of the battle; and they were further irritated by the arrogant way in which they were treated by the Danagla and their unbearable emir Wad el Hashmi, who used to call them "abd" (*i.e.* slave); they therefore decided to revolt against this tyrannical rule, and in this their emir supported them. It was agreed that they should await the great Dahiyeh festival, and when they were all out on parade, and the Dervishes were going through their prayers, they would suddenly separate themselves and, trusting to their good rifles, would be able to annihilate their hated enemies; but the thought that a number of innocent people would be thus sacrificed, decided them to await some other more favourable opportunity. It was often a matter of surprise to me how these blacks managed to keep their secret, which even all their women knew.

A clever young mukuddum lived near my hut, and did me many a kindness; he often used to bring me some meat to eat, as the soldiers who looked after the sheep and goats taken from the Arabs frequently killed some for their own food and then reported that they had died. At this time I suffered a great deal from fever, I could not remain in my close and small hut, and used to lie wide awake and tossing about on my hard bed outside. I often saw the mukuddum in secret conversation with some of his men, and then they would look at their arms to see they were all right; this made me feel certain that some plot was brewing.

Amongst the soldiers I had also another good friend, Hajji Selim, who was at all times ready to render me any little service, in return for which I used to give him a little coffee or some tobacco. Hajji Selim had a curious story. He was born in Bornu, and when young had joined his father, who was going with a caravan to Mecca. Whilst journeying through the Sahara, they came to a district in which two tribes were at war; he joined one of them, but was taken prisoner by the other, sold as a slave, and taken to Tunis; from here, he was brought to Constantinople, where he became the playfellow of his master's son, and in this way learnt the Turkish language. Soon afterwards his master was sent to Egypt as a Pasha, and he came with him, from thence they went on a pilgrimage to Mecca, hence his title of Hajji. On their return to Cairo, the master died, his property was confiscated, and Selim was taken into the army. He was sent to Sawakin, then he served under Munzinger Pasha at Massawa, and was with him at the time of his murder; from here he was sent to Darfur, then to Kordofan, and eventually to Delen, where he was taken prisoner with Mohammed Suleiman, and thus became attached to the Mahdiists.

This unfortunate man, though comparatively young, had become aged by constant travelling, he was homeless, and had neither wife nor child; he wore an old coat which had been given to him by some of Hicks Pasha's soldiers, it was riddled with bullet-holes, covered with patches of blood, and very dirty; however, that did not much matter to him, as he had no soap to wash it; he always wore the hood of his coat over his head, which further added to his curious appearance. He made his coat into a species of Dervish uniform by patching up the holes with the pieces of an old tarbush; but withal he was a thoroughly honest man, and I liked him. I also knew I could rely on him to carry out a secret mission, and therefore, after Bonomi had fled, I had made over to him some money and two volumes of the 'Popular Educator,' which Lupton Bey had given me, and which I looked upon as a priceless treasure. I did this because I was afraid that Sherif Mahmud would confiscate my little all; but when all fear was over, the honest man brought back everything just as I had given it to him. At that time I had no suitable place in my hut to hide them, so I asked him to keep them a few days longer; but, alas! my books were to become food for the flames, which soon afterwards devoured the camp, and this was an irreparable loss. I tried to find out from Hajji Selim what plot was brewing; but all my inquiries were fruitless. He would not breathe a word, and from that time I saw no more of him, for he was afraid that my importunity might make him divulge the secret. I knew perfectly well that he must have been one of the conspirators, and as I never saw him again, I presume he must have been killed.

The above little incident is merely mentioned to show how zealously the soldiers kept their secret; but all the same, the people in El Obeid had a notion that something was going to happen, and one day an order was suddenly given that a hundred soldiers were to prepare to proceed to Dar Hamer. In this way they thought to split up the party, and then disarm them; but the men guessed that this was the intention, and therefore decided to execute their plan the following day.

That night I was lying outside as usual; the sky was particularly brilliant, and I was watching the myriads of shooting stars which, leaving bright trails behind them, burst suddenly like rockets, and illumined the night till it became for an instant almost as light as day. Every one wondered at this curious phenomenon, and foretold that it meant mischief of some sort, and, curiously, there was mischief enough in the air that night.

The next day, at about noon, I was startled by the sound of firing, and bullets were suddenly flying over my head. In my alarm I had rushed out of the hut, and saw that the firing was from the direction of the powder-magazine. To my intense surprise, I did not see a solitary soldier in the zariba; even their wives had gone, and had taken their household goods away with them. I shouted and cried out, but no one answered; a few women passed by, but they were too occupied to answer me; they, too, soon disappeared, and the whole place, which but a few moments before had been a Babel of din and ronise, became silent as the gave. In the distance I could hear continuous firing, and occasionally I caught sight of women and children running away in a northerly direction.

I now thought it time to quit the zariba myself. I seized a bayonet, and tried to push aside the thorns, but they were so firmly fixed in the ground, that I could not move them. I then made for the gate, and here there was not a soul to be seen; even the slaves in chains had disappeared. Bullets were now flying in all directions. I went towards the Emir Abdullah's house, and found him standing by his door in a state of great agitation, with only two soldiers. In reply to my question as to what was the matter, he answered in a surly tone: "These beit el mal slaves have destroyed everything." These words were scarcely out of his mouth, when fifty Dervishes with drawn swords suddenly rushed up, and with frightful yells dragged him and his men off to the courtyard of the Mudirieh. I followed them. Here an enormous crowd of Dervishes was collected, and, wild with rage, they would have torn Abdullah to pieces had not Wad el Hashmi stopped them.

The Dervishes now accused Abdullah of having incited the soldiers; but he protested that he knew nothing of the affair, and in proof of his statement urged that he had not quitted his house; but it was useless. The air resounded with cries of "Cut off his head!" and he was obliged to kneel down. With one blow his head rolled on the sand; both the soldiers were also beheaded, and their bodies thrown down near the mosque, so that everyone might see them.

I now learnt that the soldiers had taken possession of the powder magazine, which consisted of a square yard, with small towers at the corners; it had been utilized as a magazine in Government days. All arms and ammunition were stored here, and a number of Egyptians were employed moulding bullets and filling cartridges; there were also quantities of caps, and all the necessary implements. The soldiers had broken into this place, killed the guards, made loopholes, and prepared for defence; they had burnt down most of the houses in the town, and forced all they met to join them. Two Egyptians who refused to do so were at once killed. The Dervishes had rushed, in a body, to attempt to recover the magazine, but had been shot down in numbers; several emirs also fell in this assault, and no one dared to return to recover their bodies. At length, having rallied from their first failure, they again collected and advanced—this time with more order—to the attack; but the soldiers, who had learnt of their Emir Abdullah's death, fought with desperate courage, and again drove them back, with heavy loss.

The Dervishes now assembled beside the great gate of the Mudirieh, and consulted what was best to be done; they were thoroughly alarmed, and no wonder; for everyone who came within range of the fort was almost certainly shot down. Amongst these was Fiki Isa, of the Shanabla, who was struck in the neck by a bullet, and fell dead at once. Naturally, I fled as soon as possible from this dangerous proximity, and went to the house of a clerk, whose walls I knew would give me protection.

The firing now became faster, and the soldiers sounded the trumpet for the attack on the Mudirieh, intending to capture the guns which stood outside the gate; but the Dervishes had withdrawn them and closed it, so the troops were forced to retire; their ranks had been largely increased by a number of male and female slaves, who, on hearing of the mutiny, had at once left their masters.

Fighting lasted till nightfall; and at length, under cover of darkness, I made my way back to the zariba, to see what had become of my companions in adversity. I found it empty and deserted; even the cattle had escaped somehow; and only two miserable slaves, suffering from ferentit (guinea-worm), and who were unable to move, remained behind. I was feverish and restless; so returned again to the Mudirieh, to see what was going forward there. I found a crowd of Dervishes, exasperated at the idea of having been defeated by the "slave-soldiers," as they called them; more of their emirs had been killed; and the chief, Wad Hashmi, had been mortally wounded, and died the following day. When the Dervishes caught sight of me (hitherto

I had passed unnoticed), they ordered me back to the zariba, threatening to kill me if I again left it; I suppose they did this because they thought I might join the mutineers. It was believed that the soldiers would attack and capture the town the next day. How I wish they had had a good leader!

My companions and I now found ourselves in the beit el mal again, under the guard of four soldiers. Worn out with excitement, I threw myself down on my angarib; the success of the mutineers again revived in my breast hopes of release; and with this pleasing thought, I dropped off into a sound slumber.

I was suddenly roused up by one of the guard prodding me with the butt end of his rifle, and saying—"When everyone is in terror of his life, how can you sleep?" So I reluctantly had to get up, and began chatting to the guard, as I feared any display of satisfaction on my part would probably call down vengeance from them. We talked over the events of the day; and I soon realised that the Dervishes were, in truth, greatly alarmed.

The powder magazine was not far from the beit el mal, so we could overhear a great deal of what was going on there; and one would have imagined that they were engaged in marriage festivities rather than in bloody warfare. The whole night through they kept up singing; the women were dancing, and the men drinking marissa: every now and then the trumpets were sounded, which seemed to add to the women's delight; they were all laughing over the Mahdi's doings, heaping insults on him and his religion; and still further exasperating the Dervishes by shouting out to them to come and join them in a drinking bout.

But whilst these good blacks were enjoying themselves in the magazine, the Dervishes had fortified the beit el mal, and placed bodies of troops, with their flags, in different parts. Occasionally, the blacks fired a volley into them, which made them disperse, leaving their flag behind them. Everyone was in a state of most anxious expectancy for the next day; it was looked

upon as certain that a fight would take place between
the Dervishes and the soldiers, which would finally
decide matters; and that night there was little sleep
for anyone.

Early the next morning the soldiers played the
Khedivial salute, which stirred us to the quick; and
by the time the sun had risen, firing had recommenced,
and was continued up till nine o'clock. The soldiers
made a few raids on camels and donkeys, but did not
attempt to attack the Dervishes; and it was not at
all clear what they intended to do. The Dervish emir,
being certain that the mutineers were quite demoralized,
sent their imam (priest) to tell them that if they wished
to surrender, they would receive pardon; this exasperated
the blacks beyond measure; the imam was told not to
talk nonsense; and was then deliberately dragged out
about fifty paces from the fort, pierced through and
through with his own spears, and his body thrown out
in the direction of the Mudirieh, whilst the soldiers
shouted out—"This is the head in return for the head
of our Emir Abdullah." They continued to make
desultory sorties during the day, and captured a quantity
of animals.

In the afternoon they left the powder magazine;
the band playing, women and children marching in
front; then came the ammunition, surrounded by armed
men, and lastly, the soldiers, marching in good order,
and disposed in such a manner as to resist any sudden
assault.

The Dervishes, however, determined to attack, and,
marshalling their banners, they made for the powder
magazine, which they found quite deserted; the soldiers
had thrown into the wells all the powder they could
not carry. There were only five fresh graves in the
magazine, which showed that the soldiers had lost only
five men, whilst the Dervishes had lost about five
hundred.

Meanwhile, the blacks were marching gaily towards
Melbeis; but the Dervishes, more furious than ever
after their discoveries in the magazine, set off in hot

pursuit; and when they had got within a short distance of their enemy, they were received by a well-directed volley, which killed some fifty of them; the remainder fled in disorder to El Obeid. The total number of the blacks, including the slaves who had joined them, did not exceed one thousand men, whilst the Dervishes more than trebled that number. Had they only had a competent commander, there is no doubt they could easily have captured El Obeid. They continued their march, unopposed, to Nuba, and arrived first of all at Delen, where they established themselves, and selected Beshir, an old soldier of Slatin Bey's, to be their Mudir. Mahdiism was entirely renounced, and the Khedive's Government proclaimed. Anyone who swore by the Mahdi's name received eighty lashes; the regular form of swearing was—"Hakk ras Effendina" ("By the Khedive's head!") Strict discipline was enforced. Any one found selling arms or ammunition to the Nubas was punished with death, and the sentence was carried out by shooting.

Shortly afterwards, they quitted Delen and marched to Jebel Naïma, the inhabitants of which place are known as the bravest of the Nubas; but here they still seemed to think themselves too close to their hated enemies, and therefore moved on to Golfan, where they took up a position in an inaccessible mountain, were recognized by their neighbours as the rulers of the country, and were supplied by them with quantities of cattle and sesame.

In the meantime Sherif Mahmud, in Omdurman, had been fully informed of all that had occurred. He fell into a terrible passion, accused all his emirs of cowardice, and proceeded forthwith to El Obeid. He would not even enter his house, but encamped outside the town. Khalifa Abdullah had ordered him to leave the mutineers alone, and to proceed, *viâ* the Es Safiyeh Wells, to Dongola; but Mahmud entirely disregarded this order. He thirsted for vengeance against these rebels, and determined to subdue them. Added to this, he had also conceived the idea of usurping Khalifa Abdullah's authority. His object, therefore, was to increase his power by regaining the co-operation of the soldiers, and so proud and self-confident was he, that he believed they would never attempt to fight against him.

Here, underneath the great Adansonia tree where the Mahdi had stayed so long, he pitched his camp and made preparations for his advance on Nuba. He called for volunteers, saying that he did not wish to force anyone to go to war, and at the same time he endeavoured to encourage the people by telling them that the Mahdi had appeared to him in a dream, and had told him to advance and attack the rebels, promising him certain victory. In spite of this summons, very few volunteered, and getting thoroughly annoyed, he now threatened with death anyone who refused to join him. Thus did Mahmud realise that the spirit of Mahdiism had almost died out, and that in future force would be required to carry out its behests.

He rapidly advanced with a force of 2,500 men, most of them armed with Remingtons. On his way he was joined by a number of Arabs, which raised his force to some 8,000 men. On arrival at Naïma he found that the mutineers had moved on; he therefore advanced to Golfan, and sent in a letter to the effect that if they surrendered he would give them a free pardon. But the soldiers had had previous experience of Mahdieh promises, and received the messengers with volleys, which soon made them turn back. Mahmud determined, therefore, to invest his former adherents, and, putting himself at the head of his troops, he advanced towards the mountain; but the soldiers, concealed behind rocks, sent volley after volley into the Dervish ranks. Mahmud received a bullet in his side, but, nothing daunted, he continued to advance, carrying his own flag, until another bullet, hitting him full on the forehead, killed him.

Already over a hundred Dervishes had fallen, and the remainder, hearing that Mahmud was dead, turned tail and fled in disorder towards El Obeid. The soldiers did not pursue, but took up Mahmud's body and gave him an honourable burial befitting the brave man he was. In his death Mahdieh lost perhaps the boldest of its adherents, and certainly the bravest of the Mahdi's family. And though he had latterly given himself up to a life of pleasure and debauchery, as all the rest had done, still he did not fear exposing himself to every sort of danger.

Mahmud fell in the month of November 1885, and Khalifa Abdullah was by no means displeased to be rid of a rival whose prowess and popularity he greatly feared and envied.

In place of Sherif Mahmud, Abdullah despatched his brother Bakhit to Kordofan; but he was a very different class of man, and was nicknamed "Tor" ("The Bullock").

Soon afterwards Bakhit received orders to leave all his men at El Obeid and to return to Omdurman. He was succeeded by the emir Wad el Hashmi, who was followed by Osman Wad Adam (nicknamed "Ganu"), the Mahdi's nephew.

Preparations were now made to transport all Mahmud's people to Omdurman, and in order to convey so many thousand people, camels were forcibly seized. We also were released, and permitted to go to Omdurman. I had passed too many miserable years in Kordofan not to rejoice at the change: for a time I had a faint hope that someone might be sent by Father Bonomi to assist me to escape, but now it seemed useless to hope for this any longer, whereas, once at Omdurman, I might manage to escape by myself. Our departure was delayed for a month.

El Obeid had gradually become a dirty Arab village; except meat and dokhn, there was absolutely nothing to be got in the market. I suffered much from dysentery. There were no medicines to be had, so I had to trust to the recuperative powers of nature, assisted by a little rice which was grown in the marshes about Birket. I had not a civilized soul with whom to associate.

The Nubas of Jebel Dair did their utmost to harass El Obeid; they were always hovering about in the outskirts, ready to pounce down on any cattle and slaves they saw. It would have been madness to go an hour's distance from the town without an escort. The Dervishes frequently made attempts to clear the neighbourhood of these brigands, but I observed that they always returned considerably fewer in number, and I secretly rejoiced at their inability to cope with these brave Nubas. Taking everything into consideration, I was not sorry to say good-bye to this dreary and inhospitable town.

We were given four camels, whose owners acted as the drivers. It was agreed that on arrival in Omdurman we should pay them at the rate of seven dollars a camel.

On the 25th of March, 1886, we left El Obeid. What a flood of recollections welled up in my mind as we marched for the last time through the desolate ruins of the city! How strange had been the vicissitudes of this once flourishing place during the last few years! From a thriving and peaceful township it had been transformed into the theatre of constant warfare and bloodshed. It had then been the scene of the Mahdi's debaucheries, when he rested after his victories, and now it had dwindled down into a wretched Arab village.

Our road took us past the site of the El Obeid Mission-house, of which not a trace remained. In its place was the market, and a heap of white bones indicated the locality of the cook's shop. We halted that evening at Korbatsh; the next day we started very early; and after a two days' march, arrived at Bara. This beautiful little town is situated in a woody depression of the great Kordofan plain. In the distance we could see the white ruins through the high acacia trees. Formerly the place had been well planted with date-palms; but during the siege the inhabitants had cut them down, and lived upon the crushed core.

In the Government days Bara had been a sort of sanatorium for El Obeid, where the richer inhabitants used to spend the summer; they had made lovely gardens, full of date-trees, lemon-plants, banana-trees, and vines, while the vegetables used to be sold in El Obeid. The soil is exceptionally fertile, and there is an abundance of water obtainable at only six feet below the surface. But now the place was completely destroyed and neglected ; and wild bushes and thorns grew apace amidst the ruins.

As we approached Bara, we heard the thunder of guns, and were told that it was a salute announcing the arrival of Zogal, the Governor of Darfur, with his troops. It was the 2nd of April. We halted under a large acacia tree, and took down our angaribs, over which mats were tightly stretched. The arrival of two large parties, one from El Obeid and one from Darfur, soon changed this dismal graveyard into a noisy camp.

Zogal had brought with him 2,500 infantry, 4,000 black soldiers and singers, and 1,500 good horses. He had over 10,000 dollars in his beit el mal, besides what each of his men possessed—and that was no inconsiderable quantity : for everyone had enriched himself in Darfur ; and all this wealth was destined to become the Khalifa Abdullah's property. Zogal had organized bands in his army ; and the same tunes which had been played in the days of the Government, now resounded over the deserted plains of Bara. Zogal's camp was a scene of pleasure and merry-making. Marissa was publicly sold and drunk openly ; all idea of being within the Mahdi's jurisdiction seemed to have been forgotten. Zogal was a liberal man ; his principle was " live and let live ; " and he thoroughly enjoyed the good things of this life, which the Mahdi's revolt had placed within his reach. He was a powerfully built, stout man, of about sixty years of age, with a white beard, which gave him a patriarchal appearance. He was known as the father of many children, and was of an open-hearted and generous disposition.

Zogal's camp was pitched on the ruins of Bara ; rich carpets were spread over the sand, and there he sat, ready to see anybody and everybody at any time of the day ; abundance of food was always ready for all his guests. The only thing for which Zogal should be blamed was his shooting to death twenty-five Sanjaks and Turks, who had surrendered with Slatin, on the fall of Darfur. These Sanjaks had sworn to revolt against Mahdiism, but had been betrayed. With this exception, he had conducted his rule with great moderation; he did all he possibly could to further trade; and when in Bara I saw some French calico, which had come from Tunis, viâ Wadai, to Darfur. Zogal's Bazingers made a great impression on me; they were a wild and turbulent lot, capable of great marching power, and able to support long-continued privations.

Lupton Bey often used to tell me of the cannibal propensities of these black warriors. In many instances, their only dress consisted of the leather bandolier, or cartridge case, and a big leather bag, from which a human leg could often be seen protruding; and in almost every bag some human flesh or bones could be found. When I used to go to the market, crowds of these swarthy warriors would collect to gaze on my white skin, which, in truth, the sun had long since tanned to a very brown colour.

Zogal's nine days' halt in Bara soon came to an end. News came that disturbances had occurred in Omdurman between Khalifas Abdullah and Sherif; the latter had frequently written to Zogal to come to Khartum at once, as he was most anxious to have him there. News was brought at the same time that Abu Anga had arrived at El Obeid viâ Birket; it was rumoured that Abu Anga had been sent by Abdullah to arrest Zogal, for it was reported that Zogal and Sherif had agreed to combine and wrest the authority from Abdullah. Zogal was quite strong enough to overturn Abdullah; but unfortunately he was no soldier, and Abdullah had secretly won over a number of his emirs to his side.

Abu Anga pressed on from El Obeid, and, arriving at Bara, summoned Zogal to surrender. The latter, however, prepared to fight; but most of his Bazingers and emirs went over to Abu Anga's side, and he was soon left with but a few followers, and easily fell into Abu Anga's hands; he was at once put in chains and handed over to Said Bey Guma, who was at that time commander of the artillery. All his property was confiscated. Abu Anga did this in revenge, for Zogal had done exactly the same to Said Bey when he took possession of Darfur. Zogal was now dragged in chains to El Obeid, where he was left for a year to think over his changed state. His emin beit el mal, Ibrahim Ramadan, was also seized on his way to Omdurman, and brought back in chains to El Obeid, where he was mercilessly flogged to make him disclose the hiding-place of the money; but nothing would induce him to tell. He was subsequently taken to Omdurman, where Abdullah received him well and gave him a situation in the beit el mal.

Zogal's arrest was the signal for ill-treating all the Khalifa Sherif's adherents; these were deprived of all their positions, and were replaced by Abdullah's nominees. I had relied considerably on seeing a change for the better if this attempt of Sherif and Zogal to upset Abdullah had succeeded; but it had failed, and we again moved on towards Omdurman, still further depressed by the feeling that Abdullah was growing more and more powerful. By the time we arrived near Omdurman my camel had died; the poor Arab wept bitterly for his loss, and I could do nothing towards repaying him. On the evening of the 24th of April, 1886, we encamped close to the town. A fearful sandstorm was blowing, and we were enveloped in clouds of dust—a fitting advent to the capital of the Mahdi's empire!

CHAPTER XII.

OHRWALDER'S IMPRESSIONS OF OMDURMAN.

Ohrwalder's arrival in Omdurman—His first impressions of the Dervish capital—Khalifa Abdullah's intentions to conquer Egypt—Wad Suleiman of the beit el mal—Wad Adlan succeeds —Gordon's clothes, medals, &c.—Adlan reorganizes the beit el mal—The slave market, museum, mint, and system of coinage —Counterfeit coining—The lithograph press—The Khalifa's system of justice.

THE next morning—the 26th of April, 1886—we rose covered with dust from head to foot, and by the time we had got under way again, the sun was already high in the heavens, and was unusually hot. This was the worst season of the year. The first place we came to was the Mahdi's old camp, which was marked by a line of mud walls. From this position the fort of Omdurman had been besieged, and innumerable human and animal bones marked the site of this long-sustained conflict. To our right lay the White Nile, flowing between its green banks, beyond it the Blue Nile could just be seen, and the ruins of Khartum were visible behind the thick belt of palm-trees.

Emerging from the arid deserts of Kordofan, the Nile with its green banks was a most refreshing sight; on the other hand, the view of Khartum in ruins awakened the saddest recollections. Of the vast crowd which had beset Gordon on every side, some were scattered far and wide, while others had settled down around their new master in Omdurman. The little hill on the west bank just opposite to the junction of the two Niles was called Omdurman, hence the name of the Mahdiist capital. Previous to the revolt, there had been merely a few huts; but it was always considered a place of importance, as the hills in the vicinity supplied lime and stone in quantities for building works in Khartum. In those days, the lime-pits were in Omdurman, and the place where the Mahdiist capital now stands was a thick and thorny bush—the abode of the Batahin robbers.

What a change had now taken place! From the old fort at the south end, right up to Khor Shambat, and even further, the new capital extends, a countless conglomeration of straw huts (tokuls), surrounded by small zaribas; here and there a few mud huts, some of which, larger than the others, denote the residences of the Khalifas and principal emirs—they are looked upon as palaces.

Formerly the mosque consisted merely of a square enclosure, surrounded by a hedge; but this had now been replaced by a wall of sun-dried bricks. In the distance we could see the galvanised-iron mosque where the Mahdi used to perform prayers. The Mahdi's original camp had been situated some kilometres' distance to the north of the fort, where the plain widens out.

On our arrival we at once made inquiries about the market, and sought news of the other Europeans. The market was a sort of maze, and arranged with no idea of system. Merchants never left their goods there overnight; but always took them to their own houses. A Greek had made a bakery, and drove a good trade, as long as people had money to buy. There were such crowds of people that it was almost impossible to make one's way through; there were quantities of provisions for sale, and trade seemed very lively. Egyptian merchants brought their goods as far as Ed Damer, whence they were brought by Arab merchants to Omdurman. The only tax levied by the Khalifa's order was $2\frac{1}{2}$ per cent. zekka (*i.e.* alms for the poor), and people seemed generally contented and happy. There were quantities of money in the beit el mal, and at that time there was no occasion to oppress the inhabitants.

There were numbers of Greeks, Jews, and Syrians, all of whom were doing fairly well in business. I also saw Klootz. Slatin at that time happened to be absent, he was commanding some troops under the Emir Yunis at Wad el Abbas.

Khalifa Abdullah was full of ideas of conquest and pretensions; he used often to announce publicly that the end of the Turks' rule in Egypt was approaching. He was most anxious to obtain possession of that country, and thought the time had now come. Several of the sheikhs and ulemas in Cairo and in other parts of Egypt had written to him inviting him to take possession of the country where, they assured him, he would be most cordially received.

The Mahdi's summons and proclamations were sent in all directions. Pilgrims arrived from Samarkand, Bokhara, India, and Mecca, to examine Mahdieh with their own eyes. All this tended to make Abdullah more desirous than ever to conquer Egypt. He despatched Nejumi and his men to Dongola, whilst Yunis was instructed to collect all the men he could in the Gezireh. Sherif Mahmud's followers were also sent to Dongola; thus did Abdullah dispose of the adherents of those emirs whom he knew to be hostile to him. Zogal once arrested, Abdullah had now little to fear. Hitherto he had treated his two brother Khalifas, and the Ashraf and Danagla with the utmost respect; but now he conducted himself in a very different manner, and could not bear to have anyone in the smallest degree associated with him who was of almost equal rank; he therefore did all in his power to weaken the opposition party, and to increase the influence of his own party. The first blow he struck fell on Ahmed Wad Suleiman, emin of the beit el mal. The day that we arrived in Omdurman he was put in chains, and his house and the beit el mal were put under guards. Wad Suleiman had been one of the Mahdi's most fanatical adherents, and whenever he passed the Mahdi's tomb he used to stretch out his hands and weep like a child—indeed he had every reason to do so, for the Mahdi had raised him from a low position to a post of great honour, and the thought of losing this position distressed him greatly.

Suleiman's wheel of fortune had come round at a good time, when the amount of money in the beit el mal was considerable. The immense quantities of loot taken at El Obeid, Shikan, Khartum, Sennar, and Berber, had all passed through his hands, and any Dervish who was in need of anything always came to him, and in this way he acquired great influence. Since the Mahdi's death there had been great enmity between Suleiman and Abdullah, and on the pretext of examining the accounts, Abdullah had him arrested, and intended to send him away, while he appointed Mohammed Osman (Zogal's son) in his place.

In Suleiman's house some 5,000 grammes of unstamped gold was found, and it is more than probable that this was but a small portion of what he had previously appropriated. He was therefore thrown into chains, where he remained for a year and more. A month after his arrest, a certain Ibrahim Wad Adlan, of Wad Medina, on the Blue Nile, and sometime merchant in El Obeid, was appointed emin beit el mal. He had frequently been in Cairo, was a pleasant-looking man, and had enlightened ideas. At one time, when a dispute arose between the commercial house of Arbib in Cairo, and their two partners in El Obeid, Adlan had been nominated arbitrator by the Cairo house. He had for long remained loyal to the Government, and had stayed in El Obeid until it fell into the hands of the Mahdi, who permitted him—as a special favour—to keep 2,000 of the 30,000 dollars he then had.

For a long time Adlan had nothing to do; but he was always an influential man, and was continually trying to help those in distress. After the fall of El Obeid, and when all the clerks had been exiled to various parts, he never ceased until he obtained permission for their return. A short time before the Mahdi had quitted El Obeid, he had been employed in the beit el mal, and at Rahad, Wad Suleiman had appointed him his assistant. He was then despatched by the Mahdi to Berber, to secure the £60,000 which had been sent to Gordon from Cairo, and which had been left in the

Berber treasury, owing to the interruption of communications with Khartum. Ibrahim brought the money, clothes, medals, decorations, and other valuables belonging to Gordon to the Mahdi. The clothes were sold, and cut to pieces to repair other garments, the metal of the medals, &c., was melted down, whilst the precious stones were sold, and eventually found their way to Cairo.

Adlan soon gained considerable influence over the Khalifa, and had sufficient tact to moderate the inborn tyranny of his master. His desire to continually give assistance when he could, had made him very popular. He soon set to work to reorganize the beit el mal, and began by removing it from its original position to the river bank, thus avoiding the unnecessary transport of articles brought by boats to the stores.

Here he built an extensive yard of sun-dried bricks, which he divided off into sections for the various departments of the administration. He made a large cornstore, in which a mountain of dhurra was collected—indeed, so high was it, that it could be seen from a considerable distance. This store was placed in charge of his assistant. Another yard was built containing a number of rooms, in which the slaves were kept under a guard of soldiers. Here the slaves were shackled, twenty or thirty together in one long chain, with iron rings round their necks. Any obstreperous slaves were generally shackled with one or two makias or iron rings round their ankles, joined together by a small chain or iron bar, which made walking very difficult.

Slaves received a little dry dhurra from the beit el mal as food until they were sold. The female slaves generally grind the dhurra, and make a sort of polenta out of it, which is either eaten with water or boiled and eaten as balila. The dhurra ration of a slave is generally so small and so bad that numbers of them die of starvation long before they are fortunate enough to be sold.

Slaves are sold by auction in the beit el mal, and a written certificate is given to the purchaser, stating in detail the description of the slave, whether male or female, and that the purchase was effected in the beit el mal. Before an auction the slaves are generally well rubbed with oil, to improve their appearance. The bulk of the slaves sold are females, as male slaves are generally attached to the army. A special woman is also employed, together with the other officials, to see

A SLAVE WOMAN FROM EQUATORIA.

to the female slaves. Adlan also railed off a part of the beit el mal for the reception of cattle—camels, sheep, goats, donkeys, &c.; these are also sold by auction.

The Mint forms a distinct sub-department. When the Mahdi was alive, gold and silver coins were struck by his order, not so much to supply the demand, but rather to prove his independence of Egypt and the establishment of his new kingdom. He ordered guineas to be coined, just like the Egyptian pounds; they were made out of the gold ornaments captured in Khartum. Dollars were coined, and made similar to the Turkish Medjidie dollar. A certain Hajji Abdullah Granteli, of Bokhara, formerly jeweller in Khartum, and Elias el Kurdi, watchmaker, were made chief coiners. In 1889 the latter lost his hand and foot for issuing counterfeit money. Almost all coins bearing the stamp, " By order of the Mahdi," have disappeared.

When I arrived in Omdurman there was a great scarcity of small coins, and in consequence pieces of damur (a twilled cotton fabric manufactured in the Sudan), valued at ten, five, and two and a half piastres, were made currency; but these rags soon became so dirty, from being passed from hand to hand, and so covered with oil and grease, that people refused to accept them. Khalifa Abdullah, when he heard of this, threatened those who refused with confiscation of property and imprisonment, and employed spies in various parts of the market to report the names of those who objected; but the spies were bribed to keep silence, and Abdullah was obliged to give in. Merchants had recourse to every sort of deception to evade his orders, so the dirty rags were withdrawn from currency.

Adlan had organized the Mint rather with the object of making a profit than of supplying a want. Silver was cheap, and he was able to make 50 per cent. profit on the manufacture of dollars. At that time gold coinage was no longer current. On one side of the dollars was stamped the Mohammedan date, with the words, " Struck in Omdurman," while on the reverse was the Sultan's Toghra, underneath which was written the word, " Makbul" (accepted); hence the dollar became known as the " Makbul dollar." Pieces of five and ten piastres value were also coined, as well as a few single piastre pieces, on one side of which was stamped the Toghra, and on the other the word " Omdurman." The Mahdi on his coins had written, within the Toghra, the words, "By order of the Mahdi," but Khalifa Abdullah did not follow his example.

Besides these coins, English sovereigns were also current in Omdurman, and were known as "khayala" (cavalry) pounds, on account of the St. George and the dragon being engraved on them. Egyptian pounds were also current, but now all gold coins have become rare.

The principal currency is the Medjidie dollar, and these have been in such constant use that they are much obliterated. The Maria Theresa dollar (also known as the "Abu Nokta") is current as well, but chiefly with Sawakin, Massawa, and Abyssinian traders, and notably with the last. The French 5-franc-piece and the Spanish dollar (known as Abu Madfa) are current in a very minor degree. Egyptian piastres and half-piastres, introduced by the Hicks Expedition, are occasionally seen. The Austrian quarter-gulden piece (fiorini) is considered to be worth 2 piastres. In addition to all these silver pieces, copper coins of all descriptions are current.

The Khalifa Abdullah had no small trouble in circulating the Makbul dollar; the merchants refused to value them at 20 piastres, and, in spite of most stringent orders, and continued threats of confiscation of property, imprisonment, &c., the order was somehow continually evaded.

Merchants set high prices on their goods, and would never accept until the buyer had shown all the different sorts of dollars he possessed; he was thus obliged to do this or to buy at exorbitant rates. Complaints became rife, and eventually they reached Abdullah's ears. He got very angry, and one day in October 1887, he sent troops to the market with instructions to bring all the goods in the market to the beit el mal. It was useless to resist; the owners were obliged to look after their own goods, which were piled up near the big gate of the beit el mal, in the open, and under a burning sun. Abdullah was now raging, and publicly made the following curious statement :—

"That unbeliever Gordon induced merchants to accept miserable bits of paper as equivalents for money, and now I offer you silver and you won't even take it."

For fourteen days these wretched people sat by the gate, trembling for their property. All sorts of rumours were flying about. Some said that the Khalifa intended to throw all the goods into the river; others said that he was going to burn them, and perhaps the most likely notion of all was that he intended to confiscate the lot and transfer it to the beit el mal. By this time the merchants were thoroughly alarmed, and begged some of their influential friends to mediate with the Khalifa. At length the latter summoned the principal merchants, and asked them if they would accept the Makbul dollar at the value of the old dollar, whereupon they not only accepted gladly, but declared their readiness to accept any sort of money he chose to issue, even should it be made of leather.

Thus was a reconciliation effected. The Khalifa treated the merchants well, gave them plenty of food, and condescended even to eat with them on this festive occasion. After this episode there were no more difficulties about making the Makbul dollar current in Omdurman, though to this day the Arabs refuse to accept it.

But gradually silver became dear, and the Mint began coining bad dollars, made of two parts silver to three parts copper; consequently the value of the old dollar has now gone up to 25 piastres. This gave further opportunities to the counterfeit coiners. The silver-workers in the Mint began making dollars on their own account, and, those being different from the others, caused great confusion. These false dollars were very well coined, and it required a practised eye to notice the deception; indeed, it was not until a very large quantity of these false coins had got into circulation that the fraud was found out.

An inspector was now sent to examine all dollars; all false coins were broken into pieces, and no compensation given to the owners. Thieves and smugglers purchased the bad dollars at 10 piastres apiece, and then, of course, every description of bribery and corruption was practised. For instance, an Arab would agree to sell his camel for 150 dollars, on condition that the money should be submitted to the examining commission. The president, who was of course bribed, gave out as his decision that the dollars were all good, and received a good round sum from the purchaser for his falsehood; thus it happened that the Arab was generally defrauded of 40 or 50 dollars. In spite of several false coiners being punished with the loss of a hand and foot, still the evil practice continued, and it is only within the last few years, since the price of silver has increased so much, that false coining has, to a great extent, ceased.

A printing and lithograph press was also established in the beit el mal; it had originally been set up in Khartum, and was now used for pulling off numbers of Mahdi proclamations. Several "Ratibs," or Mahdi's book of prayers, were also printed and distributed.

A museum of curios also formed part of the beit el mal. It is known as the Beit el Antikat, and contains numbers of interesting things, such as trophies from Darfur, Abyssinia, and Egypt. The Abyssinian section is the largest, and includes King John's throne. Amongst the Darfur articles are the robes of Sultan Yusef and of the Sultan of Masalit. The robe of one of the Ababdeh sheikhs, who was made a Bey by the Government, and then came to Omdurman and submitted to the Mahdi, represents Egypt.

The beit el mal also contains a dispensary, in charge of an Egyptian doctor; here are numbers of shelves, laden with medicines, which have long since gone bad, but the doctor has taken entirely to native remedies, of which cauterization and burning are the most usual.

Amongst the Khartum survivors was a certain Greek soap-boiler, who had established a soap manufactory in the beit el mal, and had handed over to it his large supplies of soda; but gradually other private individuals began to establish soap works, and soon they began to sell soap so cheaply that all the beit el mal customers came to them. The consequence was that the Khalifa at once issued an order that the beit el mal held the soap-boiling monopoly, and anyone who infringed this rule would lose one hand, and all his property would be confiscated.

A careful system of accounts was elaborated in the beit el mal showing all revenue and expenditure. If an expedition is ordered to any part of the country, money, clothing, and other necessaries must be supplied from the beit el mal. The staff to work this large administration consists of an emin beit el mal, his assistant, head clerk, and a host of smaller officials and clerks. When the merchants refused to accept the Makbul dollar the staff was increased, as at that time the whole of the boats and canoes were also confiscated. Of these there were upwards of 1,000, and they were eventually hired out by the beit el mal. Wad Adlan always tried to secure for the beit el mal the services of those clerks who had formerly served under the Government; but this plan did not please the Khalifa. Adlan naturally preferred the old clerks, who thoroughly understood their work; besides, they were terrified of the Dervishes, and thus did not dare to cheat. On the whole, Adlan's administration was very good, and he received the Khalifa's thanks.

Abdullah now turned his attention to reorganizing the system of justice. Hitherto, and during the Mahdi's lifetime, the office of Kadi had continued, but the Ashraf (Mahdi's relations) also acted in the capacity of judges, and the result was the greatest possible confusion. For instance, supposing a man was sentenced by the judge, Sayid Abdel Kader (the Sheikh el Islam) would immediately pardon him. Abdullah, not unnaturally, wanted to change this anomaly, not so much in the interests of justice as to break down the power and authority of the Ashraf. He therefore nominated Kadi Ahmed as the Kadi el Islam, and appointed a number of assistant judges, whom he called Nuab.

It was ruled that everyone, old and young, should

report all causes of dispute to the Grand Kadi, and it was his duty to look into it and give a decision. Kadi Ahmed is a particularly good man, and gives protection to the white people, more especially when they are attacked and abused by the native populace. He is, however, of rather a vacillating, timorous disposition, and is therefore a pliable instrument in the Khalifa's hands; consequently there is often a miscarriage of justice.

Thus did the Khalifa secure, in his own person, the right to pardon or to convict, and thus he became absolute master of life and death. As for the law, he only appealed to it when it suited his own convenience; on every other occasion he absolutely ignored it.

CHAPTER XIII.

THE KHALIFA DECIDES TO CONQUER ABYSSINIA.

Events subsequent to the fall of Khartum—Capture of Gedaref and Galabat—Dervishes defeated by Abyssinians at Galabat—Abu Anga's victorious expedition to Tagalla—His triumphant return to Omdurman—The Khalifa's grand review—Destruction of the Gehena tribe—The Khalifa decides to send Abu Anga's army to conquer Abyssinia—The battle of Dabra Sin—Abu Anga sacks Gondar—The victorious Dervishes return to Galabat—Rejoicings at Omdurman.

THE preceding pages have given a glimpse of Omdurman, the new Dervish capital of the Sudan ; let us now turn briefly to the military events which had occurred since the fall of Khartum.

Whilst Khartum was besieged on all sides, so also were the various other garrisons still holding out, closely beset. Gedaref, also known as Suk Abu Sin, the name of the patriarchal sheikh of the Shukrieh tribe, was situated in the midst of a fertile plain which produced such quantities of corn that it was the common saying, three camel-loads could be sold for half a dollar. The ground was so productive that anything could be grown. There was no want of water. The Greeks and several Egyptians had made gardens, in which there was found every description of fruit-tree ; grapes grew in abundance, and were of particularly good quality ; they were to be had all the year round ; for it was of no consequence in what month the vines were pruned. Quantities of sesame were also grown as well as a special kind of dhurra, with a sweet stalk, from which a substance something like honey was extracted. Water-melons, cotton, tobacco, and all sorts of vegetables were grown in the greatest profusion, and everything was of exceptionally good quality.

The garrison of Gedaref consisted of only two hundred men, and on being summoned by the Jaalin to surrender, they did so, in April 1884. This is hardly to be wondered at, for the inhabitants of Gedaref are, for the most part, Jaalin, and resistance would, under such circumstances, have been next to impossible. The principal merchants were permitted to keep their goods, and the change of hands did not, for the moment, greatly alter the situation; but we shall see, later, what became of this rich and valuable province after a prolonged Dervish occupation.

As regards Galabat, the difficulties were considerably greater. This town was situated about six days' journey from Gedaref, and was the residence of the well-known Takruri, Saleh Bey Shanga, who was Mamur of the district. This brave official remained loyal to the Government throughout, and was bitterly opposed to Mahdiism. He succeeded in gaining the friendship of the neighbouring Abyssinian tribes, and, through their assistance, inflicted great losses on the Dervishes. In November 1884, he severely defeated the besieging Jaalin; but a few days later, the Dervishes, being heavily reinforced, beset him very closely.

Through the intermediary of the English, King John sent a relieving force of Abyssinians, which reached the vicinity of Galabat on the 27th of January, 1885; and making known their approach to Saleh, the latter made a sortie, while at the same time the Dervishes were heavily attacked by the Abyssinians, who drove them off, thus enabling the entire garrison, men, women, and children, to escape; they marched *viâ* Gondar to Massawa, under the protection of an Abyssinian force. Galabat was subsequently occupied by the Dervishes, who collected here in great force under the Emir Wad Arbab.

Meanwhile, Saleh Bey, who was now staying with Ras Adal, the chief of Amhara, was not idle, and was continually urging him to take possession of Galabat;

he was shortly afterwards joined by the Fiki Medawi, formerly a wild, fanatical adherent of the Mahdi, and who, together with Abu Girgeh, had been one of the first to lay siege to Gordon in Khartum; this man, after the Mahdi's death, began to find out that he had been following an imposture, and fled from Omdurman; he stayed in Abyssinia for a time, and eventually reached Cairo. Abdullah was furious at his flight, and put a number of his friends in chains, believing that Fiki Medawi had been instrumental in pushing on Ras Adal to attack Galabat.

Shortly after the festival of the "Three holy kings," in commemoration of the baptism of our Saviour in Jordan, known as "Ghittas," which means immersion (on this occasion—the 5th of January—a cross is always immersed in the river); Ras Adal, having collected a large army, amounting, it is said, to 100,000 men, of whom 20,000 were horsemen, advanced across the mountains and descended on Galabat.

Sheikh Egeil, of the Hamran Arabs, who had always been loyal to the Egyptian Government, and had combated Mahdiism continuously, also joined Ras Adal, and entered Dervish territory. Wad Arbab, who had received full information of the Abyssinian movements, was awaiting their attack, strongly entrenched within Galabat. He had 16,000 well-seasoned troops, mostly Jaalin, and a quantity of rifles and ammunition. In a few minutes the Abyssinian cavalry, dashing down with wild impetuosity, completely surrounded Wad Arbab; the fight did not last long; the Dervishes were driven out, pursued in all directions, and Galabat was soon in flames. Arbab's men could not face the wild rush of the Abyssinians, and fell in great numbers; the high wind caused the flames to spread with terrible rapidity, and soon the powder magazine blew up with a terrific report, burying hundreds in its ruins; amongst these was a Greek who had come from Sawakin the year before to Omdurman, where he was imprisoned for a time, then released, and came to Galabat, hoping to escape into Abyssinia, just a few days before this fight which took place in January 1887. The Abyssinians captured a large number of women and children, whom they dragged off as slaves.

A few months prior to this action, Gustav Klootz had died in Galabat. He had left Omdurman in September 1886, for Galabat, intending to escape into Abyssinia; but having no money, he was forced to walk the entire distance, and the great fatigue he had undergone made him seriously ill; he lingered on for a time, but eventually died; and perhaps it was fortunate that he did die, for only a few days afterwards an order arrived from the Khalifa Abdullah at Gedaref, ordering him to be thrown into chains and brought back to Omdurman, where a miserable death awaited him.

Whilst the Abyssinians were attacking Galabat, Sheikh Egeil fell upon Doka, a place situated between Galabat and Gedaref, which he succeeded in capturing, and putting its inhabitants to the sword. The Abyssinians now returned to their own country, after having sacked and pillaged Galabat, which they left absolutely empty.

The disaster at Galabat was a great blow to the Dervishes; Abdullah now appointed his nephew Yunis as emir of the district, and ordered him to reoccupy the town. Yunis, on his return from Wad el Abbas, had encamped south of Omdurman Fort, at a place which is still known as Dem Yunis; his force consisted of about 1,000 men, armed with Remingtons, and 2,000 sword- and spearmen, of whom the majority had been amongst the Mahdi's original followers at Abba. Abdullah himself now crossed over to Khojali, and led Yunis's troops for some distance.

The equipment and transport of the force were not expensive items; each man received about half a dollar; and perhaps that was sufficient, for the troops always plundered the villages for their food as they went along. Yunis marched direct to Abu Haraz, on the Blue Nile, and thence followed the Khor Rahad up to Galabat, which he found quite empty and deserted. He now settled down, and, to his credit, he occasionally made raids into Abyssinia, destroyed a few villages and churches, and sent the ornaments he took to Omdurman. This so delighted the Khalifa that he dubbed him " Mismar ed Din " (or the " Nail of Religion "), and had special poems about his deeds sung in his presence.

But soon Yunis abandoned hostilities, and guaranteed free passes to merchants travelling in the country; the Abyssinians believed in these assurances of peace, and descended into the Galabat plain at various times in the year, bringing with them for sale thousands of mules, donkeys, and horses, also quantities of coffee, garlic, lentils, beans, wax, and honey. Things went on quite peaceably for some time; but one day Yunis suddenly fell on all the merchants collected within their zariba, killed numbers of them, seized their goods, and sent off about 1,000 of them as prisoners to Omdurman. Several died of starvation on the journey, and on their arrival in Omdurman the remainder were released, but had to go about the markets begging their bread. It frequently happened that they would take shelter for the night in the merchants' empty stalls; and on the latter arriving with their goods in the morning, they would find their shops full of dead and dying Abyssinians; afterwards, slaves were left by the merchants to guard the shops and prevent these miserable creatures from making use of them. These wretched, gaunt, half-starved people used sometimes to come to us to beg for food; they knew no Arabic, but knowing that we were Christians, they would repeat that word, or sometimes "Wad Maryam" ("Mary's child") to excite our pity. Their wretched condition at length reached the Khalifa's ears, and he ordered the beit el mal to take charge of them; the emin beit el mal now sent a crier to the market to warn all Abyssinians that if they came to the beit el mal they would receive assistance. The poor starving creatures dragged themselves there, but were still kept two or three days without food; numbers of them died, and their bodies were thrown into the river, whilst the remainder were at last given a miserable pittance of dhurra, which served to keep body and soul together for a time; but these, too, at length succumbed to starvation; and after that, I never saw an Abyssinian prisoner again.

In July 1887, Khalifa Abdullah wrote a letter to King John, offering to make peace, on condition that he would become a Moslem, and that he would return all the women and children he had captured, but more especially was he to surrender the persons of Saleh Bey, Fiki Medawi, and the Sheikh el Egeil. If he refused to accept these terms he must expect war. King John did not deign to reply.

During the feast of Bairam on the 31st of July, 1887, Khalifa Abdullah summoned Abu Anga to Omdurman, and here I must give a short description of this renowned warrior.

Hamdan Abu Anga had been a slave, and had been brought up in the Khalifa Abdullah's household; he had been well treated by his master, and was eventually looked upon as a member of the family, a custom which was formerly in vogue amongst the Baggara, Rizighat, and Taisha tribes. In fact, these Arabs used not infrequently to give their daughters in marriage to their slaves. It was amongst the Baggara that Abu Anga had first learnt to ride on horseback and to go out hunting, and it was from them that he had acquired such dexterity in handling and throwing spears, for which he had frequent opportunities in the continual raids which took place on neighbouring tribes.

Abu Anga had taken part in the campaigns against Zubeir Pasha, by whom he and his entire family had been captured, but subsequently released. When the Mahdi declared himself he joined with his master, Abdullah. During the siege of El Obeid little was known or heard of him, but after the fall of that city Khalifa Abdullah handed over to him the charge of all captive soldiers in El Obeid, as well as in other places. The astute Khalifa had for long had his eye on these blacks, whose fighting powers he well knew, and he was most desirous to bring them under his direct control, and utilize them.

Previous to the Hicks Expedition Abu Anga had already secured a number of them, and they were largely instrumental in compassing the complete downfall of that ill-fated army. Then, again, his blacks had shown the greatest bravery in their campaigns against Jebel Dair, when they had acquired a great name for themselves, and, finally, it was through their means that Gordon's Fort of Omdurman had been compelled to surrender. After the fall of Khartum these brave but undisciplined troops, having no more fighting to do, took to highway robbery. Numbers of them hovered about in the desert a few hours' distance from Omdurman, and amused themselves by falling on caravans coming from Kordofan or Berber, and pillaging and killing to their heart's content. Their depredations became so constant that the Mahdi decided that he must employ them somewhere, so he ordered Abu Anga to proceed with them to the still independent Dar Nuba country, which he was to conquer, and obtain from thence recruits for his Jehadieh, or Black Army.

But there was also another reason which induced the Mahdi to undertake this campaign. During the siege of Omdurman a certain Baggara Sheikh, of Birket, named Noaïa, deserted, and gathering a number of malcontents in Dar Nuba, he defied the Mahdi's authority. When I was at El Obeid there were all sorts of strange stories current about the doings of Noaïa, who had gathered numbers of horsemen from the Howazma and Miserieh tribes, and had made himself decidedly formidable. All those disappointed slave-hunters and slave-dealers who—annoyed with the suppression of their trade by the Egyptian Government—had flocked in numbers to the Mahdi's standard, now had begun to find out that they were rather worse off than before, and were, in reality, little better than the Mahdi's slaves. These people sought every occasion to desert to Noaïa. Abu Anga therefore received orders to hunt him down and annihilate him. He collected his men, quitted the now debauched and pleasure-loving Omdurman, and proceeded to the Tagalla Mountain, at the foot of which he encamped.

After the death of King Adam, his followers had again thrown off the Dervish yoke and were now in open revolt; against these Abu Anga conducted several successful expeditions, and captured numbers of slaves, but suffered some loss as well. As long as Abu Anga was in the neighbourhood, Tagalla was more or less in a state of submission; but the moment he moved off they again broke out into active opposition.

Abu Anga now advanced on Noaïa, whose adherents, alarmed by the presence of the soldiers, dispersed. These blacks are greatly feared in the Sudan, not only on account of their great bravery in battle, but also it is well known that they are merciless to their conquered enemies.

Sheikh Noaïa was eventually secured and thrown into chains, and a few days later he died of small-pox. Abu Anga attacked almost all the Nuba mountains; at times he was successful, at other times he suffered reverses. Tolodi, Gedir, and lastly Naïma, were scenes of bloody combats, and at the last-named place Abu Anga, in spite of his artillery—which was commanded by Said Bey Guma—was heavily defeated and driven back.

One of Abu Anga's most capable assistants was Abdullah Wad Ibrahim, who, on account of his unparalleled cruelties, made Abu Anga's name a terror throughout the land. Abu Anga was now recalled from his campaign by Khalifa Abdullah to take possession of Zogal and his army, who was then on his way from Darfur to Bara. We have seen how rapidly and skilfully he carried out this order.

Now all that was left for Abu Anga to do was to punish the mutinous troops of El Obeid who had killed Sherif Mahmud. Wad Ibrahim was sent on this duty, and after a severe fight, in which numbers were killed on both sides, he succeeded in capturing several of the mutineers, whom he attached to his troops; but some of them escaped to the Nubas, and Wad Ibrahim proceeded in consequence to Golfan-

Naïma, which he besieged, took, and reduced the inhabitants to slavery; the heads of Bishir and three other leaders were sent to Omdurman, where they were exposed for a month on the gallows as a warning to all mutinous-minded persons.

By all these various actions Abu Anga had succeeded in adding considerably to the numbers of his troops, and he moreover drilled them constantly and instilled a spirit of discipline which had been hitherto unknown—thus he raised up a power which it was almost impossible to defeat. Khalifa Abdullah now sent instructions to Abu Anga to return to Omdurman in time for the Bairam festival, and at the same time he sent orders to all the inhabitants of the Gezireh and Nile Valley to collect at Omdurman for a great review. Abu Anga, as usual, complied with the order with alacrity, and making forced marches, *viâ* Tayara, Shatt, and Om Sadik, he reached Omdurman in a very short time. Abdullah sent numbers of emirs to meet and welcome him.

In Omdurman the only topic of conversation was about Abu Anga and his great army. The Khalifa himself also prepared a magnificent reception for his faithful general, in which he strove to do him all possible honour. On the night preceding the great festival, criers were sent through Omdurman announcing that any one who failed to present himself at the great review the following morning would be seriously dealt with; this order was willingly complied with, and at the foot of the hills near Kerreri were assembled enormous crowds, who waited—as the malcontents said—on the pleasure of that "slave," Abu Anga. The guns had all been drawn out in line the evening before, and the festival was ushered in by prolonged salutes.

In the meantime Abu Anga had arrived at Om Sadik, where a careful inspection was made to see that no one was in possession of unlawful booty; numbers of female slaves were found, who were subsequently sent to the beit el mal. He then moved on to his camp near Omdurman, and prepared to make his formal entry the following morning.

By the time the sun had well risen, the Dervishes were assembled in endless lines under their various flags. Khalifa Abdullah left his residence accompanied by his bodyguard; he was mounted on a magnificent camel, and advanced to the sound of the great onbeïa trumpet. Abu Anga, mounted on a pony and clad in a casque and coat-of-mail, now advanced to meet him, and his magnificent figure created no small impression on the assembled multitudes. His bodyguard, consisting of his very best soldiers, accompanied him, as well as a number of mukuddums. On approaching the Khalifa he adroitly dismounted and kissed his hands; he was warmly greeted, and ordered to mount again.

Then the march past began. Upwards of 31,000 black troops, armed with Remingtons and formed up in long lines, went by to the sound of drums and trumpets; but the latter, on which the players attempted to produce some specially Dervish music, raised the most discordant sounds, which gave an intensely comic aspect to the whole proceeding. Each emir, with his flag, rode at the head of his division; the chief emirs were Ibrahim Wad Abdullah, Nur Angara, Zeki Tummal, and Ibrahim Wad Abu Tagalla. When the Jehadieh had passed, the sword- and spearmen followed, some 20,000 in number; then came the inhabitants of Omdurman in countless numbers. There could not have been less than 60,000.

After the march past all were formed up again, and then the Khalifa, dismounting from his camel, stood on his sheepskin and conducted prayers. The shout of "Allahu Akbar" from over 100,000 throats was impressive in the extreme, and, as the sound rolled down the immense lines, it was echoed again and again through the hills, lasting for over a minute after each shout.

On the conclusion of prayers the guns pealed forth salutes, and such wild fanaticism and enthusiasm prevailed that several men dashed up to the very muzzles of the guns and were blown to pieces. Of course the Khalifa announced that the souls of these stupid people had gone straight to paradise. The salutes over, the lines were once more inspected, and then all the flags were collected in one place, in the centre of which stood the Khalifa ; this was the signal for the whole force to gather around and vie with one another in their shouts of loyalty that they would die a hundred times over for him and his cause. Khalifa Abdullah became so wildly impressed by the enthusiasm of these savage hordes that he could scarcely contain himself, and it was as much as his bodyguard could do to keep the impetuous crowds from crushing him to death. Numbers were bruised and kicked by the horses; but they were left quite unnoticed—a mere remark, "Umru Khalas" ("It is the end of his life"), was all the sympathy these heartless men ever offered.

From that day to this I do not think the Khalifa has ever had such an ovation. At that time Omdurman was unusually full, trade was brisk, and it was thought that he would now undertake the invasion of Egypt. But, as it soon transpired, he had still a good deal of work to do in the Sudan itself. One enemy he undoubtedly had—this was El Merhdi Abu Rof, a descendant of the ancient Kings of Sennar and sheikh of the great Gehena tribe, which, amongst the mass of Arabs allied to the Mahdi, had persistently held aloof. This tribe possessed a large number of camels of a curious dark-coloured breed, and also quantities of gray-coloured cows.

El Merhdi had instigated a purely local movement of his own against the Government, and had once besieged and set fire to Sennar ; long before Abu Anga's arrival he had shown hostility to the Khalifa, and had annihilated a number of small Dervish garrisons; his power extended as far as Karkoj, and he levied taxes on all boats going north. For a long time the Khalifa had let him alone, but now finding himself in possession of

DESTRUCTION OF THE GEHENA TRIBE.

such an enormous force, he decided to attack El Merhdi, more especially as at this time his audacity considerably endangered the navigation of the Blue Nile, from whence Omdurman drew its main supplies of corn. He therefore despatched Ismail Wad el Andok up the Blue Nile, while Abdullah Wad Ibrahim was sent up the White Nile.

El Merhdi, attacked thus on both sides, was powerless ; he was unable to withstand the advance of the victorious black troops, and he and almost all his Arabs were killed. El Merhdi's head was sent to Omdurman, where it was exposed for a long time on the gallows, and was at last thrown into the pit in which lay the heads of Bishir and those who had been slain with him.

Thus one by one did the Khalifa's enemies become subdued. The vengeance wreaked on the unfortunate Gehena tribe by the Dervishes is almost beyond description. The property of the survivors was seized, men, women, and children were dragged off to Omdurman, and there, naked and helpless, they were left to starve on the river bank. One would see wretched mothers of three or four children, who looked just like skeletons, miserably abandoned in a place utterly unknown, and subject to the insults and indignities of the proud and cruel Dervishes. Numbers of them, especially children, died of starvation, whilst those who still had sufficient strength would wander about begging their bread ; if any one had money enough he would buy a waterskin, and would go half a mile to the river, fill it, carry it back and sell it in the market for a quarter of a piastre ; thus they eked out a miserable existence. Men who but lately had ridden on good horses and had owned hundreds of camels were reduced to this mode of gaining their livelihood, whilst poor women could be seen, with babies at their breasts, toiling under the heavy weight of a filled waterskin towards the marketplace ; then they had no rest, for in the evening they had to grind the dhurra and make a sort of pap which the poor little mouths of their infants could hardly masticate ; they had but one meal in the twenty-four hours.

It was impossible not to be struck by the mother's love of these poor people for their offspring, and at the same time to feel bitterly incensed against the Khalifa and his cruel followers who could thus intentionally inflict on people of their own race such untold cruelties. Thousands of Gehena camels were brought to Omdurman and sold at low prices; thus was the wealth of their country utterly destroyed, and now the terrible famine, which was so soon to fall upon the land, was close at hand.

In the meantime Abdullah was considering with his advisers the desirability of permitting war to break out with Abyssinia. The great power of which he now felt himself possessed inclined him to war, and of course the majority of his emirs, whose sole desire was to pander to his will, agreed with him. Then news reached Yunis that Ras Adal was making gigantic preparations; this finally decided Abdullah to wage war, and with this object in view, he despatched his faithful Abu Anga to conduct the operations.

The three Khalifas, Abu Anga's brother Abdel Maula, who commanded the Jehadieh in Omdurman, and several other important people embarked on the steamer and proceeded to the east bank, where Abdullah himself led off the troops. For some days before, every boat had been requisitioned for transport, and these were now laden with provisions for the army; but what with overloading and the strength of the current, several foundered and numbers of persons were drowned; however, this was of little consequence, for human life is of small value among the Dervishes.

The troops advanced in divisions along the banks of the Nile, and before finally taking leave of them the Khalifa addressed Abu Anga and his emirs, urging them to be ever united, and to keep always before them the rewards which would be theirs on their return, promising them the divine help of the Mahdi and a certainty of victory.

This speech was delivered in such an impressive manner that there were few dry eyes amongst these

THE BATTLE OF DABRA SIN.

hardy warriors, and the Khalifa himself was by no means ignorant of the gravity of the step he had now taken, for Abyssinia was looked upon as even a more powerful country than Egypt. Abu Anga followed his troops in a steamer as far as Abu Haraz, near which the Khor Rahad joins the Nile, and which during the winter is quite full and navigable almost up to Galabat.

Some time before, Abdullah Wad Ibrahim and Ismail Wad el Andok had been sent to collect people in the Gezireh; they now joined Abu Anga, whose entire force numbered 81,000 men. After a short halt at Galabat, Abu Anga advanced into Abyssinian territory, leaving Wad Ali in Galabat. Making forced marches, the troops made their way over hills and across valleys, through the most rugged country. Numbers died of exhaustion, but still they continued to move on; they met with no opposition, the villages through which they passed were deserted, and wherever they went they found provisions in abundance. This magnificent country was a source of intense astonishment to the Dervishes.

Meanwhile Ras Adal had collected his forces in the great plain of Dabra Sin, some six days' journey from Galabat, and here he patiently awaited Abu Anga's advance. As the Dervishes approached, numbers of the Gezireh troops who could not keep up with the force lagged behind, and were invariably killed or mutilated by the Abyssinians.

Abu Anga, on arrival on the plain, formed up in battle-array, and putting himself in the centre of a square composed of his best troops, he advanced on the Abyssinian camp, which was much extended, and stretched as far as the eye could reach.

The Abyssinians now attacked in wild disorder; they fought with the courage of lions, for their religion and fatherland, against the hated Moslems who had dared to enter their country. The horsemen especially fought with the most reckless bravery; but Abu Anga's blacks here as elsewhere showed their sterling fighting qualities; they mowed down the masses of Abyssinians in thousands with their well-aimed fire, whilst the latter were vainly endeavouring to break through their solid ranks; and soon Abu Anga's victory was assured. He had conquered through his good discipline, the arrangement of his troops, and the galling fire of the Remingtons, and now the rest of the fight was merely a massacre, which was continued until the troops were quite tired out. Most of Ras Adal's principal chiefs had fallen, and amongst the captives was one of his sons, who was well cared for and sent to Galabat.

The entire camp, with its countless tents, donkeys, and mules, fell into the hands of the Mahdiists. The captured animals were in such quantities that the victors could not possibly carry them off, and in consequence they either hamstrung them or cut their throats. Amongst the other things captured were two guns.

The road to Gondar, the former capital of Abyssinia, was now clear, and Abu Anga advanced towards it, hoping that he would secure great quantities of treasure. It was a march of only thirty miles from the battle-field, and was soon reached; sacked, plundered, and reduced to ashes; the churches were pillaged and then burnt; priests were thrown down from the roof and killed; the population massacred, and women and children dragged in hundreds into slavery.

Abu Anga only stayed a short time in Gondar, the change of climate had already caused the death of a number of his troops, and, laden with booty, he returned to Galabat, which he reached at the end of December.

Meanwhile there was great anxiety in Omdurman. Abdullah could not conceal his alarm, for it was well known that the Abyssinian army was very powerful. Abu Anga had crossed the border thirty days before, and still no news reached Abdullah: those who did not wish the Dervishes well, rejoiced at the thought that a great part of the army must have been destroyed, and the anxiety so told on Abdullah, that he was seen to visibly age in this momentous time. Besides, there was the prophecy of Mohammed, who had forbidden his followers to make war against the Abyssinians, unless the latter first provoked it. Abu Anga's expedition was in direct disobedience to this order, and it was thought that he must suffer defeat as a punishment, and it was urged that if Abu Anga returned in safety, then the Prophet Mohammed must be a liar as well as the Mahdi.

At length the arrival of twelve heads which Abu Anga had sent to Galabat proved conclusively that a great victory had been won, and now the news of the destruction of Gondar and the return of Abu Anga's victorious troops was indeed a welcome relief to the terrible suspense.

This news was followed up soon afterwards by the arrival of numbers of women and children, and quantities of loot. Several of these miserable captives had died on the journey, and those who had not been already sold, had their ears cut off, and were sent to the beit el mal.

Abdullah, without the smallest shame, went himself to the beit el mal, and chose all the best-looking girls for his harem, and each of the principal men of his household received an Abyssinian girl as a present.

Abu Anga received great praise at the hands of the Khalifa, and many verses were made in his honour. Shortly before the victor's arrival in Omdurman, criers were sent out to say that he should no longer be called Abu Anga, but Sidi Hamdan, and Abdullah himself went out to meet the conqueror, and shed tears of joy on seeing him. The booty included thirty thousand Maria Theresa dollars, of which Khalifa Abdullah at once took sole possession.

CHAPTER XIV.

KING JOHN OF ABYSSINIA KILLED IN BATTLE.

Destruction of the Kababish tribe and death of Saleh Bey—Events in Darfur—Revolt of Abu Gamaizeh—His death and destruction of his army—Rabeh Zubeir—King Theodore's son visits Omdurman—The conspiracy of "Sayidna Isa"—Death of Abu Anga—King John of Abyssinia attacks Galabat—Success of Abyssinians, but the king killed—Victory turned to defeat—The king's head sent to Omdurman.

LET us now leave Abyssinia for a moment, and turn to the course of events in other parts of the country. The most powerful and determined opponent to Mahdiism was Saleh Bey Fadlallah Wad Salem, the brother of Sheikh Tome of the Kababish, who had been executed in El Obeid. This tribe has enormous quantities of camels and sheep, and occupied the desert between Dongola and Kordofan; they formerly paid taxes to the extent of 100,000 dollars a year to Government. They did all the carrying trade between Dongola and Kordofan. It will be remembered that, during the siege of El Obeid, Saleh Bey had come to the Mahdi's camp; but had left it quite suddenly, and thenceforth had become one of the Mahdi's bitterest enemies.

In 1884 he had given considerable assistance in camels to the English expedition, and had been in constant conflict himself with the Dervishes.

When Khalifa Abdullah had consolidated his authority he determined to rid himself of this rebel. Saleh Bey was at that time weak, for many of his tribe had joined the Mahdiist ranks, and had fought against him. He learnt that Abdullah intended to strike a serious blow to his power, he therefore appealed to the Egyptian Government for help, and sent fifty of his slaves to Wadi

Halfa; the Government granted them two hundred Remington rifles, forty boxes of ammunition, and £200 in cash.

Neufeld, a German merchant, joined Saleh's men on their return to Kordofan, intending, if possible, to re-open a trade with the Arab sheikhs in gum and ostrich feathers.

Nejumi, who was then at Dongola, having learnt through spies of their departure, occupied the wells of Selima on the Arbain road, through which the Kababish would probably pass. Fifteen days after leaving Halfa the little caravan arrived at the oasis, only to be received by Dervish bullets. Most of them were killed, and a few, including Neufeld, were taken captive to Dongola; there they were beheaded, with the exception of Neufeld, who was sent on to Omdurman, where he arrived on the 1st of March, 1887.

The capture of the caravan and arms was a great blow to Saleh, and now Abdullah no longer delayed to carry out his intentions. He despatched the Emirs Greger Hamed and Wad Nubawi, of the Beni Jerrar, against him. In the first fight Saleh was successful; but lost his brother and a number of men. After this, a number of Dar Homr Arabs, who had formerly been allied to him, now deserted to the other side, and with the Dervishes occupied the wells of Mahbas. This being the only water in the neighbourhood, there was now nothing left but to fight, and Saleh and his men performed prodigies of valour, killing great numbers of the Dervishes; but he was hampered by numerous camp-followers, women and children, whom it was impossible to defend; and at length, seeing his third brother fall before his eyes, he dismounted from his horse, sat on his "fur" (sheep's skin), and waited to receive his death-blow, which was dealt by one of Greger's relatives, between whom and Saleh a blood feud existed; the latter having killed both Greger's father and uncle.

Another account relates that Greger had severely wounded Saleh in the head with his axe, but Saleh plunging his sword through Greger's body, they both fell from their horses, and died together. This fight took place on the 17th of May, 1887, and by Saleh's death Abdullah succeeded in ridding himself of the enemy he most feared. Wad Adam was despatched with Saleh's head to Omdurman, where it hung on the gallows for a month, and where I myself saw it.

After Saleh's death the Kababish were dealt with in the most cruel manner; several of them were brought to El Obeid as prisoners, where they were executed. On one occasion Wad Adam had one hundred of them hanged together, and then threw their bodies into a well. The same evening groans were heard from the well, and it was found that one of the victims was still alive; he was taken out and allowed to live. The camels and sheep of this wealthy tribe were all brought to the beit el mal at Omdurman. Most of the she-camels were killed and sold for about two dollars apiece. In this way the Dervishes ruined the possibility of breeding, and destroyed the prosperity and well-being of the country.

The once powerful Kababish tribe has now almost disappeared, and is seldom even mentioned. Abdullah having thus vanquished his last enemy, now seriously set to work to mature his plans for the conquest of Egypt.

But before entering on this part of my story, it may be as well to give a brief historical sketch of Darfur, and the recent events which had occurred there.

Darfur had, for the last four centuries, been governed by its native sultans, who had gradually extended their authority into Kordofan, and it was here that they first came into contact with the Egyptian Government. Mohammed Ali had sent his son Ismail Pasha to take possession of the Sudan, and whilst he was engaged in subduing the petty kings of Shendi and Halfaya, his general, Ahmed Bey Defterdar, had advanced from Dongola into Kordofan. This province was then administered by a Magdum appointed by Sultan Musallem, of Darfur, who, hearing of the advance of the "Turks," collected a large force, and awaited the invaders at Bara. Spies had told him that it would be impossible to fight the Turks, as they used fire ; but the Magdum laughed at the idea, and said he had no fear of fire. Moreover, to prove his word, he had an immense quantity of thorns and brushwood collected, which he set fire to, and then ordered his cavalry to dash through it; these bold and fearless riders did so, and received no great harm. Thus did he impress his followers that they need have no fear of the Turks ; but the good man had no notion of firearms and what they were. He met the attack of the Turks in the most heroic manner ; but he and most of his followers fell, and the province became an Egyptian possession, though no steps were taken to establish a government there.

It was not until August 1874, that the bold slave-hunter Zubeir Pasha attacked and took the ancient kingdom of Shakka, and thus did Ismail Pasha extend the Egyptian authority over Darfur.

From that date the country knew no peace; there was a constant series of little wars. Slatin had fought no less than twenty-seven battles. Then after the defeat of Hicks Pasha came the Dervishes, and Zogal became Emir of Darfur, residing at El Fasher ; but his rule was not peaceful. The Sultan Dudbenga was fought, overcome, and sent to Omdurman a prisoner in 1884 ; thence he was sent to Galabat, where he died. After this, Zogal was left undisturbed, and succeeded in accumulating a considerable amount of riches ; but when the Mahdi died, Zogal, as we have seen, was summoned to Omdurman, and left Darfur in the hands of Sultan Yusef, Dudbenga's son ; this sultan was entirely submissive to the Khalifa ; and when Sheikh Madibbo, of the Rizighat tribe, revolted against Karamallah, the Dervish Emir of Bahr el Ghazal, and fled to Jebel Marra, Sultan Yusef took him prisoner, and sent him back to Karamallah, who passed him on to Abu Anga, by whom he was decapitated in El Obeid.

But Abdullah did not wish Darfur to continue in this semi-independent state ; he therefore instructed Karamallah to raid the country from Dara. Yusef sent word, begging that their respective boundaries might be adhered to, but Karamallah only raided the more. In self-defence Yusef sent out his army, and thus a war broke out, which was just what Abdullah wanted. Yusef allied himself with Sultan Said, of Jebel Marra, and their combined forces defeated Ketenbur, who had been sent by Karamallah in command of a force.

In consequence of this disaster, Abdullah despatched his uncle, Osman Wad Adam (nick-named "Ganu"), with a strong force to Shakka, where he joined Karamallah. Yusef, fearing that he had been betrayed, sent a very strong force, and in the month of December a great battle took place, in which the Furs were almost annihilated, and it is said that Karamallah's brother, Kerkesawi, killed so many men with his sword that his right arm became bent.

Darfur once a prey to the bloodthirsty Dervishes, Osman Wad Adam continued his victorious march to El Fasher. Sultans Yusef and Zayid then fled to Jebel Marra, and sought the assistance of Sultan Jabrallah. Osman sent troops in pursuit. Yusef detached himself from Jabrallah and fled again, while Jabrallah betrayed and murdered the brave Zayid and sent his head to Osman. Shortly afterwards Yusef was captured, brought to El Fasher, and there decapitated. The heads of both these sultans eventually reached Omdurman, and were hung up beside the Abyssinian heads, where I saw them in January 1888.

After this the captor of Zayid returned to El Fasher, whilst Jabrallah, anticipating a great reward for his treacherous conduct, was sent with his five sons to see the Khalifa in Omdurman. He was allowed his liberty for a time, but having once attempted to escape, he and his sons were thrown into chains; four of the latter died in prison, and just before I escaped I saw the unfortunate Jabrallah and his surviving son in a pitiable state in the streets of Omdurman.

For the second time Darfur had now become a Dervish province, under the direction of Osman Wad Adam.

The Khalifa believed that all opposition was over, and that he had nothing to fear from that direction. Indeed, the majority of the inhabitants had been killed, and the few surviving sheikhs had taken refuge in the Dar Tama and Masalit districts; but they did not remain inactive; there were constant meetings, in which they discussed how they should rid themselves of these "enemies of Islam," as they called the Dervishes.

The Masalit people are savage and cruel to a degree; they are in the habit of making waterskins out of the skins of their slain enemies. Slatin Bey told me that when in Darfur he had two of these skins—of a male and a female—which he had kept as curios. Some of the Darfur sheikhs had gone as far as to apply to the Sultan of Borgo for help, but he had refused to interfere in any way with Mahdieh. Then a man suddenly appeared amongst the Masalit about whose origin little was known; he represented himself as the arch-enemy of the hated Dervishes, who, under the guise of Mohammedanism, robbed, plundered, ravished, and murdered all they could lay their hands on.

Such influence did this fiki, or religious teacher, gain over the superstitious masses of the west that some said he must be the true Mahdi; others said he was the fourth Khalifa (Osman); then again many said he was the celebrated Sheikh es Senussi, the great religious head of all the North African tribes, and whose influence has extended far into Central Africa. Several asserted that he was merely a delegate from the great Senussi.

This religious reformer and adventurer styled himself "Abu Gemaizeh" (Gemaizeh is the Arabic name for the sycamore fig-tree), because it was said that the shade of this tree always accompanied him. At Omdurman all sorts of extraordinary stories were current about his supernatural gifts. Some said that he had the power of miraculously increasing food; an ordinary plate-full he would make sufficient for hundreds of people; others said that they had seen him produce milk from his finger-tips, and it was said that he could produce, in a moment, all sorts of things pleasant to the palate. He could raise a palm-tree out of barren ground, which, in the space of an hour, would become covered with fruit. In his sermons and letters he reproached the Khalifa for having oppressed and slaughtered Moslems, and having taken their wives for himself—a crime only committed by the "unbelievers"—and with God's help, he declared his intention of coming to Omdurman to annihilate "God's enemies," as he called the Dervishes.

The sayings and doings of this extraordinary being attracted great attention throughout the entire Sudan. The Mahdi had first appeared in the west, and now an anti-Mahdi had sprung up from the west. Immense numbers of adherents flocked to his standard. Not only did the Furs, thirsting for vengeance, join him, but people from Bornu, Borgo, and Wadai collected around him.

Osman Wad Adam despatched a force against him, which was annihilated, and he now begged the Khalifa to send him reinforcements. In answer to this appeal a number of Beni Jerrar Arabs were sent to him, but these also were destroyed almost to a man. These two important victories increased Abu Gemaizeh's prestige enormously, and when Abdullah saw that the oppressed Sudanese were secretly rejoicing at his discomfiture, he himself began to tremble for his authority.

A third expedition, despatched by Osman, met with a similar fate to the other two, and now the Khalifa vented his wrath on his unsuccessful lieutenant. In October 1888, he wrote to him to retire at once to El Fasher, to confine himself entirely to defensive operations, and on no account to attack the enemy. There was great excitement in Omdurman, where the importance of Abu Gemaizeh's victories had been enormously exaggerated. It was even said that Osman had been killed, El Fasher captured, and Kordofan on the point of being invaded. Then came the news that El Obeid had been captured, and now the rejoicings at the Khalifa's defeat were an open secret. But these highly-coloured rumours were merely the outcome of an intense desire and longing on the part of the wretched inhabitants of the Sudan, groaning under the Dervish yoke, to see themselves once more free from the tyrannical oppression which their own short-sighted conduct had brought upon themselves.

Abu Gemaizeh had, it is true, been very successful. He had three times defeated Osman, who was now besieged in El Fasher, and in great want of food. All Darfur had sided with Abu Gemaizeh, and the Dervishes were almost powerless; but in the zenith of his success the great religious sheikh was suddenly struck down by small-pox, and died at Kebkebieh in February 1889. His death caused many of his adherents to quit the cause, and his successor—who, had he not attacked El Fasher, might have succeeded in compassing the downfall of Osman, who was then entirely cut off and in great straits—felt that he must do something to keep his army together. But his force was hampered by a large number of women, children, and camp followers. He was deficient in firearms, whilst Osman was well supplied with rifles and ammunition, and his Shaggieh troops fought magnificently.

The final action took place under the walls of El Fasher, on the 22nd of February, 1889, and resulted in the death of the leader and the massacre of thousands of his followers. This was the death-blow to the movement, and is an example of how easily Moslems are imposed upon by religious adventurers. Numbers of those who had joined and left Mahdiism, thoroughly convinced of its fraud and deception, had unhesitatingly allied themselves to this new religious movement, which they inspired with almost greater enthusiasm than that they had just quitted. The collapse of this new delusion was therefore comparatively greater. The heads of Abu Gemaizeh and a number of his important leaders were sent to Omdurman, where they found a place on the gallows, and were subsequently relegated to the pit in which lay the whitening skulls of Merhdi, the Abyssinians, and the mutinous blacks.

Osman's victory delighted the Khalifa even more than Abu Anga's success in Abyssinia, because he had always considered Darfur a place of refuge, to which he had a secure line of retreat in case of attack from the north.

The victorious Osman now vented his wrath on the tribes who had supported Abu Gemaizeh's movement. The Beni Helba tribe especially fell under his merciless hand, and was almost exterminated; but the country took some time to recover its normal state, and, in consequence, the Khalifa had to forego the pleasure of summoning Osman to Omdurman, and loading him with benefits as he had done to Abu Anga. However, he had a special house built for him near the mosque, and prepared to do him all honour when his presence could be spared from Darfur.

But this was not to be. The successful Osman fell ill, and died shortly afterwards at El Fasher. He was succeeded by the Khalifa's brother Mahmud Wad Ahmed, who was also accompanied by the kadi Suleiman el Hejazi. This latter individual was deported to Darfur because he had had a disagreement with the Khalifa's principal spy, Hajji Zubeir.

Mahmud was ordered, on his arrival at El Fasher, to send to Omdurman all the money found in the late Osman's safe, and to take over all his horses, wives, &c., and keep them for himself. He left Omdurman with a large number of followers, and travelling *viâ* El Obeid at length reached his province. Here he found the country desolate; during the recent wars all cultivation had lapsed, a terrible famine had set in, and he was unable to find food for his troops. On reporting this to the Khalifa, he received orders to retire to Nahut in Kordofan, which he did, but his black soldiers disliked the change, and conspired together to kill Mahmud and desert back to Darfur. They attempted to carry out this project one night, but failing to secure the ammunition, which was essential to the success of their undertaking, they deserted from the camp, about 1,000 strong, and set off to join Rabeh Zubeir.

This Rabeh had been originally brought up in Zubeir Pasha's family, had shown military ability, and at the time of the suppression of the revolt in Bahr el Ghazal by Gessi Pasha commanded with Suleiman (Zubeir's son) the supposed rebel army. On Suleiman's capture and death, Rabeh fled with the remnants of the force towards Bornu, and after a host of strange adventures and constant fights with the kingdoms of Borgo, Wadai, &c., he succeeded in establishing himself in an independent position on the banks of the Sharé river which empties into Lake Chad. Here he has collected a considerable force, and appears to have at last established friendly relations with his neighbours. The Khalifa has frequently sent messages to him to return to Omdurman, where he would be most honourably received, but Rabeh has persistently refused.

Osman, when at El Fasher, also communicated with him in the same sense; but Rabeh, who had a shrewd idea of the Khalifa's intentions, summoned to his aid a Fiki who had been in Omdurman, and who quite understood Abdullah's character. On Rabeh telling the Fiki of his message from Osman, the Fiki asked that a cock should be given him, and he proceeded deliberately to pull out the feathers of its wings. He then bound its legs together, and plucked it completely; and last of all cut its head off The Fiki said not a word, but Rabeh thoroughly understood the moral of the proceeding, and came to the wise conclusion to stay where he was. The last news is that a portion of his force has re-entered Dar Fertit, the country to the north-west of Bahr el Ghazal.

As for Mahmud, after the disturbance at Nahut, he retired on El Obeid in 1890, and left Darfur to its fate. All that portion of it bordering on Kordofan is entirely depopulated. Herds of elephants roam the plains as far as El Fasher. There is continual internecine warfare, which is still further reducing the population, and creating a wilderness of this once populous district.

Let us now revert to the operations against Abyssinia. In consequence of Abu Anga's victory over Ras Adal, the tribes on the north-western borders of Abyssinia, and who are known as Makada, embraced Mahdiism;

and it was at this time that Todros Kasa, the son of the Todros Kasa (King Theodore), who had been vanquished by the British at Magdala, suddenly appeared at Galabat, and offered his services to the Dervishes to fight against his own countrymen. He was at once sent on to Omdurman, where he was received with great pomp by Khalifa Abdullah, who promised to place him on the throne of Abyssinia, and in return for this promise Todros agreed that all the Abyssinians should turn Moslems, and should pay the Khalifa an annual tribute.

Before going further, it may be as well to explain briefly who this Todros was. He was the second son of the King Theodore who had been subdued by the English army. The eldest son had been taken to England, where he died. At that time the Todros of whom I speak was a mere child, and had been concealed by his relatives from King John, who wanted to kill him. When he grew up he wandered about Abyssinia, and happened to be in the neighbourhood of Galabat when Abu Anga made his successful descent on Abyssinia. It at once occurred to Todros that an alliance with the Dervishes might secure him his father's throne, and we have seen how successfully he had deceived the Khalifa, who implicitly believed in his good faith.

Todros had two children of twelve and fourteen years of age, who always accompanied him when he went about in Omdurman, and he always carried a red umbrella, which made him the laughing-stock of the place. He did not speak Arabic, and all intercourse with him had to be through an interpreter.

Amongst the female slaves taken by Abu Anga were two girls, who accidentally came into the possession of one of my friends. These girls were related to Todros, and when he heard of them, he at once bought their release, and eventually took them with him to Galabat. We used often to talk to him, as he was not in the least afraid, and told us of his real projects and intentions. Suddenly Abu Anga, without any previous warning, set off for Galabat, no one knew why, and it was generally supposed that some very important information had reached the Khalifa. Abu Anga took Todros Kasa with him.

Before leaving, Abu Anga asked the Khalifa to whom he should refer in case of his (the Khalifa's) death. Abdullah replied to his brother Yakub, and from this it was generally understood that he intended to retain the succession in his own family.

ABYSSINIAN DANCING GIRLS.

Shortly after Abu Anga's departure, the Khalifa received a small note in Amharic, written on parchment, from King John. Two of the Abyssinians in Omdurman interpreted it to the Khalifa, and it was to the effect that he (John) was prepared to make a reasonable treaty of peace with the Khalifa; basing his argument on the fact that they all—both Sudanese and Abyssinians—had a common descent through their mutual forefather Ham, and that, being neighbours, they should rather combine to fight against their common enemies, who were the Europeans, and whose power was always extending. To this the Khalifa replied that if he would become a Moslem, they would become good friends; but if he refused to do this, he (the Khalifa) felt obliged to brand him as the enemy of God and His Prophet, and that he had no other course open but to exterminate him.

On Abu Anga's arrival at Galabat, the most violent jealousy sprang up between him and Yunis. The latter separated his camp from Abu Anga's, and lost no opportunity of showing his hatred and envy of the "slave" (as he called him), who had so successfully combated the Abyssinians. Even on the usual Friday review, in spite of Abu Anga having been appointed to the supreme command, Yunis always drilled his men separately from the rest. This Abu Anga reported to the Khalifa, who at once instructed Yunis to place himself under him in every respect.

Meanwhile a conspiracy was brewing amongst the emirs in the camp of Yunis. One of the ugliest types of Takruris that have ever been seen took to calling himself "Sayidna Isa" ("Our Master Jesus"). Yunis and his emirs believed in him, although he subsequently betrayed him. It is impossible to understand how it is that these fanatical people could believe in the nonsense told them by Isa; yet, if he heard that any one disbelieved in him, he would at once have him summoned, and there, in the presence of four witnesses, he would convert him. He asserted that he was the Messiah foretold by the Mahdi who should wrest the power from the Khalifa. Indeed the day was actually fixed when it was decided to kill Abu Anga and proclaim Isa publicly; but Yunis betrayed the conspiracy to Abu Anga, and after afternoon prayers on the following Friday he summoned the sixteen mutinous emirs and threw them into chains; he then wrote to the Khalifa asking his instructions. The latter despatched some judges to Galabat, who were told to instruct these deluded people in the right way. They were tried one after the other; but none of them would deny their belief in Isa; then they threatened to kill them; but Isa laughed, and said he was immortal. At length the judges, seeing that further talking was useless, condemned Isa to death, and in a few minutes he was dangling on the gallows. Even this was not proof enough for the sixteen deluded emirs, who still believed he was not dead, and so one by one they were hanged, and their heads sent to Omdurman, where they also remained on the gallows for a month and were then relegated to the pit. Yunis was summoned to Omdurman, and for some time was quite out of favour.

Thus did Khalifa Abdullah score success after success over his enemies, and there is little doubt that, had Abu Anga failed to act as quickly and decidedly as he did, Isa's rapidly-increasing power might have become a serious menace to the Khalifa's authority. There is no doubt that these sixteen emirs had been instigated by Yunis to revolt against the Khalifa and put him at the head of the movement; they knew perfectly well that Isa was a mere fraud and deception; but I do not think it is possible ever to start a movement on a large scale in a Moslem country unless it is based on some religious grounds. The Mahdi only succeeded by working up the fanaticism of his own countrymen. Such motives as liberty, freedom, and the love of the fatherland are entirely unknown factors in the composition of feelings which go towards creating a national movement amongst Moslems.

Abu Anga, who was now growing old and fat, did not live long after the events just described. He was attacked by typhus, which at that time was prevalent at Galabat, and in a few days this great warrior, who had shed such quantities of blood, was dead. His soldiers mourned him bitterly, and his name is still held amongst them in affectionate remembrance; they loved him because he himself had been a slave, and knew how to discriminate between severity and kindness. He was one of the best emirs of Mahdieh, and of an infinitely more generous nature than Wad En Nejumi or others. Once a poor woman came to him and complained that a soldier had forcibly taken her milk, which was all she had to live upon. Abu Anga sent for the soldier and asked him if the woman's complaint was true; the thief denied it most emphatically and abused the woman unmercifully. Abu Anga was almost convinced that he was speaking the truth; but the woman still persisted in the most violent manner that the man had drunk the milk. After a moment's thought Abu Anga gave the following judgment: "The man's stomach to be ripped open, and if no milk is discovered, the woman will be executed." The woman accepted this judgment with delight, while the unfortunate man had to undergo this terrible operation. The milk was found in his stomach, and Abu Anga made good to the woman her loss. Thus did he maintain discipline amongst his men, and as long as he commanded in Galabat there was no fear. In battle his cruelty knew no bounds, and the most horrible atrocities were perpetrated by his men, especially in Abyssinia. His death was deeply felt by the Khalifa, and with reason, for he was not only a brave and capable leader, but he was absolutely honest; any other man in his place would have, long before, abused his power. He was buried in Galabat in 1888, and his men have canonized him as a saint.

When dying, Abu Anga nominated Wad Ali as his successor, until the Khalifa's orders should be received; but very soon after his death there was discontent amongst the men and want of harmony amongst the emirs, with whom Wad Ali was by no means a favourite. These dissensions reached the Khalifa's ears, and he despatched the Kadi Ahmed, in whom he placed great reliance, to Galabat, with instructions to do all he could to put down discord, and to nominate some one as leader who was popular with all ranks. After several meetings, the Kadi at length succeeded in quieting the people, and it was agreed, by common consent, to nominate Zeki Tummal as Abu Anga's successor. This appointment was subsequently confirmed by the Khalifa.

The Galabat army was now made into four divisions—Zeki Tummal commanded the first division, and was also Commander-in-chief of the whole; Abdallah Ibrahim, Nur Angara, and Mahmud Wad Ali commanded the other divisions. In addition to these four great emirs there were also other well-known men in the Galabat force—such as Sheikh Abu Tagalla, Faragallah (Gordon's old commandant of Omdurman Fort), Omar Wad Elias Pasha, Sheikh Nuri, of the Bederieh tribe, Ismail Wad el Andok, and others. The immense zariba was now further fortified and strengthened.

There were already rumours that King John was making preparations to take Galabat, after which it was said he would advance on Omdurman and utterly destroy Mahdiism. King John was accompanied by all his most important chiefs—Ras Adal, Ras Aria Salasseh, Ras Michael, Ras Mariam, Ras Alula, Saleh Shanga, and several others. In all, the army numbered some 150,000, of whom 20,000 were horsemen.

This news caused the greatest alarm in Galabat and Omdurman; but it also had the effect of making us indulge in pleasant dreams of release. Zeki Tummal took counsel with his emirs whether it would be better to await the enemy's arrival in the zariba or whether it would be advisable to advance and fight in the open. Kadi Ahmed urged that it would be better to stay in the zariba, and his advice was adopted; there is little doubt this was the wisest course to take, as the Abyssinian cavalry would undoubtedly have struck confusion into their ranks. Zeki's force now numbered 85,000 men, and was well disposed in the zariba to resist attack. Criers went through the market-place summoning all people to leave their business and take up arms for the defence of the town; messengers were also sent to the Khalifa to beg his blessing—in fact, great fear prevailed. Spies reported that the enemy were as numerous as the sand, that their numbers stretched beyond the horizon, and that when they moved such clouds of dust arose that the sun was quite obscured.

This news created almost a panic in Omdurman; besides, there is an old prophecy that the Abyssinians should come to Khartum; that their horses should wade knee-deep in blood, and that the King should tether his horse to the solitary tree on the White Nile near Khartum.

At the end of February the King quitted Gondar, and marched out to make holy war against the most bitter enemy to Christianity. When near Galabat he sent word to Zeki to say he was coming, lest it should be said that he had "come secretly as a thief." Numbers of women had also joined the Abyssinian army; they were, for the most part, the wives and concubines of the soldiers, and many others had fled from their parents to follow their lovers to battle.

On Saturday, the 9th of March, 1889, the King began his attack on Galabat. Such clouds of dust were raised that it was almost impossible to see anything. The zariba was stormed; some attempted to drag away the thorn bushes, others tried to set fire to it, whilst the Dervishes opened a terrific fire on the masses. Some Takruris, who had deserted Zeki's camp, reported that the part of the zariba held by Wad Ali was the weakest, and, in consequence, the Abyssinians made a supreme effort to break in at that point.

The din and noise was beyond description. At length, after a very hard fight, the Abyssinians succeeded in forcing an entry, and then their masses rolled in like a great storm stream, carrying everything before them. The thousands of Dervish women within now raised terrible cries as the enemy approached, killing and destroying all in their path; they set fire to the straw huts; the din of the firing, the shouts and screams of the men and women, mingled with the crackling and wild rush of the flames, were terrible beyond description. Already the Abyssinians had

VICTORY TURNED TO DEFEAT. 249

taken possession of the beit el mal, and had occupied the house in which Abu Anga's harem lived, and now they were searching for his body, which they wanted to pull out of the ground and throw into the flames, in revenge for the burning of Gondar.

The strength of the Mahdiists was now almost exhausted, ammunition was running short, and it was thought the fight was nearly over, when suddenly the news spread amongst the Abyssinians that their King had been struck by a bullet. This was the signal for a general retreat: everyone seized all the booty he could lay his hands upon, and soon the zariba was evacuated; several of the women were carried off as captives, including Abu Anga's harem, and the Abyssinians then made for the river Atbara.

Now was the time for the Dervishes to reverse their defeat; they had suffered very heavily, Wad Ali's division had been almost annihilated; but they lost no time in cutting off some of the Abyssinians' heads and sending them at once to Omdurman, with the information that they had gained a great victory, for Kadi Ahmed well knew how anxious was the Khalifa, and how fearful that defeat should overtake his forces.

The Dervishes thought the Abyssinians would renew their attack the next day, but to their surprise no one appeared; then spies were sent out to discover their whereabouts, and they brought back information that the Abyssinian force was now in full retreat towards the Atbara. This information decided Zeki to pursue, and on the 11th of March the Dervish force came up with a large portion of the Abyssinian army encamped on the river bank; a battle ensued, in which the Abyssinians lost heavily and fled precipitately, leaving the dead body of King John in the hands of the Dervishes. It was discovered carefully packed in a long box, and sealed with wax; at first it was thought to contain treasure, but on opening it the odour of decay left little doubt that the body they had attempted to embalm was none other than that of the unfortunate John, and this was confirmed by the Abyssinian prisoners. The King's head was cut off and sent to Omdurman.

Here the wildest excitement prevailed, the Khalifa Abdullah ordered the great war-drums to be beaten and the onbeïa to be sounded. A large review took place. The Abyssinian heads were paraded and said to be those of Ras Alula, Ras Mariam, and Saleh Shanga; but this was not true. However, the Khalifa's delight knew no bounds, and our sorrow was proportionately great. Once more our cherished hopes had been dashed to the ground, and it seemed as if all chance of escape was now quite at an end.

The heads were put upon the gallows, and left no doubt that a great victory had been won, then three days afterwards came the news that the King had been killed. Fixed high up on a camel's back, John's head was paraded up and down through the market-place, preceded by a herald shouting out that the mighty Negûs had been slain, and that now was a time for festivity and rejoicing. The Khalifa was quite intoxicated by his success. He publicly exposed the articles captured with the King's body, amongst which was the throne from which the cross had been removed; this was afterwards replaced in Omdurman and retained in the beit el mal.

A wonderful copy of the New Testament had also been taken; it was written on parchment in Amharic language, was profusely illustrated and illuminated, and bound in a triple leather cover; then there was a gold watch marked "Crosdi, Paris," which showed the day of the week and the month of the year; a telescope, and also an original letter from Her Majesty Queen Victoria to King John, dated November 1887. I myself read this letter, in which the Queen inquired after King John's health, and asked him how he and his family were; that England having occupied Egypt had become a near neighbour to Abyssinia, and that it was Her Majesty's earnest wish to continue to live on terms of peace and friendship with the Negûs. The letter concluded with good wishes for the King's health, happiness, and long life, and was signed by Lord Salisbury. Amongst other things I also saw the King's tent and a number of richly jewelled crosses.

On the same day of its arrival, the Khalifa ordered the King's head to be sewn in a piece of leather and sent it on to Dongola, from whence it was to be sent on to Wadi Halfa as a warning to the Khedive and the English that a like fate would await them if they did not at once submit.

It now seemed that the Khalifa was at the very zenith of his power. There in a dirty pit near the market-place lay the decaying heads of all his principal enemies, the Sultan Yusef, Abu Gemaizeh, the Abyssinians, Sayidna Isa, all huddled up together in a heap, and I could not help reflecting deeply on all these strange events every time I passed that pit. Gradually the skin and hair dropped off, leaving only the bare white skulls, deep eye-holes, and grinning teeth, and yet these were the skulls of crowned heads, prophets, and patriarchs gathered together in a narrow pit from far-distant countries—a solemn evidence indeed of the far-reaching power of Mahdiism. Passers-by struck them with their sticks, and yet for what thousands of lives had these now empty brain-pans been responsible, which lay rotting on far-distant battlefields—proof in truth of God's judgment on the Sudan!

Abdullah now thought himself master of the whole world. In his moments of wildest enthusiasm he had never dreamt of gaining such a tremendous victory over the Abyssinians, and yet another such victory would have almost destroyed his power; he had lost thousands of his best warriors, and the women and cattle captured could never compensate him for such a loss. Of course Zeki and his emirs did not always adhere to the truth in writing to the Khalifa, nor was the latter anxious they should do so—indeed, it would have been tantamount to a crime on Zeki's part to report that the Galabat garrison was weak; had he done so, and even if he had been the Khalifa's own relative, he would probably have been relegated to prison. It would have been treason to have said anything which would detract from the Khalifa's idea of his own power, and he was surrounded by wretched flatterers and trimmers who were the last to tell him the truth.

But all these wars and disturbances had now almost completely ruined the country, and then came the terrible famine, which lasted almost a year and brought untold sufferings on the people. The Khalifa, however, was blind to all this misery and distress. His only idea was self-aggrandisement, and he did not realize that hunger was likely to prove by far the worst and most dangerous enemy with which Mahdieh had to cope; but this he eventually learnt by bitter experience.

After the death of King John there was a certain amount of intercourse between the Dervishes and Abyssinians, and not a few of the latter used to come to Galabat and promise to lead Zeki to where the late king's treasures had been hidden; but this they probably did with the intention of trying to draw him into an ambush. It was eventually hunger which compelled Zeki to take some active measures. He despatched Abdullah Ibrahim into Abyssinia with several thousand men, and a few words respecting the career of this emir may not be amiss.

He was a nephew of Ahmed Bey Dafallah, of Kordofan, and had come to notice during the siege of El Obeid. Whenever he saw any cattle near the town he was always on the watch with his slaves, and generally succeeded in making a successful sortie, capturing them and bringing them into the fort. It was said that on one occasion, when the Mahdi was approaching El Obeid, Ibrahim left the fort and made straight for him, intending to kill him, but was twice wounded by his revolver; he however succeeded in returning to the fort, and after its fall the Mahdi, already greatly impressed by his bravery, pardoned him, and placed him in command of a division under Abu Anga. He accompanied his chief in all his numerous fights, and displayed even greater bravery in fighting for the Mahdieh than he did in fighting for the Government. Had he only been a Baggara he would undoubtedly have succeeded Abu Anga in command.

This Abdullah now penetrated Abyssinia; for a long time nothing was heard of him, and it was thought he must have been annihilated; but at length he returned to Galabat, having lost a large portion of his force. The actual events which happened in this expedition are wrapped in obscurity, and it is more than probable that it fared badly.

After the King's death Abyssinia became a prey to civil and internecine war, which left the inhabitants no time to revenge themselves for the death of their King. The Dervishes, too, were quite exhausted, and had to combat a terrible famine, which swept them off in thousands. This famine induced the sensible emirs at Galabat, such as Abderrahman Wad Abu Degel, to enter into commercial relations with Abyssinia, which have continued uninterrupted up to the present time.

CHAPTER XV.

DEFEAT OF NEJUMI AT TOSKI, AND OF OSMAN DIGNA AT TOKAR.

The Khalifa's intentions regarding Egypt—Wad en Nejumi despatched north—Various operations on the Egyptian frontier—Battle of Toski—Defeat and death of Nejumi—Subsequent events in Dongola—Osman Digna's operations against Sawakin—Is defeated at Tokar—Emin Pasha and events in Equatoria—Recent events in Uganda and Unyoro.

HAVING briefly considered the Khalifa's operations within the Sudan, let us now turn and follow his movements and intentions regarding Egypt. Ever since the annihilation of Hicks Pasha's expedition the conquest of Egypt had been the dream of the Mahdi's life. Those of his followers who had seen Egypt described it in the most glowing terms to the Sudanese, whose cupidity was fully aroused. The immense wealth in Cairo, the lovely women in the harems, had excited their most ardent desires.

The Mahdi himself had decided on the Khedive's palace of Abdin as his place of residence, whence it was his intention to proceed to Syria, and after conquering it, to advance on Mecca. He had prophesied that the conquest of Egypt should be carried out by Khalifa Sherif's flag, and he himself had done all in his power to incite the Egyptians to revolt. He wrote numbers of letters to the leading sheikhs and principal people in Cairo, and had he not died, there is no doubt his influence would have permeated, in no small degree, into Egypt. Several people in Egypt believed in him as the true Mahdi, and besides, he was now the ruler of hundreds of thousands of people. With his death belief in Mahdiism began to decline. His successor, it is true, was a man of boundless energy, and had just as ambitious ideas as his predecessor in regard to the conquest of Egypt, but circumstances had entirely altered.

The Mahdi's death and the Khalifa's accession had caused Mahdiism to break up into two distinct parties, viz. the Baggara Arabs, who called themselves the Arabs of the Sudan, and the "Aulad Belad," or country

AN ARAB SHEIKH OF UPPER EGYPT.

people, such as the Danagla, Barabra, Jaalin, and other tribes on the White Nile. This division in Mahdieh considerably weakened it. Wad En Nejumi and his emirs belonged to the section opposed to the Khalifa, and who would like to have freed themselves from his control; in consequence Abdullah always arranged that a Baggara emir should be attached to Nejumi, to keep him informed of all the latter's doings.

The Mahdi had laid down the plan for invading Egypt, which should be by combined movements from Dongola towards Halfa, and from Abu Hamed towards Korosko; and accordingly, when the English evacuated Dongola in June 1885, Mohammed el Kheir, the conqueror of Berber, together with Abdel Majid, at once took possession of the province, and the first action which took place between these latter and the British and Egyptian troops occurred in December the same year at Giniss. El Kheir was defeated, and fixed his advanced camp at Kerma.

The fall of Sennar enabled the Khalifa to send forward more troops for his operations against Egypt, and the Mahdi's prophecy that the conquest of Egypt was to be carried out by Sherif's flag, entirely fell in with his own arrangements, for he entrusted the command of the advanced force to Wad En Nejumi, who belonged to Sherif's raya (flag), and thus succeeded in keeping this powerful emir, whom he regarded with great fear and jealousy, as far away from him as possible.*

Nejumi set out from Omdurman in November 1885, and marching along the river bank to Berber, robbed and pillaged as if he were advancing through an enemy's country. He seized the goods of merchants at Berber, giving them receipts signed to the effect that they should receive payment when he had taken Assuan. He captured two Egyptian spies, one of whom he decapitated, and the other had his hand and foot cut off. During his stay at Berber he robbed and pillaged in all directions, and used to boast of his approaching conquest of Egypt. He stopped all trade with the north, and drove on the entire population towards Dongola.

It was not, however, until the end of November 1886,

---

* It was the knowledge of this fact that caused General Sir F. Grenfell, in his letter written to Nejumi, calling on him to surrender just prior to the action of Toski, to say, "I know that you personally have been the victim of a base jealousy imposed upon you by the false Khalifa."—*Mahdiism and the Egyptian Sudan*, p. 418.

that he reached Dongola, and there he began to organize his fighting force, which was continually increased by reinforcements sent from Omdurman.

Early in 1887 four messengers were despatched with letters to Her Majesty the Queen of England, His Majesty the Sultan of Turkey, and His Highness the Khedive. These envoys were permitted to come to Cairo, and to personally deliver their letters; but when they were opened, perused, and found only to contain a summons from the Khalifa to adopt Mahdiism, and submit to him, or the recipients would suffer the same fate as Gordon and Hicks, the messengers were at once sent back without any reply being given to them, and this was considered by Abdullah to be the greatest insult that could have been offered to him.

The Dervish advanced-guards continued to creep on towards the Egyptian Frontier, whilst Hassan Khalifa, the nephew of the former Mudir of Berber, occupied the desert wells, and made several incursions on the river to the north and south of Korosko. Mounted on dromedaries, these bold raiders made sudden descents on defenceless villages, carried off quantities of booty, and then disappeared into the desert.

At this time the Egyptians had retired to Wadi Halfa, and the Dervishes had occupied Sarras, a little to the south, from whence they constantly harassed the Egyptian outposts. A variety of circumstances, however, occurred to prevent Khalifa Abdullah from carrying out his projects against Egypt. The revolt in Darfur, the Abyssinian war, internal dissensions, all contributed to impede the despatch of troops north. Besides, the Dervish garrison in Dongola had already done much to destroy the well-being and prosperity of the province; they plundered the inhabitants, who, in their turn, became averse to the Dervish occupation; continued warfare had produced a famine; numbers died of small-pox.

Bahr el Karrar in 1888 occupied the wells of Haimar and Ongat, and from here was able to annoy the inhabitants on the Nile between Assuan and Korosko. He raided the village of Kalabsheh, some fifty miles south of Assuan, killed the Egyptian police guards, and carried off their officer a captive to Omdurman. All this time there was a great deal of talk in the capital, about the conquest of Egypt, but we never received any very decisive news. The captured officer was paraded through the streets in triumph, and was then brought before the Khalifa, who received him kindly, and questioned him very fully about Egypt; but he quite understood what sort of replies to make to the Khalifa's questions, and only told him what he knew would please; so he was well treated, set at liberty, and now lives in Omdurman.

From time to time the Khalifa despatched reinforcements to Dongola which never returned, and this was the reason of the main road leading north out of Omdurman being called "Darb Esh Shuhada" ("The Martyrs' Road").

The Egyptian Government had now confined itself to the defence of its own frontiers. In June 1888, Bishir Bey, a subsidized Government sheikh, turned Bahr Karrar out of Haimar; but on the other hand, the Sarras Dervishes made a sudden descent on the Dabarosa bazaar, killed a number of merchants, and escaped before the troops from Halfa could intercept them. Meanwhile, there was not much harmony between the big emirs. Nejumi and his followers were jealous of the masterful Baggaras, and it was only with the greatest reluctance that they brought themselves to show any respect to the Emir Mussaid of the Baggara Habbanieh, who had been sent to Dongola by the Khalifa to watch and report on Nejumi's doings.

The Baggaras hated Nejumi to such an extent that one of their number attempted to poison him; but he recovered after a long illness, though he never entirely got the poison out of his system. It is said that his eyesight was always bad afterwards. This constant bickering between the Baggara and Nejumi crippled his energy. Formerly he had been greatly feared by them, but now his own people were annoyed that he showed so much deference to the Khalifa and his emirs. As for the Khalifa, he was thoroughly exasperated by Nejumi's indolence, and summoned him to Omdurman.

During his absence from the province, a deserter from the Egyptian side led the Dervishes into the fort at Khor Musa, within five miles of Halfa, where they killed some of the garrison, but were unable to take the

BISHIR BEY, SHEIKH OF THE ABABDEH ARABS.

whole fort. Colonel Wodehouse having been informed of their attack, at once sent out help, and the Dervishes were surprised and annihilated.

Towards the end of 1888 Nejumi was in Dongola again. The Khalifa had threatened to throw him into chains unless he showed more energy in his operations against Egypt. He had already exhibited his displeasure by imprisoning Sheikh Idris and Makin Wad en Nur, who had shown a reluctance to go forward, for they had made up their minds that a successful attack on Egypt was an impossibility. They could not even capture Wadi Halfa. The desert roads were next to impassable owing to want of water, whilst the river was in the hands of the enemy, who had numbers of steamers, and could prevent any Dervish advance by water. All these difficulties were quite apparent to Nejumi and his emirs; but so self-confident was the Khalifa, that he could not believe there was any great difficulty in conquering Egypt; added to this, several sheikhs of Upper Egypt had assured him that when the Dervishes advanced they would be joined by the entire population.

Thus the Khalifa insisted, and Nejumi could not do otherwise than obey. He had already transferred to Dongola the entire Batahin tribe, which had showed a mutinous spirit, and early in 1889 he sent a further detachment, consisting of thirty flags, composed for the most part of Gehena Arabs, who are not warlike, and were most averse to fighting in the Dervish cause. Thus, like lambs to the slaughter, were these unwilling tribes driven forward to battle.

When the revolt in Darfur had been suppressed, and Abyssinia had been humbled, the Khalifa turned his attention more earnestly than ever to the invasion of Egypt. He despatched Yunis ed Dekeim to Dongola, and on his arrival, Nejumi was to begin his advance north.

Nejumi was now nominated Commander-in-chief, and being one of the Mahdi's most determined and fanatical emirs, he had given him the title of "Emir el Umara" ("The Emir of emirs"). He had under his command several brave emirs, such as Abdel Halim, Makin en Nur, Wad Gubara, Sheikh Idris, Osman Azrak, and several others. But the fighting conditions of these Dervishes had considerably changed during the last few years

The Ansar no longer fought for Mahdieh. All those promises of joys in paradise were no longer believed in, for by dying the Mahdi had proved himself to be false, and so were all his prophecies. They did not fight to obtain booty, for long experience had shown them that the booty was exclusively appropriated by the Khalifa and his emirs. It was now fear of the Khalifa's anger which drove them to fight, and numbers of them deserted when a favourable opportunity occurred for them to do so.

Not only were all these feelings at work in Nejumi's force, but also the conditions of the country in which he was operating were very different from those in which he had won all his early victories. Then he knew every path, almost every tree. It was his own country; the inhabitants were of his own race; volunteers flocked to his standards. He always largely exceeded his enemies in point of numbers; but now it was all entirely different. He knew nothing of the country through which he had to march; enormous difficulties blocked his every movement. Even had the population of Upper Egypt been desirous of joining him, they were much too carefully looked after by the troops and the Government to be able to do so. An enormous desert separated him from the position he desired to reach, and the result was that his force—just as Hicks's force had done—suffered greatly from want of water. As usual he was accompanied by numbers of women and children, and sometimes even five dollars would not purchase a drink of water.

Abdullah showed his mistrust of the men by permitting their wives and families to accompany them, for he thought that they could not well run away, leaving their wives and children behind, and therefore they would have to fight; but this great crowd of women and children hampered Nejumi's movements enormously, and still further increased the want which already prevailed in the Dervish camp. When in Dongola, the Gehenas were suffering so terribly from famine that they stole the Dervishes' sheepskins, on which they prayed, and ate them.

It was madness to attempt to invade Egypt with such a force as Nejumi then had, made up of almost every tribe and nationality, all huddled together, and yet absolutely wanting in cohesion. Then the enemy which they were going to fight was of an entirely different stamp to the one they had overcome in the Sudan. The Egyptian was not the same as in the old days. The army was now composed of well-trained battalions under English officers; and it is not out of place here to remark that the occupation of Egypt by England was a heavy blow to the Khalifa and his followers. Often have I heard him say, "If the English would only evacuate Egypt, I should very soon take possession of it."

Thus did Nejumi set out from Dongola with his force. At Sarras a parade was held, and some 14,000 souls counted; but of these nearly half were women and children. His intention was to avoid Halfa, and march direct on Bimban, as the inhabitants of that place had promised to join him; but in the village of Argin, he was attacked and defeated by Colonel Wodehouse. Here Nejumi lost about 1,000 men, amongst whom were several emirs, including Sheikh Idris and Abdel Kader Guru, besides many more wounded. On account of this victory, Wodehouse Pasha was known in the Sudan as "the vanquisher of Wad Nejumi."

But, in spite of his defeat, Nejumi still continued his advance, although the only food he had for his force was camels' and donkeys' meat, and his troops were more dead than alive. He was obliged to make his cavalry into a rear-guard to prevent desertion, but still large numbers succeeded in joining the Egyptian troops.

The Sirdar, General Grenfell Pasha, wrote a letter to Nejumi, in which he showed him that he understood the wretched state his troops had come to, and urging him not to expose uselessly the lives of so many of his people; but take the wise course and surrender. Nejumi, however, boldly replied that if Grenfell Pasha would adopt Mahdiism he would guarantee him happiness and contentment, otherwise he would sweep him and his troops off the face of the earth.

Only one of the two messengers who had been sent with General Grenfell's letter returned with this reply; the other—an Arab named Abdel Hadi—was sent on to Omdurman bearing the General's letter to the Khalifa, who was also informed by Nejumi, that Abdel Hadi had originally been on the Dervish side at Abu Hamed, but had deserted over to the "Turks."* On his arrival, Abdullah questioned him closely regarding the latest news of Nejumi and the condition of the opposing armies. Abdel Hadi replied that the "Turks" were very strong, and that it was probable that Nejumi would be defeated For this saying, he was thrown into prison for months, and would have starved to death had not Neufeld, who was with him in prison, given him some help; he was eventually released through the intermediary of Hajji Saad, and permitted to return to Abu Hamed, whence he escaped back to Egypt.

Meanwhile Nejumi still continued his advance; he could not and would not submit. On the one hand he was of far too proud a nature to submit to the hated Egyptian troops; and on the other, his fear of the Khalifa added to his natural obstinacy. At Toski his advance was arrested by General Grenfell at the head of the Egyptian troops, and he had no other course open but to fight. He was utterly defeated, himself and most of his emirs killed, whilst a mass of men, women and children fell into the hands of the Egyptian force.

This battle took place on the 3rd of August, 1889; by it the annihilation of Hicks Pasha's expedition was avenged, and the project of invading Egypt, which had been maturing for the last three years, entirely collapsed. The news of this defeat caused great commotion in Omdurman; it was at first rumoured that every one had been killed; and the Khalifa was in despair.

* It must be remembered that with the Arabs of the Sudan the term "Turk" is a synonym for the hated oppressor of whatever nationality. The British troops, even, were confounded under the same appellation.

He hated the Europeans and Egyptians, and though we, in our hearts, were rejoiced at the news, we suffered no small anxiety as well, for we thought it quite possible that the Khalifa would appease his wrath to some extent by venting his annoyance on us. It was, indeed, a most crushing blow for him and his followers.

The Emirs Hassan en Nejumi—a relative of Wad

WAD EN NEJUMI.

From a photograph of a drawing made by an Egyptian officer of the great Emir, as he lay dead on the field of Toski.

Nejumi—and Siwar ed Dahab, who had escaped from the massacre, returned with all speed to Dongola, and thence to Omdurman. They reported that it was madness of Nejumi to have attempted what he did; that all his emirs were opposed to it, and that they had told Nejumi that they were sure, if the Khalifa were fully informed of all the circumstances, he would never have permitted him to advance. As it was, famine, want of water, and the unseasonable time of the year, ought to have been sufficient reasons for postponing the expedition; but Nejumi turned a deaf ear to all their protests, he feared the Khalifa; his plundering and cruelties cried to heaven for vengeance, and the instruments of that vengeance appeared in the persons of General Grenfell and Colonel Wodehouse.

Saleh Bey, the son of Hussein Pasha Khalifa, and a subsidized sheikh of the Egyptian Government, drove his nephew out of Murat, advanced almost to Abu Hamed, and we fondly hoped that the Government would at least advance to Dongola, which is the key of the Sudan; but we were again doomed to disappointment.

And now Mahdiism was far too exhausted to make any further attempts on Egypt. The province of Dongola had been utterly ruined, and Yunis's ill-treatment of the inhabitants was beyond description. Complaints of his evil deeds eventually reached the Khalifa's ears, and fearing that the inhabitants might be induced to join the "Turks," he relieved Yunis of his appointment, and replaced him by Zogal, who, in spite of his former fall from power, was known to be a just man, and the Khalifa trusted to him to restore the confidence of the people. Yet the Khalifa did not entirely trust Zogal, and still left Mussaid to watch him, he also sent another Baggara called Arabi with three hundred troops to observe his doings.

Dongola now became a hotbed of spying and cross-spying. Matters became so serious that it seemed a fight between the rival parties was imminent, and every post brought letters from either section, accusing the other of malpractices. The Khalifa therefore summoned these two emirs—Mussaid and Arabi—to Dongola, and on their arrival they reported that it was Zogal's intention to deliver up the province to the Egyptian Government. Thereupon the Khalifa recalled Zogal, and replaced him by Yunis.

Zogal, on his arrival in Omdurman, was well received, and did not hesitate to refute the misstatements of the emirs; but he was not believed, and was thrown into chains, where he remains to this day. Zogal's only fault is, that he is a Dongolawi, and a relative of the Mahdi, whilst his opponents are all Baggaras, who are the governing party, and therefore he is not likely to receive any pity from them.

Besides Wad en Nejumi and Abu Anga, there yet remained one of the greatest of the Mahdi's old emirs. I mean Osman Digna, to whom I referred in the early pages of this work. He had been sent to the Eastern Sudan after the fall of El Obeid, and in July 1883, had taken up a position near Sawakin. The Mahdi had given him proclamations to distribute to all the tribes in the neighbourhood of Kassala and Sawakin, ordering them to rise against the Government. The summons was obeyed, and by the end of 1883 Osman Digna was in possession of all the principal posts in the vicinity. The most important work which Osman Digna performed for the Mahdi was cutting the communication between Sawakin and Berber, and thus blocking the shortest and best road into the Sudan. Fully alive to the importance of this route, the Government made repeated attempts to re-open it, but Osman, with his dauntless Hadendoas, caused every effort to fail.

On the 3rd of February, General Baker Pasha made a vain attempt, but was cut to pieces at El Teb, losing over two thousand men and all his arms and ammunition. After Baker's defeat, the English made another effort, and after General Graham had defeated Osman Digna at both Teb and Tamai, the proposal was made to open the road to Berber, and thus relieve Gordon, then besieged in Khartum; but it was thought impossible to fight Osman Digna's hordes, and to overcome the difficulties of the desert, so the idea was abandoned.

For seven long years Osman Digna continued alternately to harass and besiege Sawakin; but gradually numbers of the local Arabs—notably the Amarar—fell away from his cause, and intertribal conflicts ensued.

When almost quite deserted, Osman Digna came to Omdurman. In January 1887, he returned *viâ* Gedaref and Kassala, where he collected some four thousand men, eventually occupied Handub, and again besieged Sawakin. He also defeated the Amarar, and killed over seven hundred of them.

Kitchener Pasha, the Governor-General of the Red Sea Littoral, was severely wounded during his attack on Handub; in March of the same year Abu Girgeh arrived with a force from Kassala, and thus Osman became almost as powerful as ever. He continued to harass Sawakin, and to devastate the neighbouring country. It was useless for him to attempt to take the town, he therefore received the Khalifa's orders to establish himself at Tokar in January 1889, and at the same time he was permitted to open commercial relations with Sawakin. A small post was established at Handub, and Dervish merchants were actually permitted to enter the town and purchase goods.

These commercial relations existed for about two years between Sawakin and the Dervishes, and, as a famine prevailed at Tokar, the enemy drew most of their supplies through the port of Trinkitat. Suddenly news reached Omdurman to the effect that the gates of Sawakin had been closed, and all traffic stopped between Tokar and Handub. In consequence the famine increased, and merchants arriving in Omdurman said that no doubt it was the intention of the Government to attack Osman Digna very soon.

The wealthiest of these merchants was a certain Omar Kisha, who had smuggled quantities of lead and powder through Sawakin. The news they brought was soon confirmed, and in February 1891, Handub was occupied. In March a message was received from Zogal, in Dongola, to the effect that a salute had been fired at Halfa to announce the occupation of Tokar by the Government, and the complete defeat of Osman Digna. This news created almost a panic in Omdurman, and what made it worse was the uncertainty, for no news had been received either through Berber or Kassala. It was not until eight days later that a Shukrieh Arab arrived from Kassala, and said that he had heard much talk about the defeat at Tokar, but the fate of Osman Digna was uncertain, some said that he had been killed, others, seriously wounded. A month afterwards letters arrived from Osman himself confirming the news of the defeat. This caused great consternation, and the Khalifa at once assembled a council.

It was said that an Egyptian expedition had already reached Berber, and every day it was thought news would arrive of the capture of Dongola. It was decided to make a camp at Metemmeh. The whole of Omdurman was secretly rejoicing at the approaching downfall of the Khalifa, but again we were all doomed to the most bitter disappointment. News came from Berber that the "Turks" had no intention of advancing further, and were content to have occupied Tokar, where they had built a fort and securely established themselves. But, though thus temporarily relieved, the loss of Tokar was a very severe blow to the Khalifa, as the Government was now in immediate contact with the tribes on the Sawakin-Berber road, and the way was clear.

On the last Muled (the anniversary of the Prophet's birth) Osman Digna arrived at Omdurman, accompanied by a few followers. During his flight from Tokar towards Kassala his followers had nothing to eat but wild figs, and many had starved. The Khalifa received Osman very coldly, and reproached him for his defeat; he afterwards sent him to cultivate on the Atbara, where he now lives at a place called Adaramab.

Of all the opponents to Government, Osman Digna was perhaps the most bitter; he had done great things at Sawakin, Kassala, and on the Abyssinian frontier, but by his ruthless cruelty he had alienated the Arabs from his cause. In his present seclusion he has, probably, occasion to think of all his evil and bloodthirsty deeds, which have ended in the ruin of his country and the death of his followers. Almost all the Arabs who espoused his cause with so much zeal are now dead, and his present humiliation is a fitting reward for his blind adherence to a false and ruthless tyrant.

Scarcity of money in the beit et mal at Omdurman was the main reason for the despatch of an expedition up the White Nile. Since 1885 Emin had not been disturbed by the Dervishes, and Karamallah had long since retired to Bahr el Ghazal, from whence no news had been received of him for years.

There was no Dervish post south of Fashoda, which was the market to which the blacks brought their cattle for sale. The negro tribes all along the White Nile had been left quite undisturbed by the Dervishes, but now it occurred to the Khalifa to send an expedition to collect ivory and slaves and to subdue Emin Pasha. Omar Saleh was appointed to command, and was given three steamers and a number of sailing vessels; he was also the bearer of a letter to Emin informing him of the various events which had occurred in the Sudan, and calling on him to surrender to Omar. To add weight to his letter, he also ordered the Syrian Stambuli to write in a similar sense; also some of the Copts in Omdurman were ordered to write to the Copts who were known to be in Emin's service.

Omar Saleh left Omdurman in July 1888, and a whole year passed without any information of his movements reaching Omdurman; it was thought that Emin must have annihilated the expedition and captured the steamers. The Khalifa became restless, but at length one of the steamers returned, laden with ivory and slaves.

We were all naturally most anxious to hear about Emin, and the men who brought the despatches informed us that they had arrived at Regaf in October; this place they took by storm, and had sent down to Omdurman one of the clerks they had taken prisoner there. As to Emin, they stated that he and an Englishman (we thought this Englishman must be the intrepid Stanley) had been put in chains by the mutinous soldiers, because the Englishman wanted to bring Emin to Egypt, as the Khedive had sent him there for

270   TEN YEARS' CAPTIVITY IN THE MAHDI'S CAMP.

that purpose. Omar Saleh had seized this opportunity to take possession of the province, but he had been driven back by the mutineers; this last news was not told the Khalifa, but we heard it in confidence. Omar had begged the Khalifa to send back the steamer with-

A NATIVE WOMAN OF MAKARAKA, THE WIFE OF ONE OF EMIN PASHA'S OFFICERS, WHO REACHED EGYPT FROM UGANDA IN JUNE 1892.

out delay, and in consequence it went south again a few days afterwards.

A long time after this another steamer arrived from Equatoria, but it brought no important information.

It seemed that Emin had left the provinces, that on his departure the country had fallen into a state of anarchy, and that the blacks had massacred all the Arabs. The Khalifa despatched two emirs, Hasib and Elias Wad Kanuna, to Regaf in the steamer; and as it was reported that the Dervishes there suffered a great deal from the climate, he decided to make it a place of exile, and afterwards sent only bad characters there.

In 1891 the Emir Hasib arrived in Omdurman; he came as a fugitive, and reported that he was with two of the steamers which had been sent to a place two days' journey from Regaf to collect ivory; they made a zariba, and one steamer was already loaded up when they were suddenly attacked by the blacks, who killed everyone in the zariba, and he had retreated with the remaining empty steamer, but the other had fallen into the enemy's hands.

Some of the blacks who came to Omdurman with Hasib said that they had heard Emin had returned to the province and had stirred up the blacks to revolt against the Dervishes; but Hasib was of a different opinion, and believed the attack to have been purely a local affair.*

Khalifa Abdullah now felt some alarm for the safety

* The arrival of a portion of the old Equatoria garrison in Cairo in June 1892, who had travelled under the ægis of the Imperial British East Africa Company through Uganda to Mombasa, throws further light on the present situation in Equatoria. They state that after Stanley's departure from Kavalli's, Selim Bey (Emin's old commandant), who had been despatched north to collect the garrison, finding that Stanley had gone, settled down with a small number of men in his old camp at Kavalli's, while the rebel officer, Fadl Maula Bey, with the bulk of the garrison, remained in the neighbourhood of Wadelai. This place was eventually attacked by the Dervishes, who were driven off, but most of the garrison, feeling that they could not trust Fadl Maula, who was known to have been in communication with the Dervishes, deserted to Selim Bey. Emin had come to Kavalli's in April 1891, but on stating that he was in German employ had been joined by only a few of his old garrison, and had not attempted to re-enter his old province. Shortly after Emin's departure, Captain Lugard had arrived, and had taken the entire force into Uganda and Unyoro, where he had established some military posts.—F. R. W.

of his posts at Lado and Regaf, more particularly as he was now at war with the Shilluks, and his post at Fashoda was hemmed in by this warlike tribe; he therefore despatched another steamer south to obtain more information, but the Dervishes he wished to send refused to go, and had to be dragged on board in chains.

In my opinion the Khalifa will have some difficulty in retaining his posts on the White Nile. When I left Omdurman, the head of the Shilluk King was hanging on the gallows, and his brave people revolted against this act of treachery which had deprived them of their chief. The revolt had assumed large proportions, and the Emir Zeki had been despatched to Fashoda from Galabat, and had been heavily pressed by the infuriated blacks.

CHAPTER XVI.

THE FAMINE AT OMDURMAN—1888-1889.

Ohrwalder describes Omdurman—The Mahdi's tomb, and how it was built—Pilgrimage to Mecca forbidden—A description of the great mosque—The Khalifa's palace—The markets—The population—The Khalifa's tyrannical rule—The terrible famine of 1888-1889—Awful scenes and sufferings—The plague of locusts.

IN this chapter I propose to give a description of the great Mahdi capital of the Sudan. I have already given a brief account of the place as I found it on my arrival from Kordofan in 1886, but now the city is vastly increased in size.

When Khalifa Abdullah had quite consolidated his authority within the Sudan, and was contemplating the invasion of Egypt, it also occurred to him to define the limits of his kingdom, and establish an hereditary succession in his family. Indeed his only reason for carrying on his rule under the guise of Mahdiism was his fear that a change of name might involve him in difficulties, but nevertheless he adhered strictly to his intentions, with the result that now nothing of Mahdiism remains but the name. He has adopted many of the old Government systems of administration, and were it not that he feared he might lose his new kingdom, I believe that he would not be averse to substituting the Sultan's for the Mahdi's name.

It is now thoroughly understood that the Khalifa's authority is no longer based entirely on religious principles as in the case of the Mahdi: he has substituted for it—if not in name, at any rate in fact—the system of "molk," or temporary authority. He has abolished almost all the Mahdi's decrees. His predecessor had substituted for the gallows the system of decapitation for death-sentences, but the Khalifa has reinstituted the gallows, his reason for doing this was to make the mode of execution more alarming to the Sudanese, for whom he considers decapitation a too painless death.

He has changed the name of his followers. The Mahdi had decreed that the Foggara (or " poor " as the Dervishes first called themselves) should take the name of Asyad (*i.e.* masters), and this system of nomenclature was partially adhered to up to the date of his death; but the Khalifa thought the name Foggara very derogatory to the spirit of his rule, and therefore ordered that this name should be abolished and substituted by "Ansar ed Din" (*i.e.* auxiliaries or helpers in the cause of religion); it was also permitted to be called the Habib or Sahib el Mahdi (*i.e.* the friend or disciple of the Mahdi), consequently the women are known as Habiba —a play on words which has given rise to much joking on the part of the men. It took only a few days to cause the name of Fakir to be completely forgotten, and now Ansar for the men and Ansariat for the women have been adopted throughout the Sudan.

The Khalifa also abolished the name Fiki, which is given to religious teachers. There is a Sudan proverb which runs, "El Fiki yefik ed Din" (*i.e.* "The Fiki analyses religion"), and the Khalifa knew well how these fikis imposed on the minds of the people, how they wrote amulets for preservation against the evil-eye, witchcraft, diseases, and ill-luck; how they pretended to be able to give women the means of taking revenge on their husbands whose love had grown cold, and help those who desired to secure the sole affection of their husbands. Abdullah well knew how credulous were the Sudanese in such matters; already the Mahdi had given the strictest injunctions that the practice of writing amulets was to be discontinued, and now the Khalifa was even more severe; he decreed that any fiki found writing an amulet should lose his right hand, but in spite of these stringent measures it is almost impossible to eradicate the people's belief in these superstitions; the Khalifa himself has openly declared that he has not the smallest belief in witchcraft, amulets, &c., and that God, who is alone the Judge of right and wrong, has alone the power to reward or punish. However, he is a believer in the power of the evil-eye, and will never permit a one-eyed man in his presence, as it is said the one eye that is good can do great damage.

The Khalifa, like the Mahdi, is bent on the destruction of the old towns, so as to further wrap in oblivion the former Government rule. Thus old Berber has been long since deserted, and a new Berber has been built just to the north of the old town. Of course Omdurman—the Dervish Khartum—is by far the most important of all the towns; and being the place of the death and burial of the Mahdi, it is quite right that it should be the capital of the kingdom which he founded. Just as Medina is one of the most holy places of Islam, so is it considered advisable to raise Omdurman to a similar position.

By far the most important and conspicuous structure in Omdurman is the Mahdi's tomb; and in spite of the Khalifa's divergence from his Master's views, still he considers it politic to show that he is grateful to his benefactor. His desire was to build a tomb which should excel everything between Omdurman and Alexandria. It is said that the dome can be seen three days' journey from Omdurman, but on this point I am not prepared to give an opinion, as I never went beyond Khartum. From here, of course, the dome, rising high above the miserable mud hovels and straw huts, is a most conspicuous object, and it is certainly the tallest of all the buildings in the Sudan.

Abdullah spared no expense in erecting this structure. He first ordered the plans to be drawn out, and selected that of the engineer Ismail, who was the architect of the Sidi Hassan dome at Kassala. Omar, the former Government architect, was lent to Ismail to assist him. Laying the foundation stone was a great spectacle, and was celebrated with general rejoicing and festivity. Enormous crowds collected to witness the ceremony. Several people were crushed to death, and were looked upon as fortunate to have died on such a day.

The work of construction was now vigorously taken in hand. Khartum supplied the materials. Thousands of people were sent there, and the work of destruction went on apace. Walls were pulled down in order to procure the burnt bricks, which were sent across to Omdurman. The corner stones of Government house were pulled out and used as the corner stones of the dome. The woodwork was made by carpenter Mohammed Bornawi. The masons were for the most part Egyptians who had learnt their trade in the construction of the Mission house and church in Khartum; and by them the Dervish workmen were instructed how to break down walls without destroying the bricks. The foreman of works was in the habit of secretly chewing tobacco, and one day he rather unguardedly put a piece into his mouth; but he had been observed by some of the Dervishes, who fell upon him, knocked him down, and would have torn him to pieces had not Wad Adlan interposed and taken him off to the steamer, where he concealed him.

In the eyes of the Dervishes it was an unpardonable crime to chew the forbidden weed whilst working at the dome of the Mahdi's tomb. Most of the Dervishes worked without pay—" Fi shan Allah " (" For the sake of God "), as they say. A small quantity of dhurra was allowed them; but the masons received pay. Lime was obtained from Omdurman itself.

In order to push forward the work, Khalifa Abdullah, accompanied by the two other Khalifas, and all the emirs and judges, went to the river bank and assisted to carry the stones to the dome. Of course the whole town followed them. Abdullah put a great stone on his shoulder and marched off with it. The others all followed his example; and in this way it took no time to bring up all the stones required. The Khalifa promised the Mahdi's blessing to all who assisted in this work; and he solemnly assured the labourers that they should be possessors of as many palaces in paradise as stones which they carried to the dome. The women carried the water required for the work. The tomb is built much in the same style as all Mohammedan domes erected to the memory of some holy sheikh.

Several of the domes in the Sudan are made of clay; but the Khalifa had determined that the Mahdi's dome should be the grandest in the Sudan. The mud hut in which the Mahdi had died was pulled down, and a square structure about thirty feet high built round the spot, with large windows. Above this superstructure rose the dome some eighty feet above the ground. The foundations were laid very deep, and the walls were immensely thick. On the four corners of the superstructure, and just where the dome begins, are four round balls supported on four small pillars. On the summit of the dome are three large balls, the centre one being the largest; and above these again is a gigantic gilt spear-head resting on the balls.

The doorway is really a work of art which does credit to Sudanese labour. It is painted in bright colours, and was made in the arsenal at Khartum; and when it was finished, Yakub, the Khalifa's brother, himself went to fetch it, and rewarded handsomely the men entrusted with the work. The outside walls of the building are white. At first they attempted to paint the tomb with oil-colours; but as they were not properly prepared, the paint soon peeled off when it was dry, and so they had to be content with simple whitewash. The fanatics said that there had been some evil Christian substance mixed with the paint, which prevented it sticking; and by its falling off, it proved that it was not acceptable to the Mahdi.

The large windows admit a quantity of light into the tomb, which is decorated inside with the most glaring colours. The actual grave is not situated quite in the centre of the building, and is covered by a painted wooden catafalque. To reduce the glare, the windows are well curtained. Every night, and all through the night, quantities of candles are kept burning; and it is impossible not to be impressed with the solemnity of the tomb. The walls are so thick that the tropical sun cannot penetrate, and there is always a cool refreshing breeze inside. The rich perfumes with which the tomb is being continually sprinkled fill the air with the most agreeable odours. The surrounding wall, which marks the limits of the Mahdi's original enclosure, is so high as to conceal the superstructure on which the dome rests.

This tomb means to the Sudan Moslems what the Kaba at Mecca means to the thousands of pilgrims who visit it; but pilgrimage is not enjoined to the Mahdi's tomb. To come to Omdurman is quite sufficient without being obliged to go through various ceremonies. Omdurman is detested in the Sudan; and no one who is not obliged to live there would stay for a day longer than he could help; and the farther people can distance themselves from it, the better they like it.

Since the Mahdi appeared, pilgrimage to Mecca ceased, because, while he was alive, a visit to him was supposed to supply all its advantages. And when he died, a visit to his tomb was supposed to confer even greater benefits than the pilgrimage to Mecca. Several of the Fallata, who came from distant parts of Bornu, Wadai, &c., were stopped at Omdurman when on their way to Mecca.

Thus have the Sudanese become schismatic to the orthodox Moslem religion, asserting that those who do not believe in the Mahdi, even though they be Moslems, are unbelievers. Now, of course, all these ideas have quite disappeared, and all true friends of Islam in the Sudan bitterly deplore the present state of affairs. Several people used to say to us, "Our position is a most miserable one! You Christians have nothing to reproach yourselves with on the score of religion, but with us Moslems such a state of affairs as the present is too dreadful to contemplate, and we know no rest." A great number of people now repeat, in the privacy of their own homes, the daily prayers, although they have gone all through them in the mosque; but as they do not believe in the Mahdi, they consider the prayers said in his mosque to be valueless.

Quantities of women visit the Mahdi's tomb; for, though most of them no longer believe in him as the Mahdi, they still look upon him, on account of his great victories, as a saint to whom God has given a great position in the other world because of his holiness. But, after all, these ideas are held for the most part by his enormous circle of relations, whose motives are always somewhat interested.

Khalifa Abdullah did not, however, confine himself only to beautifying the Mahdi's tomb. Being now the sole monarch, he desired also to beautify his own residence. It will be remembered how, with Wad Adlan's assistance, he had organized the beit el mal. Now, close to the Mahdi's tomb, was the great mosque—not a mosque in its usual sense, but an immense yard, which would hold upwards of 70,000 men extended in long rows of 1,000. It was roofed in by enormous mats, held up on innumerable forked sticks, which gave it the appearance of a forest. This "rukuba," or kneeling-place, was capable of holding 30,000 men, whose murmuring sounded like distant thunder. At first the great enclosing wall was made of mud; but afterwards Khalifa Abdullah had it pulled down, and a good wall made of burnt bricks and lime.

The mihrab, or niche, marking the direction of Mecca, in which the Mahdi repeated prayers, is situated a little to the east of the centre, and is square in shape with mud walls, and a gable roof, made of iron plates from the Khartum arsenal; gates open in the walls on the north, south, east, and west. The mihrab is entered from the west, but is well protected by branches of trees, so as to prevent the Ansar from crowding up too close. The floor is sprinkled with fine sand; the Khalifa repeats prayers in the big mosque on Friday at noon; but he says daily prayers in the rukuba, in which there is a whitewashed platform about six feet high, on which he stands.

Close to the rukuba is a square building with thatched gable roof supported by two pillars. This is open on three sides, but surrounded by well-carved and painted wooden railings : in this there is a seat about three feet high, in which the Khalifa sits when he addresses the Ansar. As one leaves the east gate of the rukuba, the Khalifa's palace gate is visible, being built quite close to the mosque.

The Khalifa's palace is known as the "Bab," just as the Sultan's palace is known as the Bab Ali, or Porte. This palace contains a number of different divisions, all built of mud besmeared with red sand. Just within the great gate is the only two-storied house in Omdurman, which the Khalifa has purposely built in order to overlook the whole town, and from here he can see as far as Kererri to the north, and as far as Omdurman fort to the south. Gordon's ruined palace in Khartum is also visible. Near the great gate, and close to the outside wall of the mosque, is a building surrounded by wooden railings, in which the judge sits and carries on his court.

The Khalifa is very fond of going about to different parts of the town, accompanied by crowds of people, and as he found the narrow streets impeded his progress, and detracted from his splendour, he ordered his engineer Omar to construct broad straight roads to all the principal places. This necessitated the removal of thousands of mud huts, which were immediately demolished; but I never heard that the proprietors received any indemnity for the losses they sustained. A broad road now leads from the north gate of the mosque to the Hejira (or place from which expeditions start) near the Khor Shambat. This road, as I previously mentioned, is called "the Martyr's Road." The second large road leads from the west gate of the mosque to the Arda (or parade place), and is known as the "Darb el Arda." A third main road leads to the southern Hejira, whence expeditions leave for Kordofan, Darfur, &c.

In addition to these main roads are innumerable

winding streets and lanes, to traverse which a guide is absolutely necessary. The great Mahdi's dome forms an excellent landmark.

The Khalifa pays the most special attention to the requisites necessary for war, and for this purpose he has had a large building constructed a little to the south of the mosque, consisting of a large hall supported by pillars, and built of burnt bricks. This is known as the "beit el amana," and it is subdivided into various compartments, in which are stored powder, ammunition, guns, rifles, and other implements of war. This building is entered through a large vaulted gate, and no other houses are allowed to be built near it. It is surrounded by a high wall, and is carefully guarded night and day by detachments of soldiers. Within the yard the flags are all firmly planted in the ground, and present the appearance of a small forest of staves. The great black flag of the Khalifa Abdullah towers high above them all. Near the flag yard is a small two-storied building, in which the war-drums are stored, and they are purposely put high up so that they may be heard from a greater distance. In front of the beit el amana is a large open square connected with the mosque by one of the main roads.

Besides his palace, Abdullah possesses a number of other houses, which he visits from time to time. Of these one is situated close to the bank of the White Nile, and its roof is ornamented with two gigantic hippopotamus heads. He has another house at the beit el mal, from which he can easily reach the river, and embark on one of his steamers to visit his Eastern Hejira, whence expeditions start for the Gezireh, or for Abyssinia. And, lastly, he possesses a large house on the Arda, or parade ground, and at the northern Hejira. In all these houses he keeps up a large establishment of women.

Omdurman is built almost entirely of mud, the straw huts or tokuls have disappeared. Every house-owner surrounds his yard with a wall, in order to keep out thieves and spies with which the city abounds. It is not permitted to build good houses, as they might prove a temptation to their owners to hide money. Whenever a man is known to be well off, or prosperous, he is almost certain to have his wealth taken from him.

One of the most important places in Omdurman is the market, to which a broad road leads from the mosque. It is a place full of life, abounding in buyers and sellers, as well as idlers, who come to tattle and pick up any news they can. The proof that Mahdieh is not considered to be a durable régime is evident from the feverish anxiety of everyone to hear the latest news, and the market is the rendezvous for all news-seekers. Here are collected merchants from Kordofan and the Gezireh, from Berber, Dongola, and Sawakin, all earnestly occupied in learning each other's news.

It is impossible to give an idea of the wild rumours which are continually flying hither and thither. It is equally impossible to separate the false news from the true. On this account the market is looked upon by the Khalifa with the utmost distrust, and he would readily abolish it if he thought it was possible to do so. It consists of a strange medley of shops and stalls, workshops and straw huts. Khalifa Ali Wad Helu has been put in charge of the place, he has apportioned special quarters for each variety of goods, and the different marts are now separated off in lines.

At night all goods, working tools, &c., are removed, as it would never be safe to leave them there, so that in the daytime the market is the very life of Omdurman, while at night it is absolutely empty and deserted. Since, however, Wad Helu has taken it in hand, small brick huts have been run up in which some merchants lock up their goods, and leave them in charge of caretakers. Cloth dealers, druggists, greengrocers, salt and meat vendors, all have their special quarters now, as well as gold- and silversmiths, blacksmiths, carpenters, tailors, and barbers. There are also special quarters for public eating-houses, coffee-shops, firewood vendors, builders, and shoemakers.

The women have their own separate divisions, and for the last few years men have been forbidden to have

THE INHABITANTS OF OMDURMAN. 283

any dealings with them. For the settlement of quarrels and disputes which frequently occur in the market, there is a special market court, presided over by a judge, and all delinquents are interned in a large zariba quite open to the sun's burning rays. Close to the zariba are three sets of gallows, besides two others in different parts of the town. The gallows are erected close to the market, in the hope that if the executions are seen by the masses, it will have a deterrent effect on crime.

The inhabitants of Omdurman are a conglomeration of every race and nationality in the Sudan : Fellata, Takruris, natives of Bornu, Wadai, Borgo, and Darfur ; Sudanese from the Sawakin districts, and from Massawah; niggers as black as ebony, down to a light chocolate colour, Niam Niam and Mombuttu cannibals, Bazeh, Dinka, Shilluk, Kara, Janghé, Nuba, Berta, and Masalit ; Arabs of every tribe — Baggara, Rizeghat, Taisha, Homr, Howazma, Miserieh, Kababish, Habbanieh, Degheim, Kenana, Gowameh, Bederieh, Beni Jerrar, Gehena, inhabitants of Beni Shangul, and of Gezireh, Shukrieh, Batahin, Hadarba, Hadendoa, Barabra, Jaalin, Danagla, Egyptians, Abyssinians, Turks, Mecca Arabs, Syrians, Indians, Europeans, Jews ; and all these various nationalities have their own quarters, and marry into their own tribes and sections. Arabic is the universal language, and all free inhabitants of the Sudan speak it or corrupt dialects of it.

The Danagla, Barabra, and Hadendoa have their own special languages; but being derived from Arabic, they are called "rotan," as if Arabic were the only original language in the world—the language of Adam and Eve, and the language of paradise. Arabic is not compulsory, so the blacks still talk in their local dialects.

The population of Omdurman amounts to about one hundred and fifty thousand persons; but it is by no means fixed, for during the winter numbers quit the town and go off into the Kordofan or Gezireh districts to cultivate. But when the Khalifa orders a general assembly, the numbers of course increase considerably.

In 1888 the city was perhaps larger than at any other time, for in that year the Khalifa ordered all the inhabitants of the Gezireh to come and live in Omdurman. The reason for this was never exactly known, but it was thought he feared a revolt on the part of the Ashraf.

All the principal towns and villages on the Blue Nile as far south as Karkoj have been destroyed, such as Kemlin, Messalamieh, Wad Medina, Abu Haraz, Wad el Abbas and Rufaa; the inhabitants of all these towns, men, women, and children, under great fatigue, had to come to Omdurman, where they settled in the north of the town near Khor Shambat.

All these severe measures quite alienated the people from the Khalifa; wives were furious with their husbands for having so abjectly submitted to his yoke, and it was now quite plain that they feared him greatly. One word from him was sufficient to make them pull down their houses, pack up their goods, load them on camels, donkeys, and mules, and transport them to hated and dreaded Omdurman. How they longed for the Government they had so bitterly abused. "Alf turba wala rial tulba" ("Thousands of graves are better than a dollar tax") had been their watchword in the beginning of the revolt; it had proved true with a vengeance, and how bitterly they repented of their folly when it was too late! Khalifa Abdullah now gripped them in the palm of his hand, and the utter disunion and discord which he created between tribes and nationalities, made all hope of future liberty and freedom quite out of the question.

Those who detested Mahdiism prior to 1888 had much greater cause to do so in 1889 and 1890; the first of these years brought a terrible famine on the land, and in 1890, though the actual period of want had passed away, everything was excessively dear.

The 1888 harvest had turned out badly; during the summer of that year the Khalifa had issued stringent orders that no one should keep more than one ardeb of dhurra in his own house, under penalty of severe punishment; all over and above that amount was ordered to be

BEGINNING OF THE FAMINE.

brought to the landing-stage at Omdurman; and as there were but few transport animals to carry the dhurra into the town, their owners charged exorbitant rates for its carriage, consequently large stores of it lay on the bank, and quantities were stolen.

Soon the price per ardeb rose from twelve to twenty dollars, and latterly to sixty dollars. Even the most aged people, in the whole course of their existence, had never seen such a famine as now fell on the land. Continual wars had prevented cultivation, and want of rain into the bargain were the main causes of this terrible calamity. In 1878, when there was a scarcity of rain, the price of dhurra never exceeded sixteen dollars the ardeb, now the price was almost four times as great. The supplies of corn received from Fashoda alone saved Omdurman from absolute starvation. The supplies from the Blue Nile were quite exhausted. Up to 1889, Fashoda continued the supply mart; the native cultivators receiving in exchange glass beads, pieces of copper, iron, cowries, and old Medjidie dollars; and in return for all this, the Khalifa despatched Zeki Tummal and an army from Galabat, who treacherously murdered their king, and fought these people who had actually saved him and his capital from the jaws of death!

The dhurra thus imported to Omdurman by the merchants was unloaded there under the strictest watch, and was sold to the Baggaras only at six dollars the ardeb, under absolute compulsion, whilst the other tribes had to purchase it at ten times that amount. This called forth the bitterest complaints against the Khalifa's injustice.

The awful scenes enacted by the starving inhabitants in the market-place at Omdurman are beyond description. People flocked from Berber, Kassala, Galabat, and Karkoj, thinking that the distress would be less there than it was in the provinces; but here they were quite mistaken. As one walked along, one could count fifty dead bodies lying in the streets, and this quite irrespective of those who died in their own homes.

In the provision market the sellers stood over their

goods with big sticks in their hands, to turn away the poor wretched skeletons who, with eyes deeply sunk in the back of their heads, would cast wistful glances at the food which was denied them. Sometimes twenty or thirty of these miserable starving people would join together, and, regardless of the blows showered upon them, which covered their bodies with wounds and bruises, they would wildly attack the sellers, madly seize whatever they could lay their hands upon, and swallow it on the spot, begrimed with dust, and probably besmeared with their own blood.

Others would sneak about like wild beasts, their loins covered with the merest rag, and if they saw anyone alone carrying eatables, they would pounce down on him like tigers, content even to seize a handful. These were called "Khatafin" (*i.e.* snatchers, or birds of prey), and at first they were fairly successful in their sudden attacks; but gradually people understood what to be prepared for, and the wretched creatures would be beaten off with sticks: hunger seemed to make them insensible to pain.

One could see hundreds of these starving people wandering about, mere bags of skin and bone, and almost shapeless; they would eat anything, no matter how repulsive. The skins of the camels which had been killed after the defeat of the Kababish and Gehena, and which had been used as coverings for the roofs of the houses, were now taken down, roasted, and eaten in that condition.

Perhaps the most horrible scenes occurred at the places where animals were slaughtered. Hundreds of starving men and women would be seen standing around with cups or gourds in their hands, ready to catch the blood before it fell, and then, as the animal would be writhing on the ground in its death-agony, they would fall upon it to catch the blood as it flowed out of its wound, whilst a crowd would be seen struggling on the ground for the few drops which had escaped and become mixed up with the dust and sand; these struggles generally ended in fights, in which the receptacles were broken, and the people besmeared with their contents, which added to the grim ghastliness of this dreadful sight. No power on earth could have restrained these poor sufferers—the pangs of hunger had driven them mad.

Although famine swept off hundreds, still people poured in from the provinces. Male camels and bullocks had become scarce, and the females were now slaughtered without mercy, even should they be with young. Old bones of animals were ground to powder and made into a sort of bread, which was eaten with avidity; even the decaying carcases of donkeys were consumed in this terrible struggle for food.

But in all this wretched misery the Khalifa showed no mercy, pity, or a desire to relieve these terrible sufferings. He took good care that his Baggaras should be fed, but for the others he cared not a jot. Hunger certainly had the effect of bringing to the front all manner of inventive genius; as it was now no longer possible to rob and steal, the khatafin decided to let the sellers alone, provided they would not hinder them in their attempts to get what they could out of the buyers.

Omdurman was full of strangers who had no notion of the existence of the "khatafin," and would carelessly go to market to buy their food; but no sooner had they placed their money in the shopman's hands than the "khatafin," with wild yells, would seize the money in a trice, and leave the purchaser standing with empty hands. Naturally, the shopmen would not deliver to them the goods, the price of which had been stolen by the "khatafin."

One could fill a book with the thousands of strange episodes which occurred during this awful famine. Children, deserted by their mothers—poor, wretched, starving little things—would beg in the most pitiful, heart-breaking way for alms. Beggars would follow one about till late at night, and would stand about one's house; they would beg for hours even for a grain of food. A poor naked little boy one day broke into our house, crying, "Gian Gowi!" ("I'm very hungry!") The tone in which it was said, the wistful, sunken eyes, and the wretched condition of the boy, could not but excite our pity, though hundreds of beggars had been turned away before he came; we fed him, and he survived the terrible year of famine, but he had forgotten his name, so we always called him "Gian Gowi." Often did I see poor little skeletons of infants trying to get nourishment from their dead mother's breasts.

The following instance will give the reader some insight into the horrors of this famine. One day a poor woman came to me with three starving children; she carried one in each arm, while the eldest clung to her skirt, the whole four looked like wandering skeletons. With a voice of agonised supplication, which could come from a mother only, she earnestly begged me to take the boy and feed him, and that if he survived he could remain for ever my slave. Here was a poor mother who preferred to see her child a slave than to look on whilst he died of starvation before her eyes. This touched me to the very heart, but I could not accept the offer, for I had scarcely enough food for myself, so I dismissed her with a handful of dhurra.

The next day the mother came with one child less, and the third day she came with one child only; and at last she came alone, saying that she was now going to follow her three loved children. After that I never saw her again. If grief did not kill her, hunger must certainly have claimed her as a victim.

One day a girl presented herself before the judge of the market court, and reported that her mother had roasted her little brother and eaten him, and that now she had run away, as she was afraid she might suffer the same fate. The Kadi at once sent some soldiers with the girl to seize the unnatural mother; they found a poor half-starved woman with an ear and a piece of a leg. She was taken before the Kadi, and took a solemn oath that the only child she ever had was the girl; she was immediately interned in the zariba, and the matter reported to the Grand Kadi, who ordered the leg and ear to be exposed on the gallows. Even the savage blacks, who were hardened by constant warfare, were impressed with the horror of the poor woman's action, and crowded round the zariba to gaze at her; but it was soon discovered that the wretched creature was raving mad, so the Khalifa pardoned her, but she died a few days afterwards.

It was never safe for children to appear in the streets at night, or they would certainly have been seized by the starving people. One evening I heard a cry at my door, and myself and several neighbours at once ran out to see what was the matter. We saw a man dragging a boy away: we at once gave chase, and the man dropped the boy and fled; he intended to have a good meal off the boy that night.

During the famine several sold themselves or their children into slavery; but when it was all over, the Khalifa ordered all such to be set free without remuneration to their masters.

Dervishes, who had heaped insults on the Turks during the siege of El Obeid for eating donkeys, and other unclean animals, were now feeling Heaven's vengeance, for not only did they eat unclean animals, but their own children as well. There were so many dead bodies about that it was not possible to bury them all. At first they used to bury them within the city, but the Khalifa put a stop to this, and they were then taken out to the north-west side, and up to this day, if anyone walks in that direction he will find the plain scattered with innumerable skulls and human bones, which lie there glistening in the sun, as white as snow; the driving sand and burning sun have polished them like glass.

How many dead bodies were carried away by the Nile, God only knows; if people thought of it I do not think they would ever eat any more fish, for the fish must have had a surfeit of human flesh. The scent of the dead bodies brought hyenas everywhere, and they became so bold that they would come almost up to my door. As for the vultures, their name was legion, but even they with the help of the hyenas were unable to consume all the bodies.

Let us leave Omdurman for a moment and trace the course of the famine in the provinces. In Dongola and Berber the price of dhurra rose to one hundred dollars an ardeb. The entire districts between Omdurman and Berber had become depopulated. In a hut might be found a man, his wife and children all lying dead on their angaribs. Even in the salt districts near Shendi, almost the entire population had died of hunger. In Kassala and Galabat matters were even worse; here the price of an ardeb had gone up to two hundred and fifty dollars, and even for this enormous price it was almost impossible to get it, for there was really none in the country. The great Shukrieh tribe had eaten almost all their camels, and its numbers had dwindled from forty thousand to four thousand souls.

The large tribe of Wad Zayid (the Debaineh) in the neighbourhood of Gedaref, who for his opposition to Mahdiism had been thrown into prison in Omdurman, had become almost extinct. The population of Kassala, Galabat, and Gedaref had dwindled almost to nothing. Zeki Tummal, to obtain food for his troops, had mercilessly robbed the corn merchants and compelled them to give up their very last supplies; he left them without even a handful.

Around Galabat the hyenas became so bold that they would sneak into the villages almost before the sun was down and drag off the wretched half-dead people. Out of Zeki's force of eighty-seven thousand souls before the famine there remained, after it was over, only ten thousand, including women and children. Karkoj and Sennar, which were generally called the granaries of the Sudan, were desolated by famine. It was, indeed, Heaven's terrible retribution on a people who had practised untold cruelties and shed rivers of innocent blood.

So great was the distress that it became a general saying that any one who did not die in 1889 would never die; and this year, corresponding to the year 1306 Moslem era, will remain engraven for ever on the minds of those who went through the famine in the Sudan and had the good fortune to survive it.

When the first supplies of the new harvest reached the market, there was the most heartfelt joy throughout the country, and every one congratulated his neighbour on the termination of their distress; but even the new harvest was not good, and dhurra did not go below twenty-four dollars the ardeb. The locusts did much harm to the harvest, and this plague has devastated the land now for nearly four years.

There are two sorts of locusts, the yellow and the bright red, and they have infested the whole country from Kordofan to Dongola and to Tokar. They came in such swarms that at times the sun was obscured; on one occasion they passed through Omdurman, and took from two to three hours to do so. The rushing sound they made alarmed the people greatly, and wherever they established themselves they left the place completely bare. They demolished the hard palm leaves so completely that it seemed as if they had been cut with a pair of scissors; even the bark of the trees they did not spare. Wherever they settle they look like a big cloud, which completely covers streets, roofs, and walls. Sudanese, as a rule, sleep out of doors, so that their beds were covered as well, and as soon as one swarm was driven off another settled.

Locusts are considered by the Sudanese as a great delicacy, and when well roasted in butter they taste like fried fish; the locusts generally came between June and September, just when the harvest is ripening or the new crops sprouting after the rains. There is no attempt made to destroy their eggs. Another plague was mice: these little animals, which are of a reddish colour, came in such quantities as to drive the cultivators to despair. No sooner was the seed in the ground than the mice had rooted it up and eaten it. Often the fields had to be planted two and three times over; and then when a heavy rain came the mice would all be drowned, and as the water subsided the ground would be covered with the dead bodies of these little animals.

It seemed as if the entire Sudan lay under a curse. The people knew it too, and looked upon it as God's righteous judgment on them for the evil deeds they had been prompted to do at the instigation of a wicked and false Mahdi.

CHAPTER XVII.

THE KHALIFA AND HIS GOVERNMENT.

The Khalifa's system of government—His household—An outline of his character—His system of prayers in the mosque—His visions and dreams—His espionage system—His household troops—His great activity and circumspection—The great Friday review described—The emigration of the Baggara and western tribes to Omdurman—The flight of Sheikh Ghazali—Management of the beit el mal—System of taxation.

THIS chapter I propose to devote to a brief description of Khalifa Abdullah and his system of government.

Abdullah is a Baggara of dark chocolate-coloured complexion, with a long and prominent nose; he wears a short beard cut according to the Moslem custom. When I first saw him at the siege of El Obeid he was very thin, but now he is extremely stout, and his skin hangs in great folds underneath his eyes; he has a strong clear voice, and though well instructed in Arabic, he cannot conceal his Baggara dialect and accent.

His dress consists of the usual Dervish jibbeh and drawers, he also wears sandals, and over his jibbeh, which is generally reeking with grease and fat, he wears a tob or light cotton cloth; on his head is the usual Mecca takia, round which a turban is bound.

As regards food, the Khalifa is more moderate and simple than the Mahdi; he still adheres to his native dishes—asida (a sort of polenta), eaten with milk or meat, over which a strong sauce full of spices and pepper is poured. Sometimes he eats roasted chicken and drinks quantities of milk and sugar, especially camels' milk, to which all Baggaras are devoted. He has no fixed hours for food, but eats whenever he feels so inclined; and it is perfectly astonishing the amount of food which a Sudanese can consume at a sitting.

Like his master the Mahdi and all important persons in the Sudan, the Khalifa is much addicted to harem life. Shortly after he had established himself as supreme ruler, he thought to surround himself with all the pomp and splendour of a Sudanese Sultan, of which the most important item is a very extensive harem. As the Mahdi had done before, so did he take to himself numbers of wives. Wherever a pretty woman is to be found, he at once gets information about her from his spies, and she is immediately brought to the harem.

Each of his wives has her own house, kitchen, and slaves quite apart from the rest, consequently the expenditure of his household is considerable. His first wife is head of all the other wives, who now number one hundred and fifty. She is a Baggara woman, and is waited on by numbers of eunuchs, who were formerly in the service of the Turkish and Egyptian pashas; and although the making of eunuchs is strictly prohibited by Mahdi law, nevertheless the Khalifa secretly employs numbers of persons who arrange to supply eunuchs when required.

The chief eunuch is a certain Abdel Gayum, who is head of the entire household. He has under his orders numbers of female slaves, who grind dhurra and prepare the food; it is estimated that three ardebs of dhurra a day are consumed in the Khalifa's household.

Abdullah is endowed by nature with a good constitution, but his irregular mode of life has gone far to destroy it. Twice he has had severe attacks which have all but killed him; on both occasions he was delirious, and his body became enormously distended. The last time he was ill all hope of his recovery had been given up, and the doctor who was attending him, and had given him a purgative, was on the point of being beheaded, when at the last moment the medicine took effect, and was the happy means of saving the lives of both the Khalifa and his doctor.

The Khalifa's illnesses are always kept secret, so that

whenever he fails to attend prayers, it is generally thought that he is sick. Fifteen days after the last crisis, and when all danger was over, Abdullah summoned the other two Khalifas and the judges to show them that he had recovered, whereupon Khalifa Ali at once offered up a prayer of thanksgiving, though, if his real feelings had been analysed, it would have been found that he was anything but thankful. After leaving Abdullah, the Khalifas announced to the people in the mosque that he had been very dangerously ill, but that God in His mercy had spared him.

This news was the signal for a wild shout of delight, which reached the Khalifa's ears and pleased him not a little. Eight days afterwards he appeared for the first time in the mosque, then the rejoicings knew no bounds, and the shouts were heard miles off; all the emirs congratulated him on his recovery, and the air resounded with the cries of "Allah etawil Omrak!" ("May God prolong your life!") All this flattery pleased the Khalifa immensely, and this eye-service is a particularly highly-developed characteristic of the Sudanese.

And now a few words as to the Khalifa's character: he is an intensely vain and proud man, very cruel and quick-tempered. Occasionally his ideas are good, but he is surrounded by so many fanatics that his ideas, however good they may be, generally die almost before they are born. He is of a most distrustful nature, because he knows he is surrounded by enemies—thus he is a curious mixture of resolution and inconstancy. He listens eagerly to calumnies, and delights in hearing evil spoken of other people; this causes his decisions to be changeable and capricious; he is guided a good deal by what low slanderers tell him, but they have to watch his temper very closely, and have become great adepts at humouring him. He is fearful and jealous of his authority, and the very smallest infringement of it is looked upon as a most serious crime and punished accordingly. He has surrounded himself with spies, who pander to his jealous and tyrannical nature.

These spies are everywhere, they get into private

houses, attend every meeting, and often start a discussion against the Khalifa and against Mahdiism, merely to draw the unwary into a trap and make them divulge their real feelings and opinions. He is told about the most trivial thing, and sometimes during his speeches and sermons he will give way to the wildest denunciation of his unfavourable critics. He knows perfectly well that he is hated, but he will never allow it to be said openly; for, though he cares little whether he is liked or disliked, he does not wish anything to intervene between him and his authority.

The Khalifa adheres most strictly to the prescribed forms of prayer; every day he attends five times in the mosque and enforces the presence of all the principal emirs. He does not like the Ansar to get into comfortable and luxurious modes of life, but insists on their always being hardened and in readiness to withstand the fatigues of war; all prayers end with the "fatha,"* after which is an invocation for the victory of religion, the long life of the Khalifa, and the continual success of his arms; then follows a prayer calling down God's vengeance on unbelievers and those who have erred from the paths of Mahdiism, and asking that their wives and children may be given as booty to the true believers; at the end of the prayers the whole congregation joins in a loud "Amen."

After afternoon and evening prayers, the Khalifa generally holds short political conversations, in which the affairs of the empire and of the capital are discussed; he receives his emirs and gives them instructions; he frequently gives discourses from the place in which he repeats prayers, and sometimes turns and addresses in the most benevolent manner those who are gathered around him with heads bent in obedient submission. If he bears any one a grudge, he never attempts to conceal it, but refers to it in the most open manner in the mosque, when the culprit generally

* The first chapter in the Kuran; it is held in great veneration by Mohammedans, and is used by them very much as the Paternoster is recited by Roman Catholics.

comes hurriedly forward, throws himself at his feet, and implores forgiveness : if he fails to do this, he is generally threatened with imprisonment.

The mosque is at the same time both barracks and prison, for here he teaches his followers humbleness, obedience, and submission. He frequently repeats his orders that all should be most punctual in their attendance at the mosque, and if, when the appointed hour comes, people are found in the streets, they are invariably flogged and carried off to the zariba. This is the way the Khalifa tests the obedience of his people, and assures himself that they are at all times ready to obey his smallest behest.

The highest punishment possible for an absentee is that he shall attend regularly at the mosque five times a day for eighteen months, under a police guard, who is as a rule a Baggara, and who never lets him out of his sight. A man under such a sentence may, if he have money, pay a fine or bribe his guard ; but if he cannot do this he must attend, no matter how far off his house may be. Some unfortunate people who live a long way off spend their whole day in going backwards and forwards between their dwellings and the mosque. The emirs even, if they neglect this order, are very severely dealt with. This enforced attendance at prayers has greatly added to the unpopularity of the Khalifa, for work is being continually interrupted, and all real feelings of religion are subverted.

Formerly every important emir and fiki had his own rukuba, in which he prayed with his own people ; but the Khalifa put a stop to this, fearing that all such meetings would have a tendency to conspiracy and mutiny. He himself is much more a supporter of authority than of religion, but he induces the former through the latter. Personally, he cares little for religion. All his absurd dreams and imaginary visions only make him a laughing-stock of the people, and he is considered by the orthodox Moslems to be an absolute heretic.

On one occasion, when his spies reported to him that

he was very unpopular, and that it was the general wish that he should die, he withdrew for three days. This considerably alarmed the people, for they had no notion what form of revenge he might not be preparing for them. At the end of this period he reappeared, and from his place in the mosque he announced as follows:—

"I have been taken in the spirit to the third heaven, where I beheld the Mahdi, the Prophet Elias, and Jesus Christ; when I saluted the Mahdi, he introduced me at once to the two prophets; the Prophet Elias had a very ruddy and sunburnt appearance, and took me very roughly by the hand; but the Prophet Jesus was white and soft as wool. These two prophets were pleased to know me, and I represented to the Mahdi that I had no desire to quit this pleasant heaven; I begged him, therefore, to send some one to rule my people instead of me, as I was tired and exhausted by trying to govern people who did not care for me; but the Mahdi told me not to lose heart, and that he would give me power to please all; the Mahdi also told me that he was quite satisfied with my ruling. He afterwards took me into the presence of God, who also showed pleasure at knowing the Khalifa of the Mahdi."

All true Moslems who heard this extraordinary tissue of lies were very angry that he should dare to take God's name in vain in this way, and thoroughly understood his reasons for having such absurd and blasphemous pretensions.

On another occasion he was told that the two Khalifas were very dissatisfied with his arbitrary ruling, and resented being excluded from a share in the government of the country. This induced another vision, in which he declared that the Mahdi had told him he should live eight years more, after which the Prophet Jesus would appear. In this way he gave them to understand that they had not much hope of being given any authority; but this vision appeared to have exactly the opposite effect on the Khalifas, who became more clamorous than ever. He therefore instructed his "vision secretary" to withdraw this vision from circulation, and added that should any one ever be heard talking on this subject again, he would be punished by the loss of a hand and a foot. And then he tried to justify his action by declaring that it was the fault of his secretaries, who had put an entirely different construction on the vision to what he had intended, and indeed to what he had actually seen!

After noonday prayers he ordered extracts to be read from the book dealing with the early wars of Islam. This was quite a new departure. To keep any book on religion or religious history, it was necessary, in the first instance, to obtain the Khalifa's permission; and indeed it was very difficult to keep any such books safe from the wild fanaticism of the Dervishes. It was the Mahdi's intention to destroy, as far as possible, everything which would serve to remind his people of the old days, so that they should believe the more readily in his revelations only.

The Khalifa will not accept written petitions, as he himself cannot read. If any one has a complaint to make, he must call out, as the Khalifa enters the mosque for prayers, "Khalifat el Mahdi!" or "Sidi!" or he may cry out, "Ya Sidi ana mazlum!" ("Master, I am oppressed!") Abdullah then listens to what he has to say, and decides the matter. Whether the decision be favourable or not to the complainant, he must be satisfied with it.

Gifts and alms are frequently besought of the Khalifa, chiefly because he is not of such a benevolent nature as the Mahdi, and moreover, he has less to dispose of than his predecessor.

If the Khalifa does not at once dispose of a case that is brought before him, it is a sure sign that he has no intention of giving a decision on it, and woe to him who dares to again bring forward the question! Abdullah gets very angry if he is interrupted when speaking. The various expressions of content, restlessness, and revenge are so clearly portrayed on his face that one seldom mistakes the frame of mind he is in at any particular time, though he often vainly tries to conceal his actual feelings.

There are some people in Omdurman who make the expressions of the Khalifa's face their study, and are wonderful adepts at knowing what is passing in his mind. They listen attentively to every word he says, and their estimates of his moods go the round of their friends, but are often rather distorted in course of transmission. These thought-readers assign causes to his various moods, which they put down to a variety of reasons, such as ill-health, a disaster, or a quarrel with one of his many wives. All these reports spread at once throughout the country, and one would think that the people had nothing else to do but to discuss the Khalifa and every incident of his daily life. And perhaps this is not to be wondered at, since he exercises so indiscriminately the powers of life and death. One word from the Khalifa is able to rouse up the energies of all those spies whose special duty it is to report the smokers and marissa-drinkers. The liberal payment to them of bribes by these law-breakers occasionally serves to make them neglect their duties; but should the Khalifa wish to replenish the waning supplies of the beit el mal, the reporting of a few delinquents rapidly fills the exchequer again.

The Khalifa is a man of great activity, and personally directs all important matters. He receives reports on the most trivial affairs, and is always overwhelmed with business. This, however, helps to keep him in health, and prevents him leading a life of sensual ease to which his inclinations undoubtedly tend. He has nothing but his activity to thank for the fact that he is still alive, though during the last few years he has greatly deteriorated in this respect, consequent on his indulging more than usual his uxorious appetites.

After morning prayers he generally takes a short sleep, and during the remainder of the day he is busy with the affairs of State. Posts are continually coming and going; and the telegraph having been destroyed, a camel postal service has been organised, but is exclusively used for official letters. Any one who wishes to send private letters must do so through the intermediary of merchants and travellers.

After the day's work is over, the Khalifa delights in gossiping till late in the night, surrounded by his emirs and judges. Sometimes just before midnight he will again enter the mosque, and will summon the poets to sing his praises. He delights in music, and keeps a number of Dar Fertit and Niam Niam singers, who accompany themselves on the rubaba (a sort of native guitar), and their strange and weird melodies delight the Khalifa's soul. These native musicians have a sort of school of music, in which they practise all day; but they never seem to learn anything new.

Abdullah is by no means a ruler in name only. His palace is crowded with male and female servants, slaves, eunuchs, and young boys, who continually wait upon him, and carry after him the inevitable "ibrik." One slave is especially told off to carry the "farwa" or sheepskin to the mosque. The other servants are called mulazimin, and act rather in the capacity of spies than personal attendants. A good or bad word from them has no small weight with the Khalifa. Of course they are all submission to their master; and if they have been brought up in the Khalifa's service, when the time comes he permits them to marry, and gives them a horse as well—the two things they long for most. The Khalifa has also his special barber, who is a slave; and his master of the horse, who is an immensely tall Dinka. He has also a sort of giant slave who lifts him on and off his horse. His life-guards consist of 500 black slaves armed with Remington rifles, who always accompany the Khalifa whenever he rides out. They wear a very short jibbeh—not unlike a soldier's tunic—and short knickerbockers. Amongst them are about 100 Taisha and Homr Arabs, whose special duty is to prevent any one approaching the Khalifa's person. To further add to his prestige, he has also appointed an honourable council, composed of all the principal sheikhs of the great Sudan tribes.

His mulazimin el bab, or "household cavalry," are obliged to be in continual attendance at the great gate of the palace, and never quit their posts until Abdullah has retired for the night. He occasionally selects one or two of their principal officers to despatch on important missions into the provinces. The household cavalry rank next to the judges in the mosque precedence. If any man seek employment, he must attend at the mosque at prayer-time and humbly make known his request to the Khalifa; and if he wishes to succeed, he must not be sparing in the lavishness of the compliments with which he prefaces his demand. The Khalifa is specially open to such eye-service, and always selects for his servants persons who possess this qualification in a marked degree.

The business affairs of State are conducted by an army of clerks, of whom the most influential are Fauzi, Muntasser, Abu el Gharem, and Ahmed; these are all men who possess a good knowledge of Arabic, and know something of history and the Moslem laws; they read all incoming letters to the Khalifa, and answer them in accordance with his directions; one of these clerks is his special seal-bearer; all letters are supposed to be strictly confidential, as well as the deliberations and discussions of the council. If he ever mentions a matter in public, in which he conveys blame or censure, then it is understood that this is merely a warning; if he wishes to inflict punishment, then the culprit is seized unawares, and the chastisement or imprisonment inflicted without further ado; thus does he bring the men of the Sudan low before him, and tramples on their necks.

Abdullah specially delights in a display of magnificence; whenever large expeditions start from any of the hejiras, he generally proceeds there in the afternoon, returning in the evening. Latterly he has made fewer of these excursions, as much work and an irregular life are beginning to tell upon him. He never announces beforehand what he intends to do, but just before noonday prayers the onbeïa is sounded, and a herald shouts

"Khalifat el Mahdi yerkab" ("The Khalifa of the Mahdi is about to ride out"); then everyone who owns a horse prepares to mount and accompany him. The horses in Omdurman have become so accustomed to the sound that whenever they hear the onbeïa they begin to neigh and prance, as if rejoicing in the honour of being allowed to join the Khalifa's ride.

Immediately after prayers the giant slave puts him on his horse, and as he proceeds, hundreds of horsemen and thousands of men on foot follow him shouting and showing all the signs of joy. He always carries a large spear, and is little different from other riders. These latter do not march quietly behind, but continually dash forward in groups of four and eight, their spears poised to strike, then suddenly pull up and re-enter the ranks; this "fantasia" delights the mob, who shout the most violent applause.

During these excursions the Khalifa observes carefully all that is going on around him and what the people are doing. On one occasion, when he rode to the beit el mal and was surveying the mighty river, a woman wearing man's clothes was brought to him from a ship close by. In reply to the Khalifa's question what she was doing, she said she was preparing the crew's food; he then asked if she was married, and she said no, thereupon he began joking and presented her to Wad Adlan; but the latter, seeing that she was neither young nor pretty, readily answered that he was already possessor of the four lawful wives. The Khalifa could not of course violate the law, so he summoned the captain of the ship and insisted on him marrying this old creature on the spot; he also casually remarked that the sailors had a noggara (copper drum) on board, and he immediately gave a general order that no drums were to be allowed on board boats.

On another occasion he noticed a very thick cloud of smoke, and on inquiry he found that it came from a soap manufactory; he therefore immediately issued orders that the soap monopoly rested with the beit el mal, and that any other manufactory was prohibited.

In this way he deprived numbers of people of a means of livelihood.

One day he remarked a large heap of sewage in the centre of the town, which spread a most foul odour all around; this was the cause of the Khalifa himself stating in the mosque that if, when he inspected the town three days hence, he found any refuse, the trespassers should be very severely punished.

Everyone now became directly responsible for the cleanliness of his own dwelling and its vicinity, and this order had a most excellent effect; it was further enforced by the presence of horsemen, who took good care to see that the instructions were carefully carried out. The Khalifa also went so far as to order that if any impurity should be found in the public streets, the owner of the defiled place should carry it away himself with his own hands to the appointed place. This was a cause of great delight to the street-arabs, who heaped insults on the disgraced individual by shouting after him "Shalhu!" ("He has taken it away!") But as it was with the Mahdi, so it is with the Khalifa—at first orders are obeyed with the greatest alacrity, and then people get as careless as ever. Omdurman at the present time is by no means a particularly clean or sanitary town.

The occasions on which the Khalifa appears in the greatest splendour are when he rides to parade. In accordance with the Mahdi's orders, these reviews have always taken place on Fridays, no matter what the weather may be, rain, sunshine, or sandstorm. The review, or "Arda," as it is called, is a religious ceremony, and those who take part in it are supposed to obtain special blessings and advantages. The Mahdi of course wanted to keep up the martial spirit of his followers, and therefore he based his reviews on religious grounds. Sometimes Khalifa Abdullah is absent from these parades, in which case his brother Yakub takes his place.

On parade days the great war-drums begin beating two hours before sunrise, and the slaves whose duty it is to beat them have two varieties of cadence, whilst a small drum beaten in quick time completes the call to

A TROPHY OF ARMS, BANNERS AND DRUMS CAPTURED FROM THE DERVISHES.

arms. The people apply all sorts of expressions to the beating in quick time, such as "Nakelkum" or "Naktulkum" ("We will eat you up," or "We will kill you"), *i.e.* their enemies. In the stillness of the night these drums are heard a very long way off, and in the terrible times of the Mahdi wars their weird and monotonous roll created a most sad and depressing effect on me.

Immediately after morning prayers the leaders proceed to the flag yard, each takes his flag, and they all stand in line in the open space in front of the beit el amana.

The flags of the Khalifas Abdullah and Ali Wad Helu are kept quite apart. Khalifa Sherif seldom goes out, and keeps himself as much as possible from appearing anywhere in public with Abdullah, with whom he is on very bad terms, because he has been deprived of all authority.

The four drum-beaters stand in front of the flags, and gradually the followers all collect round their respective leaders. As soon as the sun rises they begin shouting, and then march to the parade ground. Arrived here, the flags are all placed in line. The horsemen follow Yakub or any other person whom the Khalifa may delegate.

The Ansar are drawn up in a long line facing eastwards, and all the people immediately rush to get into the various divisions to which they belong. Then the onbeïa sounds to indicate that the great master himself is arriving; this is the signal for all those who have stayed behind, attempting to shirk parade, to rush helter-skelter to the ranks, as the Khalifa gets very angry unless the review is well attended. He is generally mounted on a very good camel led by Wad Beshir; he sits with drawn sword, and moves very slowly, surrounded by his black life-guards formed in square.

The four onbeïa-blowers march just in front, and take it in turns to sound the great elephant's tusk. Behind the Khalifa follow the mulazimin riding. Arrived on parade he first inspects the whole line, and occasionally performs some cavalry manœuvres in the hills which stretch towards Kererri. These hills are supposed to be the abode of the Jinns,* who are said to be the Khalifa's auxiliaries in battle, and he frequently indulges in visions, retiring into a small hut, while the Ansar have to stand outside waiting for hours in the burning sun.

At length he gives the signal to march off; again the flags unite in two groups, followed by the shouting Dervishes. The horsemen keep dashing round the flanks to see that no one goes away. All must march back to the beit el amana, where they await the Khalifa's arrival to be dismissed.

The orders respecting the arms and equipment to be carried by the Ansar on parade are all strictly adhered to; everyone must carry at least three spears, *i.e.* one large and two small ones; also a sword, which is slung round the shoulder, and a girth as well; anyone appearing deficient of any of these articles is flogged.

At large festivals the reviews are most imposing. Months before, orders are sent in all directions for the Ansar to assemble. On these occasions there are generally about 1,000 horsemen. The Khalifa, wearing a suit of mail armour and a helmet, is generally mounted on a good charger, and is surrounded by some 200 horsemen, also clad in mail, wearing helmets and greaves; the horses also wear brass head-armour lined with thickly-quilted stuffs, which are intended to protect from sword-cuts.

The riders wear thick red turbans, which they wind round the helmet, and then tie tightly under the chin, thus leaving only very little of their face exposed; they also wear red girdles, which they throw over their shoulders. The combination of red with the dark Baggara complexion is peculiarly effective, and gives them a most martial appearance. The red turban and girdle are entirely the Khalifa's idea. At first the horses were

---

* Jinn is the Arabic equivalent for genii, in the existence of whom the Mohammedans are believers, and by whom they are divided into "believers" and "unbelievers." The Mahdi always asserted that in battle thousands of Jinns fought on the side of the Dervishes.

not shod, but recently Abdullah ordered some thousands of horse-shoes to be made in the arsenal.

The wild excitement and confusion prevailing on these occasions can readily be understood. The guns are all brought out, arms distributed amongst the Ansar, and the shouting and yelling is endless; crowds of horsemen dash hither and thither at a wild gallop, raising clouds of dust.

Horses and horsemanship are a great delight to the Sudanese; the best breeds are from Dongola and Abyssinia. At one time there were quantities in Darfur, and there was no difficulty in raising 4,000 of them, but since Mahdiism has fallen on the land the numbers have greatly decreased. Every horse-owner is entitled to half an ardeb of dhurra from the beit el mal.

The reviews which I have just described tend to keep alive enthusiasm, and also to intimidate those who are secretly opposed to the Khalifa, and whom the sight of such numbers of foot- and horsemen cannot fail to impress. The best riders are the Khalifa's own countrymen—the Baggaras—who are brought up on horses from their early childhood. The Khalifa has craftily arranged that all horses remain in the hands of the Baggaras. At first not many of this tribe joined the Mahdi, they preferred to remain in their own happy hunting-grounds, rearing horses, and living in unfettered liberty in their great plains and forests, and in consequence the Arabs nicknamed them "Arab el Shedera" (Arabs of the forests), but when the Khalifa succeeded to supreme power, he thought that his authority would be considerably strengthened by collecting his own countrymen around him.

After conquering Sultan Yusef, of Darfur, the Khalifa ordered Osman Wad Adam to gather his own countrymen—the Taisha—nearer Omdurman. The youthful Osman gave to those wild nomads a most glowing account of the magnificent countries near the Nile, and of the Khalifa's enormous power and authority, and to prove the truth of what he said, he showed them all sorts of glittering dollars, and various kinds of cloths; nor did he rest until he at last persuaded them to leave their homes.

They set out with all their movable property—women, children, and flocks—all bound for Omdurman; they plundered the inhabitants of the various countries through which they passed, and forcibly seized their camels for transport. The Dar Hameda tribe alone, through whose country they passed, lost 4,000 camels. When they reached El Obeid, a special tax was levied for their maintenance, but, quite regardless of this, they broke into the houses, and laid hands on all they could find.

From El Obeid they passed on to Tayara and Shatt, whence the Khalifa had them conveyed in steamers to Omdurman. There were, in all, 7,000 warriors, exclusive of women and children; their arrival in Omdurman was viewed with a certain amount of alarm, and not without reason. As the Arnauts and the Bashi Bazuks were utilized by the Government in the old days, so were the Taisha to be now utilised under the Khalifa's rule; he favoured them in every possible way, the beit el mal was made responsible for their maintenance and pay. After they had partially settled down, and some had been given the richest patches on the Nile banks, as well as several of the islands, the others were then removed to Berber, Abu Hamed, Dongola, and the Gezireh.

In all these places they very soon made themselves masters of the situation, and the Khalifa gave them the most important Government posts to fill; but notwithstanding all this favoured treatment, still they were not content: the more they had, the more they wanted. Upwards of 4,000 of them deserted from Omdurman, to proceed to their own country; but they were overtaken, and, as an example to the remainder, the right hand and left foot of three of them were cut off, though it was with the greatest reluctance that he ever punished his own countrymen in this way. Two hundred of the deserters were put in prison, where some of them died in a few days: the horrors of this prison so impressed these wild children of the desert, that to this day they tremble at the thought of it.

The sheikh of the Taisha was a man named Ghazali, who was by no means happy in his new position; and though he was well received by Abdullah, still he could not brook the feeling of being under the authority of a man who at one time had been one of his lowest menials. It was reported to the Khalifa that he was discontented, he was therefore summoned before him, and addressed as follows :—

"When you were sheikh in your own country, were we not obliged to kiss your hand, and show you all reverence and respect? Yes: and it was quite right to do so. But now God has placed me over you as your master, then why do you now refuse to give me the same honour and respect which you required of your own subjects when you were in a similar position?"

Ghazali made no reply, but then and there decided to run away. This showed a spirit of independence which had been dead amongst the Arabs for centuries, and to find it we have to go back to the time of Saladin. Sheikh Ghazali was a man who knew no fear, and he confided his plans to his wife and daughter, and they —far from deterring him—rather encouraged him to carry it out. His wife saddled his horse, and urged him rather to die than to submit to a position so far beneath him.

Ghazali, accompanied by two of his relatives, mounted his horse in the middle of the night; without shedding a tear, his wife bade him farewell, and wished him all success in his undertaking. In order to put his enemies off his track, he at first went in a northerly direction till just below Kererri, then turned south-west, and made for Kordofan. But Ghazali made a fatal mistake in using horses for such an enterprise, for, winter being over, there was a scarcity of water in the desert; it would have been far better had he used camels.

The poor man had to pay dearly for his error. Scarcely was he out of Omdurman than one of his own tribesmen reported his flight to the Khalifa, who became very angry, cursed the Taisha for their ingratitude, and ordered the fugitives to be pursued at once. They searched the desert around Omdurman in every direction, and, thinking they must have taken camels, they did not at first take any notice of the horses' tracks, but eventually they decided to follow up the latter, and were soon convinced that they were on the fugitives' heels.

Some distance after leaving Kererri, they came up with the horses which Ghazali and his companions, owing to their fatigue, had abandoned, and had continued their flight on foot. The pursuers were now two days distant from Omdurman, and were on the point of giving up the chase, when they heard a shot fired from a thickly-wooded khor. It was Ghazali, who, suffering greatly from thirst, had separated from his companions in search of water; he had been digging about in the sand, and, discovering the longed-for liquid, he had fired a shot to let his companions know he had been successful.

This shot was his betrayer; the pursuers rushed to the spot, surrounded him, and although he killed and wounded several, he was overpowered and fell riddled with bullets. His head was cut off, for the Khalifa had given orders that on no account was he to be brought back alive. His two relations submitted, and were subsequently pardoned by the Khalifa, who is always more lenient to his own tribesmen than to others. Ghazali's head was brought to Omdurman, and thrown amongst the heap of "unbelievers'" heads.

There is no doubt that if Ghazali had succeeded in regaining his own country, he would have become a dangerous rival to Abdullah. Most of the Taisha infinitely prefer the liberty of their native forests to holding high posts in Omdurman, and would have rejoined Ghazali in large numbers.

One of the most important measures taken by the Khalifa to get all power into his own hands was his attempt to gain possession of all firearms. He had over and over again given orders that any one found with a gun would be punished by the loss of a hand and a foot, and, of course, the natural result was that every one feared to deliver up his gun, dreading the punishment which would inevitably follow. This plan having failed, the Khalifa then ordered two Jew merchants to buy up all firearms for the beit el mal, and the people having no fear of Jews freely sold them.

In this way about 1,000 Remington rifles were secured: in a like manner the Khalifa got possession of the coats of mail; but, as may well be imagined, the Jews did not make much profit out of the business. They were put into chains for eight months, and had to pay back a considerable sum of money as well.

Thus did the Khalifa gradually concentrate all power in himself. The emin beit el mal is obliged to give him a daily statement showing all revenue and expenditure; the Sheikh es Suk (or sheikh of the market) has to render a daily report of everything that has taken place in the market, and the chief judge must keep the Khalifa fully informed of all important cases which come under his notice. The Khalifa reserves to himself the powers of life and death, although the judge passes the sentence.

Every province has a governor or emir, *i.e.* Dongola, Berber, Galabat, Karkoj, Gezireh, Fashoda, Kordofan, Lado, and Jebel Regaf. All these emirs are Baggara, and have several emirs under their commands. Each emir has his own beit el mal, and has the power of appointing his own emin beit el mal and kadi (judge). The emir is the supreme civil and military governor of his province, and is entirely responsible for its administration.

The beit el mal at Omdurman is known as the "Beit el mal el Umûm," and the head of it gives orders direct to all his provincial assistants. Each emir is obliged to report all events of importance to the Khalifa, they are frequently summoned to Omdurman to give an account of their administration, and to take the Khalifa's instructions.

Abdullah watches most carefully all events in frontier provinces, such as Dongola, Berber, &c., and spies, disguised as merchants, are continually sent to Egypt to get the Arabic newspapers, which are always read to the Khalifa by his secretaries. An emir should never pay a visit to Omdurman empty-handed, or he is likely to fall into serious disgrace.

In addition to the emirs are the omala (tax-gatherers), who visit the provinces annually and collect the ushr (one-tenth) and the zeka (alms for the poor, two and a-half per cent.). These appointments are let to the holders at an enormous rate—several thousand dollars a year. The omala have to cover all their own expenses, which they do, and get a very considerable profit besides.

It is therefore apparent that the inhabitants are grievously oppressed. The emirs and omala act in the most arbitrary manner in their own provinces; their will is absolute, and horrible systems of cruelty prevail everywhere. One of the omala, Wad Hamdu Allah, by way of extorting money from a man, bound his hands so tightly behind his back that when released they remained quite powerless. The poor man went to Omdurman to seek redress, and the Khalifa, on the principle of " an eye for an eye and a tooth for a tooth," ordered that the amil's hands should be cut off, or that he should pay the injured man a sum of money. The man, of course, chose the latter, as the cutting off of his oppressor's hands could not have done him any practical good ; so he received 200 dollars compensation and four slaves. But this is an exceptional case ; as a rule these cruelties seldom reach the Khalifa's ears, and if the instigator of the crime is a Baggara it is never noticed.

The Khalifa's brother Yakub is his principal supporter. He and Abdullah are not of the same mother, and Yakub is a few years the senior; he has a somewhat lighter complexion, but if possible he is even more cruel than his brother, and is in charge of the harem. The two brothers work entirely together, and Abdullah, being satisfied with Yakub's integrity, gives him the fullest liberty. Orders given by Yakub are carried out with the same alacrity as if they were given by

Abdullah. He receives every day from the emin beit el mal all surplus cash, and moreover has charge of spare leather, sacking, &c., with which to supply the wants of the Baggaras. It is said that Yakub is already possessor of great stores of wealth.

Thus do the brothers, Abdullah and Yakub, hold the entire Sudan in the most cruel bondage, whilst the inhabitants are harassed by the merciless Baggaras, who have made themselves the ruthless masters of the whole country.

CHAPTER XVIII.

A CHAPTER OF HORRORS.

The revolt of the Batahin tribe—Revolt suppressed with appalling cruelty—Wholesale executions—Method of hanging—Punishment by mutilation—The execution of Abdel Nur—Trade with Egypt—Wad Adlan, the emin beit el mal—His imprisonment and death.

ANOTHER example of the Khalifa's cruel and merciless treatment of all who oppose him is shown by the manner in which he dealt with the Batahin tribe.

This small but warlike tribe inhabits the right bank of the Blue Nile near its confluence with the White, and extends as far as Rufaa; also portions of this tribe are found scattered in the Gezireh. They are the most daring robbers, and, mounted on swift camels, they lie in ambush awaiting caravans and merchants, whom they generally kill and make off with their goods. Bruce, in his 'Travels,' remarks that the wooded country around Omdurman was their favourite haunt. They were the staunchest adherents of the Sheikh el Obeid, whom Gordon's "fighting pasha," Mohammed Ali, had so severely defeated.

During the massacre in Khartum the Batahin were most cruel and pitiless, and for their evil deeds God's just vengeance overtook them before long. Abdullah had sent an emir with a few soldiers to collect the ushr tax, but the wild Batahin, whose own system was to rob and plunder the poor, leaving them not even the wherewithal to live, resisted the emir and his men, and forced them to flee their country. When this news reached the Khalifa, he was infuriated, and determined to deal in the harshest possible manner with this rebellious tribe. He therefore despatched the emir Abdel Baki with a considerable force, with instructions to seize every Batahin he could find, put him in chains, and bring him to Omdurman.

This tribe was now hunted down over the whole country, and Abdel Baki succeeded in securing a few hundred of them, as well as Taher Wad Sheikh el

Obeid, who had been instigating them, and these were all brought to the capital. The influential El Obeid family had taken a very prominent part in the siege of Khartum, but after the Mahdi's death they had become discontented and were not on good terms with the Khalifa; Taher had, therefore, been ordered to leave Rufaa and settle in Omdurman.

On reaching Khojali, which is just opposite to Omdurman on the other bank, he wrote to the Khalifa to say that his father, who since his death had been revered as a saint in the Gezireh on account of his holiness, and who had received innumerable presents on account of his power in preserving the lives of infants, had appeared to him in a dream, telling him to stay at Khojali and make that the headquarters of the family; he was not, therefore, able to come to Omdurman. Taher showed his sagacity in refusing to comply with the order; but Abdullah, whose earnest desire it was to abolish the "saints" of the Sudan, agreed to give Taher twenty-four hours to decide whether he would come to Omdurman or not, so there was nothing for it but to go. However, after a time he was permitted to return to Rufaa, leaving his family as hostages in Omdurman. This is the Khalifa's usual mode of acting with all influential persons whom he suspects of disloyalty.

But to return to the Batahin. Most of them died of starvation and ill-treatment, sixty-nine were taken to the square opposite the beit el amana, where they were kept under a soldiers' guard whilst the Khalifa held a consultation regarding their fate. No decision was come to for some time, and this was because more gallows were being prepared. Hitherto there was only one, now there were three near the "court" zariba—two at the south end of the market-place, and one at the west end; all were provided with camel-hair ropes.

Early the following morning the war-drums were beaten, the onbeïa sounded, and eighteen Batahin were executed, three on each gallows. Such executions have always a great attraction for the Sudanese. The eighteen men were all brought up to the gallows with their hands tied behind their backs. Without a sound or even a change of expression, they gave themselves up to their fate, or, as the Moslem says, they gave themselves up to "El Mektub" (*i.e.* "to that which is written"), for it is supposed that God writes down in a book the birth, experiences, and death of everyone, which things cannot be changed.

Below the gallows is an angarib, on which the condemned stands, while an immensely tall Dinka called Bringi puts the noose round the man's head, pulls it tight, fastens it to the gallows, and then draws away the angarib; and in this way the whole eighteen were soon swinging in the air, whilst the assembled masses sent up shout after shout of exultation.

It was a most horrible sight. The poor creatures wore only a miserable cloth round their loins; they had had nothing to eat for some days, and presented a most wretched condition as the wind blew their emaciated bodies backwards and forwards. All were powerful young men, and the bystanders—as is always the way with the Dervishes—vituperated them freely, accusing them of every description of wanton cruelty, whereas it is more than probable that all these just executed were entirely innocent, and were expiating the crimes of those who had been fortunate enough to escape. When all contortions were over, the bodies were untied to make room for the remainder, who had been quietly gazing at the fate of their brothers which was so soon to be theirs.

On this occasion—as it had often happened before—the cord broke under the last man's weight; but Bringi was very quick, he lost no time in joining the ends and completed his brutal work. The impressions which all those dreadful scenes left on my mind can never be obliterated. But if the fate of the eighteen was cruel, the fate of the remaining fifty-one was even worse.

The Khalifa now rode out accompanied by the cavalry and thousands of spearmen, and taking the wretched Batahin with them they marched towards the parade ground. Every now and then on the way he ordered one of them to be decapitated, and in this way twenty-four more were killed; there were now only twenty-seven left, and on arriving on the ground he sent for the butchers to cut off their hands and feet; soon there was a heap of these bleeding members, whilst the bodies of the poor Batahin lay writhing on the ground, beads of anguish pouring from their brows·; yet not a cry did they utter; most of them died in a very short time. Even the most stony hearts were touched on beholding this terrible spectacle, but no one dared show it—in fact everyone tried to force a laugh or a jeer, because the Khalifa himself revelled in scenes of useless bloodshed and cruelty, while in truth the whole population of Omdurman secretly lamented it.

The bodies hung on the gallows for a day, so that everyone might see them, whilst the mothers and sisters of those who had been mutilated on the parade ground begged the Khalifa's permission to go to the spot and see if any of their relatives were still alive; they were allowed to go, and there they found a few still living; they dressed their bleeding limbs and carried them on their backs to the market-place, where they begged food for them.

Never shall I forget the face of one poor woman. With tearless eyes she bore her mutilated son in her arms, and it would be hard to say which of the two was suffering more—the mother or the son—the latter lifting up his mutilated right arm while he rested his mutilated left leg on his right to prevent anything striking the wounded stump.

It was indeed a shocking and pitiful sight. Several of the survivors of Khartum would pass by these wretched people, and staring at their wounds would shout out, "Have you forgotten Khartum?" Long after this I used to see these poor creatures dragging themselves about in the market-place begging for alms.

Soon after this the Khalifa pardoned the Batahin, and sent Ahmed Wad el Bedri to try to persuade them to come and settle in Omdurman; eventually they formed part of Nejumi's force, and were almost all killed at Toski. Thus did God's vengeance overtake them for their untold cruelties during the massacre in Khartum. It is said that the Khalifa has repented of his wanton slaughter of this tribe.

After this, fear took possession of even the bravest, and no further attempts at resistance were made; discontent was everywhere rife, not in Omdurman only, but throughout the provinces, and even the Baggara, who were favoured in every way, and given every possible advantage, longed to return to their own country.

It is usual, when the day's work is done, for neighbours to collect together in the lovely moonlight nights, for which the Sudan is so famed, and talk over matters. The conversation always turns to politics; the latest news from all directions is eagerly discussed, and often the most unlikely and impossible stories are credited. The fact is that the people long for freedom, and their smallest hopes become exaggerated into not only possibilities, but certainties. The proverb, "El gharkan yemsik fi shaaru" (*i.e.* "The drowning man catches at a straw"—literally, a hair), is being continually exemplified. Talk also turns much on what the Khalifa said and did, what he intends to do, what has taken place in the last council, &c. But the Khalifa, fearing that all these conversations might lead to conspiracies, ordered them to be discontinued. But nevertheless they are still carried on secretly.

Near the market-place there lived a certain fiki named Abdel Nur (*i.e.* the slave of light—that is to say, the slave of the light of the Prophet; though, when the Copts are called by this name, the reference is to the light of the Redeemer). The fiki's neighbours used to assemble in his house every evening, and of course the conversation always turned on Mahdiism, and the Khalifa was abused freely. Abdel Nur would talk more excitedly than the rest, and used to say that the Sudan no longer formed part of Islam, that both the Khalifa and the Mahdi were unbelievers, and this he proved by quotations from the sacred books. All this was reported by a spy to the Khalifa, who at once despatched a company of soldiers by whom the unsuspecting party were suddenly surrounded and carried off to prison.

Early the following morning Abdel Nur was brought before the judges, who asked him if he had really spoken against Mahdiism. Seeing that he was now lost, he thought this a good opportunity, in the presence of such a large audience, to prove his assertion; he declared that the true Mahdi should not die in Omdurman, and that true Mahdiism would not be confined to the Sudan alone; that the people having been once deceived, the paths of wickedness should be avoided, the paths of truth followed, and the oppression of the Moslems abandoned once and for all.

The judges, who in their own hearts were convinced of the truth of Abdel Nur's assertions, were unable to browbeat him, whilst all those who listened had little doubt in their own minds of the truth of the statements of this outspoken man, but fear of the Khalifa intervened to stop them from admitting their convictions. One of the judges at length stood up, and, desiring to make an end of this dangerous and humiliating position, said to Abdel Nur: "We are with the Prophet, the Mahdi, and his Khalifa; are you with us or not?" The fiki replied, "I am not with you," whereupon the Khalifa sentenced him to death, and at ten o'clock the same morning his body was dangling from the gallows; his friends were not executed, but were severely reprimanded.

This execution was so sudden and unexpected that everyone was asking what his crime could have been, but the Khalifa was careful to send spies to all quarters to spread false reports about him, to the effect that he was an unbeliever and a magician; these spies were also told to ascertain exactly what the people said, but the latter knew they were being watched, so they said nothing and retired; the spies set fire to the fiki's clothes, and the next morning reported to the Khalifa that hell-fire had burnt them up.

But the matter was not ended here; according to the Moslem law, if an unbeliever be discovered, all his neighbours within a forty yards' radius are considered guilty, and their houses may be plundered and destroyed. This law was carried out in the fiki's case, and several families with all their goods were dragged off to the beit el mal, while their homes were occupied by the soldiers; several men were threatened with the gallows, and there was a good deal of disturbance in the town. The Khalifa's adherents were shouting, "Away with these unbelievers!" Several suspected persons were seized and kept for three days in continual fear of death.

On the third day several of the wives and families came to the Khalifa and begged his forgiveness, throwing dust on their heads and making every show of Oriental grief. On this occasion the Khalifa thought it was sufficient to thoroughly frighten them all, so on the expiration of the three days he released them and returned their property. He took this opportunity of giving an order that it was the duty of every one to report to him any fiki who was in the habit of writing amulets; spies and informers soon produced numbers of such fikis, who only saved their lives by making most solemn promises to the Khalifa that they would never again be guilty of this disobedience of orders.

On another occasion a boat-boy was accused of having said something against Mahdiism; he was hurried before the judge, confessed his crime, and was then taken off to the parade-ground, where the Khalifa ordered him to be beheaded. Ahmed el Talia was the executioner, but he made a false stroke and only gashed the youth's shoulder, but with the second blow the head was clean severed from the body.

Abdullah's jealousy and alarm for the safety of his kingdom now induced him to turn his attention to Wad Adlan. As I have already narrated, Adlan had rendered the Khalifa great services: he had put the beit el mal in good order, had regulated the accounts on the old Government system, and in order to increase the revenue without having recourse to force, he had persuaded him to open trade with Egypt.

It had been the Khalifa's original idea to erect a sort of great wall of China between Egypt and the Sudan, to prevent all ingress into his newly-acquired dominions; but Adlan was a very tactful man, and by degrees he induced the Khalifa to agree to his proposal. Ivory and gum were declared to be the monopoly of the beit el mal. Ivory comes in small quantities from Regaf and Lado, while gum, which is purchased by the beit el mal for five dollars a hundredweight, is sold out by the beit el mal to merchants for twenty dollars; the beit el mal will also accept gum as payment in lieu of money. A lively trade soon sprang up between Berber, Sawakin, Assuan, and Korosko; and Omdurman merchants were allowed to come to Sawakin and purchase goods; the beit el mal made considerable profits, and the people were less oppressed than before.

Thus did Adlan render a great service to the inhabitants of the Sudan, and through his influence many of the cruel measures of the Khalifa were altered. As long as he was in charge of the beit el mal he was very popular with all, the capital was in good hands, the markets throve, and even when the funds in the exchequer were low he had no difficulty in raising loans from rich merchants on payment of bills of exchange. Usually a loan of 5,000 to 6,000 dollars could be raised between fifteen or twenty merchants with ease, because of the feeling of security which Adlan's presence induced. The white people also owe him a deep debt of gratitude, for he gave them continuous protection.

On one occasion, when it was rumoured that the Sudan was to be invaded by Egypt, the Khalifa proposed separating all the whites and scattering them amongst the Arabs in various parts of the country, but Adlan impressed upon him the necessity of retaining them all under his own eye in Omdurman, and thereby he rendered us an immense service; his main idea was to lighten the Mahdiist yoke and relieve the oppression of the people.

But this growing contentment gradually began to be displeasing to Abdullah, whose main object was to reduce every one to poverty and to enrich his own tribe, the Baggara; thus his and Adlan's views frequently clashed, but Adlan was most prudent, and knew when to give way. What displeased the Khalifa most was to see numbers of people assembling every morning outside Adlan's door waiting for him to go to the beit el mal, where they would lay their complaints before him.

The honour they paid and the praises they heaped upon him excited the Khalifa's jealousy, and the latter frequently rebuked him sharply; but he took no notice of these outbursts, and in a fit of anger he was, on one occasion, thrown into chains for fourteen days. On his release Adlan now thought that the Khalifa could not get on without him, and began to show less submission to his master's will than before. This still further widened the breach between him and Abdullah, which was made worse by Adlan's many enemies, who envied him his high position.

The Khalifa's brother Yakub was his most dangerous rival, as Adlan's popularity had rather detracted from his authority. He and others represented him to the Khalifa as a dangerous man, who might at any moment bring his influence to bear in direct opposition to the Khalifa. It is therefore not to be wondered at that Abdullah grew suspicious, and one day, when Adlan was presenting his daily report, the Khalifa took occasion to tell him that he was far from pleased with him, and blamed him for his delay in sending corn to the starving Dervishes in Dongola. Adlan answered: "What can I do? The people won't have Mahdiism any longer, and that is why I meet with so much opposition." Some say that he even said much more than this; but the Khalifa was not accustomed to be talked to in this way, so he ordered Adlan to give up his sword, and the same night he sent him to prison. This gave his rivals ample occasion to speak against him, and Yakub insisted that he should suffer death.

EXECUTION OF WAD ADLAN.

Adlan was very heavily chained, and forbidden all intercourse with the outside world. His arrest did not at first create much excitement, but this was due to the many false reports which were circulated regarding the cause. On the following day it was announced that he might have to suffer death, on the third day this sentence was confirmed, and a messenger was sent to Adlan to ask him if he had any choice between being hanged or having his hand and foot cut off. Adlan chose the former.

To the beating of war-drums and the sound of the onbeïa, he was led, with his hands bound, to the market-place. Here numbers of Baggara horsemen formed a square round the scaffold, and Adlan, escorted by a guard, entered the square with firm footsteps. When he reached the foot of the gallows, the judge called on him to repeat the Shahada or Moslem creed, which he did with a clear voice, then jumped on to the angarib, adjusted the noose himself, which Bringi pulled taut, and he swung into space, whilst at the same instant the Baggaras drew their swords and flourished them in the air, to signify that a like fate would surely befall all the Khalifa's enemies. But grief was read on every face, and never before had there been such heartfelt lamentations in Omdurman.

Ibrahim Wad Adlan was a most intelligent Sudanese, with black face and aquiline nose. He was about thirty-five years of age.

After his body had been suspended for half-an-hour, Yakub, accompanied by several others, took it down, and laid it out on the angarib; the bystanders say that Yakub could not conceal his look of half repentance, half terror, as he gazed on the corpse of his victim. It was wrapped in a cotton shroud, and taken to the cemetery outside the city, where it was buried, Yakub leading the procession. That night robbers pulled out the body and stole the clothes in which it was laid, leaving the corpse on the sand to be food for hyenas.

The Khalifa's reason for sending Yakub to attend Adlan's funeral could not well be misunderstood, for every one knew that Yakub had been the prime instigator in securing his condemnation; and yet Abdullah was short-sighted enough to imagine that in thus sending his brother he might to some extent dissipate the bad impression which Adlan's execution had created.

The mourning for Adlan was both general and sincere; during his whole administration he had done no harm to anyone; he had done his utmost to smooth over difficulties and lighten oppression, and I can confidently affirm that he is the only man of whom this can be said, for, as a rule, Sudanese who rise to positions of power and authority invariably become most cruel and arbitrary.

Now what good could this execution have done for Mahdiism? No doubt the Khalifa thought to justify himself in the public estimation, because Adlan was too popular, but the real reason was, that the Khalifa feared him, for he knew that his justice and prudence had made him beloved by the people.

With the one exception that Adlan had opened commerce with Egypt, chiefly through the secret intermediary of a former Khartum merchant named Abdel Majid, I do not believe there was anything else against him. It was said that letters had been found, purporting to have been written by Adlan, in which he had begged the Egyptian Government to retake possession of the Sudan; but this statement, had it been true, would have been announced far and wide by the Khalifa; this, however, had not been done, and it was generally agreed that it was entirely fear on the Khalifa's part which prompted him to take Adlan's life.

All his property was confiscated, and his friends persecuted. Some of the latter, after his death, remembered that he had told them how, when studying in Cairo, an old woman had foretold that he would die a violent death. For long he paid little attention to this prophecy; but during the siege of El Obeid, he called it to mind, and thought it would perhaps be fulfilled there. But when he eventually rose to high position in Omdurman, he used to laugh at the old woman's saying. However, during his last imprisonment, he had been firmly convinced it would come true, and that was what made him so bold and firm when he actually came to look death in the face.

In place of Adlan, the Khalifa nominated his relative Ez Zaki, now Emir of Berber; but he fell ill shortly afterwards, and resigned. The Khalifa then appointed Nur el Gereifawi (that is, a native of Gereif, near Khartum). He had been in charge of the beit el mal at Berber; as Nur was an intimate friend of Adlan's, it was thought that he might suffer a like fate, but he was a crafty individual, and had sent the Khalifa 30,000 dollars, which he knew would have the desired effect.

On arrival at Omdurman he stood by the great gate to see the Khalifa; but Abdullah did not summon him that evening, so he lay that night on the ground beside the Khalifa's door—an act of humility which quite won his heart—and the next morning Nur was officially appointed Adlan's successor. In order to thoroughly impress Nur with the dangers of his new situation, the Khalifa announced to him that on the previous night he had beheld a vision, in which he had seen hell, and Ibrahim Adlan suffering untold agonies in the lowest abyss, with a long chain fastened round his neck; Nur was shackled to the other end of the chain, and Adlan was trying to drag him down into the abyss; but the Khalifa had unfastened the chain and released him.

Thus was Nur completely overawed, and did his utmost to comply with the Khalifa's and Yakub's wishes. He discharged all the Copts employed in the beit el mal, and replaced them by blacks. Awad, formerly head clerk of the Kassala Mudirieh, he appointed as his assistant, and through his astuteness and knavery he lost no opportunity of forcibly extracting money from the people.

CHAPTER XIX.

SOCIAL LIFE AT OMDURMAN.

System of public security and justice in Omdurman—The court of small causes—Bribery and corruption—The story of the slave and her mistress—How the Khalifa deals with quarrelsome persons—Thieves and pickpockets—The story of Zogheir—Usurers and their trade—The chief of police—Brigandage—Disproportion of males to females in Omdurman—How the Khalifa overcame the difficulty—Immorality—The marriage ceremony.

IT may be imagined that fear of the Khalifa and his tyrannical rule would produce at least a feeling of public security and immunity from lawlessness; but the following chapter will show that this is not the case.

In the early years of Mahdiism there was no discipline, and laws were entirely put aside, because the whole population was at war and everyone on the move. They were living on the captured wealth and prosperity of the Government. At that time there were not many robbers. When we were living in Kordofan we were perfectly safe, and could sleep with our doors open at night. No one ever thought of taking precautions against thieves, though nothing would have been easier than to break into our loosely-built straw huts.

After the capture of Khartum, and when Omdurman became a large city, the former prosperity of the country gradually began to wane, famine broke out, and then public security became seriously threatened. Thieves increased in such alarming numbers as to be a terror to all; and in 1888-89 they became so bad that people scarcely dared to go to sleep. It is true the punishment of cutting off hands and feet was freely exercised; but even this had little effect, chiefly because robbery and corruption went hand in hand, and a thief had no difficulty in disposing of a bribe.

As I have already narrated, the Khalifa nominated his own judges, with Ahmed the Kadi el Islam as their head; a special court was also established to deal with the innumerable marriage disputes which form so large a part of Moslem legislation. Abdullah specially instructed his judges to consider these cases from their external rather than from their internal aspect.

The usual proofs required are the evidence on oath of witnesses. The witness is obliged to wash himself before taking an oath, so that he may be pure. He then places his right hand on the Kuran, and says, "Hakk kitab Allah" ("By God's book"), following it by his statement. In cases of complaints, the defendant only has the right to take an oath, whereas the complainant must produce witnesses. If no witnesses are forthcoming, the defendant has only to take an oath, and is then acquitted.

The real sense and meaning of an oath is absolutely ignored. Hundreds of oaths are taken every day in the market court on the smallest trifle, perhaps not exceeding a piastre. The falsehood of the individual taking the oath is frequently quite apparent; but unless the witnesses come forward, the most flagrant case will go unpunished.

It is the popular idea that if a man swears falsely on the Kuran, he will immediately fall down dead. This constant perjury is very clear evidence of the depth of moral degradation and religious decadence which the followers of the Mahdi have now reached.

In cases relating to debt, acknowledgment on the part of the debtor of his liability is considered sufficient; but if this is not forthcoming, then two witnesses are required. As a consequence of the widespread mistrust and duplicity which exists, everything, even to the smallest matter, is generally written down on paper; or a bargain may be struck in the presence of witnesses; but this is not considered a safe proceeding, owing to the prevalence of bribery. The Khalifa has given very strict injunctions that all debts must be repaid, and if there be a delay, the debtor is to be put in prison, and brought to reason by hunger.

Let us glance for an instant into the court of justice in the market-place of Omdurman, where most of the small cases are tried. Here we find the sheikh es suk (or sheikh of the market), together with the judge, some soldiers, and (latterly only) a few Arabs, as a police guard. The sheikh generally rides to the court at eight o'clock every morning on a donkey. One of his guards places his sheepskin on a small straw rukuba (latterly this has been constructed of clay), and on this the sheikh seats himself. He has the Kuran beside him.

The parties in dispute arrive, and the case turns, for example, on fraudulent dealing, debts, payment in false coinage, &c. As there are no lawyers, each party must defend himself. As a rule the Sudanese are clever and astute in their conversation, and the man who can talk best has already gained half the victory. The noise and shouting is deafening; and the Sudanese have a wonderful display of sly cunning. The sheikh's last resource is the Kuran.

Sometimes bystanders attempt to mediate between the disputing parties, and this course generally prolongs the talk and noise indefinitely, and does not often succeed. The usual punishment is flogging, which is inflicted on the spot. Marissa-drinkers and tobacco-smokers receive eighty lashes. The individual sentenced has to lie prone on the ground, supporting his head with his hands, while two slaves take it in turns to belabour him with whips made of hippopotamus hide. The first few strokes generally draw blood, but as a rule the victim remains immovable, whilst the bystanders applaud him for his courage. If he utters a cry or a moan he is laughed at and derided. The sheikh and his supporters are much addicted to bakshish, which enables many a culprit to escape punishment.

Should the dispute be of a very serious nature, it is

THE SLAVE AND HER MISTRESS. 331

brought before the high court at the Bab el Khalifa; but here money plays even a more important part than in the smaller court. The success or failure of the case depends on the ability with which the opposing mediators influence the judgment; a hint or a sign with the hand is quite sufficient to make the judge understand, and with marvellous astuteness he will contrive to give the case an entirely new aspect, and one which, probably, only a few moments before he has most strongly condemned, but which now he thinks it advisable, under the circumstances, to adopt; and this change of front is carried out without the smallest hesitation.

I will here give an example of what is considered justice in Omdurman. A female slave who had for a long time had a quarrel with her mistress decided to have her revenge, and the fact that her mistress was in the habit of smoking and wearing jewels aided her in her design. She took her lady's tobacco and cigarette papers, which were generally kept hidden under ground, tied them in a little bundle, ran off with them to a soldier who was her relative, and who belonged to Yakub's bodyguard, and reported her mistress's evil doings.

Meanwhile the lady, finding that her slave had run away, sent her brother-in-law in search of her. The family were now thoroughly disturbed, and anticipated all sorts of bad consequences. The lady's husband hastened to Yakub's house, thinking that perhaps the slave might have gone there, and there, sure enough, he found her, surrounded by a crowd of Ansar. The latter, espying Ahmed (as we may call him), surrounded him and were carrying him before Yakub, when Ahmed, who did not lose his head, explained to the Ansar that he had always been under the impression that the Khalifa had appointed a judge to inquire into all such matters, and that he was ready to bow to the judge's decision; so he, the female slave, and the Ansar all went to the court. The slave produced from her pocket the bundle, laid it before the Kadi, and then stated her complaint against her mistress.

Meanwhile Ahmed had met a friend, and told him how that for a long time the slave had been on bad terms with her mistress, and had seized this opportunity for revenging herself on her, adding that she had probably obtained the tobacco and cigarette papers from elsewhere, and had trumped up this case to harm her mistress, who had never smoked in her life nor worn jewels; indeed, if they liked they might go and inspect the house.

The mediator gave a sign to the judge, who at once decided the case in Ahmed's favour, and ordered him to go to the sheikh es suk, who had been instructed to send some one to inspect his house.

It was not a difficult matter to circumvent the sheikh es suk, and when they all arrived at the house, the slave was called upon to show the place in which she had been ordered to hide her mistress's tobacco. Without a moment's hesitation the slave came forward and began scraping away the earth in a corner. It was evident that she had often done this before, and that the hiding-place had been carefully prepared—indeed, the slave found some tobacco still there which she had not noticed before, and this she exultingly produced; but at that instant one of the Ansar gave her a slap on the face, saying, "Look at this bint el kelb (daughter of a dog), she brought some tobacco here which she purposely dropped into the hole whilst she was clearing the earth away." Heaped with insults by the bystanders, the poor slave was dragged off to the market-place, where she received eighty lashes because she had failed to prove the truth of her assertion. Such is Omdurman justice.

Although this is but one amongst thousands of cases of the most disgraceful corruption, still all this serves to keep the slaves in order, and were it not so, there is little doubt that masters would stand in constant danger, and would be at the mercy of their slaves. Indeed, many slaves have succeeded in getting their masters into great disfavour by informing on them, and this makes the masters in great fear of their slaves

Even if a slave has been born and brought up in his master's house he cannot be trusted, and if he receive some slight punishment, it is more than probable he will go off and report his master as a smoker, marissa-drinker, or that he has become lax in the cause of Mahdiism; and, as likely as not, he will be flogged, or receive some worse punishment.

According to Moslem law a slave's evidence against his master is considered invalid; but this law, as well as all other laws, is only applied according to the Khalifa's wishes and the circumstances of the case: the same remark applies to the value of evidence given under torture.

Curiously enough, murders are seldom committed, and when the wild nature of the Sudanese is considered, it is contrary to what one would expect. Quarrels and disputes are endless, but in spite of being armed, both parties seem to expend their energy in violent talking and gesticulation. The Khalifa has given the strictest orders regarding "assault and battery;" if a man hits another man, he will be liable to have his hand cut off, and this order is generally unflinchingly carried out, unless the condemned man be well off, and he will then have his property confiscated, as the following case will show:—

A dispute once arose between a merchant named Yusef Kurdi and a certain Mohammed, son of the rich Ben en Naga; both were intoxicated at the time, had drawn their swords and slightly wounded each other. The affair reached the Khalifa's ears; he ordered both of them to be arrested, and threatened to cut off their hands; but, as a matter of fact, he really wanted to secure some of their money. Old Ben en Naga, a man of ninety years of age, threw himself at the Khalifa's feet and begged that his son's punishment might be altered, and after a few days' confinement and continued threats, the Khalifa was at length graciously pleased to commute the sentence into confiscation of property. Yusef Kurdi paid 6,000 dollars and Ben en Naga's son 5,000 dollars, while both of them were kept in prison for many months to expiate their hasty step. With no less energy did the Khalifa deal with thieves and swindlers.

There are various classes of thieves: there are the pickpockets, whose field of labour lies principally in the markets, the small bazaars, and landing-places. They are principally Khartum people or Egyptians, and their feats of dexterity are marvellous. The removal and cutting out of purses and money-bags is for them a quite simple operation, and is generally performed when people are engaged in a violent dispute. The thief has generally a confederate with whom he works. They will sit in the crowded ferry-boats, and whilst one of them attracts the attention of his fellow-passengers by singing or telling an exciting story, the accomplice is busily engaged in pocket-picking; or sometimes one of them will begin rocking the boat whilst the other takes advantage of the passengers' alarm by robbing them. They hover about all day long in the market, watching their opportunities to steal both from purchasers and vendors. Stolen goods are sold to a particular set of men who are in league with the thieves, and the money obtained is quickly squandered. The art of pocket-picking has become quite a science, and so skilful are they that detection is almost impossible. The stolen goods are passed on so readily from hand to hand that even if the original thief is caught the person robbed will probably never secure what he has lost. Over and over again thieves are apprehended *in flagrante*, but when brought up before the judge, no trace of the stolen article is ever found. Frequently the judge does not fail to get his share of thieves' profits; so that the latter have every inducement to continue their nefarious practices.

But far more dangerous than the pickpockets are the housebreakers. Of the latter there is a regularly organized body, of whom the chief is known as the Sheikh el Haramieh. The band is made up of strong and bold slaves, who are experts at breaking through walls or climbing over them, armed with a long knife, with which they would not fail to stick anyone who attempted to stop them. They employ women and children as spies, who go about begging from house to house, and then give the housebreakers full information, whereupon the thieves, stripped almost naked, and armed with swords and daggers, break into the house. One of them is always told off to stand over the sleeping owner, and to give him his quietus if he should attempt to rise, whilst the others ransack the dwelling, and are off again as quickly as they came, to divide the spoil. Whenever the cry of "El Harami" ("Thieves") is heard at night, all sleep is banished, and a careful watch kept till morning.

Formerly watch-dogs were most useful to warn against housebreakers, but the Khalifa decreed that they were impure animals, and forbade them to be kept. Not a dog is now to be seen in the whole of Omdurman; but in spite of this injunction, the Arabs living in the desert still keep them. If one of these poor animals by chance strays into the town he is at once pursued by a multitude armed with spears, shouting "Arian!" ("Naked!") and he is soon despatched.

A man called Zogheir—an Egyptian, born at Bara—became quite one of the most celebrated of thieves. From an early age he was brought up to steal, and became most skilful. To a strong constitution he added a courage which was worthy of higher things. As head of a band of thieves he led many a daring undertaking, and had the most wonderful knack of always escaping all harm himself. On one occasion, when there were scores of complaints made against him, he was sent to the lock-up of the market. The sheikh es suk, who was at that time rather short of money, promised to release the prisoners if they could collect fifty dollars amongst them.

Zogheir agreed to get the money, and was given one hour's release from prison. He at once went to the market, and very soon found a victim in the person of a dammur (cloth) vendor, who had sold almost all his goods, and sat with his purse full of money in front of him. Zogheir seated himself down beside him, and started a conversation about the cloth, which he began turning over piece by piece, and with great dexterity he succeeded in seizing the purse, which he secreted under his jibbeh. He then went off to the judge, to whom he presented the purse, in which were seventy dollars, and then quietly returned to the lock-up, and told his guard to again put his chains on.

The cloth merchant soon discovered the theft, rushed off madly to the market court, and there represented that a thief—and it could have been no one else but Zogheir, for he had been sitting with him—had stolen his money. The sheikh severely reprimanded the merchant for making a false accusation, asking whether he was a liar or was mad, and then, taking him off to the prison, he showed him Zogheir heavily bound in chains; and after this the unfortunate merchant had to thank his good fortune that he himself did not receive a flogging.

During the famine Zogheir drove a thriving trade. On one occasion he discovered some Arabs in the market who had just sold a quantity of dhurra, and were counting out their money, which amounted to 700 dollars, which they were carefully examining, to see that all were good. This sight made Zogheir long to get the money, so he winked to his accomplice, and then seated himself near the Arabs, and began asking them whether he could offer them "Medjidie" in exchange for "Makbul" dollars.

When the agreement was nearly concluded, Zogheir took two dollars out of his pocket and gave them to one of his accomplices, to buy some dates, and when the man returned with the dates he began throwing them about in all directions, calling out "Karama! Karama!" ("Alms! Alms!"). The starving beggars flocked to him in crowds, and began quarrelling over the dates, whilst the leather bag in which were the 700 dollars suddenly disappeared.

The cries of the Arabs, searching for their lost money, could scarcely be heard in the frightful din occasioned

THE STORY OF ZOGHEIR, THE THIEF.

by the distribution of the dates, and all this time Zogheir kept on condoling with the Arabs over their loss, and then he seized a favourable moment to make off and divide the contents of the leather bag amongst his friends. At length complaints against him became so numerous that he was sentenced to have his right hand and left foot cut off. He submitted quite cheerfully to the operation, which is really a very simple one.

A butcher is called up, who ties the arm and foot tightly with string just above the place where the cut is to be made. This butcher, who has had an immensity of practice, knows exactly where to cut, and it takes only a very few moments to sever the hand and foot at the joints. The tightly-tied string keeps the victim from bleeding profusely, and in order to prevent gangrene or mortification setting in, the mutilated members are at once dipped into boiling oil or fat, and are then smeared over with katran (a sort of mixture of tar and grease), or sesame. In the course of about two months the cure is complete—that is to say, the cure of those who survive the first shock; but several succumb as well. However, the enormous number of cripples in Omdurman is practical evidence that the nerves of Sudanese are strong.

Zogheir survived the operation, but hardly had he recovered than he began his old tricks again. He now was possessor of a fine donkey, on which he rode about in far better clothes than he had before, and altogether, with his diminished members, his condition seemed to have generally improved. But continual thefts again drove him into prison, where he wore two chains on his foot and two on his neck; still he thought it beneath him to take to crutches, and contented himself with hopping about on one leg. He remained in prison for two years, and during the whole of that time he was well looked after by his friends, who supplied all his wants. At last he was released, and is once more the best professional thief in the Sudan.

But thieves are not all—there are swindlers as well. Several people wished to give their money out to interest, and of course there were numbers found ready to give them what they asked. The Prophet, however, forbids money to be lent out at a monthly rate of interest, and the Mahdi renewed this injunction with threats that an infringement of it would involve confiscation of property; this led the swindlers to adopt a variety of subterfuges. For instance, some men would induce the Arabs to give them 200 to 300 dollars, with which they set up a restaurant, promising the lenders half profits in the concern. As long as the cook has money in hand everything goes on well, and the Arab will probably make daily inquiries as to the progress of the business. "It is going on capitally," is the reply, and the cook entertains his patron, who in turn is much gratified at his generosity, and generally makes a very excellent meal.

A careful account is kept, and prices are high. At the end of the month the profits are divided, and the Arab gets from say eight to fifteen dollars. The business goes on perhaps for a year, the Arab is content and lavish in his praises, but he is not aware that the cook has paid him his share of the profits out of the original money he put into the concern. At the end of about a year the cook begins to complain that "es suk barid" ("The market is getting cold")—*i.e.* business is slack, meat is dear, customers are few, and instead of profit there is a distinct loss. Finding he is the only customer, the Arab patron eats quickly and goes away. At last the shop is closed, and the Arab, coming for his money, is met with the simple answer, "There is none." The case is brought before the judge, the cook hands in a statement of his accounts, showing that the profit amounted to 150 dollars, of which eighty were passed to the credit of the patron in food, and the rest had been lost owing to general depression of trade. The accounts are all right, and the Arab is thoroughly puzzled as to why he should have to pay so dearly for his cook's proffered kindness.

Several Arabs, who have considerably less knowledge of the world than the Gellabas, have lost all they possessed by these swindles. The Omdurman market is, I suppose, the scene of more swindling and deception than any other place of its size in the world. There is no shame in being a thief or a swindler; it is only when one is found out that some shame attaches.

Several masters keep slaves for the express purpose of getting them to rob and steal, and share the profits with them. Slaves of this description are valuable commodities, as, if they are discovered, it is generally pretty certain that their master can bribe the judges; but this, of course, all depends on the relations which exist between the individual and the local authorities. Thus tobacco-smokers and marissa-drinkers must pay a monthly sum to the sheikh es suk, which enables them to carry out their lawless practices with impunity. If any such individual refuse to pay, his habits are at once reported, and he is severely punished, the confiscated tobacco being then sold by the police.

Complaints against these evil practices, and regarding the absence of public security in Omdurman, grew so continuous and so serious, that at length the Khalifa was obliged to interfere, and the following case brought the matter to a head. A drunken slave had shot one of his fellow slaves. In accordance with the law, the master is permitted to take the offending slave's life; but he forgave him, because he did not wish to lose two slaves at once.

When the Khalifa heard of the case, he at once ordered the slave to be executed. After this, every one came and told him about the smokers and marissa-drinkers; and then and there he appointed a certain Wad er Reis, also named Hussein Wad ed Dayim, as sheikh of the market.

This man, who had been formerly Mamur of the Berber police, succeeded in making himself feared by the thieves. He openly told the Khalifa that it would never do to treat thieves according to the law, and that only the strongest and most energetic measures would effect the breaking up of the band.

The Khalifa agreed; and at once the new chief of

police seized all the well-known thieves and put them in chains. They were then bastinadoed, and forced to confess what they had stolen, to whom the goods had been sold, and their value. And thus they got to know the names of almost all the thieves in the town.

These measures created a great sensation in Omdurman, for it was found that several people in high places were implicated, and they were convicted. The thieves, too, seized this opportunity for extorting hush-money; but Wad er Reis soon re-established public security. To increase the supervision, he divided the market into quarters, over which he appointed sub-sheikhs (known as sheikh el hara), who were responsible, with the assistance of the inhabitants of the quarter, for preserving security at night. Numbers of marissa-drinkers were apprehended, and a large quantity of confiscated tobacco was publicly burnt in the market-place. All the principal thieves were transported to the convict-station at Regaf, a course which the Khalifa thought preferable to mutilation of the hand and foot.

Just about this time an Egyptian convict, who had escaped from Sawakin, arrived in Omdurman. He had been convicted of false coining in Egypt, and had been sentenced to ten years penal servitude at Sawakin. While in the prison there, he and a companion had come to an agreement with the soldier guarding them, and all three had escaped and set off for Berber. The soldier and the other man had died on the journey, and the survivor, having reached Omdurman, begged to be presented to the Khalifa; but Abdullah thought it beneath his dignity to interview an escaped convict. He was therefore transferred at once to the steamer bound for Regaf with all the thieves and other exiles, whilst the Khalifa was heard to remark that anyone who came from Egypt was invariably a criminal or dishonest man.

The new posts of sheikh el hara were unpaid, and as the holders had to live, they were forced to make money by unfair means. This led to the old tobacco and marissa abuse, so that matters soon drifted back into much the same condition as before.

The caravan roads into the interior are fairly safe, but merchants always prefer to travel in parties of twenty to thirty; though, as a matter of fact, the Baggara garrisons at the various posts are a much greater source of danger to the merchants than are the thieves and brigands. These Baggara wring money out of the merchants, and steal their goods; but if the caravan is large, they are afraid to do anything which may lead to reprisals. The Khalifa has, however, done much to improve public security in the provinces, and punishes severely when cases are brought to his notice.

The state of public morality in the Sudan is very bad, and in Omdurman it could not well be worse. Before the Mahdi appeared, matters were bad enough. Almost all the large towns, such as Khartum, Messalamieh, Metemmeh, and El Obeid—especially the latter—were hotbeds of immorality of the very worst description.

The Mahdi was utterly opposed to all these evil habits, and during his life matters greatly improved; but this was due rather to the fact that the whole country was under arms, and that the towns were practically deserted. Besides, punishment for such crimes was ungrudgingly given, and the stoppage of marissa-drinking also tended to lessen the evils. Marriage ceremonies were simplified and made less expensive, and a distinct advance in public morality was apparent.

But when the principal fighting was over, and the victorious emirs gave themselves over to a life of luxury and debauchery, when idle town life took the place of religious campaigns, when houses were built of mud and bricks instead of rough straw huts, and when the Mahdi died, then immorality broke forth with the redoubled violence of long compression, and the state of affairs became infinitely worse than it had ever been in the old Government days. I refer especially to

Omdurman. Constant warfare had greatly diminished the male population. Omdurman was full of women who had neither husbands nor male relations ; and this is the real cause of the evil state of affairs.

Matters reached such a pitch in 1888 that the Khalifa issued an order that every unmarried woman must be provided with a husband within three days, or she would be handed over to a Baggara as a slave or concubine. In consequence of this order, for the space of three days the whole town was continuously occupied in marriage ceremonies. Men seized this opportunity of taking women whom they would never, under other circumstances, have been allowed to marry ; and of course these forced marriages could not be of long duration—in a month or two most of the couples were separated.

Another cause which tended towards immorality was the fact that numbers of men had been sent off to far-distant parts of the country on expeditions, unaccompanied by their wives, most of whom were left in Omdurman for years ; and it is hardly to be wondered at if in time they began to forget their husbands and to form unlawful connections, in which the Khalifa had frequently to interfere.

On one occasion upwards of eighty women, whose infidelity to their husbands was unquestionable, were put in prison, and a council held to consider what should be done to them. It was decided to make an example of one, and the victim selected was an unfortunate who had borne two illegitimate children. The poor creature was led into the women's quarter of the market, and there she was lowered into a grave with her last child tied to her bosom, and both stoned to death by a cruel and hard-hearted crowd, who seemed to take a fiendish delight in this inhuman piece of work.

This, however, was the only execution of the sort which took place during Mahdiism. The other women were released ; but the only effect of the above example was to induce women to take criminal means to rid themselves of these evidences of illicit connection; and the open sale of abortive medicines only tended to further increase the moral decadence of the people. One can truthfully say that feelings of horror and shame scarcely exist in the Sudan. From slaves of all ages and sexes, to the little child of six years old, all are instructed in the very worst forms of immorality; but on this painful and disgusting subject I will say no more.

Gradually the simple marriage laws introduced by the Mahdi gave place to the old former customs. For example, the Emir of Berber, Abdel Majid, married the daughter of Abderrahman Bey Ben en Naga, and received from her father 2,000 grammes of gold. The marriage ceremony, which was celebrated with dancing and singing, lasted about a month; but when the Khalifa heard of it, he had the emir imprisoned for some months, declared the marriage dissolved, sent the bride back to her father, and forbade him to let the bridegroom ever take her again.

But the Sudanese have a passion for such ceremonies involving dancing and singing, and will never be restrained by any of these new laws. The women wear jewellery as before; they dance, sing, and prepare marissa; games of chance too are quite in vogue; but of course everything is carried on secretly. From time to time the Khalifa raises his voice against it, and then for a few days everything stops; but it soon breaks out again, and goes on just as before.

The festivals consequent on the termination of Ramadan, on Bairam, on the occasion of births, circumcisions, &c., are not carried out with any degree of their former brilliance. Perhaps a meat meal is given, and visits paid two or three times in the year. The old days of rejoicing have vanished, all is anguish and fear, no man's life and property are secure; every one has perforce to break the laws, which are most of them quite impracticable, and at the same time are in constant fear of spies, who are everywhere. There is no security, justice, or liberty; and happiness and content are unknown.

CHAPTER XX.

THE KHALIFA'S TREATMENT OF THE WHITE CAPTIVES.

Description of the prison, or "Saier"—The "Abu Haggar"—The imprisonment of Charles Neufeld—Terrible sufferings of the prisoners—Domenico Polinari—The danger of corresponding with the European prisoners—Neufeld threatened with death—He is given charge of the saltpetre pits—The fate of Sheikh Khalil, the Egyptian envoy—The Khalifa's treatment of the "Whites"—Exile to the White Nile.

IN the preceding pages frequent reference has been made to the prison. This is an institution of so much importance in connection with Mahdiism that it merits a description in detail.

"Saier!" In the Sudan the bare mention of this word causes a shudder. The ordinary word for prison is "siggen," but Saier is really a contraction for beit es Saier (*i.e.* the house of the Saier). Saier is the name of a terrible individual of the Gowameh tribe of Kordofan, who has been gaoler since the early days of the Mahdi, and his name has become the synonym of the horrible place of which he is the guardian.

A curious story is told about his name which is said to be true. The Gowameh women are not renowned for moral virtue, and when Saier was born his mother was asked whose son he was; she was unable to say, and when brought before the authorities and again questioned, she replied that it was "Saier" (*i.e.* it was the custom of her country); the boy was therefore called Saier, and the name clung to him.

Up to the time of the fall of Khartum, the prison had been merely a large zariba, and it was only after the Mahdi's death that a wall, built by the prisoners themselves, took the place of the thorn hedge. It is situated on the river bank, and consists of a large yard, in the centre of which is a building made of mud, straw, and stones, known as " abu haggar " (or the stone hut), with small square openings for a window and a door; near the hut is a well. In one corner are the cells, which are scarcely large enough to contain a man, and which had been built by Charles Neufeld.

The ordinary prisoners are not kept apart, but lie under the shade of the wall during the day, and at night they are packed, some into the abu haggar and some left to lie about in the yard. A few of the well-off prisoners, who are in for long terms of imprisonment, have been allowed to build little huts for themselves. And just behind the gate is a small sun-dried brick building, which belonged to Wad Gazuli, late sub-Mudir of Khartum, who deserted to the Mahdi before Gordon's arrival; this hut is only big enough for two people, and so low that it is impossible to stand upright in it.

It is considered a very great favour to be given a hut of this description—a favour which is only conferred on very privileged prisoners; it is, moreover, very expensive, but it has this merit, that the occupier can at any rate live separately. There are only three huts of this description in the prison.

Prisoners are not allowed to use mattresses, but the owner of a hut can have a small platform slightly raised from the ground, on which he is allowed to sleep. The ordinary prisoners generally lie on their sheepskins or on mats stretched on the ground.

All prisoners are in chains, the number of which depends on the nature of the crime committed. The chains, called makias, consist of large iron rings forged to the ankles, and joined by one and sometimes two thick iron bars. The whole thing is very cumbersome and heavy, and most tiring to walk with. To lighten this difficulty, the prisoners generally attach a piece of string to the chains, with which they lift them up as they walk. If the connecting bar is twelve inches long walking is greatly facilitated. Prisoners who have fallen under the Khalifa's special displeasure are generally laden with four makias, which make it almost impossible to rise; besides these, a long heavy chain is fastened round the neck, and to prevent the skin being chafed, leather stocks can be bought of the prison warders. Close to the prison gate is a large anvil and several hammers; the foot is placed in the open ring, the ends of which are so tightly hammered together that it is quite impossible to withdraw the foot; the anvil is in such constant use every day that it is almost worn out.

Prisoners have to arrange for their own food; if they have any relations or friends they are generally supplied by them, or if they have any money they can buy their own food from hawkers who are permitted to come into the prison. But woe to the unfortunate prisoner who has neither relations nor friends—he must inevitably die of starvation.

At night, as I have remarked, the prisoners are locked up in the stone hut, and sometimes the Saier crowds it up to such an extent that the inmates are almost suffocated or crushed to death. When he is in want of money he does this, for a man will give anything to be released from this awful black hole, in which he packs them like sardines in a box and then closes the door. The walls of the hut become heated during the day, so that within the temperature is like an oven. A little air gets in through the small opening, but the pestiferous atmosphere caused by scores of perspiring human beings tightly huddled together is beyond measure unbearable. Several may be suffering from various illnesses, but there is no possibility of getting out once the door is closed. These horrible scenes can, however, be better imagined than described; suffice it to say that the noise and quarrelling amongst the prisoners, occasioned by the revolting operations which go on, is generally quelled by the guards coming in with whips, with which they lay about them roundly, and then go out and close the door again.

Sleep is almost quite out of the question, for there is no room to stretch out the legs, the heat is unbearable;

scorpions abound, and every now and then a yell shows that some unfortunate individual has been stung; but no one takes any notice. Cases of heat apoplexy often occur, and deaths on this account are frequent. When a person falls down in a fit, the only remark passed is, " ed dam darabu " ("The blood has beaten him"). Thus, in utter anguish and misery, the night is dragged through. The moment the door is opened a rush is made for the open air, the dead are dragged out, their chains knocked off, and then they are buried.

Prisoners who have special permission to sleep outside are all chained together to prevent flight, and are guarded by numbers of soldiers. The slightest show of resistance on the part of a prisoner is punished by flogging. Unless the Khalifa gives special orders to the contrary, prisoners are allowed to receive visits from their friends and relatives. There are no fixed periods of imprisonment, except in the case of smokers and marissa-drinkers, the usual punishment for them being confiscation of property, eighty lashes, and forty days imprisonment; but latterly a fine, estimated at the value of their property, is levied instead of complete confiscation; the two other portions of the sentence are, however, always inflicted.

Prisoners are generally divided into three classes: the first class comprise those who are sentenced by the chief of the beit el mal, and although there is a special prison for offenders against the beit el mal, all serious cases are brought to the Saier.

Second-class prisoners are those undergoing sentences of the judges; both these classes hope for release whenever a sufficiently influential person will pay a sum of money for them, which sum must also be accompanied by a certificate from the Saier that they have been conducting themselves properly during their stay in prison.

The third class are those on whom the vials of the Khalifa's wrath have been poured out; their crimes are for the most part political, and all mediation in their cases is quite useless, no one, not even the judge, is allowed to say a good word for them to the Khalifa. It is only when his wrath is somewhat abated that it may occur to himself to make inquiries about them, and then, perhaps, he may consider recommendations for their release; but the Saier's opinion goes for much more than any other person's, and therefore it is a great point to secure this individual's favour and get into his good graces. One bad word from the Saier can do an infinity of harm, and may indefinitely postpone a release which has been on the point of being made.

The Saier thoroughly understands how to work his influence, for he benefits considerably by his exercise of power; he receives no pay, and therefore he is entirely dependent on what he can make out of the prisoners. The richer his victims, the more pleased he is, for he knows he can wring money out of them freely. Once a month the judge or his representative goes with a clerk to the Saier and makes a list of all the prisoners, showing how long each prisoner has been in confinement. On these occasions numbers of the inmates throw themselves at the feet of the judges and beg to be released because they are starving. This list is shown by the judge to the Khalifa, and Charles Neufeld's name always appears at the top. Abdullah goes through the list, makes careful inquiries about the prisoners, some are released and others passed over in silence, a sign which bodes them no good.

The Saier has seen and heard not a few of the misfortunes of both Sudanese and Europeans. The first Europeans he knew were Slatin Bey and Lupton Bey. Gustav Klootz was put into chains in Abu Girgeh's camp. During the siege of Khartum it was thought the Europeans might attempt to escape to Gordon, they were therefore put in chains; both Slatin and Lupton spent upwards of ten months in chains under the Saier; they suffered dreadfully from hunger and ill-treatment, and were frequently threatened with death. After the fall of Khartum they were released, and were told by the Khalifa that they should feel thankful to have been in prison, otherwise they would undoubtedly have shared Gordon's fate.

DOMENICO POLINARI.

One of our Mission brothers, Domenico Polinari, was also kept in prison for six months; he was imprisoned the same day that I arrived from Kordofan.

After the fall of Khartum, Polinari's brother had been working as gardener in the Mission grounds, under his new master, the Khalifa Sherif. The former gardener, a Dongolawi, had been dismissed for dishonesty, and before he left, Sherif ordered him to be carefully examined, as it was thought he might have taken some of his master's property. Polinari, who was a most conscientious man, and had never even taken a lemon without his master's permission, carried out the search most carefully, and succeeded in getting back quantities of things the thief had made away with. For a time the thief said nothing, but soon his innate Danagla astuteness came to his assistance, and he concocted a plan to revenge himself on Polinari, and again become chief gardener.

The war material, just as it had been left by Gordon in the Mission house, was still there, and it happened that one day some powder was stolen. In spite of the most careful inquiries, it was impossible to trace the thief, and now the ex-gardener began to throw out hints that Polinari was implicated in the theft. A certain Hajji Zubeir was entrusted with the inquiry. Polinari's hut was overhauled, but nothing found in it; his honesty was so well known that no one would credit any evil reports or slander against him. But the ex-gardener was not to be put off. Having failed in his first accusation, he now began to spread reports that Polinari drank liquor and chewed tobacco, and in proof of this he produced a large glass bottle and some dried herbs; there were some fresh dates in the bottle, with which Polinari intended making vinegar, which the gardener insisted was liquor; the dried vegetable was a sort of cabbage which Polinari intended cooking for his food, but this the Dongolawi asserted to be tobacco.

The unfortunate Polinari was obliged to walk through Omdurman with the bottle on his head, followed by an insulting and disorderly crowd, until he came before the judge. Kadi Ahmed, who was well known for his partiality to Europeans, at once recognised that this was all a trumped-up slander, and was anxious to release Polinari; but Hajji Zubeir, who had still great influence with the Khalifa, and instigated by the ex-gardener, sent him off to the Saier. Every other day we used to send him some bread and dates, but the slave to whom the food had been consigned never delivered it, as we afterwards discovered, and had it not been that two of the sheikhs, who were fellow-prisoners with him, had given him some of their food, he must have died of starvation.

Amongst the many Sudanese who have at various times been inmates of the Saier, may be mentioned the aged sheikh of the Shukrieh, who had been most loyal to Gordon, Awad el Kerim Abu Sin—he died in prison : Wad Zaid, of the Debaineh tribe, had been kept in prison four years; then there were Ahmed Wad Suleiman, who had been the Mahdi's chief of the beit el mal; Saleh Pasha Wad el Mek, one of Gordon's principal officers; the Ashraf Sayid Abdel Kader and Sayid Abdel Kerim; Wad Adlan we have already referred to; Jabrallah, Sultan of Darfur, and his five sons, most of whom died; Wad en Nejumi; Sheikh Idris; Makin Wad en Nur, and many others.

When the Khalifa's tribe, the Taisha, first arrived, they plundered the market, and Abdullah threw 200 of them into prison, "to teach them," he said, "the right way." Every night fifty of them were driven into the stone hut, which was, indeed, a terrible change from their forests and plains. Every day several died of typhus fever, and now the mere mention of Saier makes them tremble; even their head sheikh, El Ghazali, whose misfortunes I have already narrated, spent some months in prison before he made his unsuccessful attempt to escape.

Yasin, a Jaali, who had fallen into the hands of the English at Toski, and who was subsequently released, and given a letter to take to the Khalifa from the Egyptian Government, had to pay dearly for saying to Abdullah that they could not fight against the English. Another of the captives taken at Toski, but who also returned to Omdurman, was much more crafty in his interview with the Khalifa; this individual related that, when in Cairo, an old monk had said to him, "Is not the Khalifa of the Mahdi called Abdullah?" to which he replied, "Yes; it is so." "Is he not slightly lame?" "Yes." "Is he not marked with small-pox?" "Yes." Then the monk said, "Do you see this book? It contains the history of the Mahdi and his successor, and it is stated in it that Khalifa Abdullah shall conquer Egypt, Syria, and Mecca." The Khalifa was so delighted with the story that, turning round to his people, he said, "You see the Christians know perfectly well that Mahdiism is not false." The wily author of the story was then given a present of money.

Occasionally the Saier treats his prisoners very cruelly. Two fikis who were suspected of being unbelievers were given 1,000 lashes each; one died on the spot, and the other a few days afterwards. Occasionally he relieves the monotony by giving his prisoners 400 lashes, which is not considered an out-of-the way punishment.

On one occasion, two Ababdeh Arabs coming from Korosko as merchants, were discovered south of Metemmeh with rifles in parts, carefully concealed in bales of cloth; letters were also found on them. They were at once considered to be spies, and taken before the Khalifa. As soon as it was rumoured that Arabs carrying letters for the Europeans had been caught, a friend came to me at once, and told me that the letters were sure to be addressed to me. This threw me into a fever of anguish and alarm; I was made a prisoner, and spent that night in the greatest terror. The Khalifa had warned us most distinctly not to correspond with Egypt, and threatened to imprison us if a letter should ever be discovered.

On this occasion I had every reason to be alarmed, for I had already had a similar experience. After

Father Bonomi had escaped, he sent a Kababish Arab to Kordofan to try and secure my escape. The Arab remained with Sheikh Saleh Bey, and did not, to my knowledge, ever come to El Obeid. When Saleh was killed in 1887, they found amongst his papers a letter from Father Bonomi to me, advising me to trust the Arab, who would not fail to guide me safely to Halfa. This letter was brought, with the other correspondence, to the Khalifa, and was translated to him: he was furious, and had not my guardian angel protected me, I must have been relegated to prison.

Arabic letters are less dangerous, for they are read out to the Khalifa by his secretary, but he is always mistrustful that European letters are correctly translated. How I had longed for letters, even a word from the outside world, or from my relations or friends; but now in my captivity how earnestly I prayed that no letter for me should be found amongst those brought by the Arabs!

As soon as it was daylight I went out in search of news, and to my delight was told that the letters were in Arabic and were not for me, but for some one whom I knew very well. The contents of the letters were quite harmless, merely an interchange of compliments between families in Cairo and Omdurman, and news of a wedding which had taken place in Cairo. However, the two men who brought the letters were in no little fear, thinking they would certainly be executed; but the Khalifa had thoroughly mastered their contents, and though it was evening, he mounted his big white horse, in which position he usually made his important speeches to the Ansar, and he told them that letters had been captured which had come from Egypt and were addressed to the "Ansar el Gudad" (*i.e.* the "new Ansar," or inhabitants of Khartum and the Blue Nile, in contra-distinction to the "Ansar el Gudum," or old Ansar of Kordofan, who were the original adherents of the Mahdi); that he did not intend to mention the names of the persons to whom the letters were addressed, but he was sure they would spend a sleepless night.

The next morning the two Arabs were sent to the Saier, but their lives were spared. A few days later I went to see Neufeld in prison and inquired about the Arabs. I saw them both chained, and when they saw me they at once asked me for something, addressing me as Baladieh (*i.e.* one of their own countrymen), as they took me for an Egyptian; and then they told me in strict secrecy that they had come with the intention of securing the flight of two persons—one Mankarius Gottas, who had died in Galabat, and the other a resident in Berber, by whose imprudence they had been betrayed; these unfortunate men had had nothing to eat for three days, so I gave them a few piastres which I had brought for Neufeld, and as I did not dare to stay longer with them I begged Zogheir to look after them.

Fifteen days afterwards I returned and found the poor men stretched out dead under the wall, they had died of starvation, and the guards had just come to knock off their chains and carry their bodies out of the yard. The sight of these two Ababdehs filled my heart with sadness; there they lay, nothing but a mass of skin and bone; they had come to help poor captives to escape, and this was their own miserable end. This, indeed, was a warning to me to act with increased prudence and caution.

An Egyptian, born in the Sudan, was also sent to the Saier for a few months for declaring that he was the fourth Khalifa—*i.e.* the Khalifa Osman. One day this individual had presented himself to the Khalifa and begged to be heard for a few moments as he wished to tell him of a dream he had had. It is quite an ordinary occurrence for the Ansar to relate dreams flattering to the Khalifa, in the hope of getting some bakshish.

Thus did our Khalifa Osman relate that in his dream or vision he had beheld the Mahdi, who told him to declare himself the fourth Khalifa, and therefore he begged that Abdullah would confirm him as such and permit him to take his share of authority with the other Khalifas; he also begged that all the honour due to him as Khalifa Osman should be forthwith paid to him.

This poor madman paid dearly for his dream. Abdullah merely made a sign to one of his body-guard,

CHARLES NEUFELD.

on which he was hurried off to the Saier, where he received fifty lashes twice a day, and was eventually obliged to confess that the devil had tempted him to strive after this position.

Charles Neufeld remained in the prison longer than

any one else. I have narrated in a previous chapter how he had daringly joined Saleh's people with the intention of establishing commercial relations with the Arabs, and how he was entrapped by the Dervishes at the oasis of Selimeh. This good man knew nothing of the Sudan and nothing about Mahdiism, and it was just at this time that the Khalifa had made up his mind to crush Saleh and his Kababish.

On the 7th of March, Neufeld arrived in Omdurman —a prisoner under a strong escort. News spread like wildfire that an English pasha had been captured, and this caused a great stir in the capital. The Khalifa considered him a most important capture, and Neufeld was ushered into the presence of the three Khalifas and two Europeans, who were entrusted with the examination of his papers. Neufeld spoke Arabic, and was quite fearless. His papers showed that he was a Prussian and had studied in the Leipzig University. All the documents were most carefully translated to the Khalifa, as it was most important to assure him that Neufeld was not an Englishman, as otherwise it would have gone very hardly with him. There was one letter, however, in English, which, if it had been truthfully translated, would have probably got him into great danger.

After the preliminary examination, Abdullah's mind seemed to have been put at rest, for he delivered from his high seat a long speech to the inquisitive Ansar regarding this great English pasha, who he said had come to the Sudan with arms and ammunition, intending to seize Kordofan and fight against Mahdiism, but fortunately the brave troops of Wad en Nejumi had met him near Dongola, killed his soldiers, and captured him.

It was the Khalifa's habit to exaggerate facts and thereby encourage the Ansar; he also made out his capture was a most important event, for hitherto they had not succeeded in taking even one of the hated English. Poor Neufeld was therefore thrown into chains and carefully guarded by soldiers; during the whole of that night a fanatical Dinka negress, who used to dress in men's clothes and wear a sword, shrieked continuously at him, "Allah hu akbar alal kufar!" ("God's power is most great over the unbelievers.")

It was decided that Neufeld was to be hanged the next morning. Very early the Khalifa sent orders that the great drum should be beaten, while the blast of the huge onbeïa close to Neufeld's ears almost made him fall down from fright. The slaves made game of him as if he were a monkey; but he still kept up courage and answered all these insults with a manly spirit; the rope had been fixed on to the scaffold, and already crowds of people were collected to see the Englishman executed. But the condemned man had not yet arrived, for the Khalifa's final decision had not been taken. Hitherto he had never executed a white man in this open way, and he delayed, because he was still uncertain about his being a Prussian. Had Neufeld been an Englishman, there is not the smallest doubt he would have been killed.

At length Abdullah made up his mind not to kill him, but he determined to frighten him; about midday, therefore, Neufeld was taken to the market-place escorted by horsemen; the crowd raised a yell of delight when he appeared, but Neufeld fearlessly walked on, and on reaching the gallows he jumped on to the angarib and bent his head so that Bringi might adjust the rope round his neck. Just at the last moment the judge stepped forward and said that the Khalifa had been graciously pleased to repeal the sentence of execution, and Neufeld was, therefore, again removed to the lock-up.

Three days later he was laden with three heavy chains, put on to a camel, and led through all the streets of Omdurman, so that every one might see him. He was also taken to a review where the Khalifa asked him if the Turks possessed as many troops as he now saw before him, to which Neufeld replied that the Khalifa's troops were more numerous, but that they

NEUFELD'S MISERY IN PRISON.   357

were not so well drilled in exercises and movements as the Turks were.

This answer did not please the Khalifa; and in order to make him take an interest in the Mahdi and his Khalifa, he was taken over to Khartum and was there shown the Mission building, which the Mahdi had seized; he was then taken back to the prison, where he remained four years. He was frequently attacked with typhus fever, dysentery, and other ailments, and was terribly stung by scorpions; had not the Europeans in Omdurman supported him he must have starved to death.

The depth of misery to which poor Neufeld was reduced may be readily understood when it is known that he spent a whole year in the stone hut, and it was not until he had completed two years in prison that, through the intermediary of a friend, he was allowed to build a little cell for himself in one of the corners of the yard, where he could sleep away from the other prisoners. This little building was about twelve feet square and very low, and here poor Neufeld used to sit all day long; his jibbeh was very dirty and swarming with insects, which allowed him little rest at night, and in despair he used to get one of his companions in adversity to rub him with wet sand, which made his skin less irritable; some sympathizing Arabs told him to soak crushed cloves in water and then rub his body with the paste; this Neufeld found a capital remedy, though it made his skin smart a great deal at first. Neufeld's kindness of heart soon won over his guards, and often they allowed him to remain undisturbed in his little hut for the night instead of dragging him off to the stone hut.

One evening, hearing that the Saier was in a bad humour, he told his guards that he wanted to spend that night in the stone hut; but the soldiers assured him that the moment they knew there was to be an inspection they would at once let him know. So Neufeld settled himself to sleep in his cell, when suddenly, about midnight, one of his guards awoke him, saying, "Get up quickly! the Saier has sworn he will give any one he finds outside the stone hut 100 lashes."

Neufeld got up as quickly as possible and made his way to the hut, but the chains prevented him from moving rapidly, and when he got to the door he could not turn the key; just at that moment the Saier came into the yard, and seeing him, ordered him to be given 100 lashes on the spot; but the soldiers refused to obey —one said he had fever, and the other said that he had been flogging people all day and was too tired. The Saier was therefore obliged to call slaves from his own house, who administered the 100 lashes, and left poor Neufeld covered with deep scores all over his body.

In 1889 Neufeld obtained a new companion in adversity in the person of a Bohemian baker, who had been employed with some Greeks at Halfa. One day, in a state of semi-intoxication, the baker had left Halfa with nothing but his violin, intending to go to Sawakin; but he lost his way in the desert, was overcome by thirst, and wandered towards the Nile, which he at length reached. Quite ignorant of the direction in which he was going, he struck out towards the south, and fell in with a patrol of Dervishes, by whom he was passed on to Omdurman.

On his arrival the Khalifa sent him to prison, where he remained two years. Neufeld shared his every mouthful with him; but during the famine he suffered dreadfully from want. At length, through the intermediary of the mukuddum in charge of the Europeans, he was released; but a few months afterwards he made off to the Gezireh. The mukuddum, who had guaranteed him with his head, sent several camelmen in search of him; but there was no trace to be found of him. After a time it was reported that he had died of starvation at Rufaa on the Blue Nile, and this information greatly relieved the Khalifa's mind.

As for Neufeld, we did our utmost to obtain his release; but the Khalifa would not hear of it; moreover, false reports were circulated about him. Some people who came from Dongola said that Neufeld, in disguise, had been sent by the Egyptian Government to find out whether the Mudir—Mustafa Yawer—was still loyal or had thrown in his lot with the Dervishes ; but in reality it was Kitchener Pasha who had been entrusted with this mission.

On another occasion an Arabic newspaper, printed in Cairo, was brought to him, containing a paragraph to the effect that an English officer had been captured by the Dervishes in Dongola. This amazed the Khalifa greatly, for at once he believed that he had been deceived and that Neufeld was actually an Englishman. Being, in truth, a mere savage and an ignorant man, he believed that all news in a newspaper must be true, and blamed himself for not having executed Neufeld in the first instance ; he ordered him, however, to be more heavily chained than before.

Others again spread rumours abroad that Neufeld had come with the intention of aiding Slatin to escape—news which enraged the Khalifa perhaps more than anything else. Thus did Neufeld spend four years in prison, and his release seemed hopeless ; but we left no stone unturned. We secured the good-will of all the most influential people in Omdurman, including even the Om el Muminin (Mother of the Faithful—*i.e.* the Mahdi's widow) and the Sherifa Sitt Nefisa (the daughter of Sidi Hassan el Morghani), who petitioned very earnestly for his release ; but the Khalifa would listen to no one.

When powder was scarce in Omdurman, some one suggested, at one of the Khalifa's councils, that it would be much better to make the unbelievers work for religion instead of remaining all day long idle in the Saier, and that Neufeld ought to undertake the saltpetre refinery. The Khalifa said, " Do what you think right—I am content." And on the same day Neufeld was sent to Halfaieh in search of saltpetre ; he found some, and a month later was moved to Khartum, where he is now working in the old Mission-house with an Egyptian assistant named Said. He still wears one chain on the feet, which, from constant rubbing, has become as bright as silver, while there are great black marks round his ankles. In Khartum he is allowed greater liberty than he had in Omdurman.

In 1891 a Jewish merchant came from Massawa to Kassala, where the Emir Abu Girgeh was then commanding. The latter was in favour of opening commercial relations by means of Jews, and permitting non-Mussulman dealers to come and sell their goods at Kassala, or let them go on further into the country. When, therefore, the Jew had disposed of his goods, he went, on Abu Girgeh's advice, to Omdurman. On being presented, the Khalifa summoned another Jew, named Passioni, whom he made responsible for the new arrival. But, as usual, the voice of slander was not silent; it was whispered that he was an Italian spy, and that it would have been better to have him under surveillance. He had scarcely left the Khalifa's presence, when he was recalled and sent to the Saier, there to be "educated as a true Ansar."

The fate of Olivier Pain and the experiences of Neufeld and this Jew are sufficient evidence to prove the utter uselessness of attempting to personally enter into commercial relations with the present ruler of the Sudan. Any one who comes to Omdurman need expect nothing but chains, the most terrible form of imprisonment, insults and ignominy from the Sudanese.

A still worse fate befell Sheikh Khalil, who was sent from Egypt to the Sudan on a special mission to the Khalifa. In company with an Ababdeh sheikh, he arrived at Abu Hamed, where Zogal was at the time. The latter being accurately informed of the nature of his mission, allowed the two messengers to travel without escort to Omdurman, and on the journey Khalil had opportunities of speaking to the people, and ascertaining how they were disposed to the Egyptian Government. He saw with his own eyes the devastation wrought by the Dervishes and by famine in all the towns and villages along the Nile. For some days before he actually reached Omdurman, we heard of his approach, which occasioned no small stir in the place. Some people thought he was bringing proposals of peace, which, if refused by the Khalifa, would oblige the Egyptian Government to again advance into the Sudan; rumours of all sorts were rife, but there was no possible means of knowing the truth.

Late one evening Khalil arrived, dressed as an Egyptian, with a long flowing abayeh (mantle). He was taken before Yakub, to whom he made over his letter, and was then taken before the Khalifa, to whom, it is said, he freely spoke his mind. That same evening he was sent under escort to Kererri, where he was put into a hut under a strong guard, but he was not chained. He was supplied with meat, butter, corn and sugar, and a female slave was placed at his disposal by the Khalifa, who had purposely sent him out of Omdurman to prevent him conversing with anyone, and to keep all information regarding his mission quite secret.* In this way the Khalifa thought he would give him a different impression of Mahdiism, while Hajji Zubeir was told off as intermediary between Khalil and Abdullah.

It was generally believed that Khalil had blamed the Khalifa for his ill-treatment and oppression of the Moslems, and had shown him how his rule was ruining the Sudan. He had begged him to abandon the evil of Mahdiism and return to the true orthodox religion. Whilst in confinement at Kererri he was frequently threatened with death. No one knew what his mission could be, and the Khalifa knew how to guard it secretly, so that gradually people began to forget all about him, and great was the surprise when one day Khalil and his companion appeared riding on mules at the great parade held during the Bairam festival.

The Khalifa brought Khalil here to show him how immense was his power and authority, and just before the parade was concluded Abdullah and all the cavalry galloped up to him, surrounded him, and asked whether

* Khalil had been entrusted with a few lines of a purely non-political nature, politely asking the Khalifa to return to the bearer any clothes, papers, &c., belonging to the late General Gordon, which his family were very desirous of procuring. He was also given lists of all prisoners captured at Toski, showing how they were disposed of in Egypt, and a remark was added that when peace and tranquillity were restored between the two countries, they would be permitted to return, but in the meantime they were well cared for.—F. R. W.

he would not rather stay in the shadow of the Mahdi's dome than return to Egypt. Khalil, who had now been for upwards of five months in confinement, and thinking that he should never be allowed to leave, and at the same time longing to be allowed to return and report to the Government all he had seen, replied diplomatically that having once been in the light he had no wish to return to darkness.

This reply delighted the Khalifa, who ordered him to be set free, and at prayers in the mosque on that day he sat in the centre of the long line of Ansar just behind the Khalifa.

It is the custom at festivals for all European prisoners, Greeks, Syrians, Jews, &c., to go and offer the Khalifa their good wishes. When they arrived on this occasion the Khalifa ordered them to be seated around him—he does not allow them to kiss his hand, as he might thereby become contaminated with their impurity ; he usually makes a speech, pointing out the punishments which may fall upon them ; but this time he was particularly gracious, asked how they were all getting on, and if they had met with ill-treatment or injustice at the hands of anyone. He gave them to understand that they must look on him as their protector, and that should they die their children would become their heirs, and that if a family had no children, the property would be sold and divided amongst the other prisoners.

This kindly speech was a great surprise to us all ; but the astute Khalifa only wanted to show Khalil how well he treated his prisoners. It is possible, also, that Khalil had observed to him how badly we really were treated, but this is only surmise on my part. Abdullah's kindly speech, however, did us much good, for of course all he says goes the round of the whole town, and when the people knew that we had been well received, they showed us much greater kindness and respect. If, on the other hand, the Khalifa ever imputes a word of blame to any of us, the reaction on the people is immediate, and we are at once insulted and maltreated. It is always said that " the whites "—which is the name by which we are known in the Sudan—"live under the shadow of the sword."

The Khalifa then asked Khalil's companion if he wished to return or stay where he was. The man replied that he was a messenger, pure and simple, and that as such "he should return to him who sent him," and on the same day the Khalifa gave him permission to depart.

But now evil reports were spread abroad regarding Khalil. It was said that he was a great friend of Mustafa Yawer, the ex-Mudir of Dongola, and that it was mainly through his influence that he prevented him adopting Mahdiism; it was also said that he was the chief of the spies sent by the English, and a bitter enemy to the Mahdi. It was imprudent under such circumstances of Khalil to go as an envoy to Omdurman. He had given his services to the Government for this purpose, and he bravely adhered to it; but he was well known to the inhabitants of Dongola and Dar Shaggieh, and it was quite certain that the Khalifa would never permit such a man to return to Egypt. Even in Omdurman he would not allow him to be at large.

Two days later the judges were assembled to consider Khalil's case: false witnesses came forward who asserted that they had seen Khalil worshipping the sun and frequently turning towards the west at prayers, and all sorts of stories were trumped up to induce the Khalifa to put Khalil in chains.

The pliable judges condemned the sheikh, and he was relegated to the Saier. Neufeld had to give up his cell, which was made over to Khalil. None of the prisoners were allowed to speak to him—thus was the poor man left without a friend or acquaintance to help him; everyone shunned him as if he were the victim of some foul disease. From the earliest days of Mahdiism it was always the fate of those who fell in favour to be deserted by all, and this was more especially the case with all those on whom the Khalifa's wrath fell. Thus everyone —fearing for his own life—avoids all intercourse with such prisoners.

When Khalil had expended the little money he possessed, he sold his sword, sheepskin, and clothes, and bought bread—such bread too!—even Sudanese, who are accustomed to eat all sorts of stuff, could only eat prison bread when hunger had made them like ravenous wolves; but Khalil had come from Egypt and its flesh-pots, and the Sudan bread made him ill.

At length he had no more money to buy even bread, and then he suffered the pangs of hunger. For a month before his death his beard had grown quite white, and he himself had become like a skeleton. His wretchedness and loneliness brought on sickness, and he died a miserable death. It occurred on a Friday whilst the Khalifa was attending a review, and Abdullah accidentally fell from his horse on that day, but was caught before he reached the ground. This was considered a very bad omen by the people, who thought that Khalil had been unjustly condemned. They believed it pointed to the overthrow of the Khalifa's rule, and he himself was very much disturbed.

The disloyal Ababdehs of Hassan Khalifa were also locked up in the Saier. Hassan was a nephew of the former Mudir of Berber, had been for a long time emir of Abu Hamed, and during Nejumi's advance on Egypt had occupied the wells of Murat. It was said that when there, he had acted in a most reprehensible manner, and had wrung quantities of money out of the merchants. It was also said that when Saleh Bey advanced from Korosko on Murat, he came to an arrangement with him—for he was not a Mahdiist at heart—and had retired on Abu Hamed without attempting to fight.

All sorts of reports about him reached the Khalifa's ears, but he refused to believe them. When, however, a certain Abadi named Karrar, one of the Khalifa's spies, who had been captured by Saleh at Murat, for having letters in his possession for the sheikhs in Egypt, and had been kept in prison for some months, was released and returned to Omdurman, the Khalifa then became convinced of Hassan Khalifa's disloyalty; he sent four of his mulazimin to Abu Hamed, arrested him and his people, and confiscated all their property. About forty men were thrown into chains, dragged to Omdurman and there relegated to the Saier; several died of typhus, and the remainder, after two years' imprisonment, were sent as exiles to Fashoda, except Hassan, who still remains in prison at Omdurman.

Near the Saier is another small prison for females, but there are not so many of them.

CHAPTER XXI.

LUPTON BEY AND THE AMMUNITION.

The Khalifa's powder and ammunition begin to fail—Lupton Bey makes fulminate—Unsuccessful attempts to make powder—Yusef Pertekachi at last succeeds—The explosion in the powder factory.

As a result of constant warfare and the careless expenditure of ammunition, the want of it now began to be sensibly felt by the Khalifa, and it eventually became an all-important question. The principal want was caps for the Remington cartridges, for, though there were quantities of empty cases there was scarcely any fulminate left.

Many a starving Egyptian began to try and invent some substance which would act as fulminate; there were still a few books on chemistry to be found, but all attempts failed to produce satisfactory results. At last, a certain Hassan Zeki, who had formerly been a doctor in Khartum, invented the substance required. The Khalifa told off Lupton Bey, who at that time was living in the most abject poverty, as his assistant.

The first trials of the new fulminate were made in the presence of Yakub, and were most successful; the invention proved of the greatest use to the Khalifa. The unfortunate Lupton Bey died on the 8th of May, 1888, and Hassan Zeki continued the work. Within a comparatively short time he prepared a very large number of caps. Abdullah had a special laboratory made, and employed a number of boys as cartridge fillers. It was principally owiug to this invention that the Khalifa was enabled to conduct his successful campaigns against Abyssinia.

KAMAL ED DIN, THE INDIAN.

And now another difficulty arose—this was the scarcity of powder; numbers of persons presented themselves as prepared to make this commodity. An Indian, named Kamal ed Din, came forward amongst others; he had come from India to join the Mahdi, passed himself off as a doctor and proudly called himself "Physician-in-chief to the Khalifa." He had a ready tongue, and soon acquired respect and wealth; he painted his beard red with henna.* He had immense powers of persuasion, and thereby obtained a concession from Abdullah to make powder. He demanded that a special laboratory should be built for him in Khartum, so as to be quite out of observation, and he asked for a quantity of money for the purchase of the chemicals he required.

The laboratory was built in the course of a month in the old corn store in Khartum, and the work was taken in hand. The Indian declared that it was most necessary to obtain phosphorus, and therefore he had all the bones and skulls of the people who had been massacred in Khartum, collected, and these he pounded in mortars into very fine flour, much to the annoyance of people who objected to this desecration of the dead.

Every now and then he applied for more money from the beit el mal, which was supplied to him at once, and now he began to work quite alone and in secret; he put the bone flour in earthenware vessels, poured water on it, and then sealed the vessels hermetically; he now declared that to prepare the chemical substance only, another month was necessary. He therefore stopped work and lived at his ease. At the expiration of the month he secretly opened the vessels; no one had a notion what he was going to do with the bone-paste, but he affirmed that so far everything was most successful, and invited the head of the beit el mal, as well as several emirs, to be present at the trial of the powder.

The emirs came and sat in a circle round a furnace

---

* This worthy was taken prisoner by the Egyptian troops at the capture of Tokar in February 1891.

which slaves were blowing up with bellows; then the Indian produced the vessel, asked the emirs to take some of the substance and throw it into the fire. This they did, and it exploded with a loud report, which greatly astonished the spectators, one of whom then and there, knelt down and offered up a prayer of thanksgiving for the success of the invention.

The emirs accompanied Kamal ed Din to Omdurman in triumph, where he also gave proof of the excellence of his powder in the presence of the Khalifa. Abdullah was wild with joy, and presented the inventor with 200 dollars and a concubine. The Indian now returned to Khartum with profuse promises that he would supply several hundredweight of the new powder in the course of a month.

But soon people began to talk of him as being a cheat and a deceiver; a month passed and the powder was not delivered; the head of the beit el mal became anxious, and reported the matter to the Khalifa, who at once sent his brother Yakub and Wad Adlan to make inquiries on the spot; they went, and it was very evident that the Indian had been duping them all the time. He was brought before the Khalifa, and, strange to say, was not punished. Abdullah merely remarked that he was a poor foreigner, and, of course, had to do his best to make a living. It is a curious thing that Abdullah has a much greater insight into the ways of foreigners than most natives.

A certain mukuddum, however, of the Jaalin tribe did not get off so easily. In the days of the Government he had practised an extensive fraud in Khartum, and also in Sennar as an alchemist, and now he came forward to offer his services for the manufacture of lead. At first he had been occupied in making gold, but now to the Khalifa lead was even more precious than gold, and the want of it was causing him grave apprehension.

The mukuddum's offer was accepted, he received presents from the beit el mal, where he was given a special place in which to carry on his work, and numbers of slaves were placed at his disposal; he was given all the money he required to purchase various things in connection with the manufacture, and which he asserted were absolutely essential. Four slaves were told off to keep up an enormous furnace, whilst the mukuddum, his head and shoulders swathed in a great mantle, beat the ground madly with a long whip in order to call the Jinns to his assistance. His curious antics greatly astonished the people, and he soon became the principal topic of conversation in Omdurman. After fourteen days an enormous lump of lead was drawn out from the furnace, and his reputation was made.

The Sudanese are great believers in alchemy; and it was thought that the preparation of one of the ingredients required the greatest secrecy. The mukuddum, therefore, worked fully on the superstitious nature of the people, and a thick cloud of foul-smelling smoke was seen continually issuing from his mysterious and dark laboratory. The lead was at once sent to the Khalifa, who appeared thoroughly convinced of the miraculous power of the maker, and indeed had the piece brought into the mosque to expose it publicly. The sycophants of course told him that this was an undeniable miracle on the part of the Mahdi, who had been the means of supplying the precious metal to his successor through this mukuddum.

The manufacturer was now in high favour, the Khalifa pressed him to continue the work, and supplied him liberally with money and female slaves. One of the Europeans had urged him to desist, telling him that it was quite impossible to manufacture lead; but the mukuddum answered him three times in the most solemn manner : " Do you think that you know the knowledge of God ?" and then went on with his work. From time to time he continued to send pieces of lead to the Khalifa, but his supply only lasted a few months; the more sensible people began to talk, they urged that if he could make one piece of lead, he could also make several hundred-weight. The voice of the detractors grew stronger, the Khalifa's suspicions were aroused, and the mukuddum was summoned into his presence. He asked him in the most kind manner if it was a fact that he really knew how to make lead, or if he was only attempting to deceive; if the latter—and he confessed to it—then he might receive forgiveness.

But this kindly warning was entirely without effect; the mukuddum boldly answered that he did know how to make lead, and moreover abused his detractors, calling them enemies of Mahdiism, who hated the Khalifa, and did not wish him to be possessor of the precious metal. He added that, if given sufficient time, he would prove his enemies to be liars. The Khalifa permitted him to continue his work a little longer; but the results were still the same, and he was again summoned before Abdullah, who now threatened to cut off his hand and foot unless he confessed that he had been practising a fraud; but still the mukuddum persisted in his denial, and the Khalifa ordered three chains to be forged for his feet, and had him sent back to his laboratory under a strong escort; he was to be permitted to work for three days longer.

He now redoubled his antics, making the dust whirl in clouds about him, and crying on the spirits to aid him. He put a few pounds of substance into the fire—all that was left of his lead-scrapings—but this time the spirits left him in the lurch. Bathed in perspiration, he anxiously raked about the coals; but there was no lead to be seen. He begged and prayed for more time, which was granted. But at length one of his slaves let out the secret; he said that the mukuddum used to purchase in the market the lead bullets which had been dug out of Khartum, he filed them into thin shavings, mixed them with some concoction, and threw them into the furnace; the melted lead was then drawn off and allowed to cool. On the last occasion he had failed, and now his fraud was fully exposed; the Khalifa ordered his hand and foot to be cut off, "not," he said, "so much for the fraud, as for the continual denials." The operation was carried out, but the mukuddum died eight days afterwards of tetanus.

The failures of this man and of the Indian to manufacture powder and lead did not deter others from continuing their experiments, and amongst the latter was a Greek named Yusef Pertekachi, who continued working on with the most dogged determination. He had tried every plan to gain a livelihood; but whatever he put his hand to, it seemed to fail, and he was soon deeply involved in debt. In his desperate position he determined to study the manufacture of gunpowder. For a whole year he continued his experiments, and in his case the truth of the proverb, "Necessity is the mother of invention," was fully exemplified; he succeeded in making fairly good powder.

The experiences of the Indian and the mukuddum pointed to extreme caution; he did not, therefore, tell Adlan, who he thought would not believe him, but after his death he applied to Yakub.

Yakub is a man whom even the leaders of Mahdiism find a difficulty in approaching, and poor Pertekachi tried for months before he obtained a hearing; but at length he was attended to, and the various trials and experiments of the new powder, both in guns and Remington rifles, proved most satisfactory.

Pertekachi at once rose in favour in the eyes of Abdullah and Yakub, and was soon comparatively well off. The Khalifa ordered a bottle of the powder to be placed in the Antik Khana, on which was written: "Powder invented by the Osta (Master) Pertekachi."

At first Pertekachi set to work to improve the damaged powder, of which there were quantities of old barrels taken out of the Government magazines, but, having been left in damp places, it had become crusted. For several months he continued his work, to the complete satisfaction of Abdullah, but the poor man was soon to come to a terrible end.

On the 26th of January, 1891, Pertekachi as usual went to the market-place at an early hour to have a chat with the other Europeans. He happened to say: "To-day is the anniversary of the fall of Khartum—Gordon's day—a black day!" In the Sudan it is the custom to call a day on which a misfortune has occurred "Yom aswad" (a black day). And to the survivors of Khartum, the 26th of January is always looked upon as a day of grief and sorrow; several people give alms for the rest of the souls of their murdered friends.

Pertekachi had intended to go and look at the new house he had just built; but being the 26th of January, he would not go to it, and decided to go to the beit el mal instead, where he had some work to do. He found the workmen busy opening one of the barrels of damaged powder, and after taking a cup of coffee, he went to help them, as they seemed to be in difficulty. He had scarcely reached the spot when—owing to a sudden blow or shock, or clumsiness on the part of the workmen—the powder blew up with a most terrific explosion which shook the whole town, and terrified the inhabitants, who rushed wildly about in all directions to see what had occurred. I happened at the time to be sitting at my loom, and at once ran up to the roof of my house, and there, in the direction of the beit el mal, I saw a column of thick smoke ascending.

My first thought was for poor Yusef. I hastened to the beit el mal, which was half an hour's walk from my hut, and found crowds going in the same direction. The Khalifa himself appeared on the scene, he came riding along on a donkey, with only one or two men. His first question was, "Osta Yusef fi?" ("Is the Master Yusef alive?") "Taish enta!" ("May you live!") was the reply. These are the words in which Arabs always announce a death.

A poor Egyptian woman, whose only son was employed as Pertekachi's clerk and had been killed, was weeping and wailing in the most heart-rending way —her husband and another son had been murdered in Khartum—and now wild with grief she was cursing the Mahdi, through whom her dear ones had been brought to an untimely end. Some of the Ansar approached, and threatened to beat her with a whip if she did not stop. But she shouted at them, "Kill me as well! Why should I live any longer? You have killed my dear ones—may God kill you!"

The Khalifa, who was standing near, rebuked his officious followers, saying: "Let her weep, she is 'maharūka'" (*i.e.* consumed with the pain of affliction). He did not stay long at the scene of the accident, but went away very sadly.

All Pertekachi's fellow-countrymen hastened to the spot. Of the large square house built of rough sun-dried bricks, only the four walls were left standing; the wooden roof had been blown to pieces, and it was no small difficulty to collect the shattered remains of those who had been victimized. A pair of legs were found fifty yards away, a head was found half buried in the wall; there was not a hand to be found anywhere.

Another Greek had been killed with Pertekachi, named Yusef Angeli. His head and feet had disappeared, and his body was so shattered as to be almost unrecognizable; he had been in chains, and his foot makia was found fixed in his leg. Poor Angeli had led a miserable life in Omdurman; he had neither home nor friends, and had lived in the market as a Greek hawker. Towards the end of 1890 he had been sent by another Greek to Berber, to try and recover a debt for him. This mission was to be carried out in secret, for Europeans are strictly forbidden to leave Omdurman, and the mukuddum in charge is obliged at once to report any absentees.

But Angeli was a man of no account, and could easily have gone to Berber and back without anyone being any the wiser. A Syrian, however, who bore a grudge to the Greeks, hearing that Angeli had left, went secretly to the Khalifa, but as he was at that time staying at his house in the northern hejira, he saw Yakub instead; he said that, in accordance with the orders of the Khalifa el Mahdi, he had to report that Yusef had deserted to Berber in a sailing boat. Yakub at once informed the Khalifa, who imagined that it was I who had deserted (my Arabic name being Yusef), and at once ordered Nur el Gereifawi, head of the beit el mal, to send camelmen in pursuit. The latter was eventually very annoyed when they found out which Yusef it was, for he would not have thought it worth while to send after Angeli. The pursuers, however, had gone, and found Angeli in the market at Berber; they secured him and brought him back to Omdurman.

Pertekachi, who was a countryman of Angeli's, had begged that he might be spared, and had obtained a promise from Yakub that he should come to no harm. He was brought before the Khalifa, and said that he was very poor, and had only gone to Berber to recover a debt, in proof of which statement he produced the man's written receipt for the money; but when the camel-men who had captured Yusef were asked whether they found any letters on him, they denied it, and in consequence Yusef had been sent to the lock-up in the beit el mal. This was only a very special favour, for the *régime* here is not so severe as in the Saier, and prisoners confined in this place generally obtain a speedy release.

Angeli had to thank no one but Pertekachi for this lenient treatment, and his benefactor did not cease begging until he procured the Khalifa's permission for him to work at the powder factory at a fixed monthly rate of pay; but he had still to wear one makia, and this Pertekachi was arranging to have removed when the terrible catastrophe occurred—he had only been working for three days altogether in the factory. There were, of course, slanderers found, who affirmed that Angeli used to smoke cigarettes, and had purposely set fire to the powder in revenge for his captivity, but this time the Khalifa would not listen to them. He merely said it is "Amr Allah" ("God's will"), and added that he was sure Yusef would never have deliberately tried to destroy his own and his countryman's life. The force of the explosion had driven the iron into Yusef's leg, and it was impossible to take it off; we therefore collected all that remained of the two poor fellows and buried them.

The Khalifa's enemies secretly rejoiced over his misfortune about the powder, for now, they thought, there will be no one to make it; but one of Pertekachi's labourers, who had learnt the manufacture from his master, replaced him as head of the factory. After the catastrophe the factory was removed to Tuti Island, where a large yard was built, around which the necessary workshops were constructed.

CHAPTER XXII.

AGRICULTURE AND COMMERCE IN THE MAHDI'S KINGDOM.

Remarks on the agriculture and commerce of the Mahdiist kingdom —A sandstorm in Omdurman—The paucity of cattle—System of taxation on imports—Provincial beit el mals—Local manufactures—Slavery and the slave-markets—Torture of slaves.

In the following chapter I propose to make a few remarks on the agriculture, commerce, and business of the Mahdiist kingdom. The greater part of the Sudanese live by agriculture and cattle-breeding. Agriculture goes on most of the year; the lands are sown during the tropical rains. The winter is called the "kharif," and in Omdurman begins in July and lasts till the end of September. During this period there are three or four very heavy falls of rain, usually at night, and occasionally during the day there are heavy storms, which are at times very grand.

These outbursts are preceded by great sultriness, the whole ground is hot, everything is burning, even in the shade one dare not touch metal; then in the east a cloud of dust arises, which indicates the coming storm; the clouds bank up with astonishing rapidity, and now it is time for people to make the best of their way home as quickly as they can. The dust-clouds, lighted up by the evening sun, show the exact direction of the storm; some are of an inky black, others gray, and in the distance they can be seen dashing up against one another, and forming, as it were, a series of hills and valleys; yet there is scarcely a leaf moving, and all nature seems hushed.

Then the storm-clouds seem to touch the earth, there

is a sudden rustling of the leaves; the distant houses are lost in obscurity, and now it is time to shut oneself up in one's house. In a few minutes day has been turned into night, the wind howls round the house, windows and doors creak and rattle, till one begins to think in another moment the house will fall about one's ears. Lights are used, for now it is blacker than the darkest night; the fine dust penetrates everywhere and covers everything; the heat is overpowering, one perspires at every pore, and the dust cakes on one's face and hands, giving one the feeling of being intensely begrimed and dirty; but there is nothing for it but to wait patiently for the return of daylight, when one rises with one's eyes and mouth full of dust, and nothing but a complete bath makes one feel in any degree clean again. These sand-storms are generally followed by heavy showers, which completely lay the dust.

A tropical thunderstorm is also full of solemn grandeur—deafening peals of thunder and howling wind, followed by a veritable deluge, which seems to transform the country into a lake in a few minutes.

These sudden storms are a source of no small danger to Omdurman, especially in the quarter where the mosque and market are situated. Here there is no outlet for the water, which overflows into the yards and houses, and melts the mud-built walls like sugar. During the first year or two of Omdurman's existence, and before the people had much experience, several of the huts collapsed during a storm, burying the inhabitants in their ruins. The intense obscurity which always accompanies these deluges adds still more to the general alarm. However, after about two days the whole town becomes dry again; the hot sun and thirsty earth soon absorb all the moisture, and one would scarcely know that rain had fallen.

Generally about a month before the rains begin, and when the Khalifa permits it, the people leave the town in crowds and repair to the fields, which they set to work to clear. After the famine year of 1889 the Khalifa did everything in his power to induce the people to turn their attention to agriculture. Plentiful rain and hard work produced excellent crops in 1890. Dhurra, dukhn, cotton, sesame, onions, and various sorts of beans are grown.

The operation of sowing requires little time or trouble; the fields are cleared of all the stumps, roots, &c., of the preceding harvest, which are burnt, then every one raises a small bank of earth around his ground, so as to retain the water and enable the earth to become thoroughly saturated. This measure is specially necessary in the Gezireh, where the clay soil does not absorb quickly, whilst in the sandy plains of Kordofan it is exactly the reverse.

As soon as the parched ground has absorbed the first rains, sowing is begun without delay; the soil is turned over with iron or wooden hoes, and the seed thrown down. Weeds spring up in great profusion, and it requires endless trouble to prevent their choking the young growth. Dhurra ripens in about two months, dukhn in three. The fine quality, such as Shilluk dhurra, takes six months to come to maturity. The gathered corn is threshed, and then stored in holes in the ground, where it can be kept without deteriorating for upwards of ten years.

Along the Nile, sowing and reaping goes on the whole year through. Water is drawn up by the sakiehs, or water-wheels, and distributed over the fields. After the wars, numbers of these water-wheels which had been destroyed, were reconstructed. Now there are a great number in working order, and the banks are covered with green. All work is done with the iron or wooden hoe, and the plough is not used at all. The only plough I ever saw in the Sudan was one worked by an Egyptian in Khartum, and it caused no small astonishment amongst the natives. Wheat and maize —or, as it is called in the Sudan, "Aish er rif" (Egyptian bread)—ripens in forty days.

In Kordofan quantities of broad beans are grown, as well as sesame, sugar-cane, cotton, onions, garlic, bamiahs, radishes, tomatoes, cucumbers, and water-melons; while Indian figs, pomegranates, lemons, oranges, citrons, bananas, and grapes are grown in profusion in the Khartum gardens. Date-palms are plentiful on the Blue Nile and further south; but it is not possible to dry them, for they at once become full of insects. Rain often spoils the date harvest.

Besides agriculture and cattle-breeding, the Sudanese may be called a thoroughly pastoral nation. During the long wars against the Government, as well as in the internal disturbances, the camels and oxen were almost exterminated; and in 1889 a cattle plague still further reduced the numbers.

When Fashoda was occupied, quantities of cows were taken from the Shilluks and sent either to Gezireh or on to the Berber market, in order to try and stimulate breeding. There are quantities of goats and sheep, as only a comparatively small number of these have been killed; but the greatest loss has been in camels, and it is not so easy to replenish the country in this respect. There are still a considerable number of donkeys, which are used both for riding and as pack-animals. A good donkey will fetch from forty to two hundred dollars.

The Sudanese are born traders and dealers; it is almost a passion with them, and they like the travelling which trade involves. Of course the flourishing commerce of the old days has been quite destroyed. The import of goods to the Sudan from the north and east was formerly in the hands of one merchant. The Berber-Sawakin and Berber-Korosko roads were opened through Wad Adlan, and the re-occupation of Tokar by Egypt has done a great deal to help commerce. Wad Adlan's successor, Nur Gereifawi, established the ushr (or one-tenth tax) on all important goods, in addition to the "zeka," or two and a-half per cent., which was formerly the only tax levied.

This increase in taxation has rather impaired than improved trade, but it is still fairly brisk. However, the "ushr" was levied twice, in both Omdurman and Berber, so that the beit el mal obtained twenty-two and a-half per cent. profit on all imported goods. This exorbitant taxation led to goods being smuggled into the town by night. In spite of every precaution being taken, smuggling still continued; and at last it was decided that all merchants should have their goods stamped at the beit el mal.

This stamp bears the words, "Ushr beit el mal el umum" ("The tenth—general beit el mal"), and no goods are allowed to be sold unless they are thus marked. The head of the beit el mal himself also went to the market and personally stamped all the private goods of merchants; and in this way the fraud was stopped. A merchant selling unstamped goods would have all his property confiscated.

All went well for a time; but soon it was discovered that false stamps were in use. This led to another inspection of all goods in the market, and the confiscation of a considerable quantity of property, an operation which caused business to be suspended for about eight days.

Large quantities of printed cotton stuffs are imported; also perfumes, medicines, cloves, rice, sugar, and dried fruits. The home-trade is, of course, much brisker than imported trade, and consists for the most part of provision dealing. Dongola and Dar Shaggieh supply Omdurman with dates; Berber sends salt, mats and baskets made of palm leaves; from Kordofan comes gum, sesame, and dukhn; the Gezireh exports dhurra, dammur, and cotton; Karkoj supplies sesame and a small quantity of gold. Omdurman is thus the great wholesale and retail mart, which in turn supplies the provinces. Here the whole population—men, women, and children from eight years of age—are all dealers.

The older women have their own quarter of the market, in which they sell oil, grease, pearls, vegetables, drugs, dhurra, and dates. Young women are not allowed to go to the market; but they send their slaves, who take charge of the goods. The latter are obliged to render full accounts when they return in the evening; and woe to the unfortunate slave who makes a mistake in his calculations! Quantities of vegetables are grown in the gardens in Khartum, Buri, and Gereif, and are brought to Omdurman for sale. The Baggara women are naturally good dealers, and have now secured almost the entire custom.

In the early days of Mahdiism everyone lived in the most simple way, and dressed even more simply. The staple article of food is dhurra, which is merely boiled, made into a cake and eaten. Bread, which is generally known as "kesra," is eaten with a sauce which is usually made of pounded bamiehs boiled with red pepper and salt. Sometimes beans are used instead of bamiehs. Meat is scarce, but a meat sauce boiled in milk and mixed with pounded dried fish is a favourite dish. Quantities of fish are obtained from the Nile, and tortoises, which sometimes take the place of meat, are not uncommon. But whilst the rich live in comparative luxury, the poor people exist in the greatest want and misery.

Good clothing is seldom considered; the richer a man is, the dirtier will his dress be. This is, of course, meant to blind the eyes of inquisitive slanderers. The Baggara chiefs have no reason to conceal anything; but it must be quite apparent to all that a form of government which preaches a continual despising of the good things of this life is not likely to promote any of the higher comforts of civilization.

In matters, however, regarding war and the preparations required for a jehad, it is entirely different. Blacksmiths are always busy forging spears and knives; and in this description of work the results are remarkable. Saddlers make every description of leather ornament for horse and camel decoration; tanners prepare the leather, and dye it red or black; tailors now make much better jibbehs than before; the patches are generally made of good cloth, and the best garments are now valued at about sixteen dollars each. The women spin the cotton, and the men weave the dammur from it. The best dammur comes from Berber and Metemmeh. The Darfur women are also famed for their good and even spinning; but Abyssinian dammur is generally considered better than any of Sudan manufacture.

Tin-smiths make drinking cups and tin receptacles of various sorts for household use. Cooking-pots are made of copper. Jewellers make gold and silver

A SLAVE-GIRL FROM EQUATORIA.

filigree work for the ladies; but this work is not nearly as good as it used to be in the days of the Egyptian Government. All these various trades are carried on in the market.

Mahdiism has re-established the slave trade, which is now in full vigour, and almost all those slaves who were

SLAVERY AND THE SLAVE-MARKETS. 383

liberated in the Government days have been sold again as slaves. Wherever there is a beit el mal there is also a slave-market. The largest is, of course, in Omdurman, to which all captured slaves are sent. The beit el mal sells the slaves by auction. Well-grown male slaves are generally taken into the army.

Close to the beit el mal is the female slave-market, where generally fifty or sixty women of various ages are to be found. The slave-dealers are for the most part Egyptians. The slaves are arranged in lines under the open sky; their bodies are generally well bathed in oil to preserve the gloss of their skin. Intending purchasers make the most careful and minute examination, and the price varies from twenty to a hundred dollars.

Young females are kept apart from the rest, as they are generally selected as concubines, and as such they are subjected to a most critical scrutiny; the shape of their hands and feet, and the form of their mouth, nose, ears and teeth are all carefully noted. Black are preferable to copper-coloured slaves, and the latter colour necessitates a considerable reduction in price.

Young male slaves are sold at from thirty to sixty dollars each, and these have generally to learn a trade. Purchasers ask all sorts of searching questions as to whether they have good moral qualities, are likely to run away, &c., &c. The salesman must produce a certificate showing the tribe, a full descriptive return, and the legal authority entitling to ownership.

During the early days of Mahdiism the slave trade received an enormous impetus, more especially subsequent to the capture of Bahr el Ghazal and the occupation of Darfur. After Gessi Pasha's victory over Zubeir Pasha's son and the dispersion of the slave-dealers, several of the latter fled into the interior, where pursuit was impossible; then followed the era of liberty under the Mahdi's banner, the slave-dealers emerged from their hiding-places, and, with quantities of slaves, proceeded to Omdurman.

When at El Obeid I often saw as many as 500 of them marching along to the sound of music. Slaves were dragged from Darfur, bound together with leather thongs round their necks in batches of thirty. Abu Anga brought thousands of them from the Nuba hills. The only districts untouched hitherto were those in the vicinity of the White Nile, but quite recently the garrisons of Fashoda, Regaf, and Lado have been busily engaged in this human traffic; these blacks, however, who during the intervals of peace had been gradually recovering their strength, now determined to resist the Dervish authority, which was not very strong in those far-distant districts. It would have been a great thing if the Dervishes could have been turned out of Lado and Regaf. The Abyssinian campaigns also brought quantities of slaves to Omdurman, but these are little fitted for hard work, and are employed for the most part in grinding corn, carrying water, and as concubines.

Slave-hunting, too, is not carried on in the same way as it used to be. The Khalifa is too knowing to send large raiding expeditions for slaves into the distant provinces, as he fears they might possibly become independent and turn upon him; besides, private individuals are no longer permitted to be in possession of firearms.

Blacks captured in the Khalifa's various wars are sold as slaves, and, while the free Mussulman tribes have been greatly weakened and reduced in numbers by war and famine, the blacks have, on the other hand, been growing both in numbers and in strength. There is abundant proof of this in the great difficulties which the Dervish force at Fashoda is now experiencing, being scarcely strong enough to quit their steamers and sailing boats. The inhabitants of Jebel Nuba are once more almost independent, and now the Dervishes do not dare even to go to the foot of the hills. The withdrawal also of the various Baggara tribes from the neighbourhood of Shakka, &c., to Omdurman has rid the local blacks of their hated presence in their country.

The once notorious Jaalin and Danagla slave-hunters are now beginning to experience in a degree what a slave's life is, and, indeed, it almost seems as if the

TREATMENT OF DOMESTIC SLAVES.

Khalifa Abdullah was an instrument of Heaven's vengeance on those bloodthirsty and ruthless slave-hunters.

The lot of a slave is indeed a miserable one. He is looked upon as an animal created, as the Sudanese say, to make the life of Moslems easy; he must do all the hard work, both in the household and in the field. It is the idea of the Sudanese, that if a slave gets sufficient food he always becomes proud and unmanageable. His dress consists merely of a rag tied round his loins: whatever money he may make by his work is the property of his master.

The female slaves carry water and grind corn, in return they are continually blamed and cursed; any disobedience or dishonesty is punished by flogging, or their bodies are gashed with razors, salt being rubbed into the wounds, and, lest they should have any cause to forget, their half-healed cuts are often ripped open again and salt rubbed in afresh.

In the treatment of their slaves women are more cruel than men, more especially if jealousy is the cause of their anger. Woe to the unfortunate female slave who shows any love for her master! She suffers a species of torture which it would be impossible for me to describe here, and what wonder is it that in despair they often fly from their masters and mistresses?

Yet it is only by this harsh treatment that slaves can be made obedient; it is a very true saying that a person who is forcibly deprived of liberty can only be brought into subjection by force. Slaves under Mahdiist *régime* have so many different ways of revenging themselves on their masters that they never fail to seize an opportunity when it is offered.

The immorality of slaves is quite beyond description; but it cannot be the fault of the unfortunate creatures themselves, for in their own savage homes it is not so. They learn all the vices of their masters, and, indeed, are forced to participate in them or submit to a flogging; consequently, disease of the most loathsome kind is everywhere prevalent, and to be free from it is thought to be the mark of a poor creature. In many cases which have come within my own knowledge, the offspring of such people die young, putrid by disease; of fifteen children of one father, thirteen died in five years. At first the Baggara were not infected to any large extent, but contact with the inhabitants of the Nile valley has communicated the pest, which is now eating into the constitutions of this, the most powerful and warlike tribe in the Sudan.*

Export of slaves to Egypt and the Red Sea is forbidden, because the Khalifa fears that the English may intercept them and make soldiers of them; but a certain number of female slaves are still smuggled through. By the re-occupation of Tokar the Red Sea route, which had been extensively used, was closed to the Dervishes. It is permissible to give male and female slaves papers of freedom, but the custom is never practised. If a female slave bear a child to her master she cannot be sold, and after her master's death she becomes a free woman; if she bear a child to a freed man, who is not a black, her position remains unaltered, and the child grows up a slave, because it is considered to be illegitimate.

Omdurman is full of slaves; even in the poorest houses one female slave at least will be found. Hard work and ill-treatment ages them very rapidly. Many of them long for their native homes and detest slavery, but the great majority of them submit without a murmur to their wretched fate.

* The disease lies dormant in the summer, but acquires virulence with cold weather. The medicines used are iodide of potassium and sarsaparilla.

CHAPTER XXIII.

THE BAGGARA MASTERS OF THE SUDAN.

Relations between Abdullah and the rival Khalifas—Mahdiism practically dead—The Khalifa's son, Osman—His marriage to Yakub's daughter—His intentions regarding the succession—The Baggara and the Aulad-Belad—The Baggara masters of the Sudan—Examples of their tyranny—Emigration of the Rizighat tribe—Hostility between the Khalifa's and the late Mahdi's households—The Ashraf conspiracy—Witchcraft—The dispute between the Khalifas—Riots in Omdurman—The Mahdi's widows.

I PROPOSE to devote this chapter to a brief outline of the relations which exist between the ruling powers in Omdurman, and a description of the present situation in the Sudan. The overthrow of Nejumi at Toski, the destruction of Abu Anga's immense army during his constant campaigns in Abyssinia, the year of famine in 1889, and finally the capture of Tokar and total defeat of Osman Digna in February 1891, have all tended largely towards the diminution of Khalifa Abdullah's power.

Whilst the operations against Abyssinia and Egypt were being carried on, the provinces in the interior of the Sudan were slowly recovering from the terrible strain through which they had passed. Dongola, Kassala, and Darfur suffered most. The depredations of Nejumi's wild Dervishes had entirely desolated the once fertile province of Dongola, and is it any wonder that its wretched inhabitants should cast longing eyes towards wealthy and prosperous Egypt?

But the cunning Khalifa was quite capable of coping with this revulsion of feeling on the part of the inhabitants, who were now thoroughly tired of Mahdiism, and who were undoubtedly desirous that the rule of the Government should again be extended to them. He decided to change the policy of oppression, and to establish a milder rule. For this purpose he had a convenient vision, in which he affirmed that he had been instructed to appoint Zogal as emir of the province.

This man, it will be remembered, was a native of Dongola, an uncle of the late Mahdi; had been a Government official in Darfur, and had more liberal and enlightened views than most of the Dervish leaders. The Khalifa thought—and thought rightly—that he alone would be able to re-establish contentment in Dongola. Thither Zogal proceeded, accompanied by an enormous family, and under his mild and just rule the province rapidly recovered.

The Sudan, as a whole, has considerable recuperative power, and, in spite of the Khalifa's senseless rule, would soon recover if placed under good subordinate governors. The desolation in Darfur, however, had been more widespread; there was not enough cultivation even to supply the wants of the garrison required for its occupation; it was therefore abandoned, but the Khalifa is still very anxious to re-occupy it when he can.

Abdullah employed himself, during the period of rest and cessation from war, in consolidating his power, and from the various means which he employs it is quite evident that his intentions are to establish an empire for himself, his family, and his Baggaras; he proceeded, however, in this task with prudence and caution.

It is natural that the struggle for mastery between the spiritual authority represented by the religious side of Mahdiism, and the temporal authority of the Khalifa, should constantly clash and lead to a state of insecurity and uncertainty throughout the Sudan. What the inhabitants desire is that the Khalifa should tell them the truth plainly; let him abolish Mahdiism, which exists merely in name, and let him proclaim himself Sultan of the Sudan. He has the power and authority sufficient to do this, but he fears that it might give his enemies another arm which might be turned against him; he therefore advances very slowly with the project on which his mind is bent.

From the way in which his eldest son Osman is being brought up, it is evident that Abdullah seeks to establish an hereditary succession. This youth was, until recently, of a most overbearing disposition. Whenever he saw anything he wanted, he insisted on its being given to him. If he saw someone riding a good donkey, he would order the rider to dismount, and would deliberately cut the poor animal's throat; but in spite of these foolish and cruel acts, his favour was much sought after, and many a present did he receive from people who looked for a favourable means of bringing their demands before the Khalifa; but the latter eventually became exasperated by his son's conduct. He rebuked him openly in the mosque, forbade everyone, under pain of severe punishment, to give him a present of any sort, and he made him over to a tutor with a few Taisha mulazimin.

This strict *régime* has already done the boy good. He is now about eighteen years of age. It was said that the Khalifa's brother Yakub was very jealous of his nephew, for he had looked on himself as Abdullah's successor; but, to flatter Yakub and curb his jealousy, the Khalifa expressed a wish that Osman should be betrothed to his daughter. This proposition was most acceptable to Yakub; and further, the Khalifa arranged that his daughter should be married to the Mahdi's son.

Great were the preparations for these princely weddings, which were carried out with a splendour entirely at variance with the late Mahdi's laws. The betrothal ceremony was accompanied by dancing and merrymaking in both the Mahdi's and the Khalifa's households, and the air reeked with perfumes. All the principal merchants and emirs gave rich presents in the shape of brides' dresses and varieties of costly perfumes; nor were gold and silver ornaments and velvet missing. The goldsmiths have invented a new form of jewellery, which has been named " the Khalifa's stirrups." These ornaments, although absolutely opposed to Mahdi laws, are extensively worn in both households. Hundredweights of sugar were brought to Yakub's house, besides dhurra, wheat, butter, oxen, and fat-tailed sheep, which latter are valued at from twenty to thirty dollars a head.

It is usual for the bridegroom, or the bridegroom's father, to offer presents of provisions to the bride, as well as clothes and ornaments, which are all handed over to her with great ceremony on an appointed day. Then there is the festival of "tefail," to which women only are admitted, after which comes "henna day," when the hands and feet of the bride are dyed red with henna. All these ceremonies are accompanied by banquets, dancing, and singing. Every evening Yakub entertained hundreds of the Ansar with rich food, and distributed several ardebs of dates.

On the occasion of the "dakhul" the bride is taken to the bridegroom's house late in the evening; for seven days afterwards they receive the congratulations of their friends, and then the ceremony and festival are ended.

From the pomp and ceremony with which the Khalifa surrounded his son's wedding, it is evident to all who thought about the matter that he had secret intentions. After the wedding he had a princely house built for his son, in the place known as Abu Anga's yard, near the mosque; this he quite disfigured by building houses all around it, which are considered the best in the town. When the palace was completed, the "heir apparent," who had hitherto been living with his father, moved into it with great ceremony. The Khalifa gave alms in a most liberal manner, so that his son's residence might be blessed.

Sayid Osman already takes part in the conduct of affairs, and opens and reads the letters to the clerks. Almost every morning he rides round with the Governor on his inspections, but he does not live much amongst the people. The Khalifa has changed his name into Sheikh Ed Din Sayid Osman, and now he is generally known as Sheikh Ed Din only; he quite understands the *rôle* he has to play. He is a lover of good food, and rejoices in the little specialities which the merchants bring from Sawakin and Egypt, such as kamar ed din, dried figs, raisins, and all sorts of cakes and biscuits, which are brought in abundance to Yakub's house. The Khalifa treats him with marked respect, occasionally hands over the command of the parade to him, and the soldiers always present arms to him.

From the above it is quite evident that Abdullah wishes to secure the succession to his son. This is perfectly understood by the people, who make no secret of it. The Khalifa's plan is to go slowly but surely. He wants to secure the ascendency of the Baggara over the Jaalin, Danagla, Barabra, and other smaller tribes of the Sudan.

Until the appearance of the Mahdi, the Baggara were, perhaps, the most despised of all the Arab tribes. The " Aulad-belad," as the Jaalin, Danagla, and Barabra are called, had become more civilized in virtue of their geographical position, and are far more crafty by nature than the Baggara; they despised the latter, and under the leadership of Zubeir Pasha, they defeated the great tribes in the neighbourhood of Shakka, and it is these same Baggara who are now their masters.

All the Mahdi's early victories had been gained by the Aulad-belad, who held the Baggaras in much the same contempt as they did the Fellahin of Egypt. They are cunning, corrupt, and utterly untrustworthy, and from the beginning have practised far more cruelty than the others. Even now they are still the Khalifa's spies and advisers—indeed, he was brought up entirely in their school, but has now completely turned the tables on them. The intertribal discord and mutual distrust which prevails amongst the Aulad-belad only tend to further the ends the Khalifa has in view. Wherever craft and subtlety are required, thither he despatches them, in the full assurance that as long as they are engaged in finding out the misdeeds of their own countrymen he will be well and loyally served by them.

When the Baggara are sent to search a house in

which it is supposed marissa-drinking or smoking is going on, they are almost certain to find out nothing; but with the Aulad-belad it is exactly the reverse; they poke into the walls and tap the ground to hear if there is any hollowness in the sound; they search every corner most thoroughly, and seldom leave empty-handed; but the Baggaras have now got the upper hand, and the Aulad-belad must bow down before them. In spite of this, however, they manage to deceive their new masters, and in all matters where cunning is required they are far superior to them.

It is only right that the Baggara, who have been brought up in the forests and plains, and who are far more simple-minded, honest individuals, should rule the corrupt Aulad-belad; their emigration to Omdurman and their submission to the Khalifa's rule has had the advantage of taming them, and their advances in civilization are quite astounding. Being now possessed of power and money, they have begun to build better houses, to wear cleaner clothing, and to occasionally wash their jibbehs, which were reeking and besmeared with oil and fat; the Khalifa has done much to improve their manners and customs in this respect. Their west-country Arabic dialect has greatly improved; now the two opposition parties can thoroughly understand each other, and the Aulad-belad no longer make a laughing-stock of their western brethren.

The Khalifa's policy is to weaken the power of the Aulad-belad and to strengthen the Baggaras. Just as a good father watches his children, so does Abdullah watch for every opportunity to further these ends by a clever combination of leniency and severity. He frequently blames his own countrymen for their want of gratitude to their benefactor, who has heaped favours upon them at the expense of the Aulad-belad. On one occasion he cursed the day on which he had brought them to Omdurman, calling it a "black day;" but, in point of fact, he is not really serious when he upbraids them, he rather does it to satisfy the complainers, and he takes every opportunity of sending the Aulad-belad as far away from headquarters as possible, so as to strengthen his central authority by the presence of Baggaras only.

I have already narrated how in the famine year he made the Baggaras pay only six dollars for an ardeb of dhurra, whilst everyone else had to pay sixty dollars for the same quantity; thus the Baggara suffered no hardships and want during that terrible time. They do not like dhurra as well as dukhn, which is more nourishing, and which they grind in wooden mortars. During that period of awful want, when hundreds of natives were dying of starvation in the streets, these great strong Baggaras were eating to their hearts' content, completely regardless of all the suffering creatures around them.

The revenue of the beit el mal is expended almost entirely on the Baggaras; all the fertile islands in the neighbourhood, and the best-cultivated portions of the Nile banks as far as Berber, have been made over to them, whilst the original owners of the soil have been turned out without a piastre's compensation; they are, therefore, owners of all the best lands, and serve as a foreign garrison in occupation of a conquered country.

Woe to the native who happens to have a Baggara as his neighbour! His cattle are robbed, and he must share the product of the fields with his overbearing master; wherever they go the Baggaras take their horses with them, which must be fed and cared for at the expense of the local inhabitants; complaints against Baggaras are not taken the slightest notice of, or—as it more often happens—the complainant receives a heavy punishment for having ventured to make a statement which is invariably construed as untrue and incorrect. Thus these bold tribesmen have every inducement to become more and more truculent the further removed they are from the Khalifa's supervision. I will cite an example.

A rich native of the Gezireh had a dispute with a Baggara, and struck his oppressor a blow with a stick in self-defence. Fate decreed that the Baggara should die twenty-eight days afterwards, but his death was not caused by the blow; the other Baggaras, however, seized the opportunity of demanding blood-money, and if refused they threatened to report the matter to the Khalifa. The stupid native was actually intimidated into giving the Baggara 10,000 dollars, and the matter was declared to be ended; but somehow it came to Yakub's ears, and learning that the supposed murderer was a very rich man, he advised the friends of the deceased Baggara not to accept blood-money, but to insist on the native's death. This was agreed to. The poor man was arrested, dragged to Omdurman, and hanged; whilst his property, consisting of a number of goats and 30,000 dollars, was confiscated.

Not content with this, the Khalifa also ordered that the seven villages in the neighbourhood should be burnt, on the plea that the inhabitants had made common cause with the murderer in resisting lawfully constituted authority; and it was only when the inhabitants of these villages went *en masse* to the Khalifa, begging to be spared, that he at length acceded to their request.

When it was found that the revenue of the beit el mal was insufficient to provide for the rapidly-increasing Baggara population, Abdullah ordered half the produce of the Gezireh lands to be given to the beit el mal, the other half being retained by the owners. This was published as a solemn decree, and all judges enjoined to see that it was properly carried out. Ibrahim Nur, the son of Nur Gereifawi, was sent with a body of soldiers and Baggara to assist in carrying out the order in the Gezireh, and he gained an unenviable notoriety for the ruthless severity with which he enforced his authority.

In accordance with the Khalifa's instructions, out of every hundred ardebs he seized a half, and on the remaining half he levied the "ushr" and "zeka" taxes, so that eventually the unfortunate cultivator retained only thirty-seven and a half per cent. of his original quantity; besides, he was made responsible for the transport to the river of the sixty-two and a-half per cent. Frequently the fields were far distant from the river, which involved hiring camels to carry the grain, so that finally the owner was probably left with absolutely nothing. In this way Ibrahim gathered upwards of 60,000 ardebs from the Blue and White Niles.

Ibrahim gained the title of the "Gordon of the Gezireh" from the extraordinarily rapid way in which he moved from one village to the other and gave his instructions.

Here is another proof of the Khalifa's injustice when dealing in matters concerning his own countrymen. About two days' journey from Omdurman up the White Nile are certain very highly-cultivated districts, and it occurred to the Khalifa to send there the Taisha who were not then employed, so that they might cultivate and at the same time remain in touch with him. He therefore sent a certain Sheikh Wad el Bedri to select the most favoured spots in which the Taisha were to settle.

When the inhabitants of these districts learnt what was intended, they begged and prayed Wad el Bedri to avert this terrible calamity which threatened them, assuring him that if he would assist them they would do anything he wanted, short of having the Baggara as settlers in their country; this request they accompanied with a good round sum of money.

Bedri then returned to Omdurman, waited on the Khalifa with a most beaming countenance, and reported that the inhabitants of the White Nile were very pleased that the Khalifa of the Mahdi* had been graciously pleased to think of sending the Taisha to their country; but at the same time they most humbly begged to submit to him that possibly the Taisha might find it a trouble to move so far with their families and followers. If, therefore, the Khalifat el Mahdi should, in his great wisdom, deem it advisable, they were quite ready to

* Abdullah does not like being addressed as Khalifa only, but if he be approached as Khalifat el Mahdi, and if the words "aleh es salam" ("on whom be peace") be added—a term which is only used when speaking of the Prophet—he is even more gratified.

send to their masters everything they required, and so spare them the toil of making this extended emigration.

Abdullah seemed delighted with this proposal, praised Sheikh Wad el Bedri for his services, and agreed that his suggestion should be carried out. The sheikh appealed to his countrymen, and in one year collected over 20,000 ardebs of dhurra, besides a quantity of money, which was distributed amongst the Taisha, who from that day looked on him as one of their best friends.

There is among the Baggara a curious ejaculation of "Hai! hai!" constantly interspersed throughout their conversation. The Sudani feels far more terror at this sound than he ever felt at the sight of the Egyptian officials' red tarbush.

All high posts are in the Baggaras' hands, or rather in the hands of the Khalifa's nearest relatives. The emirs of Kordofan, Regaf, Fashoda, Galabat, Kassala, and Berber, are all Abdullah's relatives. Dongola was the only place of importance not confided to a Baggara, but now Zogal has fallen in favour and has been replaced by the Baggari Yunis. Some of the subordinate posts are, however, still in the hands of the Auladbelad, but, gradually, as the Baggaras become capable of carrying out the duties, they will replace the natives.

Not content with having brought the Taisha, Homr, and Habbanieh Arabs from the west to the Nile, he has still further weakened the Aulad-belad by obliging the powerful Rizighat tribe to emigrate from their country, south of Darfur, to Omdurman. Their young Sheikh Musa—son of Madibbo, who had been killed by Abu Anga at El Obeid—was entrusted with this mission, and he marched through Kordofan with some 30,000 souls, besides quantities of horses and cattle; his vanguard had reached Shatt on the White Nile just at the time that I effected my escape.

The Khalifa had appointed a committee under the notorious Hajji Zubeir to organize a great reception for the new arrivals, and had made a long speech in the mosque calling on everyone to come forward liberally with gifts for their brethren. He urged that alms

EMIGRATION OF THE RIZIGHAT TRIBE. 397

should not be stinted, but that clothes, corn, and all sorts of provisions would be gratefully accepted, even to the " fartaga " (or smallest copper which is coined).

Every emir was instructed to let his followers know of the Khalifa's wishes; he was to collect the gifts and hand them over to the committee. If the gifts were considered too small they were returned with a strong hint that it would be advisable to increase them. Merchants were especially called upon to give largely, and if they failed to comply they invariably incurred his displeasure.

The list of gifts was scrutinised by the Khalifa daily, and his favours apportioned in accordance with what he found there. He was careful not to allow the rich to give sparingly; for instance, Kadi Ahmed presented 200 ardebs of dhurra, 100 complete suits of clothes, consisting of 100 takias, 100 turbans, 100 jibbehs, 100 pairs of drawers, 100 leather girths, and 100 pairs of sandals; still Abdullah was not satisfied and asked why he had not given any money, and immediately the Kadi, terrified at the Khalifa's displeasure, laid a considerable sum at Hajji Zubeir's feet.

The merchant Omar Kesha, who had acquired much wealth, had on one occasion been deprived of 30,000 dollars by the Khalifa on the plea that much money was apt to take his mind off heavenly considerations. Two years later a similar sum was again taken from him. On the occasion of the arrival of the Rizighat, however, he presented a camel-load of sugar, a camel-load of white muslin, and another of indigo-dyed calico, besides a quantity of kamar ed din, 50 ardebs of dhurra, a camel-load of dammur, and a completely-equipped war-horse with its attendant.

Wealthy men offer lavish gifts, in the hope of immunity from plunder, and Omar Kesha, in addition to his generosity on this occasion, does not fail to frequently offer valuable gifts to Yakub. As for the Khalifa, he is perfectly aware that with one word he can, with absolute right, demand anything and everything he requires, for had not the Sudanese solemnly pledged their property, their children, and their own lives to the cause of the Mahdi and his successor?

While in Kordofan the Mahdi had professed that he was virtually the owner of all property, but that he left it in the hands of its original tenants that they might administer it until he should require it; and now no

A BAGGARA WOMAN.

stone is left unturned to enforce his theory of the true ownership. The Khalifa directs his special attention to the merchants, who, he supposes, make large profits out of commerce and trade.

Hitherto the Baggaras have had nothing to do with external commerce, they never go to Sawakin or to Egypt. All trade with the outside world is conducted by Hadarba, Jaalin, Danagla, and Barabra merchants, also on the southern frontier of Egypt by Ababdeh and Kenuz people; but in Omdurman itself the Baggaras, and especially the women, take a large share in the retail business. Although they have scarcely ever owned a piastre in their lives, the shining dollar has excited the most inordinate cupidity amongst them. They are very quick to learn, and already surpass the Aulad-belad in many branches of trade; this fact has delighted the Khalifa, and he encourages it to the fullest extent.

The continuous support which the Khalifa gives to his own compatriots at the expense of the rest of his subjects not unnaturally irritates the latter, and out of their oppression a species of courage has sprung. The Khalifa Sherif bitterly resents being debarred from all share in the government of the country. He is highly favoured amongst the late Mahdi's widows, and the Ashraf look to him as their head.

Abdullah, however, employs every means to lower his position and diminish the respect in which he is held by the Ashraf, whose loose mode of life he never loses an opportunity of exposing. For instance, Ahmed Sharfi's second son had a concubine to whom he was much devoted, and who used to saddle his horse for him herself; but in secret she was not always faithful to her master, and when one day he returned to find her absent, he revenged himself on her return by hanging her with his own hands. When this outrage came to the Khalifa's ears, he ordered the perpetrator to be imprisoned and all his property confiscated, whereas, according to Mahdi law, a master has complete power to deal as he likes with his own slaves. Another of Ahmed Sharfi's sons was discovered to be leading a very immoral life, and he was exiled up the White Nile.

Another similar and even worse discovery, of which the principal agent was one of the Mahdi's near relatives, gave Abdullah an opportunity of openly accusing the Ashraf of leading lives which did not entitle them to the smallest respect; and having established this fact, he set to work in the most public manner to show them every mark of disrespect.

The Mahdi's uncle, Sayid Abdel Kader, a very proud man, who prior to the Mahdi's appearance had gained a livelihood by doctoring donkeys, thought, under the altered circumstances, that his profession was not a very honourable one; he therefore took to doctoring human beings with the aid of a few old Arabic books on medicine which he possessed. He made no secret of his dislike of Abdullah, and openly deplored the decay of true Mahdiism; he never attended at the mosque, and studiously avoided the Khalifa on every occasion. Abdullah, however, was fully alive to the situation, Sayid's every step was dogged by spies, and at length, when his impudence got beyond all bounds, the Khalifa suddenly summoned him to the mosque, and addressed him publicly as follows—"Why should you not come to the mosque twice a-week and greet me occasionally?" The Sayid replied proudly, "I worship God and pray to Him daily in my house."

This speech greatly annoyed the Khalifa, who replied, "Pray in your house; but I shall cut off the hand and foot of everyone who associates with you, whether in your house or out of it, and I shall send to your house to have all these Arabic books removed; you can then pray to God without distraction." Suiting the action to the word, he at once had the Sayid's books seized and burnt. After this Abdel Kader thought it as well to pray five times a-day in the Mahdi's mosque.

Thus the breach between the Mahdi's and the Khalifa's households is widening daily; the former are continually holding secret meetings and consultations, of which the latter takes good care to be fully apprized.

Another individual—a certain Ismail el Kheir—who had been one of the Mahdi's most fanatical adherents, but who, after the Mahdi's death, had shown a tendency to side with the Khalifa Sherif and to be unfriendly to Khalifa Abdullah, was one day suddenly ordered to be ready to start for Regaf in half an hour. It was rumoured that Abdullah had discovered he had been attending the secret meetings of the Ashraf.

I will cite yet another case. A certain Wad el Banna, a good man and a well-educated Moslem, had the Khalifa's special permission to retain a number of historical works on Islam, which he frequently read to him and the Ansar after prayers in the mosque. Being in high favour, and a great personal friend, the Khalifa sent him late one night a very beautiful female slave; but when she arrived at the house, Wad el Banna was nowhere to be found, and it was discovered that he was with the Khalifa Sherif. The next morning Abdullah announced that he deserved to be hanged; but as he had been very fond of him, he forgave him for the Mahdi's sake; but ordered all the books to be burnt, and that he should be transported to Regaf. Just as the steamer was about to sail with Wad el Banna on board, the Khalifa recalled and pardoned him.

There was now little doubt that the Ashraf were forming a conspiracy; the immediate result of this discovery was the sudden arrest and imprisonment of Zogal, which caused no small stir. Then followed the arrest of Fadl Maula (afterwards known as Abdel Maula), which created still more excitement. Fadl Maula was the late Abu Anga's brother, and commanded the black troops in Omdurman. He was a man of great influence, not only on account of his brother's reputation, but he had also performed a number of valuable services for the Khalifa, notably at the time of the dispute regarding the Mahdi's successor. He lived near Gordon's fort of Omdurman, enjoyed a high position, and acquired a large number of the most handsome women in the Sudan for his harem.

These ladies lived in the highest luxury. He built good houses for them, and in the evening he had a band of Fertit blacks, who played before them on a variety of instruments. He was perhaps of all the emirs the most favoured. He had no scruples in going round his men's quarters picking out the good-looking women and sending them to his harem; but this debauched and extravagant mode of living soon brought its reward, and he became affected by a sort of leprosy which seemed to have touched his brain. He became violent, and had to be put in chains. He lay for months in this condition, and no medicine was given to him to ease his pain.

At length a fiki was summoned who declared the disease to be the result of witchcraft, and he volunteered to find out by whom this evil had been practised on him. One of Abdel Maula's wives was a young girl of great beauty, who was preferred to all the rest, and who lived with her mother. Love, however, soon grew cold, and he became enamoured of another of his wives; but the mother of the cast-off girl determined to be revenged, and to aid her in her object, she sought the assistance of a fiki, who gave her a number of amulets, for which she paid him well. These bits of paper she placed under the iron platter on which Abdel Maula's bread was baked, and gradually he grew worse and worse in health. At length the papers were discovered, and everyone was convinced that his illness had been caused by witchcraft. The woman was tried, found guilty, and had her hand and foot cut off. Abdel Maula did not recover for many months, and the unfortunate woman had been sacrificed to the fiki's deception.

The people are still very credulous, and it is impossible to make them give up their belief in these superstitious fikis. Once, out of pure curiosity, I quite convinced myself that this supposed witchcraft was a mere deception on the part of a clever fiki. Abu Anga's death and Abdel Maula's illness greatly affected the latter's influence, besides he was looked upon with jealous eyes by the Taisha. His overbearing manner to Yakub, which made the latter his sworn enemy, also contributed to his downfall. Detractors were not wanting who declared that he appropriated the dhurra issued by the beit el mal for his troops. The Khalifa therefore ordered his property to be confiscated, and reduced the number of his wives from thirty-one to three. Irritated beyond measure at this treatment, he openly abused the Khalifa and Yakub; but was thrown into chains and delivered over to the tender mercies of the Saier.

The upshot of a meeting of the three Khalifas and the Kadi in Ahmed Sharfi's house, still further widened the breach. Sharfi is known as the "Gidd el Ashraf" (or grandfather of the Ashraf), because his daughter was the Mahdi's mother—Abdullah himself generally addresses him as "Gidd," and, by way of a joke, his house is known as the "Mudirieh," because it is a large square yard with numbers of small rooms ranged around the inside walls in which the numerous wives dwell.

Sharfi is an astute and crafty old man; he sees perfectly well that, under existing circumstances, it is quite useless to try and overturn the present Baggara authority. He flatters the Khalifa in the most obsequious manner, constantly gives him presents, and has even gone as far as to give up associating with the Mahdi's household, lest suspicion should rest upon him.

But to return. The four met one evening, the great gate was closed, the mulazim kept guard outside, while within the discussion waxed hot. Khalifa Sherif reproached Abdullah bitterly for non-adherence to the Mahdi's precepts. He accused him of oppressing the people, and governing without the co-operation of himself and Ali Wad Helu. He urged that the proceeds of the beit el mal were reserved exclusively for him and his Baggaras; that he had built good houses for himself and his emirs, whilst the Mahdi's household continued to live in a zariba; that his brother Yakub had considerably more authority than either of the two Khalifas; that the Mahdi's wives were living in absolute want whilst the Baggaras had every luxury; in short, he accused Abdullah of having made Mahdiism into an entirely worldly and temporal power, instead of upholding the religious precepts on which it had been founded. These unreserved expressions led to a fierce dispute, swords were on the point of being drawn, when

Ahmed Sharfi and the Kadi with tears implored them to stop quarrelling.

It was now past midnight, and Yakub, alarmed at Abdullah's absence, arrived with a party of soldiers and several Baggaras at the great gate, and began rapping violently with their spears; they shouted, "Let our Khalifa out!" The noise outside had an instantaneous effect on the disputants within. Abdullah solemnly swore on the Kuran that he would act entirely on the advice of his colleagues in the matter, and with that assurance the stormy meeting broke up. His appearance at the gate was hailed with delight, and he was conducted home with rejoicing.

But in spite of these events there was no real reconciliation. Sherif continued to agitate secretly, whilst the Mahdi's wives, who looked upon him as their protector solemnly appointed by the Mahdi, added fuel to the fire. They had some cause for discontent. After the Mahdi's death they were taken little notice of; Abdullah did not trouble himself about their wants and had it not been for Ahmed Sharfi, they must have starved. Being the Mahdi's widows, they were not allowed to marry again, and were not even permitted to move beyond the palace precincts.

This enforced confinement so irritated these good women that they decided to go *en masse* to the Khalifa, and demand either their liberty or that they should be well treated. Ahmed Sharfi, learning of their resolution, did all in his power to quiet them, and promised that he would intercede with the Khalifa for them. This he did, and Abdullah feigned complete surprise, said he had been under the impression that they had been supplied from the beit el mal with all they required, and that he himself had repeatedly given orders to Nur Gereifawi to that effect. This was a fact, but—as it frequently happens—Yakub had taken it upon himself to give counter-orders; the blame was, of course, laid on Gereifawi, who was ordered to at once issue 600 dollars to the widows, half in clothes and half in cash, and so these noble ladies were for the time being satisfied.

About a month after the meeting I have just described the smouldering fire broke out with renewed vigour. About two days before the actual climax, I was told in the greatest secrecy by a friend, that in a few days a rupture must occur, that Khalifas Sherif and Ali Wad Helu, as well as the principal Aulad-belad emirs, had solemnly sworn on the Kuran either to overturn Khalifa Abdullah, or die in the attempt. I could scarcely credit this news, for Sherif was a young and inexperienced man, and had hitherto given no proof of any special ability which would induce the confidence of others; he appeared to me as a man utterly absorbed in a life of sensual pleasure. But the following day my friend again told me that his first information was quite correct; however, I persisted in saying that I would not believe it till I saw it. So well had the secret been kept, that the Aulad-belad merchants were unconcernedly taking their goods away from the market as usual, and the Khalifa and his household knew nothing of it, for one of my friends, who lived close to the palace, declared to me that the whole matter was pure invention.

On Tuesday, the 24th of November, 1891, a rumour suddenly spread through the town that Sherif had decided to resist. The market was at once closed, and people went to their homes as quickly as possible. The whole place was in a state of alarm and excitement. Baggaras seized the opportunity to plunder and rob, and I could not learn the actual circumstances which led to the outbreak, as all that day I remained in my hut, and the following day I made my escape.

Some said that the people had risen because the Khalifa intended to execute Zogal; others, that Abdullah had secretly intended to proclaim his son as his successor, but that Sherif had violently opposed the idea. Possibly it may have been that the Khalifa—on the principle of weakening the power of the Aulad-belad —had ordered that an expedition of 3,000 of them, under the command of Wad el Ireik, should proceed to Kassala to fight against the Italians; besides, Abdullah had the intention of sending Karamallah—the capturer of Lupton Bey—and his brother Kerkesawi, with a force to Bahr el Ghazal, and it was thought that these two most deliberate attempts to get the Aulad-belad out of Omdurman had been the real cause of the outbreak.

Tuesday passed without disturbance, but every one was prepared for Wednesday. On that day the Khalifa ordered that everyone should stand to his flag, and that all the Ansar should attend at the mosque. But the whole affair turned out to be a ridiculous farce. Khalifa Sherif with a few Danagla had barricaded himself in the Mahdi's zariba; he had altogether about fifty Remington rifles. How could he attempt resistance with a feeble force of this description? He had acted most imprudently; still, in secret, the Aulad-belad would all have liked to support him, but not one of them had the courage to come forward, though there were a very large number of them in Omdurman. The Mahdi's widows, however, showed far more determination. They dressed themselves in jibbehs, armed themselves with swords, and, forming a compact little body, they swore rather to die than submit.

In accordance with the Khalifa's orders, the palace, the mosque, and the road between the Mahdi's dome and the mosque, were all occupied by the Ansar on Wednesday, whilst the black troops completely surrounded the mosque. Yakub was made responsible for distributing ammunition. Possibly Sherif may have thought that the Aulad-belad would have joined him, but not one of them dared to leave the ranks. Numerous horsemen wearing coats of mail and helmets were entertaining the crowds by their furious galloping, and in Abdullah's entire force there was general rejoicing. At about 10 A.M. Sherif opened fire, and seventeen Baggaras fell; the blacks returned the fire, and killed seven of Sherif's men. Abdullah would not allow the Ansar to fire, and it was with the greatest difficulty that he succeeded in holding back the wild Baggaras.

The few shots that had been fired startled the whole

of Omdurman ; everyone went to his house and armed himself as best he could. Meanwhile the Baggara horsemen had left the actual scene of action, and were now scattered about the town looting, robbing, breaking into houses, wounding people, and seizing women, slaves, ornaments, &c. When Abdullah heard of this, he lost no time in sending Yakub's horsemen to keep order ; but many of the robbers made off with their booty. In the evening it was rumoured that a reconciliation had been effected. Khalifa Helu, Ahmed Sharfi, and Sayid el Mek had been the mediators. Sharfi had attempted to explain to the Mahdi's widows that all resistance was useless, but they tore his jibbeh, and drove him off.

On Thursday the Khalifas all met under the Mahdi's dome, and there Abdullah, with tears in his eyes, solemnly swore to accede to all his opponent's wishes, which were that he should receive one-third of the army, one-third of the arms and of the beit el mal revenue, and that, moreover, he should take part in all meetings and deliberations. It was quite apparent that Abdullah never seriously intended to fulfil these conditions. He could have instantly suppressed the outbreak had he wished to do so, but he wanted to show that he still greatly honoured and respected the Mahdi's family.

At noon the mulazimin marched through the town, heralds announced that tranquillity had been restored, and that people should return to their daily avocations. On Friday the usual review took place, but none of the notables were present, and most of the troops continued in occupation of the mosque and palace. On Saturday there was another alarm, for Sherif had declined to hand over his arms, but that evening his submission was publicly announced. I did not hear the details, for on Sunday, the 29th of November, 1891, I quitted Omdurman in the dead of night.

CHAPTER XXIV.

PREPARATIONS FOR THE FLIGHT.

Ohrwalder forms plans for escape—The fate of other Europeans attempting to fly—Stricter surveillance—Ohrwalder's means of livelihood—Letters from Cairo—The faithful Ahmed Hassan discloses his plan—Archbishop Sogaro—Miseries of captivity in Omdurman—Death of Sister Concetta Corsi—Preparations for flight.

THE reader will readily understand that all this time I had not lost sight of the object which had been next my heart, which was to regain my liberty and escape from my miserable surroundings.

When I quitted El Obeid, I then thought that, once in Omdurman, escape would not be so difficult, and during my long journey to the Mahdi's capital this thought had buoyed me up. At any rate I was one step nearer attaining my wish, for at that time the restrictions on Europeans were not so severe, and they were permitted to trade and travel as far as Ed Damer, to which place Egyptian merchants freely came and went.

On my arrival in Omdurman, a Greek offered me hospitality, which I gratefully accepted. I had resolved to search about in the town for a trusty friend, who would help me towards the attainment of my object. It had occurred to me that I might accompany a Greek or Syrian merchant to Damer, and from thence make my escape, but unfortunately at that time I had no money and little experience. I did not actually give way to despair, but I could find no one ready to give me the assistance I required; they all feared the Khalifa's vengeance in case of discovery.

THE ARAB GUIDES WHO EFFECTED THE ESCAPE OF FATHER OHRWALDER AND THE SISTERS.

I made inquiries of boatmen, with a view to going to Berber on a supposed trading journey, but none of them trusted me; and, indeed, I was afterwards thankful that they had not spoken of my design. However, in spite of failure, I did not give up hope; and during the long days, and often sleepless nights, I turned various plans over and over in my mind. On one occasion Gustav Klootz and I decided to make an attempt to reach Galabat, and escape thence into Abyssinia, but at the last moment the plan seemed impracticable. Klootz, however, set off, and without any money he begged his way from place to place; at length, utterly exhausted, he reached Galabat, only to die a few days afterwards.

I spent about eight months with the Greek, and then thought it was not fair to trespass further on his hospitality. Besides, it had occurred to me that in case a favourable opportunity for escape arrived, he would most certainly have been accused of complicity, and might have suffered on my account; I therefore built a small straw hut for myself, and lived with a Mission brother who had a small shop in the market. For almost five months an Arab held out hopes of assisting me to escape, but I eventually ascertained that he never really meant to help me. For nearly two years I had suffered from incessant diarrhœa, which had greatly wasted my strength.

Meanwhile I had managed to send one of the Mission brothers to Berber, nominally to gain a living by repairing watches, but actually to find out whether flight from there was possible. It took him twenty-six days in a boat to reach Berber, and after staying there for a time he succeeded in escaping to Sawakin, whence he despatched a man with money and goods who was to aid in my escape; but the man never came, and must have stolen all that had been given to him.

The Mission brother's escape reached the Khalifa's ears, and at the same time certain Greeks petitioned him that their bakery might not be pulled down when the market was being repaired. The Khalifa sent for the mukuddum to inquire about the matter, and casually asked about the other Greeks, and where they were? The mukuddum replied that some were ill, others were travelling. This greatly annoyed the Khalifa, who ordered all who were in Omdurman to be brought before him the following day. Finding several absentees, his eyes seemed to be opened to the danger; he severely blamed the mukuddum for allowing the lay-brother to escape; said that he should have given immediate information, and then turning on us he threatened to cast us into the river, or cut off our hands. His actual words were, " What prevents me now from throwing you into the river, and making you food for fishes?" He spoke against us in a most vehement manner for about half an hour, and ended by saying that we should not in future be permitted to move one step south of Omdurman fort, or north of Khor Shambat. Any Europeans known to be beyond the limits of his capital, he ordered to be forcibly brought back, alive or dead. This sudden change of front obliged us to put aside for the time all idea of escape.

A Sherif of Mecca, who had come to greet the Mahdi and who had become thoroughly convinced of the falseness of his claims, expressed a desire to be allowed to return; his request was not granted, so he decided to make his escape; he bought a donkey and gaily set out on his journey. On reaching Kererri, some four hours' distance, he was stopped and asked where he was going; he replied that he was come to pay a visit to Sheikh el Tayeb's tomb at Kererri; but his story was not credited. He was brought back to the Khalifa, who handed him over to the Saier, where he died a few days afterwards.

This event made Abdullah exert a still stricter surveillance over the "whites," and now escape became more difficult than ever. Moreover, Wad en Nejumi's expedition to Egypt closed the road to pilgrims, and during that period flight would have been a pure impossibility. In the meantime I had to do something to gain a livelihood. Lupton advised me to try soap-

OHRWALDER'S MEANS OF LIVELIHOOD.

boiling; so I went into partnership with him, changed my house, and now took up my abode just beyond the Greek and Syrian quarter.

I was always thinking of escape, and in consequence kept a great deal to myself, seldom paid visits, and was seldom called upon. Two of the Mission sisters were living near me; they earned a precarious living by needlework; but this hardly brought in enough money to purchase the bare necessities of life, for several of the women who had survived the Khartum massacre were employed at similar work, and the competition was considerable.

Poor Lupton died very suddenly, so our soap-boiling plan had to be abandoned, and I had to turn my thoughts to something else. It occurred to me to make hooks out of telegraph wire, which the sisters sewed on to purses, takias, &c., and this being a novelty was for a time a fairly lucrative business: but it was long and tedious work. Gradually the novelty wore off, and the demand grew less; provisions were expensive, and a famine close at hand. All idea of mutual support had come to an end, for the Greeks, Syrians, and Jews had been prohibited from leaving the town, and nothing was to be made out of trade in Omdurman itself. Thus my condition went from bad to worse, the famine was now raging, and in desperation I had to do something to gain enough to keep body and soul together.

It was the fashion for the women in Omdurman to wear long garments trimmed with various sorts of ribbons, and it occurred to me to learn how to make these ribbons; for this purpose I acquired a small and simple loom. The few men in the market, who had the monopoly of this trade, regarded my acquisition with great jealousy, and would not teach it to any one under a less payment than forty or fifty dollars, and this sum I was quite unable to raise; however, necessity knows no law, and hunger sharpens the inventive faculties. I carefully unravelled a piece of ribbon and studied the way it was made with the greatest attention. I had a dim and hazy recollection of European looms, and, after many vain attempts, I at length succeeded in making one. The work is very trying, and at first I thought my back would break from the exertion; it was only with the greatest difficulty that I managed, after working all day, to turn out four yards, which I sold for four piastres, out of which I had to purchase the thread. However, after continuous practice, I succeeded, at the end of a month, in turning out sixteen yards a day. But loom work should be learnt when one is young, and to begin it at my age was a terrible strain on my back; still, it brought in sufficient money to keep us alive.

For seven months we lived on dhurra bread and a few boiled vegetables, without oil, butter, or meat. Hard work and insufficient food were telling on our strength: however, we were far better off than hundreds of others, who were willing to work, but, finding nothing to do, were obliged to starve. During all this time I never once abandoned hope of escape, and again succeeded in getting some one to take a message from me to Cairo seeking advice; but the undertaking was so beset with difficulties that it seemed next to impossible.

My companions in adversity watched me closely—they often volunteered to attempt an escape with the sisters; but as I was responsible for them to the Khalifa, this could not be done, and the idea of myself and the two sisters ever escaping alone seemed too absurd to be thought of. It seemed most improbable that the Government would again take possession of the Sudan; though I confess that a ray of hope was kindled when Saleh Bey of Korosko suddenly arrived at Abu Hamed with his Ababdehs and killed the notorious Suleiman Wad Naaman, the murderer of Colonel Stewart and his companions. The news of this affair caused the greatest excitement in Omdurman, and we really believed that the time for our release was approaching; but Saleh Bey disappeared as quickly as he came.

The capture of Tokar, in February 1891, also raised our hopes; but we were again doomed to disappointment. In 1890 a young Ababdeh Arab had come to

Omdurman and had asked me to give him a letter to my friends in Cairo. I did not trust him, for I had written several letters which were entirely without result. I had learnt by experience that the Arabs were untrustworthy, and that the letters never reached those for whom they were intended. It also occurred to me that the man might be a spy, so I sent him away with the answer "Neshauer" (*i.e.* "I shall think about it"), a word very often used by the Sudanese when they wish to gain time to consider a matter.

Meanwhile I made full inquiries about the man, and heard nothing but good of him. Soon afterwards he returned and asked me to give him a few lines of greeting to my friends. I was told that the man expected to get some reward if he succeeded in bringing letters to the Government from the prisoners, which might give them some information on the situation in the Sudan. When I was thoroughly convinced as to his trustworthiness, we then had a consultation, of which the upshot was that I would, with his assistance, attempt to escape, provided he could obtain the necessary support from Cairo; I therefore gave him a letter to our Reverend Vicar Apostolic, Franz Sogaro, and commissioned him to negotiate verbally with him.

The man's plan was to return when the Nile was high —that is to say, almost a year later—escape in a boat or on a raft, which the swift current would carry to Berber in about three days, where camels would be in readiness to take us across the desert to Korosko. I urged him to keep these plans absolutely secret, for their disclosure would bring most certain punishment on our heads, and I further urged him to provide arms for the journey.

Ahmed Hassan—for that was the man's name—went off, and, to tell the truth, I had little hope that he would do anything more than others had done before him. Besides, who could say what changes might not take place in a year in Omdurman, which might entirely frustrate our plans? The sword of Damocles was for ever hanging over our heads. Then might not death intervene any day? Both the sisters and myself were thoroughly debilitated by constant work and hardship, and it was always possible that a slight fever might extinguish the spark of life which was then burning but dimly.

A few days after Ahmed's departure the whole matter went quite out of our heads, and before long I was again negotiating with another Arab to assist us to escape, for I did not wish to leave a stone unturned. If it had been a question of my flight alone, there would not have been so much difficulty. As a man I could have stained my naturally brown complexion, dressed in rags, and begged my way along the banks of the Blue Nile to Abyssinia; but I could not leave the poor sisters behind, and therefore resolved to wait patiently until a deliverer should come.

Several of the merchants who had been to Egypt told me that Archbishop Sogaro had often sent us money *viâ* Korosko, Halfa, and Sawakin; but the dishonest Arabs had always appropriated it for themselves. In fact, ever since 1884 our good Archbishop had never ceased in his efforts to assist us and to make our captivity more bearable. He left no stone unturned, and moved Moslems, Christians, the Government, and indeed His Holiness the Pope, on our behalf, and one of the missionaries was maintained on the Egyptian frontier with the special object of endeavouring to procure our release; they took it in turns to relieve each other, and were Fathers Dominicus Vicentini, Yohann Dichtl, Xavier Geyer, Alois Bonomi, Leon Henriot, and Alois Specke, the last of whom died at Assuan. We had many great difficulties, but perhaps the greatest was the continual bad faith of the Arabs.

The transport of letters endangered the lives not only of the bearers, but of the receivers as well, and any letter addressed to a European would, if discovered, undoubtedly end either in the intended recipient's death or imprisonment for life. But Archbishop Sogaro worked on with indefatigable earnestness. Early in 1890 he sent one of our Coptic Mission teachers, named Hanna Arraga, with money and goods to the frontier, whence, if possible, he was to proceed to Omdurman and assist us. It was thought the plan might succeed, for at that time Zogal was Emir of Dongola, and he was desirous of opening trade with Halfa. Hanna therefore sent an Arab on to find out how matters stood, while he himself remained on the frontier; but the Arab never returned.

It so happened that just at this time Zogal and the two Baggara emirs sent to watch him had a violent dispute, which resulted in all of them being recalled to Omdurman. The Khalifa decided in favour of the Baggaras, Zogal was thrown into chains, and Abdullah's nephew, Yunis, was appointed Emir of Dongola; the latter held very different views with regard to intercourse with Egypt, and that is why the Arab never returned to Halfa. About fifteen days, however, before I effected my escape, the Arab came to Omdurman and told me about the matter. His own master and son had been implicated in the Dongola dispute and had been thrown into chains; that was his reason for not returning, and after that I never saw him again.*

Meanwhile, Ahmed Hassan, whom I had sent to Cairo with the letter, duly delivered it to Archbishop Sogaro, who made a written agreement with him for our release; he also instructed Hanna to proceed from Halfa to Korosko, and there hand over to Ahmed Hassan the goods valued at £100. Through Archbishop Sogaro's intermediary, Ahmed Hassan was given every support by the Egyptian military authorities, who presented him with £20 and gave him a free passage to Korosko. On the 15th of September, 1891, he left that place for Omdurman with the goods.

At Omdurman the winter had come and gone, the Nile had risen to its full height and had subsided, but there was no sign of Ahmed. I was not surprised, for

* The Arab undoubtedly meant well. For he was at the same time entrusted by me with a letter to give to another European prisoner, and, as I write, a reply to this letter, which was delivered to him only two months ago in Omdurman, has just reached Cairo.—F. R. W.

I had long been accustomed to disappointments of this sort. I merely remarked to myself that the number of persons who had deceived us had been increased by one, and that if a deliverer did not soon come from Egypt, there was another deliverer—death—whose approach was certain. The heavy work was sapping our waning strength, I began to spit blood, felt severe pains in my chest, and was little else than skin and bone.

The poor sisters were still nearer the grave. Our moral and physical sufferings during these ten long years of captivity had told on us terribly; death was what we most longed for and for which we patiently waited. The sad prospect of never regaining our liberty, of living a life of slavery, debarred from all the advantages and progress of the world, never again to worship in our grand churches and enjoy the comforts of our holy religion; but to live and die amongst the fiery rocks and sand of Omdurman, where the burning sun turned dead bodies into mummies—to die and be buried in slavery—the prospect of living was indeed unattractive, and what wonder we should long for death to free us from such misery!

After all these sufferings it was indeed hard to see our will-o'-the-wisp-like hope, which we had pursued so often, dissolve into nothing, and to find ourselves once more the victims of a fraud and deception. How fortunate we thought those who had been killed in battle, or had died of starvation or disease! We even envied the lot of those who had been massacred in Khartum. After all, the anguish of death had been but momentary, and now all suffering and pain was over, while we seemed to have passed through a hundred deaths, we had been in his clutches over and over again; hunger, thirst, and disease had all, at one time or another, almost claimed us as their victims. We had witnessed the destruction of cities, the annihilation of armies, the slaughter of thousands, and the ruthless massacre and bloodshed of innocent people; man's dignity trodden under foot, and human life valued far below that of a sheep or a goat.

And after all this we must live and die forgotten and unknown, our lasting resting-place a strange land, and our bodies in all likelihood food for hyenas. Thus we longed for death to remove us from these scenes of perpetual cruelty and oppression. Our nerves had become so strained that the slightest knock at the door would make us start; the sound of the great onbeïa made us positively tremble. Almost half the total number of Europeans, Greeks, Syrians, and Jews were dead, and all we hoped for was that we should soon follow them.

The death of one of our sisters only increased in me the desire to die as well. On the 4th of October, 1891, Sister Concetta Corsi, who was in a very weak state of health, was suddenly carried off by typhus. According to the Sudan custom, we wound her body in a cloth, tied it up in a mat (for there were no coffins to be had), and carried her, almost immediately after death, to a spot some six miles north of the town—the direction in which her eyes in lifetime had been so often turned. All the Greeks and Syrians followed, and there in the stillness of the desert we laid her in the warm sand, protecting her body from the ravenous hyenas by a few thorns. A short prayer was offered up for her and for the souls of those who had gone before; then we turned sadly back, hoping that before long we too might be lying beside her.

But I felt that my life was in God's hands, and comforted myself with the belief that God was dealing with me as He thought best, and that I must submit to His Divine will. My hut was gloomy in the extreme; for several days I did not speak to any one, and when night came I threw myself down on my angarib, but sleep would not come to me; then I would gaze up into the great vault of heaven and think that this same sky was over my fatherland, from which I was an exile, surrounded by suffering and sickness.

On the night of the 28th of October, 1891, Ahmed Hassan quite unexpectedly made his appearance. I took him to my hut, and after the usual Arabic greetings, he said to me, "Here I am, are you coming?" For a moment I was speechless, I quite understood what he meant; but a thousand thoughts flashed through my mind, my heart was beating violently, the dangers to which my frail companions in adversity would be subjected loomed before me, and for a few moments I could make no reply; then I collected my wandering thoughts and said: "If I did not intend to go with you I would not have sent you."

Then I began asking him all sorts of questions about Cairo, and he informed me briefly that he had seen Archbishop Sogaro and had made an arrangement with him regarding our release; that he had given up the plan of descending to Berber by boat, and that he had received £100 to purchase camels. He further told me that he had not brought any letter with him. He asked about the sisters, and when I told him that one had died almost a month ago, he almost wept, and striking his forehead with his hand, said, "Oh, that I had come a month earlier!" But I told him that I would take another sister in her place.

We then set to talking earnestly about our plans; I told him to purchase at least five good camels and to see that he had sufficient arms. In anticipation of flight, I had a long time ago secured and carefully concealed a hundred Remington cartridges. When Ahmed left the hut I began to doubt if he was really sincere; it seemed almost incredible that they should have sent him from Cairo without a line or even a signature on such an important undertaking.

The next day Ahmed reappeared, bringing with him two Arabs whom he had engaged in the cause, one at Korosko and the other at Berber. Ahmed seemed a little afraid that we would not dare to undertake the flight; he told me that he had brought a letter from Archbishop Sogaro, but had left it at Berber. The main difficulty for the Arabs would be leaving the house without being observed, but I reassured them on that point. It was almost full moon at that time, so it was decided to delay our departure until it should be on the decline, and we should thus be able to make our way out under cover of obscurity. I begged Ahmed not to come to us any more, to avoid exciting suspicion.

I now began to make preparations. My first object was to get one of the sisters, who was at that time living in a Greek's house, to come to my house. This was not an easy matter, for I dared not mention one word about our intentions to a soul, or our plans would undoubtedly have been frustrated. I therefore feigned illness, and said I could no longer carry on this hard work alone, so the sister was allowed to come, and, quite unwittingly, the Greek gladly lent me her services. She had now been with me some twenty days, so I felt that the Greek could not be held responsible for her disappearance, which occurred a few days later.

Ahmed gave me Archbishop Sogaro's letter, which he had procured from Berber, and with intense excitement I read the few lines, in which he wished me all success in the undertaking. This letter encouraged me greatly, and I had now no doubt of Ahmed's sincerity. We counted the days and hours preceding our departure, and I could not bear to think of the trials the sisters would have to undergo during the journey. I had also a little black girl, whom it would have been impossible for me to have left behind, as our departure would undoubtedly have been betrayed. She was named Adila, and had been born in the Khartum Mission house. After the fall of Khartum, she and her mother had been sold as slaves and sent to Gedaref.

Amongst Abu Anga's troops was a certain Panerazio Yusef, a very bright and intelligent young soldier, who subsequently rose to the rank of an emir; he had been told about Adila, bought her for five dollars, and took her with him when he accompanied the emir Zaki to Omdurman. On his arrival he presented her to me as a remembrance of former kindness; he also gave me a quantity of coffee, for which I was truly grateful.

The day of our intended departure was approaching, and we looked forward to it with almost breathless impatience. We had lost all appetite for food; fear, mental anguish, and the idea that we should be free, kept us in a perfect fever of excitement. I could not help thinking of my companions in adversity whom I should be obliged to leave behind, and who might, I thought, perhaps suffer after our departure. These had been constantly with us for the last ten years, sharing our life of pain and wretchedness, and now I could not but feel pained at the thought of separation. But all these feelings had to be put aside, and we had to concentrate all our thoughts on the present. I longed to be off, if only to be free from this feverish anxiety which was rending our very souls. Then Ahmed came just the day before we were to have started, and said that the Arabs with whom he had come from Korosko had not yet returned, and that we must await their departure before setting out.

I now began to think that our plans had been frustrated. Several Egyptians, including some women, had attempted to fly to Berber, whence they intended making their way back to Egypt, but had been intercepted, brought back and thrown into chains. It also happened that some Greeks who had been living at Gedaref, and had had their goods stolen, were also brought to Omdurman and put in prison, because it was thought that they had intended to escape to the Italians.

All this alarmed me, and I thought it probable the Khalifa would issue more stringent orders against Europeans. Ahmed told me that he had had considerable difficulty in purchasing the camels; he did not dare buy them in the market, as that would have aroused suspicion; he had also great difficulty in feeding them, for it would have certainly excited comment if he had collected them all in one place. He had, however, managed very well. When he saw a good-looking camel, towards evening he would follow it until he reached the owner's house, then early the next morning he would return and bargain for it; in this way he had acquired three good camels at from 120 to 150 dollars a piece, which he distributed amongst his various friends, and fed them up well. Meanwhile he used occasionally to come and see us, and bid us keep up a good hope in spite of our enforced delay.

On the 24th of November occurred the disturbance between the Khalifas which I have already narrated, and this seemed a most favourable moment to escape; but Ahmed did not come, and I was wildly impatient, for I could not even find out where he lived without exciting suspicion. In all this confusion we were lost sight of, and I avoided going to see anyone lest I should become involved in anything that was going on. I had no further preparations to make, for Ahmed had promised to provide everything.

At last, on Friday the 27th, he came to my hut, and it was decided we should leave on Monday evening. When I reproached him for not coming during the first day or two of the disturbances, he said that he too had thought of it, but that one of his friends had been locked up for being engaged in a quarrel, and he was obliged to wait until he was released.

Ahmed also told me a most important piece of news. There were no riding camels in the beit el mal. All had been despatched to the provinces on business connected with quelling the disturbances. It would not, therefore, be possible to pursue us at once. These disturbances had made all the other captives think that it was a favourable opportunity to fly, but, with one exception, none of them knew that my preparations were all made and that the next day I should be gone.

CHAPTER XXV.

ON CAMELS ACROSS THE GREAT NUBIAN DESERT.

Father Ohrwalder and Sisters Venturini and Chincarini escape—The ride for life—The rencontre with the Dervish guard near Abu Hamed—Alarm of the party—The journey across the great Nubian desert—Five hundred miles on camel-back in seven days—Arrival at the Egyptian outpost at Murat—Safe at last—Arrival in Cairo.

ON Sunday evening I went to see a friend and returned at nine o'clock; this happened to be the last visit I was to make in Omdurman. Just as I stepped into my yard, there I saw Ahmed standing before me. In a few hasty words he told me to get ready as soon as possible; his friends had made a mistake and had come a day earlier with the camels. The sisters and Adila were all ready; I gave Ahmed the few small things I had as well as my arms, and told him to take the sisters to the appointed place, which was only about thirty yards from the hut, whilst I went off and informed the only person who was in the secret, of our sudden decision to leave a day earlier.

All fear had now gone, and, almost beside myself with excitement, I hastened to my friend's house and knocked at the door. "Who's there?" he asked. And when he knew who it was he was greatly surprised, and asked why I came so late. As some one else was standing near, I said that I had been seized with a violent pain, and had come to beg a few drops of laudanum, and then I approached him, pressed his hand, and whispered in his ear that we were on the point of starting.

The poor man received such a start, that had he not

caught hold of something, he would have fallen; but I roused him by asking him loudly to get me the laudanum at once; so he went off to his room, and there, with a trembling hand, he put a few drops on a piece of sugar. I took it back to the house, which I found the sister had just left. Then wrapping myself in a black mantle, I locked the door, and took the key with me. I saw something dark in the distance, which I knew must be the camels, and thither I picked my way. In a few moments I had reached the spot, and a man whom I did not know helped me on to my camel; but there was no time to ask questions. Ahmed put the sisters on the camels, on which the two other Arabs rode, whilst I took Adila behind me on my camel.

Not thirty yards from where we were was a well, around which a number of female slaves were gathered; but the little noise we made was drowned by their laughter. The moment of mounting was perhaps the most dangerous time, for the camels were restive, and longing to be off. It was with the greatest difficulty the Arabs managed to keep their mouths closed, and no sooner were we on their backs than we glided swiftly away into the darkness. Now and then we saw fires, at which the people were cooking their food, or sitting around gossiping; fortunately it was a cold night, so most of the people were in their huts. We passed the spot where we had laid the poor sister who had recently died; it was sad to think that she was not with us now. We kept steadily moving forward, not a word had passed our lips; the camels had been well fed up on dhurra, and went so quickly that we could scarcely hold them in. I tried to peer through the darkness, while my ear was ready to catch the slightest sound of possible pursuers.

Soon we had left Omdurman far behind, and in the soft sand-bed of Khor Shambat we dismounted to have our saddles re-arranged; then we mounted again, and pursued our journey at a rapid pace northwards along the river bank. We were in all seven persons and four camels: the guide Ahmed Hassan, his two friends

Hamed and Awad; Sister Catterina Chincarini and
Sister Elizabetta Venturini; myself and Adila.

A cold north wind was blowing, which our rapid advance made quite cutting. I followed the Arab custom, and bound a large turban round my head, leaving only the eyes exposed. We passed several villages, but the barking of the dogs always gave us warning, and so we avoided them. I had not heard a dog bark for years, and the sound was quite pleasing to me. We met some Gellabas riding on donkeys, on their way to Omdurman, but in the darkness they could not see who we were, and we passed them rapidly; only Ahmed remained behind, to greet them and exchange news.

Now the narrow track led through thick bushes, which we could not rightly see; our clothes, hands, and feet got torn and scratched by the thorns; but we never checked the pace, and continued our course steadily northwards. "Time is money," they say, but in our case time was life; we crossed dry beds of streams, over which the animals would sometimes stumble and fall, the riders with them; but there was no time to think of pains and bruises; to pick oneself up, catch and mount the camel, which might easily have been lost in the desert, was all one had time to think about. None of us had watches, but during the many sleepless nights I had passed, I had become used to observing the stars, and could tell the time almost to within five minutes.

Just at dawn we neared the village of Wad Bishara, and pushed on quicker so as to pass it before daybreak. This village is generally considered two days north of Omdurman. We then left the ordinary track, and turned towards the desert, as we dared not go along the river bank during the daytime. At sunrise we could just see the thin strip of green which marked the course of the stream; still we did not alight, but pushed on and on, up and down hills, across long stretches of sandy plain. Our eyes became so red and swollen we could scarcely see, and they pained us considerably.

At length, after some hours, we drew up, dismounted

ate a little biscuit, and drank some water, readjusted our saddles, then up and away again. My mind travelled back to Omdurman. Had our flight been discovered at once? What would happen to those left behind? How astonished they would be to find we had gone! But this train of thought was suddenly interrupted; one of the sisters had fallen off her camel, and was lying insensible on the ground; we picked her up, splashed her with water, and after a time brought her to; we then put her on to the camel again, and tied her firmly to the saddle; there was nothing else to be done—it was a question of life and death. So we rode continuously forward, in the desert by day and along the river bank by night.

I had asked Ahmed about the stranger who had helped me to mount my camel in Omdurman, and he told me that the animals had become so restive by good feeding that it was impossible for one man to hold them whilst the other two came to the hut to fetch us; he had therefore taken two friends into his confidence, and made them swear on the Kuran that they would not betray us. Just after sunset they had ridden the camels quite openly through the market-place, with their arms slung across the saddles, so that people should think they were post-camels, and no suspicion would be created.

Ahmed told me more too about the difficulties he had had in stabling the camels prior to our flight; two of them had been tethered in a poor woman's yard, and the two others he had placed in charge of one of his friends; but these caretakers had guessed that something was about to happen, and had urged Ahmed to depart as soon as possible, for they began to think they might become involved in the matter. Ahmed had paid them most liberally for their services; he had also had recourse to magic, summoned the spirits, and consulted a fiki, who prophesied the journey would be "as white as milk," that is to say, that no mishap would occur, for which statement Ahmed had given him a considerable bakshish.

We continued our journey always along the left bank of the Nile, there was no time to stop for sleep. Occasionally we came across Arab shepherds in the desert tending their herds of goats. They gazed wonderingly at us, and asked questions of Ahmed, who purposely always remained a short way behind. Ahmed drew a gloomy picture of the recent rising in Omdurman, describing how the two Khalifas had openly fought with each other, how nothing was heard night and day but the roar of cannon and the rattle of musketry, while the slaughter had been terrible beyond words. He represented that we were fugitives who had left the ordinary roads, fearing that the disturbed state of the country might make them unsafe, for bands of brigands were known to be roaming about.

These simple people, thoroughly detesting Mahdiism, believed every word Ahmed told them, thought we were wise to fly, and gave him as much milk as he wanted, a fact which he also regarded as a good omen.

Although Ahmed and his friends knew the usual roads well, they had never been on exactly the track we had been forced to take to avoid the inhabited places. Thus it happened that we approached the river sooner than we expected; in fact, almost before we knew it, we found ourselves amongst houses in the village of Makani, which was so concealed by trees that we had not seen it. We then met a party of Gellabas, and at Ahmed's advice at once slowed our pace so as not to provoke mistrust. These Gellabas looked at us somewhat suspiciously, and tried in vain to find out the object of our journey. Probably they remembered us afterwards when our flight became known.

At length, after some difficulty, we emerged from the village and again turned into the desert; but when I blamed Ahmed for misguiding us, he merely answered cheerfully, "Allah marakna!" ("God has delivered us!")

When we had got some distance from the river, we dismounted and had a slight meal of dates and water. Our limbs were so stiff we could not stand up straight, and our clothes were sticking to the wounds we had received when riding through the bush. How delightful it was to be on the ground again and stretch our cramped legs, and how pleasant would a short sleep have been! But no sooner had the camels swallowed a little dhurra than we were up and off again. We still went in a northerly direction, and as our scratches warmed again they pained us considerably; but the feeling that we were not pursued, and the growing hope that we should really escape, encouraged us to overcome every difficulty. We watered at Gubat on the Nile, where the English had encamped in 1885, and then we rode cautiously, well outside the great village of Metemmeh. The barking and howling of the dogs made the camels quicken their pace, and soon we were out of sight of the Jaalin capital.

We then began to discuss how we were to cross the Nile. Ahmed had a friend living in a village just south of Berber, and it occurred to him that we might cross there. We trotted quietly on towards this village, when a man suddenly sprang out in front of us and cried, "Enta min?" ("Who are you?") But we soon found out that the man was afraid, and had taken us for robbers. His sudden appearance had given us a great start, and we at once thought that our pursuers had caught us up, and that we were about to be recaptured. Ahmed, however, approached the man, and as we rode on, he turned, spoke to him, and allayed his fears.

When we approached the village, we dismounted and hid behind some thick bushes, whilst Ahmed went in search of his friend who was to ferry us across. In about half an hour he returned, saying that it was impossible, as the boat was on the other side. Besides, he had heard that two boats had just passed down on their way to Berber, and that all disturbances in Omdurman were at an end. However, they had heard nothing about our flight. We therefore mounted again, and continued marching north the whole of that night and the following day.

On this, the third day of our journey, we came in

sight of Berber, and towards evening descended to the river almost exactly opposite the town, filled our waterskins, and then made for the desert again. We did not dare keep near the river here, as numbers of Baggara were living in the neighbourhood. At about midnight we alighted, as Ahmed did not know the road. We fed the camels, and indulged in our usual meal of biscuits, dates, and water. Ahmed had also succeeded in procuring from his friend some tobacco and small earthenware pipes; so we smoked with impunity, and began to feel that our escape was now almost assured.

But we had still before us the crossing of the river, which our Arab friends in Omdurman had warned us would be one of the most critical and dangerous parts of our plan. We were in the saddle again at dawn, and continued our journey over a stony plateau which our guides did not recognize. Then all day we marched through narrow valleys, full of large stones washed down by the torrents. At length towards evening we sighted the river again, and descended towards it through a narrow gorge, where we had to dismount, as the camels could scarcely make their way across the great boulders which blocked the path. Once on the plain, our guides recognised the road, and we found ourselves near the village of Benga, where we hoped to be able to secure boats to take us across.

We advanced now very cautiously, looking round in every direction; and I espied three camelmen setting off evidently in the direction of Abu Hamed. I at once called Ahmed's attention to this; and although they were some way off, they could have seen us, so Ahmed advised us to alight at once, which we did, and concealed ourselves in a khor amongst some bushes.

Ahmed and his companions were, I could see, not a little alarmed by the appearance of the camelmen, and began to speak to each other in their own dialect; but I guessed by the expressions on their faces what they thought—viz. that our flight had been discovered, news had been sent to Berber, and now the camelmen were on their way to warn the emir of Abu Hamed to intercept us. I endeavoured to prove to them that it was quite impossible for the news to have reached Berber yet, even if our flight had been reported to the Khalifa the morning after we had left. It was most unlikely that the pursuit would have been begun before the evening, and we had thus got a good twenty-four hours' start. We were then just four hours north of Berber, and had been three and a half days out from Omdurman. Our pursuers therefore, even if they had ridden as rapidly and as persistently as we had, could not possibly have reached Berber yet. But my calculations by no means convinced our guides; and after a long consultation, Ahmed and Awad went towards the river about four miles distant, while Hamed stayed behind to look after the camels.

Now was the time to take a few hours' sleep before night came on. During the three and a half days we had been on the journey we had had only four hours' sleep. We were quite worn out; our simple meals of biscuit and water did not give us much nourishment, our limbs were so stiff that we could scarcely move, and our wounds proved most irritating. Under such circumstances it can well be understood how welcome sleep would have been; but the appearance of these three camels, the alarm of the guides, and our anxiety about crossing the river, drove away all idea of rest, and all we could do was to await with what patience we knew the return of the two Arabs.

At length, just as the sun was setting, Ahmed and Awad returned, much rejoiced. They had made inquiries about the three camelmen, and had found out that they had nothing to do with us, and that nothing was known yet of our flight. They had arranged with a boatman to ferry us across, under the pretext that they were conducting a small party of slaves whom they were going to hand over to the emir of Abu Hamed. This most satisfactory news quite dissipated our fatigue, and we ate our wretched biscuit and dates with an excellent appetite. As soon as it was dark we moved towards the river, and dismounted close to the water's edge. As yet there was no sign of the boatman, but we saw two boys rowing towards us.

Meanwhile Ahmed had gone to a house close by to get some dhurra. Then the boatman came and announced that he could not take us across that night, but we must wait till the morning. This would never have done; not only should we have lost a whole night, but we should undoubtedly have been recognised in daylight. However, it was no use talking, and the man went off to his hut; but we did not get discouraged, for if the worst came to the worst, we could row ourselves across.

By this time the two boys had reached the bank, and they now came forward and offered to take us across; of course we accepted, and in an incredibly short space of time our guides had got the camels on board. It was a large boat, so we all crossed together, and on reaching the opposite bank Ahmed gave the boys two dollars, with which they seemed highly pleased, kissed our hands, wished us a pleasant journey, and then returned to the west bank. We watered the animals, filled our skins, mounted, and again set our faces northwards.

It was now past midnight. The camels, refreshed by their rest and good feed, pushed on quickly, and during that night and the whole of the next day we rode on without any interruption or mishap. Not a soul was to be seen in this lonely desert, but we often came across herds of antelopes, rabbits, and a few hyenas; the antelopes would stand about twenty paces off, prick up their ears, and look inquisitively at the strange caravan.

It was quite cool when we left Omdurman, but now the weather had quite changed, and we felt it oppressively hot; we saw mirages constantly, and were often deceived by them. Our camels and ourselves now began to suffer. I was much struck by the change in the appearance of these animals; the high, fat hump and thick neck they had in Omdurman had both grown to half the size. At first we had the greatest difficulty in holding them in; now they were so tired that we had to keep flogging them all the time; their feet had got so worn that treading on a stone made them jump sideways, and to ease them we four men alternately dismounted and led them for some distance.

Our track lay across a broad plain, dotted about with small shrubs, and as we passed one of these, Ahmed noticed a snake, scared by our approach, trying to escape; he at once killed the reptile with a blow of his sword, then stretched out its body and jumped over it three times in a most excited way. Thereupon the guides congratulated each other, saying there was now nothing more to fear, and that we had conquered our enemies. This exhibition of courage on the part of the guides pleased me greatly. Once more we mounted and made our way towards Abu Hamed, where we intended to take water for the last time before entering the great Nubian desert.

The next night another snake episode occurred, but it ended rather differently. We were going across a stony place, when the leading camel suddenly swerved to one side, and we heard a hissing sound, which we knew must be a snake, but it was too dark to attempt to catch it. This greatly alarmed the Arabs, who looked upon it as an evil omen, and curiously enough, when close to Abu Hamed, an event did occur which quite confirmed their superstitions.

The next day, at about nine o'clock in the morning, we sighted the mountain which was our landmark indicating the place at which we intended to water. We anticipated reaching it in three hours, and there we intended to rest whilst the Arabs took the camels down to water; but somehow we went too far to the east, did not discover our mistake for some time, and it was midnight instead of midday when we reached the hill. This hill is shaped rather like two skittles, between which the road runs, and the wind, blowing through this narrow funnel, almost carried us off our camels.

Ahmed warned us to keep perfect silence as we scrambled down the rocky slope, and reached the river at last; here the mighty stream flows rapidly and silently at the foot of a great rock cliff, the stillness being occasionally broken by the splash of the many fish which delight to disport themselves in these cool depths. This watering-place is known as Meshra Dehesh, and is about six miles south of Abu Hamed. A few dôm palms and shrubs have gained a slender footing on the steep bank, and the reflection of the bright stars in the silent river could not but make one feel impressed with the grand solitude of the place. I bent down, scooped up the water in my hands, and refreshed my parched throat; then we took the saddles off the camels, filled our water-skins, and ate some biscuits; I wanted to bathe my face and eyes, which ached with the burning of the sun and sand, but Ahmed gave the word to mount.

We were too stiff and weak to be able to stand upright, and as for the poor sisters, Ahmed had to lift them bodily off the ground and put them on their camels; they were far too exhausted to speak; we led the camels out of the stony gorge, intending to mount when we reached the level. It was long past midnight, and we were congratulating ourselves on having passed the last critical point, hoping that by dawn we should have left the river, which here bends to the west, far behind us.

We had scarcely gone twenty paces from the river, when suddenly we heard the sound of a camel. We were almost ready to drop with fright, but Ahmed and the guides went towards the spot from whence the sound had come, and there they saw a camelman mounted, armed with a Remington, and peering at us from behind a dôm palm, but it was too dark for him to have recognized our white faces. Ahmed at once approached him, seized his rifle with his left hand, and extended his right to greet him, asking him at the same time to alight.

The man, alarmed probably at Ahmed's energetic bearing, at once dismounted and joined the guides. At first we thought orders must have come from Omdurman to intercept us, but fortunately it was not so; the guard (for such he proved to be) said he had been sent from Berber to see that Egyptian merchants did not export

"WE HAD SCARCELY GONE TWENTY PACES FROM THE RIVER, WHEN SUDDENLY WE HEARD THE SOUND OF A CAMEL."

slaves from the Sudan to Egypt. He related how, the day previous, a merchant with five slaves had been captured, but had been set free again on depositing the value of the slaves. The guard then asked Ahmed if he had brought any slaves, to which he replied in the affirmative.

The guard now insisted that Ahmed should go to Abu Hamed to see the emir there, and no amount of argument would convince him that it was unnecessary to do so. Hamed now came and told me about the occurrence, but, being somewhat confused, he happened to say we were lost. These words reached the ears of one of the sisters, and so startled her that she fell off her camel, and might have been very seriously injured had we not caught her.

I gave Hamed my long knife, and told him to do what he could to win the man over with money, but that if he found this was useless, "Well! we were four men to one." Hamed quite understood what I meant, and then returned to the others. The conversation still continued for a long time. At length our Arabs returned; we put the sisters on the camels at once, and then mounted ourselves. Our fatigue had fled; even the camels seemed to scent danger, for we set off at a quick pace and were soon out of sight.

This episode served to remind us very forcibly that we were still in the Khalifa's territory. Strange thoughts passed through my mind in quick succession: Omdurman, the Khalifa, the Saier, unbearable insults, then death. All these awaited us if we failed in our attempt; but then I comforted myself with the thought we should never be taken alive; we had solemnly agreed never to submit. It was in this frame of mind that we quitted Meshra Dehesh and rode for our lives night and day; the poor camels were reduced to skeletons, and we ourselves were nothing but skin and bone.

Ahmed told me that when the guard recognized him he showed himself kindly disposed, and promised not to betray us; but Ahmed did not trust him, and would not, therefore, let him go until he had accepted some money; he had pressed twenty dollars into his hand. The guard accepted the money after extracting a solemn promise from Ahmed and his companions that they would not attempt to revenge themselves on him or his tribe—the Monasir—on their return to Korosko. The guard also swore solemnly that he would not betray or pursue us, and moreover agreed to prevent the patrols going into the desert for three days, so as to keep us out of danger's way; they had then embraced and kissed each other as a sign of sincerity.

In spite, however, of all these solemn oaths, I did not trust the man; the fate of poor Colonel Stewart and his companions came into my mind, and I remembered that they had been cruelly done to death by the cowardly and treacherous Monasir; we therefore hurried forward our camels with all possible speed, leaving Abu Hamed far away on our left.

The day broke as usual, and soon the sun was risen and burning more fiercely than ever, but that did not trouble us. We were far too much absorbed in the momentous event which had just occurred. Our track ran through a perfectly flat plain, in which not a shrub or blade of grass was to be seen. We passed the tracks of the captured slave-dealer and the patrols, and that evening entered on the caravan road leading from Abu Hamed to Korosko. The track ran through great bare hills and solitary valleys; the wind had driven the sand almost to the tops of the hills, and had filled up all the crevices with sand-drifts.

Once within the hills, our courage returned, for we knew we would be able to defend ourselves; so we dismounted and ate our last mouthful of biscuit, and now all we had was our water, which, by the way, we jokingly remarked was somewhat dear, as it had cost us twenty dollars.

After a short rest we set off again, but both we and our camels were utterly exhausted; my right arm ached from continually whipping up the poor beast. Our Arab companions lightened the way with hundreds of interesting anecdotes of their own deserts. They related how, when Berber fell, an Arab and six Egyptian women had fled; but the man had brought only a camel or two and very little water, so four of them had died of thirst. They pointed out the spot which Rundle Bey had reached when he reconnoitred Abu Hamed in 1885. The road was plainly marked out by the bones of camels and donkeys, and, prior to the appearance of the Mahdi, had been a much-used trade route.

Mohammed Ali Pasha had ridden along this road under the guidance of Hussein Pasha Khalifa. Mohammed Ali had constantly expressed a desire to halt, but his guide would not allow him to dismount, except at certain places, saying, "I am commander here;" and to this Mohammed Ali had willingly consented, for he well knew that a refusal to do as he was told by the sheikh of the desert, in that awful wilderness, might have been followed by very serious results.

Our approach to a haven of safety gave us courage to undergo most terrible fatigue. By far our worst enemy was sleep; it is quite impossible for me to describe the fearful attacks this tyrannical foe made upon us. We tried every means in our power to keep awake; we shouted and talked loudly to each other; we tried to startle ourselves by giving a sudden jerk; we pinched ourselves till the blood ran down, but our eyelids weighed down like balls of lead, and it required a fearful effort to keep them open. "Ma tenamu" ("Don't sleep"), Ahmed kept repeating, "or you will fall off and break your leg."

But it was all no good; the conversation would flag, and silence follow. The camels seemed to know their riders were asleep, and instinctively fell into slower pace; the head kept nodding, until it sunk upon the chest; with a sudden start, the equilibrium which had been almost lost would be recovered, and then sleep vanished.

At times we would shout out to one another words of encouragement, then we would whip up our camels and on again, up and down, through sandy plains and rocky gorges, where the echoes seemed to repeat themselves a hundred times. Our destination was Murat, where we remembered Gordon had given orders for a well to be dug, but it had never been done. Ahmed said that we should be at Murat on the morning of the 7th of December. He told us how the Dervishes had sometimes pursued fugitives as far as this, and not long ago had killed one near here. Our poor camels were now dragging their weary limbs very slowly; the whip was now quite useless, as it had not the smallest effect in increasing their pace. Besides, it was pain to me to beat the good creatures that had helped us to escape. We were so utterly fatigued that it was with the greatest difficulty we succeeded in keeping on our camels at all; hunger, sleeplessness, and absolute lassitude had completely conquered us, and our wounds pained and irritated us; but the feeling that we were almost safe was as balm to both mind and body.

Just before sunset we turned down the khor which leads to Murat; the fort covering the wells was visible on the hills, surmounted by the red flag with the white crescent and star in the centre. "Ahmed," I cried, "greet the flag of freedom!" and our courageous deliverer seized his gun and fired shot after shot into the air, to announce our arrival to the Egyptian garrison. The echo of these shots resounded again and again in the deep valleys, as if joining with us in our joy at deliverance from the hands of the cruel Khalifa Abdullah. They seemed to announce the "release of our spirits from beneath his sheepskin." This was an expression which the Khalifa delighted to use when talking of his captured enemies, whose souls, he said, lay beneath his "furwa," meaning that their lives were entirely in his hands.

Now we were actually in safety. A prayer of the deepest gratitude went up from the very depths of our thankful hearts; it is quite impossible to find words to express what we then felt. Our camels seemed to pull themselves together for a final effort, so as to present us honourably to the Ababdehs, who were now coming out to meet us.

The reports of our rifles had at first caused some stir in the little garrison, who feared a sudden attack, and had come out fully armed; but they soon recognized us, and answered our salute by discharging their guns in the air. These good people received us most kindly, asked us a thousand questions, and, surrounding us, brought us to the commandant's hut. Here, on the 8th of December, the Feast of the Immaculate Conception, we alighted from our camels, and the hopes which had kept us alive for years, were at last realized. This supreme moment, about which we had so often talked with our companions in adversity, which we had thought about, dreamed about, and pictured to ourselves, this delicious moment had come at last, and we were free!

But the effects of hunger, fatigue, and the sights and scenes we had gone through during the last month, did not disappear so easily; our senses seemed dulled, and our first thought on entering the commandant's hut was to lie down on the floor and go to sleep, but, strange to say, that wonderful restorer would not come; we sat gossiping with the Ababdehs, who could scarcely credit that we, especially the sisters, could have survived such a ride. We had covered the entire distance of 500 miles between Omdurman and Murat in seven days, including the day we had spent wandering about in the hills before crossing the river.

The staying power of our camels had astonished me; how easily one of them might have stumbled and broken its leg as we trotted hard through the dark nights, unable to see where we were going! But Ahmed and his companions had used all their knowledge in securing thoroughly good animals; our excellent guides had been ever ready to help and assist us; full of energy and pluck, they had carried out their enterprise with the utmost sagacity and integrity.

Poor Ahmed had dwindled down almost to a skeleton, and when he dismounted at Murat was overcome by a fit of dizziness, from which he did not recover for an hour.

Meanwhile we had refreshed ourselves with a cup of coffee and some bread and milk which the commandant,

Mohammed Saleh, had offered us, and which had revived us considerably. Murat is situated in the desert, about midway between Korosko and Abu Hamed; here three valleys unite in a sort of crater, and the hill-tops are crowned with small forts built by the Ababdehs, from whence they can keep guard over the main wells, and, besides, see for an immense distance all around.

This, the most advanced Egyptian outpost, is garrisoned by the Ababdeh Arabs of Saleh Bey, the son of Hussein Pasha Khalifa; these people live very simply in the midst of this great desert, drawing their provisions monthly from Korosko. There are a number of wells, but the water is brackish and in summer almost undrinkable, though it is not so bad in the winter; but we had still some of our Nile water, which had cost us so dearly at Meshra Dehesh. Close to the wells is a little hut, built by Gordon's orders.

Murat is a most desolate and lonely spot, unbearably hot in the summer, when the fierce rays of the sun are reflected from all sides of the deep crater-like valley in which it lies. The same day that we arrived one of Ahmed Hassan's nephews had reached Murat from Korosko, and gave us some of the dates and flour he was taking into the Sudan; he left for Abu Hamed the next day, and no doubt the news of our safe arrival was soon announced in Omdurman.

During the 8th and 9th of December we rested. Mohammed Saleh supplied us with some biscuit, and on the 9th we again set off from Murat towards Korosko. Our rest had greatly refreshed us, and now we could ride quietly without any fear of pursuit. One of our guides was mounted on a she-camel, which the commander had supplied, and she gave us plenty of milk. A few days before starting her little baby-camel had died, the owner had skinned it, and now whenever we required milk, we had only to stretch out the skin in front of her and let her smell it.

We now rode only by day, and rested at night. Heavy rain had fallen about a month before, and we found a reservoir of good water about a day out of

Murat. Some of the Murat garrison had, previous to our arrival, gone into Korosko to get their monthly pay and were now returning; they happened to encamp near this natural reservoir, and seeing us took us for Dervishes, rushed to their arms, took up a position behind a rock and levelled their rifles at us, but Ahmed, who knew them at once, called out and they hurried up to us, begging pardon for the mistake they had made. They gave us some of their flour, dates, and tobacco, and we chatted with them till nightfall.

We made no further extended halt, and on the early morning of the 13th of December reached Korosko. In the deep valley which debouches suddenly on to the Nile at this place we alighted, cleaned ourselves as best we could, and then mounted our camels for the last time, and soon came in sight first of the palm-trees and then of the Nile, which we had last seen at Abu Hamed. We were at once surrounded by numbers of people, who bore us off to the fort, and here the commandant, Lieutenant-Colonel Ali Bey Haider, greeted us most cordially, and for the first time for many years we found ourselves in comfortable rooms again, and listening to the regimental band, which we greatly enjoyed.

On the evening of the 15th of December we got on board a steamer which took us down most comfortably to Assiut. Here we were greeted by Mr. Santoni and Brother Sayer, who had been directed by the Cairo Mission to come on board and welcome us. From Assiut we took the train to Cairo, where we arrived safely on the 21st of December, 1891.

The rapid transition from barbarism to civilization, our pleasant journey from Korosko to Cairo, intercourse with educated people, the incessant change of scene, all affected us greatly; but our joy and delight at being free was somewhat saddened by the thought of the sufferings of our poor companions in our adversity, whom we had left behind in slavery and captivity. Our guides accompanied us to Cairo, where they received the money agreed upon, and we felt full of thankfulness to the energetic Ahmed Hassan and his two companions;

but to our good Archbishop Sogaro we owe a deep debt of gratitude, for it was through his intermediary all arrangements for our happy release had been effected.

It may be as well to insert here the terms of agreement made in Arabic between Monsignor Sogaro and Ahmed Hassan regarding our release. The wording is as follows :—

"I, the undersigned, Ahmed Hassan el Abbadi, of Bashri Mohammed Ali's Arabs, agree to proceed at once to Omdurman to bring Father Ohrwalder and the two nuns from Omdurman to Cairo. I agree to take care of them on the journey, and to do all in my power to bring them here and to give them every satisfaction. As a reward and to recompense me for the expenses which I shall incur between Omdurman and Cairo, Monsignor Sogaro has agreed to give me :—

"1. All the goods to the value of £100 now in possession of Sheikh Abdel Hadi at Korosko.

"2. £20 in advance before leaving Cairo.

"3. On my return from Omdurman with Father Ohrwalder and the two nuns, a sum of £300, *i.e.* £100 for each person.

"This is the agreement between me and Monsignor Sogaro, and I have made it of my own free will and accord, and have been in no way forced to do so by any one. Monsignor Sogaro and myself signed this agreement, and Wingate Bey, Assistant Adjutant-General, Intelligence, stands as a witness. This agreement will be kept in the War Office until I return from Omdurman with the three persons above-named, and I shall be dealt with in accordance with its contents.*

"Signed,   AHMED HASSAN EL ABBADI,
            " of Sayala, Frontier Mudirieh.
        "LÉON HENRIOT (for Monsignor Sogaro).
"Cairo, 9th July, 1891."

* This contract and all correspondence connected with it was kept sealed in the Intelligence Office, and was opened by General Sir F. Grenfell, Sirdar, on the 14th day of December, 1891, when the news of the arrival of the party at Korosko reached Cairo.—F. R. W.

Below is written in English:—

"This is a private agreement between Monsignor Sogaro and Ahmed Hassan el Abbadi, who leaves Cairo for Omdurman on Friday, the 20th July, 1891, and will attempt to bring Father Ohrwalder to Egypt.

"Witnessed by me,   F. R. WINGATE,
"Kaimakam,
"A. A.-G., Intelligence, Egyptian Army.
"War Office,
"9th July, 1891."

I was, of course, intensely anxious to hear what had occurred in Omdurman after our departure. I thought that our flight would have remained undiscovered that night, the following day, and possibly the following night; but it was not so. Early in the morning on the 30th of November our absence was discovered by some women who had been standing before the door of my house. They had seen us and were surprised, because we did not usually leave the house after sunset.

The idea of flight did not probably at once occur to them, but their suspicions were aroused. Early in the morning they had knocked at my door, and receiving no answer, related what they had seen to my neighbour's slave, who in turn informed her master. He, in great terror, carried the information to the mukuddum of the Europeans. This man, accompanied by many of my friends, hastened to my house, and, breaking open the door, was assured of my flight by finding a letter which I had left.

The poor man had, to save his life, to at once inform the Khalifa, who ordered the sheikh of the market to find us even should we be buried in the earth. Wad er Rais therefore closed all the houses and arrested every one who could possibly have known of my flight, and threw them into chains, with threats of the gallows and the knife. My neighbours were also arrested. When he could get no information whatever from these people, the Khalifa sent to Metemmeh a certain Ibrahim

Wad el Ahmer, who had three camels, and was ordered to bring us back at all hazards. But the beit el mal had first to buy the camels at very high prices—120, 110, and 87 dollars respectively—and before they could start some busybody told the Khalifa that Khalifa Sherif had concealed me in a boat belonging to a certain Osman Fauzi, and had aided my flight in order that I should move the Egyptian Government to the support of his oppressed party. Another declared that he had seen white faces in the boat.

These statements impressed the Khalifa, who sent men at once to recapture the boat and examine the passengers. The boat was captured near Omdurman and examined, of course, with no result, on which the Khalifa was pacified, and sent off the camels. Ibrahim inquired minutely along the route to Metemmeh, but could get no information. In the meantime those well disposed towards us lived in the keenest apprehension lest we should be recaptured. Only on Ibrahim's return without any news could our friends breathe freely and feel sure that we must have got away safely. Then those who had been imprisoned were released.

Later on I received a letter from Omdurman telling me that our flight had raised a commotion throughout the whole city, and that the prisoners had to suffer very much. It may be learned from this what grave consequences had to be considered before I took the important step of flight. Should anyone else attempt it, those who remain must suffer. May God protect our poor companions!

CHAPTER XXVI.

THE PRESENT KHALIFA'S DESPOTISM IN THE SUDAN.

[The reader is reminded that all opinions expressed are those of Father Ohrwalder.—F. R. W.]

Reflections on the situation in the Sudan—The horrors of the present Khalifa's rule—How long shall it continue?

IN the foregoing pages we have glanced at a bloody period in the history of the Sudan—the rise of the Mahdi, his victorious career through Kordofan, and his conquest of Khartum. We have sketched the development of his mighty empire, founded in bloodshed and revolution, and we have seen him honoured as a messenger of God by the millions of the Sudan; glorified—nay, almost worshipped—by his own people, and watched by the Muslim neighbours of his empire with an admiration mingled with the keenest anxiety. Then, in the full enjoyment of his victories, at the supreme moment of his power, while seated in his capital of Omdurman, he revolved schemes of conquest of the whole world he knew; then dead—dead of debauchery and disease, dead at an age when most lives' promises are brightest. Then we have seen the empire tottering, Abdullah rising to its support, slowly but firmly strengthening the trembling power, and, with the strength of bigotry and ignorance, replacing a shattered superstition by the iron rule of might.

Here I may properly submit some reflections on the general situation.

Mohammed Ali conquered the Sudan, and in the train of his conquest followed all the triumphs of progress and civilization. Wide new territories were discovered, fertile and thickly populated; explorers and missionaries advanced to the very heart of negro-land; Nile's soli-

tudes were rippled by the advancing steamer. Far
beyond the Equator reached the telegraph, and the
metropolis of the Sudan formed part of the inter-
national postal system. Trade blossomed in security,
and the white man could march to the countries of the
Niam Niam, and there join hands with his brother
from the Congo. European culture spread throughout,
and the religion of Christ planted the world-saving
banner in remotest frontiers.

The progress of fifty years was ruined by the Mahdi's
revolt. The Sudan fell back into the darkness from
which philanthropy had rescued it. Civilization was
swamped in the flood of fanaticism. The sign of
salvation was blotted out, the bearers of it chained
as slaves, and the flag of tyranny waved over smoking
ruins from Darfur to the Red Sea, and from Regaf
northwards to the second cataract. Bands of fanatics
have swept over the face of the land, destroying every
Christian sign. The Sudan lies open in its desolation
and nakedness. Everything but a little cloth and a
little corn is superfluous,—nay wicked,—for those who
accept the Mahdi's promise of eternal life. The minds
of men are savage through years of warfare. The ignorant Baggara rule and the gentler Jaalin and Danagla
are oppressed; the land is fallen back to wilderness.

The present ruler, Abdullah, is marching steadily in
the path of desolation. He roots out eagerly every
vestige of Egyptian rule; all foreign influence he keeps
at a distance, for he will rule over an ignorant people.
He wants nothing from beyond his own boundaries.
If he has no money, cloth becomes the medium of
exchange; ammunition he makes himself. With his
Baggaras he rules with an iron hand. Those who
resist are pitilessly robbed, imprisoned, or exiled.

Abdullah rules in the name of the Mahdi, whose
religious prestige is the readiest weapon for swaying
the multitude. He keeps unaltered the decisions, the
visions, the wild dreams which so powerfully established the imposture. The pilgrimage to Mecca he
regards as dangerous. Even from such enlightenment

as they might find at the shrine of their faith, his people are heedfully kept away.

A Spartan habit of life was enjoined by the Mahdi. This Abdullah still attempts to maintain, for he wishes the people to be ready to follow him, and is careful that they shall have no inducement to stay at home. Like the Mahdi, the Khalifa puts his orders in the form of visions, which have the weight of divine manifestations. Often he locks himself in darkness in the Mahdi's tomb, and spends nights in pretended commune with his master.

The policy of Abdullah is directed to strengthening his power and concentrating it in the hands of his Baggaras. Once he is sure of what he has got, he will try to enlarge his dominion. Barbarism and desolation will be extended to provinces which internal difficulties have so far prevented him from absorbing. He thinks of nothing but war. Omdurman is one vast camp. All men bear arms or are flogged; whoso rides must carry a spear and five javelins. Speeches and harangues all raise the spirit of war.

The weakness of the monarchy lies in the dissensions between the Baggara and the Aulad-belad—that is, the Jaalin, Danagla, and others. The Danagla are objects of the Khalifa's special aversion, and he would gladly exterminate them. But with his Baggaras he can at present maintain himself with ease.

Mahdiism is founded on plunder and violence, and by plunder and violence it is carried on. In some districts half the people are dead, in others the loss of life is even greater. Whole tribes have been completely blotted out, and in their places roam the wild beasts, spreading and increasing in fierceness and in numbers, until they bid fair to finish the destruction of the human race; for they enter huts, and women and children are no longer safe.

How long shall this condition of affairs continue? Negotiation with Abdullah is hopeless; that has been proved by many well-intentioned efforts, but shall savagery and desolation continue for ever? Shall the roads remain always closed that lead from Halfa and Sawakin to the richest provinces of Africa? The Sudan has lost faith in the humanity of Europe, nor does it cease from wonder why Europe has not yet stepped in. Consuls of the greatest nations have been murdered, their flags torn down, their agents kept in slavery.

Interference while the revolt was at its height could not perhaps be efficient—that is understood. But now the face of things is changed. The Sudanese have been heavily punished for their mistaken trust; they have suffered to the bitter end. Where may they look for a deliverer?

For the sake of three people did not England undertake a costly and difficult war? Is not even a more worthy object the punishment of Abdullah and the delivery of the enslaved and decimated peoples? I have pined ten years in bondage, and now, by the help of God, I have escaped. In the names of the companions with whom I suffered, in the name of the Sudan people, whose misery I have seen, and in the name of all civilized nations, I ask this question:

How long shall Europe—and above all that nation which has first part in Egypt and the Sudan—which stands deservedly first in civilizing savage races, how long shall Europe and Great Britain watch unmoved the outrages of the Khalifa and the destruction of the Sudan people?

INDEX.

ABABDEH tribe, 124-5, 213, 351, 353, 360, 399, 440-2.
Abba Island, 6-7, 98.
Abbas, steamer, 127-8.
Abdel Baki, emir, 315-9.
Abdel Gayum, eunuch, 294.
Abdel Hadi (Arab), 263.
Abdel Halim, Emir, 76, 78, 86, 88, 102, 260.
Abdel Kader Pasha, 50, 164.
Abdel Kader (Mahdi's uncle), 59, 155, 164, 214, 350, 400.
Abdel Kader Guru, death of, 262.
Abdel Karim (Mahdi's uncle), 160, 164-5.
Abdel Majid, 256, 326, 343.
Abdel Maula, 228.
Abdel Nur, 320-322.
Abdel Samad, 93.
Abderrahman Wad Abu Degel, 253.
Abderrahman Wad en Nejumi, 16, 60, 96, 98, 125-6, 130, 141, 145, 149, 165, 171, 206, 233, 255-61, 350, 387, 412; vanquished at Argin, 262-5; death of, 263.
Abdullah et Taishi, Khalifa, 10-1, 14, 43-6, 64, 66, 69-71, 87, 96, 120, 131, 146, 149, 151; and King Adam, 95; and the sisters, 100; and Father Ohrwalder, 116-7; succeeds the Mahdi, 162-3, 185, 188; and revolt of black soldiers of old Sudan army 193-200; at Omdurman, 202-3, 206; and Wad Suleiman, 206-7; Ibrahim Wad Adlan, 207-8, 323-7; and coinage at Omdurman, 210-3; system of justice, 214-5, 328-335; and Fiki Medawi, 218; and Yunis emir, 219-20; and King John, 221; and Abu Anga, 224; grand review at Omdurman, 225-6; war with Abyssinia, 228-31, 242-52; and Saleh Bey, 232-4; and Darfur, 235-41; and Egypt, 254-6, 258-69; letters from, 257; sends expedition up the White Nile, 269-72; and the Mahdi's decrees, 273; followers of, 274; and the Mahdi's tomb, 275-9; palace and houses of, 280-1; and war requisites, 281, 366-75; and the famine in Omdurman, 287-92; description of, 293; dress and food of, 293-4; harem of, 294; illnesses of, 294-5; character, 295-6; spies of, 295; and political conversations, 296, 320; mosque at Omdurman, 297-8; and visions, 298-9; a man of great activity, 300; fondness for music, 301; his barber, 301; life-guards and household cavalry, 301-2; and business affairs of the State, 302; displays of magnificence, 302-4; cleanliness of, 304; grand reviews at Omdurman, 307-8; and the Taisha Arabs, 308-11; and fire-arms,311-2; his brother, see "Yakub"; and the Batahin tribe, 315-20; and Abdel Nur, 321-2; and the Saier at Omdurman, 347-52; and Charles Neufeld, 355-60; and Sheikh Khalil, 361-4; and the slave trade, 384-5; and the Baggaras, 387-405; his son Osman, 390-1; strict surveillance over the whites, 412-3; horrors of his rule, 447-50.
Abdullah Wad en Nur, 60, 98, 100, 115, 125, 143.
Abdullah Wad Ibrahim, 38, 223, 225, 227, 229; and Abyssinia, 247, 252-3.
Abu Anga (commander-in-chief of Mahdi's forces), 60, 85-9, 98, 111-2, 125, 131, 164, 171, 175, 202, 402; description and history of, 221-31; and Abyssinia, 242-4; death of, 245-6; and slave trade, 384.

INDEX.

Abu Gemaizeh, religious reformer, 237–40.
Abu Girgeh, emir, 76, 81, 94, 125, 167–8, 218, 267, 360.
Abu Habl, the Khor, 3, 78–9.
Abu Hamed, 364, 433; rebels at, 120, 128.
Abu Haraz, 219, 229.
Abu Klea, battle of, 134, 147–8, 177.
Abu Kru, battle of, 16, 134.
Abu Kuka, 56.
Abu Saud, 7.
Abyssinia, and Kassala garrisons, 166–7; and Galabat, 217–20; Abu Anga and, 229–31, 241–4; defeat of King John's army, 245–53.
Adam, King, of Tagalla, 95, 102, 223.
Adansonia trees, 34, 40, 76, 88, 170, 198.
Adila, girl at the Khartum Mission, 421, 424, 426.
Adultery, the Mahdi's punishment for, 62.
Agriculture in the Mahdiist kingdom, 376–85.
Ahmed Bey Daffallah, 10, 21, 35, 38, 59, 252.
Ahmed Bey Defterdar, 234.
Ahmed Hassan and escape of Father Ohrwalder, 415–45.
Ahmed Sharfi, 7, 140, 403–7.
Ahmed Wad Suleiman, 63, 82–4, 96–7, 111, 139, 143–5, 161, 206–7, 350.
Aigella, 77, 174.
Aisha, the Mahdi's principal wife, 157, 159.
Ala ed Din Pasha, 1, 77, 88.
Alchemy, Sudanese and, 369.
Alcoholic drinks, the Sudanese and, 17; see also *Marissa*.
Ali Bakhit, 172, 174, 199.
Ali Bey Haider, Lieut.-Col., 443.
Ali Esh Sherif, Khalifa, 14–5, 37, 41, 59, 66, 69, 88, 93, 100. 146, 163; at Omdurman, 202–3, 254, 306, 349, 399–407, 446.
Ali Pasha, 127.
Ali Wad Helu, Khalifa, 14, 146, 163, 282, 306, 403–7.
Allegiance, sheikhs' oath of, 70.
Aluba, Hicks at, 85.
Amarar Arabs, 266–7.
Andreis, Sister A., 48.
Amhara, the chief of, 217.
Amina (a black girl), 73.
Ammunition, the Khalifa's, 366–75.
Amulets, the fikis and, 274–5, 402.

Ansar, the, 306–8, 353.
Arabi, Baggara called, 265.
Arabi Pasha, 77.
Arabs; in Omdurman, 283; see " Baggaras," " Bederieh," " Beni Jerrar," " Dar Hamed," " Ghodiat," " Gowameh," " Hawazma," " Kababish," &c.
Argin, battle of, 115, 262.
Aser, American Consul, 141.
Ashaf Station, 11.
Ashraf, the, 149, 214.
Assiut, 443.
Assuan, 174, 256.
Atbara River, 249.
Aulad-belad, the, 391–2, 405–6, 449.
Austrian Mission, at Delen, 4–5, 24–30; church at Khartum, 137–8; at El Obeid, 200; see also " Sisters."
Awad el Kerim Abu Sin, 350.

BAGGARA tribe, 3, 14–5, 20, 25–6, 32, 49, 78, 106, 162–3, 178, 221, 255, 258, 266, 287, 293, 314, 325, 341; horsemanship of, 308; emirs, 312; women, 381; masters of the Sudan, 387–407, 449; see also " Taisha Arabs."
Bahr el Arab, 3.
Bahr el Ghazal, slave trade in, 8–9, 12, 176, 383; revolt in, 241.
Bahr el Karrar, 257–8.
Baker Pasha, General Valentine, defeat of, 119; at El Teb, 266.
Banners of the Mahdi's Khalifas, see " Flags."
Bara town, 11, 55, 77, 200–2, 235; fall of, 56.
Barabra tribe, 125, 255, 391, 399; language of, 283.
Bashra, the Mahdi's son, 159.
Batahin tribe, 205, 260, 315–20.
Bayuda Desert, 16.
Bederieh Arabs, the, 3, 11, 20, 106, 167.
Beit el mal at Omdurman, 208–14, 312, 323, 380, 393–5.
Ben en Naga Bey, 21, 88–9; son of, 333; daughter of, 343.
Benga village, 430.
Beni Helba tribe, 240.
Beni Jerrar Arabs, 35, 238.
Berber, 1, 14; fall of, 121, 124–5; Gordon at, 123, 208, 256, 312, 380, 396, 430, 459; Osman Digna at, 266, 268; old, 275; famine in, 290.
Berghof, a German, 9.
Birket, 3, 11, 20–1, 28, 34, 86, 91.

INDEX.   453

Bishir, 197, 224, 227.
Bishir Bey, 259.
Blue Nile, 126, 133–4. 150, 204, 227, 379; towns on the, 284.
Bonomi, Father, 1, 5, 27, 31–2, 43, 50. 56, 68–71, 73, 97, 100, 118, 170, 172–3; escape of, 178–84, 186, 352.
Books, the Mahdi and, 63; Khalifa Abdullah and, 299, 400–1.
Borgo, Sultan of, 12, 237.
Brick-making at Delen, 5.
Bringi, executioner at Omdurman, 318, 325, 356.
British East Africa, Imperial, Co., 271.
'Bruce's Travels' and the Batahin tribe, 315.
Buri village, 125, 132.
Busata village, 174.

CAIRO, 1, 254; merchants of, and El Obeid, 35; Ohrwalder's arrival at, 443.
Camels, in Kordofan, 35–6, 379; of the Gehena tribe, 226, 228; of the Kababish tribe, 232, 234; for Ohrwalder's escape, 422, 427, 442.
Cattle in Dar Nuba, 4; in Kordofan, 35; of the Arabs, 126; of the Gehena tribe, 226; breeding in the Sudan, 376–9; cows of the Shilluks, 379.
Cemetery, European, at Khartum, 150.
Chad Lake, 241.
Chincarini, Sister C., 413–45.
Clementino, George, 126, 142.
Clothing in the Mahdi's kingdom, 381.
Coins in Omdurman, 210–13.
Comboni, Bishop, 1, 2, 24; grave of, at Khartum. 150.
Combotti, Marietta, 118.
Comet, a wonderful, 44.
Commerce in the Mahdiist kingdom, 376–85.
Corsi, Sister Concetta, 57, 419.
Cripples in Omdurman, 337.
Curios, museum of, at Omdurman, 213.
Cuzzi, Joseph, 120, 125–6.

DABAROSA bazaar, the, 258.
Dabra Sin, battle of, 229.
Dair, Jebel, 3.
Damur, pieces of cloth, 381–2; used as coins, 210.
Danagla, see "Dongola."
Dara, 93.
Dar Fertit, singers from, 301.
Darfur, 12, 35; Slatin Bey, Governor of, 2; the Mahdi conquers, 93–4,

98; historical sketch of, 234–41; Zogal and, 201–3; revolt in, 260, 387; horses in, 308: women and spinning, 381; slaves from, 384.
Dar Homr (Arabs), 11, 20, 35, 106, 301, 3 9, 396.
Dar Nauli tribe of Arabs, 106.
Dar Nuba, see "Nuba."
Dar Shaggieh, 380.
Dead, the Mahdi's law about the, 19.
Debaineh tribe, 290.
Degheim tribe, 14.
Delen, arrival at, 3; Mission at, 4, 5; news of the Mahdi at, 7, 8; description of, 23–31; quicksilver at, 35; 178, 187, 197.
Dervishes, the Mahdi's, 45; at El Obeid, 57–9; and Hicks Pasha's army, 88; in Khartum, 140; and Olivier Pain, 173; revolt against, 189–200; at Galabat, 217–9; review of, at Omdurman, 225–6; and tobacco chewing, 276; and the famine in Omdurman, 289; at Fashoda, 384.
Dhurra in Omdurman, 285, 378, 381.
Dichtl, Johann, 1.
Dinka tribe, 176.
Disease in the Sudan, 386.
Dispensary at Omdurman, 213.
Dobab mountain, 3, 102.
Dogman mountain, 24, 28.
Dogs, Mahdi's doctrine about, 143, 335.
Doka, Sheikh Egeil and, 219.
Dome to Mahdi's tomb at Omdurman, 275, 277.
Dongola, 12, 14, 35, 94, 127, 163, 172, 178, 190, 255, 256, 257–65, 268, 312, 380, 384, 387, 391, 396, 399, 449; famine in, 290; language, 283.
Doorway of the Mahdi's tomb. 277.
Dreams, the Mahdi and, 110–1, 353, 449.
Drums of the Mahdi's Khalifas, 15, 44, 47, 281, 304–6.
Dud Benga, Sultan, 184.
Duem, 126; General Hicks at, 76.
Dwarf, a, at Rahad, 110.

ED DIN, Sheikh, see "Osman, Khalifa."
Egeil, sheikh, 218–9, 221.
Egypt, and Delen, 4; and the Sudan, 34; Abdullah and, 254–6, 257–69; and the Sudan, 123, 323; Wad Adlan and, 326; the Mahdi and, 110.
Egyptian troops, Hicks Pasha's, 77–90, 92–3.

INDEX.

El Eilafun, 127.
El Fasher, steamer, 128.
El Merhdi Abu Rof, 164, 226–7.
El Obeid, 2, 6; garrison of, 10, 21; the Mahdi and, 11, 20, 29, 36–41; description of, 34–6; siege of, 52–7, 232; 'Zogal at, 75; the Mahdi leaves, 85, 99–100; triumphal return to, 91–3, 170–2; King Adam at, 95; Lupton Bey at, 176; small-pox in, 183; revolt of black soldiers at, 189–200, 223; slaves at, 383–4.
El Obeid, Sheikh, 124, 127, 130, 315.
El Teb, battle of, 266.
Elephants, 3; in Darfur, 241.
Elias el Kurdi, 210.
Elias Pasha, 10, 12, 21, 35, 40, 76, 88, 93; son of, 86.
Elias Wad Kanuna, emir, 271.
Emirs, the, of the Sudan provinces, 46, 312.
Emin Pasha, 11; Gordon and, 133; and Lupton Bey, 176; Khalifa Abdullah and, 269–72.
England and Egypt, 262; and the Sudan, 450.
English mail, capture of an, 120.
English Relief Expedition to Khartum, 147–9, 176–8; and Kababish tribe, 232; at Dongola, June 1885, 256.
Equatoria, Abdullah's expedition to, 269–72.
Exports from Kordofan, 35.

FADL MAULA BEY, 163, 271, 401
Fallata tribe, 278, 283.
Famines; in El Obeid, 183–4; in the Sudan, 252–3; in Dongola, 261; in Omdurman, 284–9; in Berber, 290; in the Provinces, 290–1.
Farag Pasha, 135, 143.
Faragallah Pasha, 131–2, 247.
Farquhar, Colonel Arthur, 79, 80.
Fasher, El, 94; besieged, 239–41.
Fashoda, 9, 11, 29, 269, 272, 379, 384, 396; corn from, 285.
Fedasi, 125.
Festivals, Khalifa Abdullah and, 362.
Fiki, Abdullah and the name, 274, 402.
Flags of the Khalifas, 15, 16, 281, 306.
Furs, annihilation of the, 236.

GALABAT, province and town, 167, 217–9, 230, 242, 244; attack on, 247–8, 396; famine at, 290.
Gallows at Omdurman, 283, 317–8.

Gedaref, garrison of, 216–7, 290.
Gedir, Jebel, 3, 7, 10, 20, 223.
Gehena tribe, 226–7, 260–1.
Gellabas (traders), 14–5, 112, 189, 426, 428.
Georges Bey, Dr., 86; son-in-law of, 141.
Gessi Pasha, 2; and the slave trade, 8–9, 241, 383.
Gezireh, the Mahdi and, 14, 64, 93–4; 229, 284, 315, 380, 390.
Ghazali, Sheikh, 310–1, 350.
Ghittas, festival known as. 218.
Ghodiat Arabs, the, 3, 11, 20, 106.
Gianzara Hill, 40, 46.
Giegler Pasha, 2, 7.
Giniss, battle of, 256.
Girls in Khartum, Mahdi and, 144.
Goats in Dar Nuba, 4; in the Sudan provinces, 379.
Gold in Dar Nuba, 3.
Golfan-Naïma, 22–3, 49, 197, 223–4.
Gondar, 230–1, 248–9.
Gordon, General, 57, 96; arrives at Khartum, 97, 121–2; letter to the Mahdi, 98; the Mahdi and, 111, 119, 126, 130; English letters to, 120; at Berber, 123–4; defeat of Gordon's troops, 124–5; successful attack by, 127; besieged, and death of, at Khartum, 131–54, 177, 207–8; and Sheikh Khalil and, 361; at Murat, 440.
Gordon Relief Expedition, 147–9, 176–8; viâ Berber, 266.
Gowameh tribe, 11, 344.
Graham, General, 120–1, 266.
Greeks, the, at Khartum, 133, 142–3.
Greger Hamed (Emir), 233.
Grenfell, General Sir F., 256, 262, 444; battle at Toski, 263, 265.
Gubat, 148, 154, 429.
Guineas coined at Omdurman, 210.
Gum, in Kordofan, 35; used as food at El Obeid, 53; at Omdurman, 323.

HABBANIEH tribe of Arabs, 73, 258.
Hadarba merchants, 399.
Hadendoa Arabs, 266, 283.
Haimar Wells, 257.
Haj Ali Wad Saad, 123–4.
Hajji Abdullah Granteli, 210.
Hajji Khaled (Emir), 21, 35, 46, 71; son of, 86.
Hajji Mohammed Ben on Naga, 35.

INDEX. 455

Hajji Selim (soldier), 49, 190-1.
Hajji Zubeir, 240, 349-50, 396-7.
Halfaya, 127.
Hamran Arabs, 218.
Handub, battle of, 267.
Hansal (Austrian consul), 1, 67-9, 73, 118-9; death of, 139-40.
Hashish, use of, 17.
Hasib, emir, 271.
Hassan Khalifa, 257, 364-5.
Hassan en Nejumi (emir), 264.
Hassan Husni (interpreter), 128, 130.
Hassan Sadik, 164.
Hassan Zeki, 366.
Hebbeh village, 128.
Heddai, sheikh, 129.
Herlth, Major, extracts from diary of, 77-9, 86.
Hicks Pasha, General, 1; and Wad Makashef, 73; expedition of, 75; at Duem, 76; at Rahad, 77-85; defeat and death of, 86-92, 121, 169, 176; white horse of, 91; Bible of, 100; stable, 157.
Hilmi Gorab, 128.
Horses, the Sudanese and, 308.
Housebreakers in Omdurman, 334-5.
Howazma Arabs, 20, 106, 222.
Hussein Pasha, 120, 123, 125, 439; son of, 442.
Hussein Wad ed Dayim, 339-40.
Hyenas, 88, 289-90.

IBRAHIM NUR, 394-5.
Ibrahim Pasha Fauzi, 143.
Ibrahim Ramadan, 203.
Ibrahim Wad Adlan, 35, 207-10, 214, 322-4, 350, 368; death of, 325-7.
Ibrahim Wad Abu Tagalla, 225.
Ibrahim Wad el Ahmer, 445-6.
Idris (sheikh), 101, 111, 114-7, 260, 350; death of, 262.
Imbrien, Bishop, of the Tyrol, 118.
Immorality, Mahdi's law regarding, 62; in the Sudan, 341-3; of slaves, 385-6.
Imports of the Mahdi's kingdom, 380.
Insects, at Delen, 4, 5; Neufeld and, 357; white ants as food, 53; lizards, 150; flies, 114.
Iron in Kordofan, 35.
Isa, skeikh, 28.
Isa, fiki, of the Shanabla, 194.
Ismail el Kheir, 400.
Ismail Wad el Andok, 22, 49, 59, 227, 229, 247.
Ismail Pasha, 234-5.

Italy and Kassala, 168.
Ivory, expedition to Equatoria to collect, 271; at Omdurman, 323.

JAALIN tribe, 123, 125, 255, 368, 384, 391, 399, 449.
Jabrallah, Sultan, 236, 350.
Jebel Dair, the Mahdi and, 111-2, 114, 199.
Jebel Naïma, 197.
Jerusalem, the Mahdi and, 110.
Jew merchants at Omdurman, 312; at Kassala, 360.
Jibbehs, the Mahdi and the manufacture of, 19.
Jinns, the, 307.
John, King of Abyssinia, throne of, 213; and Galabat, 217, 247-9; Abdullah and, 221, 242; and Abu Anga, 243; death of, 250-2.
Justice, system of, at Omdurman, 214-5, 329-34.

KABA, 34, 36-7, 39.
Kababish tribe (Arabs), 35, 55, 64, 78, 178; destruction of the, 232-4.
Kadi Ahmed, 214-5, 246-7, 329, 350.
Kakum of Delen, 4, 24, 26-8, 31-2, 178; death of, 186-7.
Kalabsheh, village of, 257.
Kalakala, 130-2.
Kamal ed Din, and manufacture of powder, 367-8.
Karamallah (slave-dealer), 176, 269, 406; in Darfur, 235-6.
Karkoj, 226, 290, 380.
Kashgeil, Hicks at, 85, 87.
Kashm el Mus, Pasha, 148.
Kassala, 154, 162, 164-5, 168, 387, 396; siege of, 166-7; Osman Digna at, 266; famine at, 290.
Kavalli, Stanley's camp at, 271.
Kawakla, natives called, 7.
Kebkebieh, 94.
Kedaro hill, 3.
Kenana tribe, 14.
Kererri, 12, 307, 311, 361, 412.
Khabir, Pasha, of Darfur, 36.
Khalifas in the Sudan, see "Abdullah," "Ali Wad Helu," "Ali Esh Sherif," Hassan, "Osman," &c.
Khalil, sheikh, 360-4.
Khartum, 1, 6, 7, 72, 93-4, 96-7, 106; the Mahdi's advance on, 99, 121, 126-7, 130; Gordon arrives at, 121-3; siege and fall of, 131-54, 177, 348; in ruins, 204, 216; materials

for Mahdi's tomb from, 276; the Batahin tribe and, 315, 320; Neufeld at, 357, 359; survivors of, 372.
Khatafin (snatchers) in Omdurman, 286–8.
Khojali, 130, 219, 317.
Khojur, the, in Dar Nuba, 4, 24, 26, 28.
Khor Musa, fort at, 259.
Kirkesawi (slave-dealer), 176, 236, 406.
Kitchener Pasha, 359; wounded at Handub, 267.
Klein, tailor, of Khartum, 140–1.
Klootz, Gustav, 80–5, 88, 91, 93, 96, 109, 120, 174–5, 206, 348, 411; death of, 219.
Korbatsh, Mount, 34, 179, 200.
Kordofan, 199, 234, 380, 398; deserts of, 2–3; military stations in, 11–2; the Mahdi and, 20, 28; mountains, 34; exports from, 35–6; camels in, 35–6, 72; agriculture in, 378–9.
Korosko, 257, 442–3.
Korsi, 68.
Kudru hill, 32.
Kumbo, King, 98–9, 117–8.
Kuran, the, concerning ministers of Christianity, 104–6; first chapter in 296.
Kurun hill, 3.

Lado Station, 272, 384.
Languages in the Sudan provinces, 283.
Laws made by the Mahdi, 17–20. 61–3.
Lead, manufacture of, at Omdurman, 368–70.
Legnani (Italian consul), 1.
Leontides, Consul N., 126, 134. 140.
Lime, near Delen, 5; pits in Omdurman, 205, 276.
Limona, Bianca, 57.
Locatelli (missionary), 54, 56–7.
Locusts, plague of, in the Sudan, 291.
Losi, Father Johann, 54, 58.
Lugard, Captain, 271.
Lupton Bey, 153. 175–7, 191, 202, 348, 412–3; death of, 366.

Madibbo, sheikh, 235; son of, 396.
Mahbas, wells of, 233.
Mahdi, the, see "Mohammed Ahmed."
Mahdiism, belief in, 185; and Egypt, 265; in the Sudan, 255, 273, 326, 328, 403, 449; and the slave trade, 382–6.

Mahdiist kingdom, agriculture and commerce in, 376–86.
Mahmud Wad Ahmed, 240–1, 247–9.
Mail, capture of an English, 120.
Makada tribe, 241.
Makani village, 428.
Makbul dollar, the, in Omdurman, 210–4.
Makias (chains), 345–6.
Makin Wad en Nur. 260, 350.
Manoli, a Greek, 142.
Mansureh, steamer, 127.
Marcopoli Bey, 2, 73.
Mariani, Gabriel, 5, 41, 48.
Marissa (a kind of beer), 4; the Mahdi and drinking of, 61, 330, 340.
Market at Omdurman, 282, 339.
Marquet, 2.
Marriage ceremonies in the Sudan, 17–8, 341–3, 389–90.
Masalit, Sultan of, 213; people, 237.
Mecca, pilgrimage to, 278–9, 448; the Mahdi and, 110; a Sherif of, 412.
Medawi, fiki, 124, 218, 221.
Mek Omar, 28–32, 49–50, 178; son of, see "Naser."
Melbeis, 95, 196.
Meshra Dehesh, 434, 437.
Mesalamieh gate at Khartum, 150.
Metemmeh, 123, 268, 429.
Miracles, the Mahdi and, 7–8; performed by Sid el Hassan, 166.
Miserieh tribe of Arabs, 106, 222.
Mice, plague of, at Omdurman, 291–2.
Minneh, fiki, 11, 20, 37, 39–40, 46, 56, 59–60.
Mint, the, at Omdurman, 209–13.
Missionaries, at El Obeid, 40–51; *see also* "Bonomi," "Losi," "Ohrwalder," "Rossignoli."
Mission Stations; see "Austrian Mission."
Mohammed Ahmed, sheikh, 396.
Mohammed Ahmed (the Mahdi), rise of, 7–9; and Kordofan, 10–12; antecedents of, 12; outward appearance of, 13; Khalifas of, 14–5; military organization of, 15–6; new laws made by, 17–20. 60–3, 273; summons El Obeid to surrender, 20–1; defeat of, before El Obeid, 34, 36–41; and the missionaries, 42–51; siege of El Obeid, 53–9; finances, 62–3; art of winning over people, 66–7; and Consul Hansal's letter, 68–71, 73; victory over Hicks Pasha, 75–90·

INDEX. 457

triumphal entry into El Obeid, 91-2; and province of Darfur, 93-4; General Gordon and, 98, 130; and the sisters, 103-6; and Father Ohrwalder, on religion, 109-11; and Slatin Bey, 118; and violation of moral laws, 121; religious movement of, 122-3; and Cuzzi, 125-6; siege of Khartum, 126, 131-54; his life of ease and luxury, 60-4, 155-9, 449; principal wife of, 157; dwelling of, 157; harem, 158; death of, 160-62, 185; and Olivier Pain, 174-5; and Egypt, 254-6; tomb of, 275-80; and immorality, 341, 343; and property, 398; wives of, 404, 406; capital of the Mahdi's kingdom, see "Omdurman."
Mohammed Ali, 234, 315, 439, 447.
Mohammed el Kheir, 125, 130, 256.
Mohammed Pasha Khabir, 21.
Mohammed Suleiman, 186.
Monasir tribe, 128, 438.
Monogamy in Dar Nuba, 4.
Moral laws, the Mahdi and violation of, 121.
Moslem law, 322; the killing of priests, 46; and justice, 61-2; Sudanese and, 279.
Mosque at Omdurman, 279, 297.
Mukran Fort, 126, 147.
Munzinger Pasha, 189, 191.
Murat, Saleh Bey and, 265; wells of, 364; Ohrwalder at, 440, 442.
Murders in the Sudan provinces, 333.
Musa, sheikh, 396.
Musallem, Sultan, 234.
Museum of curios at Omdurman, 213.
Mussaid, Emir, 258.
Mustafa Hadal, 166.
Mustafa Yawer, 64-6, 358, 363.

Nahut, in Kordofan, 240-1.
Naïma Jebel, 3, 223.
Naser (son of Mek Omar), 32-3, 40-1.
Nasri, sheikh, 167-8.
Nejumi, see "Abderrahman Wad en Nejumi."
Neufeld, Charles, 233, 263, 345, 348, 353-60, 363.
News, the Sudanese and, 72-3; in Omdurman, 282.
Nesim, Major, 11.
Niam Niam, singers from, 301.
Nile, see "White Nile," "Blue Nile."
Noaïa, sheikh, 222-3.
Nuba, country and people of, 3-5, 22-32, 35, 48-9, 50, 95, 102, 112-4, 117-8, 121, 171-2, 177, 186, 197-200, 223, 384.
Nubian desert, crossing the, 433-42.
Nur Angar, 16, 56, 112, 225, 247.
Nur Bey, 164-5.
Nur Gereifawi, 327, 379, 404; son of, 394.
Nuri, sheikh, 247.

Oath of allegiance, sheikhs taking the, 70; evidence on, at Omdurman, 329.
Obeid, see "El Obeid."
O'Donovan, Mr. (*Daily News* correspondent), 80, 96, 101.
Ohrwalder, Father, visit to Mek Omar, 50; illtreated by a sheikh, 69-70; taken before Abdullah, 100; journey to Rahad, 101-3; interview with the Mahdi on religion, 109-11; treatment of, by various masters, 114-7; in Khartum, 149-50; farewell to Father Bonomi, 178-84; down with fever, 190; sent to Omdurman, 199; and famine in Omdurman, 288; made a prisoner, 351-2; departure from Omdurman, 407; plans of escape, 408-23; and Lupton, 412-3; escape of, to Cairo, 424-46; present situation in the Sudan, 447-450.
Omala (tax-gatherers) in the Sudan, 313.
Omar Kisha (merchant), 267, 397.
Omar Saleh, 269-71.
Omar Wad Elias, Pasha, 247.
Omberer, a merchant, 35.
Omdurman, the Dervish capital, 146, 151, 275, 281, 304, 328, 380; the Mahdi at, 35, 126, 127; surrender of fort at, 131, 142, 177, 222; smallpox in, 154-5; and the Mahdi's death, 162-3; events in, 202-3; hill of, 204; scarcity of small coins in, 210-3; museum at, 213; the beit el mal at, 208-9; Abyssinians in, 220-1; Abu Anga and, 224, 230-1; grand review at, 225-6; panic in, 248; Osman Digna at, 267-8; Mahdi's tomb at, 275-9; Khalifa's palace, 280; roads in, 280-1; market-place, 282; gallows at, 283, 317-8; inhabitants of, 283; population, 283-4; famine in, 284-9; plagues of locusts and mice in, 291-2; thieves in, 328-9, 334-5, 340; system of justice at, 329-33; cripples in, 337;

immorality in, 341; marriages in, 341-3; Saier, or prison at, 344-65; Neufeld in, 355-60; scarcity of powder at, 367-75; sandstorms at, 376-7; slaves in, 383-6; the Greeks in, 412; dress of women in, 413; Ohrwalder's last day at, 424; flight from, 445, 449.
Om Herezeh mountain, 34, 46.
Om Sadik, 224.
Omshanga, 94.
Onbeïa (wind instrument), 15, 44, 306.
Ongat wells. 259.
Ornaments, the Mahdi and Sudanese, 18.
Ornithology: Birds in Dar Nuba, 3-4; kites at El Obeid, 53; vultures, 77, 88, 290.
Oshra Well, 40, 47.
Osman, Khalifa, 308, 353-4, 389.
Osman Azrak, 260.
Osman Digna, 11, 64, 166-7; defeat of, 266-8.
Osman Wad Adam, 199, 234, 236; and Abu Gemaizeh, 238-41; death of, 240.
Osman Wad Dekeim, 167.
Ostrich farms in Kordofan, 35.

PAIN, OLIVIER, at El Obeid, 172-75.
Palace, the Khalifa's, at Omdurman, 280.
Passioni, Jew named, 360.
Pesavento, Sister E., 48.
Pilgrims at Omdurman, 206.
Pimezzoni, Franz, 1.
Plagues in the Sudan: of locusts, 291; of mice, 291-2.
Plough, a, in the Sudan, 378.
Poetry, the Arabs and, 67.
Polinari, Domenico, 138-40, 349-50.
Postal service in the Mahdi's kingdom, 300-1.
Powder, scarcity of, at Omdurman, 359, 367-75.
Power, Consul, 99, 129-30.
Prayers, the Mahdi and, 19; book of, 213; form of, 296.
Printing press at Omdurman, 213.
Prison at Omdurman, 344-65.
Proclamation by the Mahdi, 76.

QUICKSILVER found at Delen, 35.

RABEH ZUBEIR, 240, 241.
Rahad, General Hicks at, 77-85; the road to, 101-3; the Mahdi at, 106-21, 125-6, 169.
Rahma, fiki, 11.
Rain in Dar Nuba, 3; in the Sudan, 376.
Ramadan, fast of, 64, 158.
Ras Adal, 247; and Galabat, 217-20.
Ras Alula, 167, 247.
Rashid Bey, 9.
Ratibs (Mahdi's book of prayers), 213.
Rauf Pasha, 1-2, 6-7.
Regaf Station, 269, 271-2, 340, 384, 396.
Religion, interview with the Mahdi on, 109-11.
Reptiles, 150; snakes, 3-4, 433; scorpions, 114, 347.
Review of Dervishes at Omdurman, 225-6, 307-8.
Rizighat tribe of Arabs, 73, 221, 396-7.
Roads in Omdurman, 280; in the Sudan, 341.
Rognotto, Joseph, 100.
Rossignoli, Father, 54, 57.
Roversi (inspector of slaves), 22-3, 27-30, 48; death of, 49.
Rundle Bey, 439.

SABURI Mountain, 5.
Saddlers at Omdurman, 381.
Sofia steamer, 127.
Said Bey Guma, 94, 202-3, 223, 236.
Said Mohammed, 39.
Said Pasha, 7, 10-1, 20-1, 29, 119; defence of El Obeid, 36-40, 49, 56, 58-9, 66.
Said el Mek, 6.
Saier at Omdurman, see "Prison."
Saleh, sheikh, 55.
Saleh Pasha Wad el Mek, 125, 153, 350.
Saleh Bey, 217-8, 221, 352-3, 364, 414.
Saleh Bey Fad!allah, 232-4, 265.
Salem, sheikh, 55.
Salisbury, Lord, letter to King John, 250-1.
Sandalia, perfume called, 157.
Sandstorm, a fearful, 203; in the Sudan, 376-7.
Santoni, A., 443; and Father Bonomi, 178-9, 183.
Sarras, Dervishes at, 257-8, 262.
Sawakin, 1, 121, 166-7; Osman Digna besieges, 266-7.
Sayer, Brother, 443.
Sayid el Mek, 407.
Sayid Hamed, 167-8.
Sayid Osman, see "Osman, Khalifa."

INDEX. 459

"Sayidna Isa," 244–5.
Schuver, Jean M., 2.
Seckendorf, Baron, death of, 88; servant of, 80.
Selima wells, 233.
Selim Bey in Equatoria, 271.
Sennar, 154, 160, 162, 164–5, 226, 256, 290.
Senussi, sheikh, 4, 14, 173, 237.
Shaggieh troops, 239.
Shaggieh tribe, 143.
Shakka, 35, 59, 235, 384, 391.
Sharé River, 241.
Shatt Station, 11, 35, 77, 126, 175.
Shebba, a (forked wood), 97.
Sheep of the Kababish tribe, 232, 234; in the Sudan provinces, 379.
Shekan forest, battle near, 87, 92, 94, 171.
Shendi, 290.
Sherif, Khalifa, see "Ali Esh Sherif."
Sherif Mahmud, 20, 60, 86, 106, 169–72, 174, 176–8, 183, 186–9, 197; death of, 198–9, 206, 223.
Shilluk tribe, 272, 379.
Shirkeleh, 77, 80, 126.
Shirra, Baggara chief, 187.
Shukrieh tribe, 166, 216, 290, 350.
Sideham, a Copt, 178.
Sid el Hassan, the celebrated Moslem, 165–6.
Sidi Hamdan, see "Abu Anga."
Sieges, see "Bara," "El Fasher," "El Obeid," "Galabat," "Kassala," "Khartum," "Sennar," "Sawakin," "Tokar," &c.
Singiokai, 25, 32, 49, 59.
Sisters of the Austrian Mission, before Abdullah, 100; at Rahad, 103–6; escape of, from Omdurman, 413–5, 418–45; see also "Andreis," "Corsi," "Chincarini," "Pesavento," "Venturini."
Siwar ed Dahab, 21, 264.
Skander Bey, 21.
Skander, fate of Mulatte, 140.
Slatin Bey, 2, 73–5, 93, 118, 153, 174–5, 177, 189, 206, 348; and Darfur, 255; and waterskins, 237.
Slave trade, in Dar Nuba, 4; in the Bahr el Ghazal, 8–9, 12, 22; in the Sudan, 382–6.
Slaves, the Mahdi's law regarding, 62; of Khartum, 143; at Omdurman, 208–9, 333, 339.
Small-pox, in Omdurman, 154–5; in El Obeid, 183–4.

Soap-boiling at Omdurman, 213–4, 303, 413.
Sobei, the Khojur of, 187.
Sogaro, Archbishop Franz, 415–7, 420, 444–5.
Soil, of Dar Nuba, 3; of Bara, 200; in the Gezireh, 378.
Stambuli, George, 42–8, 54, 58, 68–71, 84, 96–7, 269.
Stanley, H. M., and Emin Pasha, 269, 271.
Starvation in the Mahdi's camp, 154.
Stewart, Col., murder of, 128–30, 177, 414, 438.
Sudan, Egypt and the, 34, 123; the Mahdi master of the, 94; English troops in the, 120; custom to drink melted butter, 175; revolt of black soldiers of army of, 189–200; witchcraft in, 44, 274–5; famine in the, 290–2; horsemanship in the, 308; immorality in the, 341–3; cattle breeding in the, 376–9; disease in the. 386; present situation in the, 387–407, 447–50.
Sudanese, the, marriage ceremony of, 17–8; and smallpox, 154–5; and alchemy, 369.
Suez, 1.
Suk Abu Sin, see "Gedaref."
Suleiman Bey, Gessi and, 9–10.
Suleiman, Capt. M., 22, 27.
Suleiman el Hejazi, 240.
Suleiman Wad Naaman, sheikh, 129–30, 414.
Superstition, in the Sudan, 44, 274–5; the Nubas and, 186; see also "Witchcraft."
Surur Effendi, 56.
Swindlers in Omdurman, 334, 337–9.
Syria, Sherif of, 111.

TAGALLA, JEBEL, 3, 7, 77, 222–3, 225, 247; see also "Adam, King."
Taha, Sayid Mohammed, 91.
Taher, sheikh, 316–7.
Taisha Arabs, 14, 221, 301; Abdullah and, 308–11, 350, 395–6.
Takruri tribe, 171–2, 217, 244, 248, 283.
Tamai, battle of, 266.
Tamarinds in Kordofan, 35.
Taxation in the Mahdi's kingdom, 379–80.
Tax-gatherers of the Sudan provinces, 313.
Tax levied at Omdurman, 205.

460 INDEX.

Tayara Station, 11, 35, 60.
Testament, King John's copy of New, 250.
Thieves in Omdurman, 328-9, 334-7, 339-40.
"Three Holy Kings," festival of the, 218.
Tira hill, 3.
Tobacco, the Sudanese and, 17; chewing, 276; punishment of smokers of, 330.
Tobji, Osman, 65-6.
Todros Kasa, son of King Theodore, 242-5.
Tokar, 267-8; capture of, 367, 386, 414.
Tolodi, Jebel, 223.
Tomb of the Mahdi at Omdurman, 275-80.
Tome, sheikh, 55, 64; brother of, 232.
Toski, battle at, 263, 320, 350, 361.
Trades in Omdurman, 381-2.
Treasure in Khartum, 145.
Trees in Dar Nuba, 3.
Tur el Hadra, 2.
Tuti Island, 147, 375.
"Turk," Arabs and the term, 263.
Turkey, Sultan of, letter to, from Khalifa, 257.

UGANDA, events in, 271.
Unyoro, events in, 271.

VENTURINI, Sister E., 413-45.
Victoria, Queen, and King John of Abyssinia, 250-1; letter to, from Abdullah, 257.

WAD ALI, 246, 249.
Wad Arbab, Emir, 217-8.
Wad Bishara, village of, 426.
Wad el Bedri, 10, 319, 395.
Wad el Besir, 94, 124, 258, 306.
Wadelai, 271.
Wad el Areik (merchant), 21, 35, 131, 405.
Wad el Banna, 401.
Wad el Hashmi, Emir, 76, 190, 193-4, 199.
Wad el Makashef, 11, 72, 164.
Wad er Reis, 445; see "Hussein Wad Dayim."

Wad Gubara (Emir), 38-9, 85, 125, 130, 133, 260.
Wad Gesuli, 96.
Wad Guzuli, 345.
Wad Hamdu Allah, 313.
Wadi Gamr cataracts, 128.
Wadi Halfa, 257, 260.
Wad Nubawi (Emir), 233.
Wad Zaid, 350.
War materials at Omdurman, 349, 381.
Waterskins, the Masalit people and, 237.
Water-wheels along the Nile, 378.
White Nile, 3, 6, 12, 93, 126, 133-5, 150, 204; expedition up the, 269-272.
Witchcraft, the Mahdi's success attributed to, 94; the bark of Adansonia tree, 170; in the Sudan, 274-5, 402.
Wodehouse, Colonel, 115, 259, 265; battle at Argin, 262.
Wolseley (Lord), 'Soldier's Pocket-Book,' 101.

YAKUB (Khalifa Abdullah's brother), 243, 277, 304, 313-4, 324-6, 361, 366, 363, 371-3, 389-90, 394, 402-7.
Yesin, Major, 59.
Yunis Ed Dekeim, 260, 265.
Yusef Angeli (Greek), 373-4.
Yusef Pertekachi, and manufacture of power, 371-4.
Yunis, Emir, 206, 219-20, 228, 396, 417; and Abu Anga, 244-5.
Yusef, Sultan of Darfur, 213, 236, 308.
Yusef Kurdi (merchant), 333-4.
Yusef Pasha, 10-1, 42, 90.

ZEKI TUMMAL and Abyssinia, 225, 247, 249, 251-2, 272, 285, 290.
Zeregga, 77.
Zogal (the Mahdi's uncle), 75, 93-4, 164, 184, 223, 235, 265-7, 360, 388, 396, 401, 417; and Darfur, 201-3.
Zogheir (a celebrated thief), 335-7, 353.
Zubeir, feast known as, 4.
Zubeir Pasha, 172, 391; Abu Anga and, 221; and Kingdom of Shakka, 235.
Zurbuchen, Dr., 2.

NOTE.—At the last moment, when this book was passed for press, the return to England of Captain Lugard enables me, through his courtesy, to give the names and positions of the forts in Uganda and Unyoro now occupied by the troops in the service of the Imperial British East Africa Company.—F.R.W.

LONDON, *October 10th,* 1892.

www.ingramcontent.com/pod-product-compliance
Lightning Source LLC
Chambersburg PA
CBHW021350290426
44108CB00010B/175